Human Rights in Europe

Malte Brosig (ed.)

Human Rights in Europe

A Fragmented Regime?

PETER LANG
Frankfurt am Main · Berlin · Bern · Bruxelles · New York · Oxford · Wien

Bibliographic Information published by Die Deutsche Bibliothek
Die Deutsche Bibliothek lists this publication in the Deutsche Nationalbibliografie; detailed bibliographic data is available in the internet at <http://dnb.ddb.de>.

ISBN 3-631-54458-8
US-ISBN 0-8204-7792-3

www.peterlang.de

CONTENTS

Contributors 7

Chapter I
Introduction

Human Rights in Europe: An Introduction
Malte Brosig 9

Chapter II
European Organisations and Human Rights

1. The Council of Europe, the Standard-setter
Karen Schlüter 30

2. Human rights before the courts: Concurrence or complementary protection by the European Court of Human Rights, the European Court of Justice and by national constitutional courts?
Hartmut Aden 57

3. The Protection of Fundamental Rights in the European Union – selected aspects
Katarzyna Cuadrat-Grzybowska 67

4. Courts, Charters and Conventions: The Institutionalisation of Human Rights Protection in the European Union
Justus Schönlau 85

5. The Human Dimension: The OSCE's Approach to Human Rights
Jens Narten 102

Chapter III
Minorities and Minority Rights in Europe

1. Minority Rights in Europe: an introduction into a fragmented regime
Carmen Thiele 120

2. Diffusing Fragmented Human Rights Standards: Minority Rights in Estonia
Malte Brosig 137

3. Minority Rights in Europe: Roms in Slovakia and the Czech Republic
Eben Friedman 153

4. Teaching Human Rights in Europe and its the role for minority movements
Claudia Mahler, Anja Mihr,Reetta Toivanen 169

Chapter IV
The EU's external Relations and Human Rights

1. EU External Relations and Human Rights
Wolfgang S. Heinz 184

2. 'Exporting' values: Tracing the EU's human rights policy towards Russia
Regina Heller 208

3. Turkeys Compliance with EU Human Rights Norms
Birsen Erdogan 225

4. Macedonia - The Imperative of Success
Harald Schenker 246

5. The European Union and Human Rights in Bulgaria
Katina Boncheva 257

Chapter V
Limits of the Human Rights Approach

1.Taking Human Rights to its Limits or Why We Need a Critical Review
David Chandler 275

References 305

CONTRIBUTORS

Dr. *Hartmut Aden* teaches law and political science at the University of Hanover and works for the Federal Audit Office at Bonn, Germany.

Katina Boncheva is a manager of the Bulgarian nongovernmental organisation Association for European Integration and Human Rights. She is a practicing lawyer, experienced in leading strategic cases and cases in front of the European Court of Human Rights.

Malte Brosig is a PhD candidate at the Centre for European and International Studies Research (CEISR) at Portsmouth University.

David Chandler is Professor of International Relations, Centre for the Study of Democracy, University of Westminster.

Katarzyna Cuadrat-Grzybowska, Ph D in Law, Policy Officer in the Directorate General Justice, Freedom and Security of the European Commission in the Unit which deals with Fundamental Rights and Citizenship of the European Union. Before, Expert in EU Law in Office of the Committee of European Integration involved in the process of harmonisation of Polish law with EU laws and standards.

Birsen Erdogan is a PhD candidate on Human Rights Law at the Netherlands Institute of Human Rights, Faculty of Law, Utrecht University

Eben Friedman holds a Ph.D. in political science from the University of California, San Diego. Since late 2002, Friedman has been employed by the European Centre for Minority Issues, where his activities have focused mainly on Macedonia and on Romani populations in post-Communist Eastern Europe.

Wolfgang S. Heinz is a senor lecturer at the Department of Political Science of the Free University in Berlin and a senior research fellow at the German Institute for Human Rights, a national human rights institution according to UN guidelines.

Regina Heller is a PhD candidate at the Institute for Peace Research and Security Policy at the University of Hamburg.

Dr. Claudia Mahler is a researcher at the Human Rights Centre at Potsdam University.

Anja Mihr is a political science researcher and lecturer at Humboldt University Berlin. She is currently researcher in the interdisciplinary research project "Teaching Human Rights in Europe".

Jens Narten is as a researcher and PhD candidate at the Centre for OSCE Research of the Institute for Peace Research and Security Policy at the University of Hamburg. From 2001 to 2004, he worked as Senior Human Rights Officer and Training Coordinator at the OSCE Mission in Kosovo.

Harald Schenker, served from 1999 to 2003 as Political Adviser in charge of minority issues in the OSCE Mission in Skopje. From 1999 to 2001, he also was spokesman of the OSCE in Skopje. In 2004, he was Senior Research Associate and Head of the South-east Europe Department at the European Centre for Minority Issues (ECMI) in Flensburg, Germany.

Karen Schlüter is a researcher and lecturer at the UNESCO Chair in Human Rights Education, Institute of Political Science, Magdeburg University.

Dr. Justus Schönlau is researcher to a Member of the European Parliament, associate research fellow at the Centre for European Policy Studies, Brussels and honorary fellow at the department of politics of the University of Exeter.

Dr. jur. Carmen Thiele is Assistant Professor at the Faculty of Law of the European University Viadrina Frankfurt (Oder).

Reetta Toivanen (PhD) is a Senior Researcher at the Department for European Ethnology at the Humboldt-Universität zu Berlin in Germany and an affiliated Senior Research Fellow at the Institute for Human Rights at the Åbo Akademi University, Finland.

CHAPTER I

INTRODUCTION

Human Rights in Europe: An Introduction[1]

Malte Brosig

In recent years human rights in Europe have gained momentum. The Charter of Fundamental Rights and the drafting of a European Constitution brought human rights issues into the heart of European Union (EU) politics. Moreover, the EU's external relations to accession candidates and third countries as well as peace-keeping missions are also framed as human rights matters. Increased cooperation between the Council of Europe (CoE) and the EU is enhancing the EU's capacity to harmonise and integrate its member states' legislation and human rights policy.

Taking these dynamic changes in human rights affairs as a foil, the essay collection focuses on the European human rights regime and its present state of the art. By taking on a regime approach we are able to portray an integrative picture of the European human rights system. The volume tries to give an overview about the European human rights system in its complexity, juridical and political dimension. Capturing developments in differently structured organisations and across varying policy areas, treating human rights in Europe as a regime allows for compiling such a single package (Donnelly 1986: 640). The notion 'regime' should be understood as comprising an international regulatory system promoting and enacting normative rules.

Analysing human rights in Europe from a regime perspective, the volume does not reduce the European human rights regime to the interpretation of a single document such as the European Convention on Human Rights (ECHR) or focus on only one institution. Aiming to characterise the European human rights regime, one almost instantly meets the term 'fragmented'. Fragmentation and lack of coherence are core features attributed to the European human rights regime, but at the same time it can also be described as the most coercive and successful regional human rights regime regarding its legal obligations and the largely positive human rights record European states display on the whole.

[1] I wish to thank everyone who has contributed to the process of writing this volume. Most especially, I would like to thank Eben Friedman for his support and comments. This work would not have been possible without him.

The first chapter gives a general overview and introduction into the topic. In chapter II "European Organisations and Human Rights" the contributors evaluate the most recent changes in the European human rights system. Starting with the Council of Europe, this chapter delivers a thorough investigation of European human rights players and their human rights policies. Apart from the CoE, the EU, OSCE, ECtHR including constitutional traditions in CoE member states and the Convention on the Future of Europe form the basis of this section. Chapter III "Minorities and Minority Rights" pays tribute to a relatively new field of human rights legislation. The European dimension of minority issues so far has not been properly recognised in Brussels. The chapter openly addresses deficiencies in norm-setting and implementation in EU member states. Case studies on Estonia, Slovakia and the Czech Republic will illustrate this point.

As the European Union becomes aware of its values and is likely to become a 'real' foreign policy actor, its external relations are at least to some extent inspired by human rights norms. Some scholars already speak of the EU as a 'normative power' (Manners 2002). Chapter IV shows in greater detail how the EU starts to expand its foreign affairs agenda into a human rights policy. Countries under investigation are Russia, Macedonia, Bulgaria, and Turkey.

Finally, the last section "Taking Human Rights to its Limits", written by David Chandler critically analyses shortcomings and deficiencies not only of the European human rights regime, but also of the relationship between human rights and democracy. Taking a broad perspective, the final chapter detects severe and oftentimes neglected tensions between the moral and normative human rights concept and democratic rights.

The European Human Rights Regime

With the end of the Second World War Europe was left in ruins and in doubts of its cultural and civilisational achievements. Europe was the continent hit worst by destruction, death and genocide. At least in Western Europe, Auschwitz became a term for the most severe crime against the human race. As a direct reaction to the Holocaust and war atrocities, already in 1948 the United Nations drafted the Universal Declaration on Human Rights (UDHR) which paved the way for the modern human rights system. In 1949 the Genocide Convention was signed, with the International Covenant on Civil and Political Rights (ICCPR) was opened for signature in 1966. However, it was not until 1976 that the Covenant, which is the most recognised international human rights document, entered into force.

Considering the tragedy of the past, it was Winston Churchill who carried the idea of a united Europe in peace, freedom and security. Human dignity and totalitarian regimes were identified as mutually excluding elements on the basis of the experiences of the 1930s and 1940s. In 1949 the Council of Europe was founded with the attempt to unify Europe on the basis of democratic governance and human dignity.[2] All European states were invited to join the Council if they subscribed to the rules of democracy and respect for human rights.[3] Council members have to ratify the CoE Statute which mentions democracy and the rule of law as preconditions for membership. Shortly after the CoE was founded, work on the Convention for the Protection of Human Rights and Fundamental Freedoms (henceforth called European Convention on Human Rights or ECHR) started. Within 15 months this document was brought on paper and in 1950 opened for signature. On September 3rd 1953 the single most important European human rights treaty entered into force. Thus the ECHR came into power 23 years ahead of the ICCPR. The western part of Europe was much faster in developing a human rights regime than the United Nations or any other regional human rights system. Both the ICCPR and ECHR build on the Universal Declaration on Human Rights. But most importantly the ECHR does not formulate programme type articles which should be reached in a distant future. Instead, the ECHR clearly forms an indispensable frame for justiciable human rights norms. It guarantees basic rights and freedoms such as the right to life, freedom of thought, conscience and religion, freedom of expression, fair trial, freedom of assembly, and the prohibition of torture.

Initially the ECHR was signed by ten western European countries. Now it is a truly pan-European document with 46 signatory states, with only Belarus not being a member of the CoE and the Convention. Hence one can claim that the rights and standards which are enshrined in the ECHR constitute a set of common European values. The European human rights regime has unique features which set it apart from the UN or other regional systems. The external control of states by an independent human rights Court and the possibility to file individual claims is unprecedented (Leben 1999: 88). A further distinctive European feature is the abolition of the death penalty. It seems that a consensus exists on the value of fundamental rights. However, the consensus is limited to these core values and minimal standards as will be illustrated in the following paragraphs.

During its more than 50 years of existence the CoE has further developed the human rights system. So far the ECHR has been enhanced by 14 protocols. One of the most significant achievements is the recognition by all member states to allow individual complaints before the Strasbourg Court in 1990. It is only the ECHR as an international treaty which grants individuals the right to litigation. A further milestone in the development of the European human rights regime was set by protocol no. 11. As a consequence of protocol 11 in 1998 a permanent Human Rights Court replaced the existing part-time Court. Reforming the Court was a highly necessary measure to secure effective supervision of the

[2] Statute of the Council of Europe, Preamble and Article 1 a).

[3] Statute, Article 4.

ECHR. To give an example, in 1981 404 cases were brought to Strasbourg meanwhile the number had exploded to 13,858 cases by 2001.

In protocol 6 of the ECHR European states have agreed to enhance the right to life (article 2 ECHR) by abolishing the death penalty. This prohibition is an often highlighted feature of the European human rights regime (Meyer-Ladewig 2003: 355-357). All CoE members have signed protocol no. 6. Indeed this development is remarkable since neither the UDHR nor the ICCPR prohibit the application of capital punishment. Most visibly Russia and Turkey have changed their respective laws or simply stopped administering the death penalty.

Besides the ECHR, human rights norms have been put into different treaties and conventions. One such document is the European Social Charter (ESC) of 1965. In 1989 the Convention for the Prevention of Torture (CPT) came into force. The ECHR and CPT are the most recognised human rights conventions in the European human rights system. After the end of the Cold War two conventions concerning minorities were drafted, namely the Framework Convention for the Protection of National Minorities (FCNM) and the European Charta for Regional or Minority Languages (ECRML). The latest human rights convention developed by the CoE is the Convention on Human Rights and Biomedicine (CHRB) of 1999. Most of the mentioned human rights conventions are accompanied by additional protocols or other amendments. It is partly because of this fact that the European human rights regime can be characterised as fragmented.

Table 1 gives an overview of all CoE human rights treaties and their status. This table illustrates the fragmented character human rights in Europe have. Since 1950 the Council of Europe has produced six human rights conventions, which are listed above. They form the legal backbone of the European human rights regime. The EU Charta of Fundamental Rights of course will be discussed later. As can be seen in the table below these six conventions have been modified by 21 protocols or amendments. 14 of these protocols are attachments to the ECHR. For each protocol to enter into force a certain number of states has to sign and ratify them. No convention can be changed or amended without the slow and bureaucratic ratification process. More than the EU the CoE is an intergovernmental organisation which has consequences. The CoE binds its member states by international treaties, which states consent to or refute. Basically there is no instrument to force countries to sign and ratify a convention or amending protocol. This fact contributes to the "historical patchwork" (Merills 2001: 328) of European human rights protection.

Table 1 clearly illustrates the degree of regime fragmentation. The most widespread consensus among European states could only be reached on fundamental rights. The ECHR and CPT get the highest endorsement of CoE members (46 ratifications). However, looking at the approval rate of the 14 protocols one can notice that three of them could not enter into force because there were not

Table 1 European Human Rights Treaties

Treaty	entry into force	Signatory states	number of ratifications	number of objections
FCNM	***1/2/1998***	***42***	***38***	***20***
ECRML	***1/3/1998***	***32***	***20***	***25***
CPT	***1/2/1989***	***46***	***46***	***6***
protocol 1	1/3/2002	46	46	2
protocol 2	1/3/2002	46	46	2
ESC	***26/2/1965***	***32***	***27***	***37***
ESC revised	1/7/1999	40	21	22
Additional protocol 1 ESC	4/9/1992	23	13	12
protocol amending ESC	not in force	26	22	2
Additional protocol 2	1/7/1998	18	11	1
CHRB	***1/12/1999***	***32***	***19***	***7***
protocol 1	1/3/2001	30	15	1
protocol 2	1/5/2006	15	5	0
protocol 3	not in force	18	2	0
ECHR	***3/9/1953***	***46***	***46***	***40***
protocol 1	18/5/1954	45	46	29
protocol 2	21/9/1970	46	46	3
protocol 3	21/9/1970	46	45	3
protocol 4	2/5/1968	43	40	9
protocol 5	20/12/1971	46	46	3
protocol 6	1/3/1985	46	45	9
protocol 7	1/11/1988	44	39	18
protocol 8	1/1/1990	46	46	5
protocol 9	1/10/1994	29	24	2
protocol 10	not in force	28	25	2
protocol 11	1/11/1998	46	46	3
protocol 12	1/4/2005	35	11	2
protocol 13	1/7/2003	45	34	4
protocol 14	not in force	45	27	5

Objections comprise documents issues by state parties which are mostly declarations or reservations

- ***FCNM*** Framework Convention for the Protection of National Minorities
- ***ECRML*** European Charter for Regional or Minority Languages
- ***CPT*** European Convention for the Prevention of Torture and Inhuman or Degrading Treatment or Punishment
- ***ESC*** European Social Charter
- ***CHRB*** Convention for the protection of human rights and dignity of the human being with regard to the application of biology and medicine: Convention on Human Rights and Biomedicine
- ***ECHR*** Convention for the Protection of Human Rights and Fundamental Freedoms

enough states ratifying the protocols which again accounts for fragmentation. Most visibly member states have submitted in total 261 objections (declarations or reservations) to the respective human rights conventions or protocols. This can hardly be interpreted as fostering coherence.

Another example, granting rights to national minorities is a sensitive issue for many countries. This can also be deduced from the relatively low number of states backing the respective treaties. The FCNM was ratified by 42 member states and the ECRML only by 32. Furthermore, both treaties have been criticised for their weak wordings (Pentassuglia 1999: 418).

With the European Social Charter the CoE entered the controversial area of social rights. Compared with fundamental rights enshrined in the ECHR, the ESC follows a different philosophy. In the former individual rights are formulated mostly as limits to state power. Social rights such as the right to work, social security regulations or equal treatment provisions, on the other hand, create far reaching obligations which states are cautious to subscribe to (Breucking 2000: 143). These rights are also much more debateable than the right to life or the prohibition of torture. It can easily be imagined that cultural values, morality, and traditional gender roles vary widely among European countries. Not surprisingly the ESC during its 40 years of existence was until now ratified by only 27 countries. In the same period, 37 objections to the charter have been made (see table 1). The revised ESC of 1999 does not score better. Here 21 states ratified the revised version. The picture becomes even more sobering when looking at the ESC additional protocols which went through ratification only in 11-21 countries.

The Convention on Human Rights and Biomedicine encounters the same problems as the ESC. Countries like Great Britain or Germany have not signed this convention and only 19 CoE member states have ratified the CHRB. Basically it was too hard to compromise on a clear set of rules regarding, for example, research on embryos which let some states abstain form the convention. While in Germany research on embryos is regulated restrictively in the United Kingdom restrictions are far more liberal.

As we have seen so far, the European human rights system appears as fragmented in many ways. First of all there are different treaties with a high number of additional protocols. But most importantly these treaties and protocols meet very different degrees of receptiveness in European countries, resulting in a high number of ratifications as regards the ECHR and CPT and much lower approval in all other human rights areas such as social rights, minority rights, and lastly biomedicine. A further problem which this chapter cannot tackle systematically is the generally ambiguous content of human rights treaties, including European human rights conventions. It is true that most often human rights conventions are the result of intergovernmental negotiations and bargaining. It is also true that this process does not take place in a vacuum that is free from domestic influence or other state interests. Generally states hesitate to subscribe to international treaties that limit their sovereign rights or oblige them to spend valuable resources for implementation. To avoid these 'negative impacts' states seek to define human rights norms on an abstract but less precise degree to give room for interpretation (Fritzsche 2004: 51). This can be seen, for instance, in the FCNM, which contains so many weak and interpretable articles that finally the contracting parties have to fill out what is left in doubt by the FCNM.

Human rights as we study them in Europe are often softly formulated legal norms arising from political compromise. Analytically one can discern a legal and a political frame in which human rights norms take effect. This fact all the more accounts for fragmentation. The soft, vague, and imprecise wording in some human rights texts pays tribute to disagreements on the level of human rights protection or in other cases to the fear of losing sovereignty to the Strasbourg Court. In turn, instantiation of human rights standards depends very much on member states and the way in which they use the existing leeway for implementation. This does not always 'lure' states into applying minimal standards. Depending on the national discourse on human rights norms, countries may choose for themselves to set a higher standard. More specifically, in the area of social rights European countries have developed diverse social security systems with highly differentiated social guarantees and subsidies. Here, fragmentation need not necessarily have a negative connotation. Rather it refers to the principle of subsidiarity and traditionally-developed national social security systems. It may also be seen as inappropriate and undemocratic to press highly controversial issues into hard law and let judges engage in politics. There are good reasons for linking human rights to the democratic legitimacy lacking in many European organisations over the years. While the EU has taken over state-like responsibilities it is a polity without a civil society and limited democratic legitimacy.

The European human rights regime accounts for different types of interaction or tasks. Within the volume one can single out at least five types:[4]

1. Norm enforcement through legal institutions
2. Monitoring of European countries by international organisations
3. Policy coordination
4. External promotion of human rights and assistance
5. National norm implementation and application

[4] These interaction types draw heavily on Jack Donnelly's introduction of regime decision-making procedures, 604.

The first interaction type is tackled by Hartmut Aden who focuses on the complex relationship between European and national constitutional courts protecting human rights. Human rights monitoring is a classical task of the Council of Europe and the OSCE but not of the EU. However, policy coordination falls within the competences of the European Union. Mainstreaming tendencies are visible in some subject areas, such as non-discrimination. The external promotion of human rights standards is analysed more extensively in Chapter IV. Finally, the volume's country studies cover seven European countries geographically located in Central and Eastern Europe. Besides external influences from the CoE, OSCE and the EU, these studies also cover in-country factors influencing the implementation and application of European human rights norms.

After all, fragmentation refers to the diverse nature of the European human rights treaty system with its confusing number of amending documents (Mykola and Busch 2003: 33), to the lack of substance in human rights norms at some points and the different types of interaction and tasks it fulfils. Consequently, the system has rightly been portrayed as 'historical patchwork'. Nonetheless, not only in recent years European countries have referred to human rights values as enshrined in the ECHR as a source of identification. Weiler (1999: 120) notes, the consensus on central human rights norms reflects core societal choices. Thus, the fragmentation of the European human rights regime applies much less to the first generation of fundamental rights than to the subsequent set of social, minority, and biomedical rights.

The OSCE and Human Rights

The OSCE's prime task is to secure peace, stability, the rule of law, democracy and respect for human rights throughout the OSCE region. A comprehensive security concept underpins the OSCE's work. Thus the focus is on conflict prevention in the broadest sense. While at the beginning the OSCE concentrated on a security notion primarily emphasising state security, through the years the notion has been widened, with the OSCE increasingly taking into account. individual human beings and their rights and freedoms.

The OSCE security notion can be divided into three subsections or "dimensions": politico-military, economic and human. The OSCE human dimension approach addresses foremost human rights issues and questions of democracy. Democracy and human rights are seen as a tandem and mutually constitutive to stability and peace. In this context it is important to note that the OSCE human dimension approach is not a legalistic one. Where formulated, standards for democracy and human rights are seen as heavily interlinked with political systems and societal actors. The focus is on long-term political processes which aim to secure and consolidate security. In contrast to the CoE, the OSCE produces norms which are only politically (rather than legally) binding.

The Helsinki Final Act of 1975 formulates respect for human rights as a foundational principle of what was then the Conference on Security and Cooperation in Europe (CSCE). Since then, the organisation has refined its human rights approach. In 1990 the Copenhagen Document listed the right to freedom of expression, assembly, association, thought and prohibition of torture as a principle which all OSCE states reaffirm. It is remarkable that in this only politically binding document minority rights find such broad recognition. Here the OSCE was the first European organisation which prepared a set of rights for the protection of national minorities.

Since issuing the Copenhagen Document, the OSCE has institutionalised its human rights approach by establishing special organs. In 1992 the OSCE founded the Office for Democratic Institutions and Human Rights (ODIHR) in Warsaw and the post of the High Commissioner on National Minorities (HCNM) in The Hague. The HCNM functions as an early warning body for potential ethnic conflicts. The aim is to monitor minority rights and engage in preventive diplomacy if necessary. The office of the HCNM with support of OSCE country missions has developed a high competence in minority protection. The HCNM constantly issues recommendations and opinions. Much of the work of the HCNM is confidential. The OSCE deliberately chose the quiet diplomacy method for conflict prevention and promotion of human rights to avoid the negative impact of media 'sensationalization'.

The Warsaw-based ODIHR provides for human rights training including OSCE staff, government officials, and civil society representatives. Its human rights strategy is focussed primarily on promoting respect for fundamental rights. It provides research and compiles dossiers on relevant human rights issues and gives assistance for states to increase human rights protection. The ODIHR human rights programme entails nine sections on which the institution works constantly: human rights and anti-terrorism, prohibition of the death penalty, freedom of assembly and association, freedom of religion, monitoring places of detention, trial monitoring, human rights and the declaration of the state of emergency, tolerance and non-discrimination, and the OSCE human dimension mechanisms. Human dimension mechanisms should be broadly understand as an interstate or intra OSCE monitoring instrument for issues that fall within the competence of the OSCE.

The EU and Human Rights

European integration in the economic area has long been the motor for change. But it is becoming evident that Europe is not only striving for economic integration. Visibly the Charter of Fundamental Rights and the draft EU Constitution deliberately attempt to formulate common values. In article I-2 it stands that:

> The Union is founded on the values of respect for human dignity, freedom, democracy, equality, the rule of law and respect for human rights, including the rights of persons belonging to minorities.[…]

While in the past decades the European Communities were focussed on economic and political integration the European Union currently reinterprets itself. From the end of WW II until recently, European human rights norms have been regarded as the Council of Europe's business. There was no comprehensive or systematic approach visible compared with the extent and competence the CoE and the Human Rights Court have developed. To some degree, human rights on the one hand and economic integration on the other established parallel regimes which produced specialised intergovernmental and supranational organisations, namely the Council of Europe and the European Community/Union. In the broader context of the EU eastern enlargement in May 2004 and progressing economic integration, the Union was to be seen under pressure to reform itself in order to keep a larger Union manageable and not to lose political legitimacy. Apart from new procedural or institutional arrangements one result that concerns this book is the drafting of the Charter of Fundamental Rights which was proclaimed by the European Parliament, the European Commission, and the Council on the European Union in December 2000 at the Nice Council.

The EU's engagement in human rights does not start with the Charter. In 1977 the European Parliament, the Council, and the Commission issued a joint declaration on human rights.[5] Two years later the Commission drafted a proposal which recommended accession to the ECHR. However, these attempts failed to influence the EC's agenda in a sustained fashion. The Parliament, nonetheless, tried to continue its line and compiled a human rights declaration in 1989. Indeed, the Parliament has worked consistently on its profile as a human rights actor. In the meantime, the annual number of human rights resolutions adopted in Strasbourg has come to exceed 100.

Fundamental rights became a major topic at the intergovernmental conferences in Maastricht (1993) and Amsterdam (1997). The Maastricht Treaty mentioned respect for fundamental rights in Article F, corresponding to Article 6,2 of the Treaty on the European Union.

> Article 6
> 1. The Union is founded on the principles of liberty, democracy, respect for human rights and fundamental freedoms, and the rule of law, principles which are common to the Member States.

[5] 5 April 1977, Official Journal 1977, No. C103, p.1.

> 2. The Union shall respect fundamental rights, as guaranteed by the European Convention for the Protection of Human Rights and Fundamental Freedoms signed in Rome on 4 November 1950 and as they result from the constitutional traditions common to the Member States, as general principles of Community law.

Fundamental and human rights are clearly referred to as values all EU member states share. Due to a lack of EU legislative acts in this area the ECHR is mentioned as the key document. While the ECHR cannot interpret itself the Human Rights Court in Strasbourg and its jurisdiction are indispensable for applying Article 6. While this is not the place to analyse the full meaning and scope of Article 6, it is not a secret that this passage does not provide the EU with a general human rights competence (McCrudden 2002: 5) or a catalogue of rights other than those enshrined in the ECHR. However, the European Court of Justice (ECJ) was further encouraged to extend its jurisdiction on fundamental rights but only on a minimal basis.

At the Cologne European Council meeting in June 1999 it was agreed to start working on a legally non-binding Human Rights Charter. A Convent under the leadership of Roman Herzog, the former German President and Chair of the Bundesverfassungsgericht, was entrusted with compiling an EU Human Rights Charter. The Convent included representatives of the then 15 EU member states, one EU-Commission delegate, and 16 members of the European Parliament as well as two MPs from each national Parliament. Representatives of the ten prospective new EU members were not invited. Nearly the entire drafting process was made public, with the genesis of the Charter viewable on the Internet. Draft papers were available online and public sessions gave nongovernmental actors an opportunity to express their views (McCrudden 2002: 11).

Although it was clear from the beginning that the Charter would not become legally binding in the near future, the Charter was written as if it is part of a European Constitution. It was rather for political considerations that the Convent did not openly proclaim to work on a Constitution. Since the drafting of the Charter, the Convent on the Future of the European Union has drafted a Constitution in which the Charter is an integral component. Classical liberal freedoms as they are formulated in Chapter II of the Charter, like the freedom of expression or the freedom of thought, were not the subject of passionate discussions. The same can be said about Chapter V (Citizens' Rights) such as the right to vote, as well as about Chapter VI (Justice), which guarantees, among other things, the right to a fair trial.

Contrary to this catalogue of the more classical rights, which can be found in some way or the other in every member state Constitution, agreement on those rights enshrined in Chapter IV (Solidarity) was much more difficult. This does not come as a surprise. As described above, the CoE experienced widespread support for the ECHR but substantially less approval for social rights as they are laid down in the ESC. The considerably lower number of signatory states and henceforth lower number of ratifications is a clear indicator.

Most of the rights protected in the Charter are also enshrined in national Constitutions or build on the ECHR. Additionally, there are some recent innovations, including Article 3,2, which prohibits reproductive cloning of human beings, Article 8 on protection of personal data, Article 38 on consumer protection, and Article 41 on the right to good governance. Furthermore, Article 37 mentions environmental protection and sustainable development.

Despite these newly created rights most articles indeed have an obvious strong relation with the CoE's ECHR. Therefore it was necessary to clarify the relation between the Charter and the ECHR. In Article 52,3 the Charter makes a direct reference to the ECHR. There it stands:

> In so far as this Charter contains rights which correspond to rights guaranteed by the Convention for the Protection of Human Rights and Fundamental Freedoms, the meaning and scope of those rights shall be the same as those laid down by the said Convention. This provision shall not prevent Union law providing more extensive protection.

The Charter does not reinvent human rights, but is rather a reflection of a set of core values all EU countries have approved. These core values then found expression in the ECHR of 1950 and five decades later have reached the European Union in a slightly different version, first in the form of a non-legally binding Charter and later as part of the draft European Constitution. Article 52,3 is important because the Charter has simplified the wording in an attempt to make fundamental rights more easily accessible. To remedy ambiguities about a possible lower level of human rights protection, Article 52,3 guarantees the same scope of protection as warranted in the ECHR. Thus the meaning of the Charters articles which correspond to rights guaranteed by the ECHR is envisioned to be the same. This is highly advisable for preventing a dual human rights system at the European level. A human rights regime which separates the EU and the CoE would indeed foster the existing fragmentation to an unjustifiable degree. Trying to establish a second autonomous human rights regime outside the Council of Europe system would start a competition between the ECJ and the Human Rights Court. Instead of searching for a coherent application and interpretation of European human rights norms, creating competing systems would actually be the "worst possible scenario" (Toth 1997:501). Finally the Charter does not mark the beginning of a separated and thus even more fragmented human rights system. In Article 52,3 it pays tribute to the ECHR and the Human Rights Court. With this article the Charter also paves the way for EU accession to the ECHR.

Taken seriously, the Human Rights Court in Strasbourg is rightly regarded as having the highest authority and competence in interpreting European human rights norms. Since the Charter proclaims in Article 52,3 to follow ECHR standards, accession to the ECHR would be the next logical step. If the EU accedes to the Convention one can speculate about future accessions to other CoE treaties. There can hardly be arguments for a selective approach on human rights, where the EU selects those rights most welcome. Such an approach would undercut the principle of the indivisibility of human rights norms. Accession to the ECHR would also sharpen the EU's profile as an international actor, as allowing the Union contract to international treaties means acknowledging the EU's general competence in foreign policy.

An exemption of EU law from external control as regards the protection of fundamental rights appears outdated and at odds with obligations all EU member states have subscribed to (Garcia 2002: 13). The Council of Europe points out that:

> In a democratic society, a system of checks and balances is essential. All member states of the European Union, honouring this democratic principle, have submitted themselves to the external supervision of the European Court of Human Rights under this Convention, without endangering national sovereignty or the principle of subsidiarity. There is no legitimate reason why acts carried out on behalf of the European Union should be exempt from this fundamental external control mechanism, thus in effect withdrawing the protection of the ECHR from persons adversely affected in their fundamental rights and freedoms by Community law.[6]

At some points the fear was given expression that if the EU accedes to the ECHR and to the jurisdiction of the Human Rights Court, then it falls prey to the Strasbourg Court. Following this argumentation the EU could claim a special position towards fundamental rights. Again it is not convincing to exempt the Union from external control which all member states were able to accept (Garcia 2002: 14).

In Chapter II the book gives an overview on European organisations and their human rights strategies. Here, while the EU stands at the centre of our investigation, it has nonetheless to integrate itself into the already existing human rights regime. The most competent actor is undoubtedly the Council of Europe (CoE) and its Court for Human Rights. The Charter's articles draw heavily on the Council's European Convention on Human Rights (ECHR). Since its

[6] Garcia, Footnote No. 52 Report on the Charter of the Fundamental Rights of the European Union (14th September 2000 CHARTE 4465/00 CONTRIB 319).

establishment in 1959 the Court for Human Rights has interpreted the Convention and has gained a high reputation in its jurisprudence. All EU member states have signed and ratified the ECHR and have agreed to the individual complaint instrument. But the EU itself has not joined the Convention and is thus not subject to control mechanisms like its members. This situation has caused many scholars and human rights activists to speak for EU accession to the ECHR. This step has finally been foreseen in Article I-9,2 of the draft Constitution. However, the future of the draft Constitution remains uncertain, posing a potential challenge to the EU's legitimacy as an honest human rights actor.

The Charter undoubtedly codifies human rights for the EU institutions and its member states. While it does extend the catalogue of fundamental human rights by adding new norms it has at the same time a unifying effect which may remedy the notorious fragmentation of the European human rights regime. Contrary to the ECHR the Charter takes an inclusive approach towards different human rights norms. More precisely the Charter is subdivided into seven sections. They encompass classical civil and political rights but also social rights, with a special emphasis on equality. Although it can rightly be pointed out that those rights set forth in the Charter lack precision and substance, the Charter nonetheless constitutes an attempt to stop further fragmentation and disintegration of European human rights norms. At the same time the Charter pays special attention to national constitutional traditions. This might be a source for conflicts and could be labelled as fragmentary, but the intention behind it is not to split fundamental rights into conflicting and competing levels of European and domestic human rights protection. The opposite is true: By acknowledging national legal traditions besides the Charter, the EU acts on the principle of subsidiarity, which should not be confused with fragmentation.

The question why the EU needs a human rights Charter has met with several responses. First, there was the fear that the power transfer from member states to EU organs could impact negatively on the degree of human rights protection in the domestic space (de Schutter 2004: 3). Second, because the EU legislation in justice and home affairs touches on human rights issues, clarifying the normative basis on which the expanding EU legislation could draw appears as a simple necessity. Third, the EU is more and more acting like an international actor; while the EU may be far away from being a nation-state, it has state-like qualities to an extent that justifies developing a constitutional order. However, a European Constitution which does not protect fundamental rights is nearly unthinkable. An entity of the importance as of the European Union suffers a legitimacy deficit if its commitment to human rights is only half-hearted. Fourth, the Charter aims at integrating member states by expressing common European values such as fundamental rights (Ress 2004: 81).

Based on these common values, the EU is reorganising its interests and trying to establish a human rights policy which would be the next reasonable step forward in establishing a coherent human rights strategy. An EU human rights policy as it is developing right now should enhance human rights protection by adding to the judicial safeguard a political and administrative dimension. The Commission has long been urged to create a Directorate General (DG) specialised in human rights as a monitoring body. Yet current plans favour the foundation of a human agency, as Cuadrat-Grzybowska describes in the next chapter.

An EU institution solely focussed on human rights matters may help the EU in creating a coherent and comprehensive human rights approach. It surely would express the EU's commitment to human rights and possibly has a positive integrationist effect on member states. At the same time critics of an expansionist and proper administrative EU human rights policy have pointed to the fact that most often human rights protection depends on national control mechanisms and domestic jurisprudence (von Bogdandy 2000: 1312). Von Bogdandy also raises doubts about whom a human rights agency should refer to in EU member states because nearly no country has a specific human rights ministry. The last argument seems only partly valid, however, as cooperation between the EU and its member states occurs on various levels at which national ministries play a role but not an exclusive one. Parliamentary and human rights commissions, ministry subsections and national human rights institutes as well as NGOs could also be appropriate addresses.

A key question which the EU has to decide on is the ultimate size of its human rights agenda. While the working fields may not be a matter of heated discussions, defining the EU's own role might be. For the near future it is most likely that the EU will adapt a promotional agenda towards human rights with limited material and personal engagement. Since the Charter is not legally binding and the draft Constitution failed to be ratified in France and the Netherlands in summer 2005, developing a promotional human rights policy based on a publicly visible human rights organisation seems to be a sensible approach.

But in view of the expanding acquis touching on, incorporating and developing human rights it might be considered adequate to establish an administrative body. At this point one should ask whether the EU is the right address. Norm-setting in the human rights area should be the result of societal choices at the end of a democratic, participatory, and deliberative process. It is rather unrealistic to assume that the EU is able to ground itself in such a way in a national discourse on core values. This points to a challenge which the EU must face: A 'thick' human rights policy with a strong human rights institution and expanding EU legislation might be criticised for being disconnected from domestic values and national constituencies which human rights decisions should not be isolated from. There are widely known democratic deficiencies in the EU institutional set-up, such that an EU human rights institution could rightly be criticised for being undemocratic and elitist in nature.[7]

Human Rights in the EU's External Relations

Human rights, democracy, and the rule of law constitute core values EU member states regard as common. This normative basis finds its expression not only in EU internal affairs but also in its external relations. Chapter IV is dedicated to the EU's external relations and human rights promotion. It is not the intention of the volume to cover all third countries with which the EU holds a human rights dialogue. Also for practical reasons we selected countries which are of continued interest and importance for the development of human rights in Europe. We found that Russia, Turkey, Bulgaria and Macedonia fall within this category. In these countries it is becoming apparent that the EU is transforming itself into a human rights actor. This transformation is shaping the EU's capacity to act nearly globally in the name of human rights. The EU's external policy is intended to be legitimised by human rights values. As the preamble of the draft Constitution reads, the EU strives for "peace, justice and solidarity throughout the world". Moreover, Article I-3,4 of the Constitution reads:

> 4. In its relations with the wider world, the Union shall uphold and promote its values and interests. It shall contribute to peace, security, the sustainable development of the Earth, solidarity and mutual respect among peoples, free and fair trade, eradication of poverty and the protection of human rights, in particular the rights of the child, as well as to the strict observance and the development of international law, including respect for the principles of the United Nations Charter.

Despite the fact that the draft Constitution in its current shape may never enter into force, it nonetheless reflects on common positions which member states could agree on in principle. Moreover it follows a direction which has been formulated earlier, as, for instance, in the Single European Act of 1986, which . states, "Respect for human rights is an important element in relations between third countries and the Europe of Twelve". Parts of the draft Constitution may also take shape as a result of political will to proceed. The Union has already taken over missions in Macedonia, Congo and is engaged in the Sudanese Darfur region. Taking the role of an international human rights promoter, the EU presently faces different challenges. One of the most compelling requirements for effective human rights foreign policy is the need to develop a coherent and substantive human rights strategy. Such a strategy should be backed by a visible

[7] See also David Chandler in chapter V.

and effectively working institutional set-up. A loose framework such as the common foreign and security policy (CFSP) might not be sufficient. The inherent weakness and lack of coordination and agreement on core foreign policy goals, as we have seen during the Iraq war in 2003, is widely known. Especially the inability of Europe to speak with a single voice was a subject of frustration and demonstrated European disunity.

This situation could have been changed with the adoption of the draft Constitution, which however failed. Article I-28 the EU would have established the post of a European Union foreign minister, who "(...)shall conduct the Union's common foreign and security policy. [...] He or she shall ensure the consistency of the Union's external action." At least reforming the institutional basis raised expectations for a more coherent and coordinated foreign policy. Independent of the Constitution, there seems to be some political motivation to build up a European Diplomatic Service (EDS) which might be able to consolidate if not streamline European foreign affairs.

It is indeed remarkable that the EU tries to establish itself as an international actor partly by justifying utilising human rights norms as a legitimate basis for its foreign policy. International interventions in the name of human rights seem to be a trend of the outgoing 20th and early 21st century. Interventions in Kosovo, Afghanistan, Bosnia, or Macedonia have been justified on human rights grounds. One gets the impression that the EU hopes to profit from two effects of building a foreign policy on human rights norms.

First, there is the optimism that human rights standards really are common values that all member states have agreed on. This should be an advantage because in many other issues – especially foreign policy matters – EU members have hugely divergent interests and strategies. Thus, building a foreign policy on common values may be regarded as a prudent and unifying approach. But the argument should not be pushed too far. Consensus on human rights norms is only reached on fundamental rights and freedoms. It may be a basis too small for a developed foreign policy or a human rights strategy.

Second, by proclaiming and promoting a human rights-inspired international agenda the EU sees itself standing on a moral safe ground. The indivisibility and supposed universality of human rights norms opens a nearly global perspective for the EU as international actor. The EU can hardly claim to act on the basis of individual national self-interests, and although its activities are often perceived with scepticism by member states, acting in the name of human rights and thus on the basis of common values is much more likely to be perceived as a legitimate ground for action. Furthermore, member states have refrained from lending support to EU activism on foreign policy because in their perception the EU does not fight vigorously enough for national interests. But now opposition to EU foreign policy may be difficult against a Union pursuing human rights. Finally, the EU is extending its foreign policy capacities by pursuing a human rights strategy.

The Union tries to transform the loose coordination of its foreign affairs to form a more consistent and coherent approach and become an internationally recognised actor. This process is still going on and will take some time until a final arrangement might be found. As mentioned above, attempts to streamline its foreign policy can be found in the draft Constitution, which establishes the post of a foreign minister and declares human rights as a policy goal. Ian Manners in 2002 stated that "[…] it is possible to think of the ideational impact of the EU's international identity role as representing normative power." Accordingly the EU envisions for itself the role of a human rights promoter. Thereby the construction of a positive human rights-related self-image and the promotion of normative standards in relations with accession candidates and third countries go hand-in-hand (Diez 2005: 614). Such a position was most visibly expressed in the EU's 1993 Copenhagen criteria which made democracy, the rule of law and respect for human and minority rights a precondition for accession. Referring to a 'normative power Europe' does not mean to idealise EU external relations as following purely moral ends and excluding economic or strategic interests. Indeed, assuming "(…) a normative sphere without interests is in itself nonsensical" (Diez 2005: 625).

Besides conditionality on accession countries other instruments have become common practice. For instance, human rights clauses have been introduced when concluding treaties with third countries. The EU can threaten to suspend political and/or economic relations and engage in a political dialogue on human rights. As stated above, the European Parliament presents annual reports on human rights which attempt to make public human rights violations. In the best case scenario, public pressure transposed by international media exerts influence on norm violating countries.

Minority Rights in Europe

Chapter III of the book is dedicated to minorities and minority rights. With the enlargement of the CoE and EU, ethnic relations figure higher on the European agenda. The experience of civil war, genocide and 'ethnic cleansing' in Yugoslavia made Europe sensitive for ethnic conflicts. Minority rights have been designed to prevent the outbreak of violent conflicts and discrimination on racial grounds through social integration, equal treatment, and cultural protection of national minorities.

Minority rights cannot be reduced to a single set of specific norms. Various international organisations have developed minority standards and there is no common definition of what a 'minority' is. Minority standards appear as lacking in coherence and clarity. Furthermore, minority rights draw on a mixture of hard and soft law. On the one hand, minority standards can be deduced from international law based on a patchwork of international treaties. On the other hand, minority rights draw on customary international law derived from political declarations and state practice. Some of the most influential documents have no legal force, like the OSCE Copenhagen Document or the UN Declaration on Persons Belonging to National or Ethnic, Religious and Linguistic Minorities. Lastly, organisations such as the OSCE, CoE, and EU have developed minority rights standards. Among these organisations, the CoE is the only one that has dedicated a whole convention to minorities, the Framework Convention on the Protection of National Minorities (FCNM) and the European Charter for Regional or Minority Languages (ECRML).

Among the three organisations, the EU is the most conservative regarding minority standards and their application. European Union member states showed great disinterest in developing legally binding minority standards. Only the Racial Equality Directive[8] may become an effective instrument to fight unequal treatment on racial grounds. The Charter of Fundamental Rights of the European Union, which entails no legal obligations, has no specific minority article there are only Article 20 and 21 that provide for equality before the law and prohibit „discrimination on the ground of race, colour, membership of national minority." No special protection for minorities is envisioned. The EC as well as member states do not want to advance EU legislation on minority issues (Hughes and Sasse 2003: 10-12). This became most visible during the drafting of the EU Constitution. In over 300 pages minority protection is not given a single paragraph.

Despite the fact that minority rights are fragmented, they revolve around some core values that reflect a minimal international consensus and belong either to international law or customary international law based on political declarations. These values include non-discrimination, preservation of ethnic identity, protection of language, and political and societal participation.

At a summit held in Copenhagen in 1990, the CSCE agreed on a paper best known as the Copenhagen Document. This document is the most comprehensive OSCE paper on human and minority rights.[9] Before the Copenhagen Document, the Helsinki Final Act of 1975 accounted for human rights and Principle VII mentioned equality before the law and equal enjoyment of human rights for minority members. Under the Copenhagen Document a whole section (IV) is dedicated to minorities. But as was the case with the Council of Europe's FCNM, the document entails no formal definition of a minority. Application of the rights provided is dependent on effective monitoring. The Copenhagen Document grants important rights and the composition of these rights in 1990

[8] Council Directive 2000/43EC of 29 June.

[9] For an overview of OSCE and minority protection read Jane Wright (1997) "The OSCE and the Protection of Minority Rights," Human Rights Quarterly, 18, 190-205.

makes the OSCE a front-runner among international organisations dealing with minority issues. In sum, the document guarantees minority members the right to maintain and practice their culture, to use their language, set up minority institutions, special protection of minority culture by the state, participation in public life including self-governance, and the right to non-discrimination. The OSCE High Commissioner on national Minorities (HCNM) oversees the implementation of the politically binding Copenhagen Document.

The FCNM of 1995 is an exceptional piece of international law. It is the most comprehensive and legally binding piece of minority legislation produced by an international organisation. Its first aim is conflict prevention and preservation of minority identity. This is not surprising because in the mid 1990s Europe had just witnessed a brutal ethnic war in Yugoslavia. A widely held fear was that other Eastern European countries could have the same potential for spreading ethnic violence as the former Yugoslavia did. Efforts resulted in a Framework Convention that seeks to formulate minimum standards for minority protection to prevent ethnic tensions from turning into violence. The FCNM grants to minority members the right to maintain their culture (Art. 5), equality before the law and prohibition of discrimination (Art. 4), freedom of assembly, association, expression, thought, conscience, and religion (Art.7), the right to use the minority language in private and public (Art. 10), as well as to learn the minority language (Art.14), and to display information in that language to the public (Art. 11). National Minorities have also the right to set up their own educational institutions (Art.13). Further, the FCNM prohibits forced assimilation (Art. 5) and encourages the contracting parties to promote the "spirit of tolerance, and intercultural dialogue (Art. 6).

It is a clear sign of progress that European states have acknowledged the rights of 338 million people living on the European continent who can claim to be minority members (Pan 2003: 3). But consensus could only be reached by softening the wording of the Framework Convention. The explanatory report to the FCNM characterises the FCs provisions as "programme type provisions seeking out objectives which the Parties undertake to pursue". Much is left to the discretion of the contracting parties. In the FCNM many escape clauses water down the rights of minorities. Phrases like "where necessary", "as far as possible", or "where appropriate" open ways for arbitrary implementation and self-interested application. Realisation of the FCNM provisions is given to the contracting parties (Pentassuglia 1999: 418-419). It depends on their decision how to interpret and implement the FCNM. A shortcoming of the FCNM is that it does not entail a definition of the term 'national minority', allowing contracting parties to define to whom they grant the rights set out in the Convention. There is no international consensus on a single approach to defining the term 'minority' and it appears rather unlikely that such a consensus can be reached in the near future. The vague wording of the FCNM makes it almost impossible to go to the Strasbourg Court for Human Rights, the rights set up in the convention are not justiciable and no individual complain mechanisms have been developed, largely ruling out litigation out as a further tool of norm promotion (Gilbert 1996: 175).

Minority rights in particular appear is highly fragmented norms. Accordingly their implementation is often a matter of discretion as the case of Estonia will show. A further case study on Roma in Slovakia and the Czech Republic highlights the urgency with which minority rights should be treated as a truly European issue.

CHAPTER II

EUROPEAN ORGANISATIONS AND HUMAN RIGHTS

The Council of Europe, the Standard-setter

Karen Schlüter

"European" fundamental rights as we know them today as element and as objective of international and supranational organisations are among the most important result of the political development after the Second World War. They form part of the international system of protection of human rights system which was established in this period.

Due to this movement, a variety of organisations were founded with different aims and duties. Especially the Council of Europe (CoE), OECD and the European Community / Union are responsible for the European development of human rights and their protection.

However, the protection of human rights by these three Organisations varies in important points. Among them, the CoE is the oldest one, founded in 1949. Its aim – regulated in Article 1 of the Statute of the CoE "is to achieve a greater unity between its members for the purpose of safeguarding and realising the ideals and principles … ". The CoE is particularly engaged to work on international legally binding treaties for the protection of human rights and for discussions of social questions. So it becomes a standard-setter in human rights, rule of law and democracy. On the contrary, the protection of human rights by OECD has a non-binding character and was focused to promote new processes especially during the seventies. The discussion concerning the European Community / Union (EC / EU) and their role to protect human rights has got a new dimension because of the draft of the Constitution of the European Union and its catalogue of fundamental rights which was proclaimed during the summit in Nice in 2000 but without any legally binding character until now.

This article gives an overview about the the CoE's structure, organs and further bodies as well as their functions and works, especially as law-setter. A special focus is made on the European Convention on Human Rights and the future amendments by Protocol No. 14 and its mechanism to guarantee this protection by the European Court of Human Rights. The relationship between the CoE and the EU which is up to now no member of the CoE and the Convention will be examined. The article will conclude with a critical analyse of the CoE's present and future work, especially whether it can remain the standard-setter of human rights protection in Europe or whether it will lose its position facing the EU because of its lack of supranational power.

Intergovernmental or supranational: recipe for success or congenital defect?

After the turbulent period of great hostilities and within uncountable human rights violations during the Second World War caused by totalitarianism and dictatorial regimes, the idea of political unification of Europe by no means of recent origin was reborn so that numerous national and international organisations sponsoring European unity, such as the United Europe Movement, the European Union of Federalists and the Economic League of European Cooperation were founded. These combined to form in 1947 the "International Committee of Movements for European Unity" which then organised a "Congress of Europe" at The Hague in May 1948 (Sands/Klein 2001: 161). Whether this development can be described as governmental or non-governmental is interpreted in different ways: Sands / Klein describe it as a non-governmental development although many prominent statesmen participated in it, but – in their opinion – "they did so as private individuals, not as state representatives" (Sands / Klein 2001: 161). In contrary, Smith portrayed the development that "around twenty countries attended the Congress of Europe" (Smith 2003: 92). In the final analysis, it makes no difference: the resolution of the Congress, formulating the will for a "united Europe", stimulated governments into action. As a result, the draft of the CoE's Statute was elaborated due to the founding declaration "Never Again" and signed by ten European governments on 5 May 1948.

The history of the CoE can be divided in two periods: the first forty years the CoE operated as a "Western European Council" (Holtz 2000: 11). After the fall of the Berlin wall, the CoE can claim to represent Europe because it extended from its ten founding members to forty-six states. So, all European States except Belarus are now member of the CoE.

Due to the Statute, the CoE was planned as an intergovernmental organisation representing the compromise between the supporters of a supranational organisation leading to the "United States of Europe" (France) and those favouring non-binding inter-state cooperation (United Kingdom); it also represented a victory for those states which favoured a "functional" (Sands/Klein 2001: 161) approach. This legal nature leads to the description by Holtz that "right from the beginning the CoE suffered because of a solid lack, the total absence of real power" (Holtz 2000: 12). In consequence, the CoE is a confederation of states, the sovereignty remaining with the member states. The CoE cannot issue directly binding acts regarding the member states; the conventions and other international treaties do only bind the member states which ratified them. So the CoE offers an integration model "à la carte" (Holtz 2000: 16), it represents a Europe of different speeds. At the same time, this fact shows on the one hand the CoE's attractiveness and on the other hand its weakness which will be shown in detail by this article.

Structure, Organs and Institutions of the CoE

The statutory aim of the Council of Europe is to achieve greater unity among its members through common action, agreements and debates. The CoE endeavours this goal with help of their organs and other institutional bodies.

The (main) organs of the Council previewed by the Statute itself are

- the Committee of the Ministers, formed by the Ministers for Foreign Affaires of the member states,
- and the Parliamentary Assembly (until 1974: Consultative Assembly) which consists of members of the national parliaments.

A "Secretariat" supported the organs; it is however not a principal organ. The Statute remains silent with regard to the competencies of the Secretary-General. According to the Committee of Ministers' resolution of May 1951 to this institutional structure envisaged the creation of specialised European authorities with competence in the economic, social and cultural, legal and administrative and other related fields.

Three of them are particularly relevant for the development of human rights[1]:

- the European Court of Human Rights,
- the European Commissioner for Human Rights
- and the European Commission on Racism and Intolerance

Committee of the Ministers (CM)

The Committee of Ministers is the Council of Europe's decision-making body. It comprises the Foreign Affairs Ministers of all the member states, or their per-

[1] Due to the overview structure and the focus on Human Rights the following CoE's institutions cannot not be examined:
- Conference and later Congress of Local and regional Authorities of Europe (1957 / 1994)
- Council of Europe Development Bank, CEB (1956)
- Pompidou Group, Co-operation group to combat drug abuse and illicit trafficking in drugs (1971)
- European Youth Foundation, EYF (1972) as well as European Youth Centre in Strasbourg, EYCS (1972) and Budapest, EYCB (1995)
- Eurimages, European Support Fund for the co-production of cinematographic works (1988)
- North-South Centre, European Centre for Global Interdependence and Solidarity – Lisbon, (1989)
- Venice Commission , The European Commission for Democracy through Law of the Council of Europe (1990)
- European Audiovisual Observatory in Strasbourg (1992)
- European Centre for Modern Language in Graz (1994)
- Group of States against Corruption,GRECO (1999)
- European Directorate for the Quality of Medicines, EDQM.

manent diplomatic representatives in Strasbourg. In 1951, the Committee of Ministers invited each member state to appoint a Permanent Representative who would be in constant touch with the organisation so that each Minister could appoint a Deputy. From 1952 onwards the practice has developed that the Deputies have the same decision-making powers as the Ministers. A Deputy is usually also the Permanent Representative of the member state.

The Committee of the Ministers describes itself as both: as a governmental body because of national approaches to problems facing European society on inter pares level and as a collective forum with regard to Europe-wide responses. In collaboration with the Parliamentary Assembly, it is the guardian of the Council's fundamental values, and monitors member states' compliance with their undertakings. The Committee of Ministers performs a triple role:

- as the emanation of the governments which enables them to express on equal terms their national approaches to the problems confronting Europe's societies;
- as the collective forum where European responses to these challenges are worked out;
- as guardian, alongside the Parliamentary Assembly, of the values for which the Council of Europe exists.

The work and activities of the Committee of Ministers include the following issues:

- Political dialogue
- Interacting with the Parliamentary Assembly and the Congress of Local and Regional Authorities of the CoE
- Admitting new member States in cooperation with the Parliamentary Assembly and suspending or terminating membership
- Monitoring respect of commitments by member states
- Concluding Conventions and agreement
- Adopting recommendations to member states
- Adopting the budget
- Adopting and monitoring the Programme of Activities
- Implementing cooperation and assistance programmes
- Supervising the execution of judgments of the European Court of Human Rights

The chairmanship of Committee changes on a six-month basis. The Committee meets at ministerial level once a year, in May or in November. The meetings, known as "sessions", are normally held in Strasbourg and usually last one full day or two half days. While the greater part of each session is usually devoted to political dialogue, the Ministers may discuss all matters of mutual interest with the exception of national defence. Although the records of the sessions are confidential, a final communiqué is issued at the end of each meeting. The Ministers may also issue one or more declarations. During the last years the changing situation in Europe in particular the changes initiated by the draft of a Constitution for the European Union including a binding Charter of Fundamental Rights and its consequences on the work of the CoE in human rights questions were discussed. The CoE and especially the European Court of Human Rights is in favour of a deeper cooperation with the European Union and its judicial organ, the European Court of Justice.

In cooperation with the Parliamentary Assembly, the Committee of Ministers is responsible for the admittance of new members. According to Article 4, 5 and 6 of the Statute, the Committee has the authority to invite European States to become members of the Council of Europe. Generally, the conditions for membership are pluralistic democracy, the rule of law and respect for human rights. Recently the invitations have included a number of conditions concerning the implementation of democratic reforms in the applicant state. Particularly, adhesion to the European Convention of Human Rights and its supervisory mechanism, as well as the commitment to abolish the death penalty have more recently been set as explicit prerequisites for the admission to the organisation. Consequently some countries were only able to join the Organisation at a subsequent stage; i.e. Portugal in 1976, Spain in 1977. Greece was obliged to withdraw from the Council of Europe in 1970 for a period of four years. In order to facilitate the process of accession of the countries from Central and Eastern Europe, the Assembly introduced in 1989 a so-called special guest status, applicable to all national legislative assemblies of European non-member states, which have signed the Helsinki Final Act and the Charter of Paris for a New Europe. On the one hand, the adhesion of the East European post-communist states were a catalyst because it attracted more attentions for Human Rights questions (Koenig 2005: 83). As a result, the European Charter for Regional or Minority Languages from 1992 and Framework Convention for the Protection of national minorities from 1994 created a new fundament of national status. But on the other hand, the problems caused by the accession of post-communist states undermined the CoE's credibility in a sustained way because the CoE set priority to integrate these new members in its system although they did not and partly still do not fulfil the standards (Brummer 2004: 437). These critics is focussed especially with regard to Russia because of several circumstances: e.g. its adhesion during the conflict in Chechnya and the Russian statement that the CoE is not allowed to interfere in internal affaires (Elvers 2000: 223) and the permanent non-implementing of judgements by the European Court of Human Rights (Keller/Bertschi 2004: 216). Besides the membership, the CoE offers the possibility of an observer status.

Concerning the concluding Conventions and agreements Article 15 lit. a of the Statute states that the Committee of Ministers "shall consider the action required to further the aim of the Council of Europe, including the conclusion of conventions and agreements". Over 190 treaties have now been opened for signature. The best known are the European Convention of Human Rights (see below) and the European Social Charter (see below). The text of any treaty is finalised when it is adopted by the Committee. Under Article 20 of the Statute adoption of a treaty requires:

- a two-thirds majority of the representatives casting a vote and
- a majority of those entitled to vote.

The same majorities are required to authorise the publication of any explanatory report. The Committee also fixes the date that the treaty will be opened for signature. Conventions are only binding on those States which ratify them.

In regard of adopting recommendations to member States, Article 15 lit. b of the Statute provides for the Committee of Ministers to make recommendations to member states on matters for which the Committee has agreed "a common policy". Under Article 20 of the Statute, adoption of a recommendation requires:

- a unanimous vote of all representatives present and
- a majority of those entitled to vote.

However, in November 1994 the Ministers' Deputies decided to make their voting procedure more flexible and made a "Gentleman's agreement" not to apply the unanimity rule to recommendations. Recommendations are not binding on member States.

Article 17 of the Statute authorises the Committee of Ministers to set up "advisory or technical committees". This has led to the creation of some 30 steering committees and a large number of ad hoc expert committees, which assist the Committee of Ministers in the implementation of the programme of activities. So, the Committee of Ministers has an elaborate and well developed structure of committees and subsidiary bodies of governmental experts, mostly established on a permanent basis and meeting regularly (Sands/Klein 2001: 163).

In accordance with Article 46 of the Convention as amended by Protocol No. 11, the Committee of Ministers supervises the execution of judgments of the European Court of Human Rights (see below). The Committee of Ministers also plays a role as "judicial authority" (Lappenküpper 1990: 83) within its essential function to ensure that member states comply with the judgments of the European Court of Human Rights. In order to strengthen this function Protocol No. 14, not in force until now, previews under the new article 46 para. 3 to empower the Committee of Ministers to ask the Court to interpret a final judgement, for the purpose of facilitating the supervision of its execution. The Committee of Ministers' experience of supervising the execution of the judgments shows that difficulties are sometimes encountered due to disagreement as to the interpretation of judgements (CoE 2004: 16). This measure is criticised (Keller/Bertschi 2005: 224): the division of competencies between the Committee of Ministers and the Court is blurred because the Court is engaged in the political process of implementation. Besides, the effectiveness of the measure is doubted.

In order to answer the initial questions *"recipe for success or congenital defect":* the Committee of Ministers is the Council of Europe's decision-making body. First and foremost, the Committee of Ministers' session ought to find out a common opinion in essential European questions. Because of the lack of supranational competencies the Committee of the Ministers cannot elaborate legally binding decisions with regard to member states. Therefore the organ is no "European government", it has the "character of permanent diplomatic conference" (Lappenküper 1990: 84). Therefore Sands/Klein (2001: 163) have stated that the Committee of Ministers "is in no sense an executive organ" because it is readily apparent that the Committee cannot take decisions binding upon governments; its only power is to recommend matters to governments. In the conclusion, wide functions provided in Article 15 "on the recommendation of the Parliamentary Assembly or on its own initiative, the Committee of Ministers shall consider the action required to further the aim of the Council of Europe, including the conclusion of conventions ..." are combined here with extremely limited powers; the only power to take binding decisions related solely to questions of internal organisation.

Parliamentary Assembly (PACE)

The Parliamentary Assembly (until 1974: Consultative Assembly) of the Council of Europe, which held its first session on 10 August 1949, can be considered the oldest international parliamentary Assembly with a pluralistic composition of democratically elected members of parliament established on the basis of an intergovernmental treaty. The PACE represents the political forces in its member states.

The Statute only previews consultative competencies. In spite of this structural deficit, the PACE developed (three main) functions which exceed the initial framework (Björk 1990: 24):

- stimulating the European integration process in general and acting as a progressive thinker with regard to the CoE's role in particular,
- pushing developments to institutionalise important CoE's aims and
- ensuring the observance of constitutional principles as rule of law and democracy.

The PACE consists of a number of individual representatives from each member state, with a President elected each year from among them for a maximum period of three sessions. Whilst in the Committee of Ministers each member state has one vote, in the Parliamentary Assembly the number of representatives and consequently of votes is determined by the size of the country. The biggest number is eighteen, the smallest two. As there are an equal number of representatives and substitutes, the total number of members of the Assembly is therefore 630, plus 18 observers. The members are appointed to the PACE in a manner, which is left to be decided by each member state, as long as they are elected within their national or federal Parliament, or appointed from amongst the members of that parliament. The balance of political parties within each national delegation must ensure a fair representation of the political parties or groups in their national parliaments. Representatives sit in alphabetical order, not in country delegations, and European political groups have formed which bring representatives together on a political rather than a national basis. At present the Assembly counts five political groups: the Socialist Group (SOC); the Group of the European People's Party (EPP/CD); Alliance of Liberals and Democrats for Europe (ALDE); the European Democrat Group (EDG) and the Group of the Unified European Left (UEL). Political Groups have to commit themselves to respect the promotion of the values of the Council of Europe, notably political pluralism, human rights and the rule of law. To form a group, at least twenty members of at least six different delegations have to decide to do so. Members of the Assembly are entirely free to choose the group they wish to join. Before deciding they can attend meetings of one or several groups and should not be bound by their national party label but choose the group which best suits their political affinities.

According to Article 22, the PACE is a "deliberative" organ, with the power to make recommendations to the Committee of Ministers upon any matter within the aim and scope of the organisation. According to the principle of separation of powers, the relationship between the representative of the people and the government contains in practice that the executive power tables a motion. Concerning the CoE and the PACE, this principle is turned vice versa: "In the CoE, the Assembly proposes and the Committee of Ministers disposes" (Robertson 1961: 55).

The conclusions of the PACE are presented to the Committee in three different types of texts:

- recommendations,
- resolutions and
- opinions.

Recommendations, requiring a two-third majority vote, contain proposals addressed to the CM, the implementation of which is within the competence of governments. In general, a motion for a recommendation or resolution generates reports. This motion has to be tabled by ten or more members of the Assembly belonging to at least five national delegations. It is then referred to a committee for report and possibly to other committees for opinion. Resolutions embody decisions by the Assembly on questions, which it is empowered to put into effect or expressions of view for, which it alone is responsible. The Assembly mostly expresses opinions on questions put to it by the CM, such as the admission of new member states to the CoE, but also on draft conventions, the budget and the implementation of the Social Charter. Resolutions and opinions require a simple majority. The difference is largely one of terminology, although in general recommendations call for action by the Committee and resolutions do not, and opinions are given on question referred to it by the Committee.

Under Article 32 the PACE is to meet annually, normally for not more than a month at a time; it presently holds four plenary sessions a year. The Assembly's plenary debates are held in public while committees meet generally in camera. The debates are conducted according to the principles observed in national parliaments. The number of representatives who may take part in a debate is not limited, except in specific cases such as debates on requests for urgent procedure or on procedural motions. Due to the general shortage of debating time available, the Bureau proposes to the Assembly a programme and a timetable for each specific debate.

The PACE is supported administratively by the Parliamentary Assembly Secretariat and has its own elastic committee structure (Sands/Klein 2001: 164) of the:

Standing Committee

- Joint Committee
- Assembly Committee

The Standing Committee consists of the Bureau (President, twenty Vice-Presidents, the Chairpersons of the political groups or their representatives as well as the Chairpersons of the general PACE Committees or their substitutes), the Chairpersons of national delegations and the Chairpersons of the general committees. It is generally convened at least twice a year and its major task is to act on behalf of the PACE when the latter is not in session. Each year one of the Standing Committee meetings, together with a number of other committees, takes place normally in one of the member states.

The Joint Committee composed of a representative of each member Government and a corresponding number of representatives of the Assembly is the forum set up to co-ordinate the activities of, and maintains good relations between, the Committee of Ministers and the Assembly.

According to its Rules of Procedure, the PACE has 10 committees with either 83 or 51 seats dedicated to different topics[2]. Although committees deal in particular with reports, they have great freedom to discuss any matter within their competence when they agree to do so. They organise hearings, colloquies or conferences on particular subjects, the findings of which can then be used for the preparation of reports to the Assembly. Committees meet either in Strasbourg or Paris, possibly in Brussels when a joint meeting with a body of the European Parliament is envisaged or in Budapest at the European Youth Centre.

[2] Political Affairs; Legal Affairs and Human Rights; Economic Affairs and Development; Social, Health and Family Affairs; Migration, Refugees and Population; Culture, Science and Education; Environment, Agriculture and Local and Regional Affairs; Equal Opportunities for Women and Men; Rules of Procedure and Immunities, Honouring of Obligations and Commitments by member states of the Council of Europe (Monitoring Committee).

The PACE stresses the importance to be a discussion forum within external relations which covers national parliaments of member states, of non-member states, international parliamentary assemblies and international intergovernmental organisations. Furthermore, the PACE has developed its contacts with other international parliamentary assemblies such as the European Parliament, the Western European Union, the Parliamentary Assembly of the OSCE, the Inter-Parliamentary Union, Benelux, the Nordic Council, PABSEC, CIS and others. For many years the Assembly has also been operational as parliamentary forum for a certain number of intergovernmental organisations, in particular the OECD, and has developed close relations with specific organisations such as the EBRD and many of the specialised agencies of the United Nations.

In order to answer the initial questions *"recipe for success or congenital defect":* on the one hand, the essential point is that the PACE is of a purely persuasive character; it cannot bind the Committee or any member State by its action, and thus, whilst its composition is reminiscent of a parliamentary body, it is very far indeed from being a true European Parliament with real legislative power (Sands / Klein 2001: 164). On the other hand, although the Pace is limited to consultative competencies, the PACE became "the CoE's driving force" and the "European conscience" (Lappenküper 1990: 86): With regard to the accession by post-communists states it was entitled as "school for parliamentary democracy" (Schwimmer 2000: 88), thus due to its intergovernmental nature it was the best prepared institution because of its flexibility to integrate the new democracies in east and middle-east Europe (Schwimmer 2000: 81).

European Court of Human Rights (Court)

The European Court of Human Rights set up under the Convention as amended by Protocol No. 11 is composed of a number of judges equal to that of the currently forty-six Contracting States. Originally, the Convention for the Protection of Human Rights and Fundamental Freedoms (Convention) drawn within the CoE was opened for signature in Rome in November 1950 and entered into force in September 1953. Taking as their starting point the 1948 Universal Declaration of Human Rights by the United Nations, the framers of the Convention sought to pursue the aims of the CoE through the maintenance and further realisation of human rights and fundamental freedoms. The Convention was to represent the first steps for the collective enforcement of certain of the rights set out in the Universal Declaration. But in contrast to the Universal Declaration, the political will has existed to accept the lost of sovereignty to provide the Convention and consequently the Court can take decisions binding upon the member states. The Convention laid down a catalogue of civil and political rights and freedoms and set up a mechanism for the enforcement of the obligations entered into by contracting states. So it gives priority to civil and political rights (Koenig 2005: 82); social rights, second-generation human rights, are protected by a separate convention, the European Social Charter which does not know a similar protection mechanism as the Convention (Fritzsche 2004: 81). In general, White (1996: 237) describes the Charter's circumstances: "the initial lack of enthusiasm for the treaty on second-generation human rights did not prevent the Council sponsoring the European Social Charter". Mostly due to the lack of political will on the part of the member states, the European Social Charter itself does not clearly impose an absolute and immediate obligation on State parties, Article 20 adopting an unusual approach by placing parties under an obligation to pursue the policy of realising the nineteen economic and social rights listed in Part 1. In addition, allowing the States parties to select the rights they wish to protect devalue them as substantive legal rights, and allows States to avoid areas of economic and social concern on political grounds. This problem is further exacerbated by the inadequacy of the supervisory system comparable with the European Convention on Human Rights.

The Convention: original, now and future

Originally, three institutions were entrusted with the responsibility to guarantee the Convention's aims: The European Commission of Human Rights (set up in 1954), The European Court of Human Rights (set up in 1959) and the Committee of Ministers of the Council of Europe.

Under the Convention in its original version, complaints could be brought against Contracting States either by other Contracting States or by individual applicants (Individuals, groups of individual or non-governmental organisations). Recognition of the right of individual application was, however, optional and it could therefore be exercised only against those States which has accepted it. The Commission and the part-time Court had shared competences concerning the examination and jurisdiction. From 1980 onwards, the steady growth in the number of cases brought before the convention institutions made it increasingly difficult to keep the length of proceedings within acceptable limits. The problem aggravated by the accession of new contracting states after 1990. The number of applications registered annually with the Commission increased from 404 in 1981 to 4,750 in 1997. By that year the number of unregistered or provisional files opened each year in the Commission had risen to over 12,000. The Court's statistics reflected a similar story, with the number of cases referred annually rising from 7 in 1981 to 119 in 1997.

The increasing case-load prompted a lengthy debate on the necessity for a reform of the Convention supervisory machinery, resulting in the adoption of Protocol No. 11 to the Convention. The aim was to simplify the structure with a view to shortening the length of proceedings while strengthening the judicial character of the system by making it fully compulsory and abolishing the Committee of Ministers' adjudicative role. Protocol No. 11, which came in to force on 1 November 1998, replaced the existing, part-time Court and Commission by a single, full-time Court. In addition, Protocol No. 11 laid down the obligatory possibility for individual application. Individual applications were previewed by the ECHR but it was compulsory and the member state could use its right of reservation according to the Vienna convention of treaties.

But the Protocol No. 11's aim, enhancing the effectiveness of the system, notably by improving the accessibility and visibility of the Court and by simplifying the procedure in order to cope with the influx of applications generated by the constant increase in the number of states (CoE 2004: 1), could not be reached. Quite the reverse occurred: Since 1990, there has been a considerable and continuous rise in the number of individual applications as a result, amongst other things, of the CoE's enlargement. Thus the number of applications increased up to 16% annually (Keller/Bertschi 2005: 206). In 2003, the number of individual application was 38435. On the 1st of October 2004, 75200 cases were pending, in contrary to 65500 at the end of 2003. The average duration of proceedings of admissible cases comes to three years (Keller/Bertschi 2005: 206).

But this increase cannot be explained exclusively by the accession of new states parties and the rapidity of the enlargement process but by a general increase in the number of applications brought against states which were party to the Convention in 1993. In 2004, the Convention system was open to no fewer than 800 million people. Although the number of individual application against Central and East European states is increasing the most, the numbers of the individual applications against states which were members before 1989 is also growing (Keller/Bertschi 2005: 206). In 2003 and 2004, 96% of the pending cases were declared inadmissible or deleted off the registry according to Article 37 of the Convention. As a reaction, the Court tried to take streamlining measures since 1999 which can be divided in measures on procedural level and on juridical level. Concerning the procedural level, already in November 2003, the Court itself had taken steps by amending its Rules of Court based on the recommendation submitted by an internal working party established in 1999. *Inter alia,* it abolished the so called "warning letters" to those applications that are likely to be rejected as inadmissible. Moreover, it substituted formal decisions on the inadmissibility of applications taken by a three-judge-committee under Article 28 of the Convention by a mere informal letter lacking any further reasoning (Laubner 2004: 696). In regard of the juridical measures, the Court developed its jurisdiction, namely in the field of:

- Convention's violation because of length of proceedings and
- so called "repetitive cases".

The development of the Court's jurisdiction in cases which deals with violation because of length of proceedings can be distinguished in two steps, firstly violations against Article 6 para. 1 of the Convention because of too long proceedings; secondly violations against Article 6 of the Convention referring to Article 13 of the Convention (right of effective appeal). The first step is originally linked with applications from Italy complaining about the delay of proceedings. At first, the Court judged by global assessments and handled simultaneously several applications (Breuer 2004c: 446). On the 28th July 1999, the Court stated in the sense of an appeal that the high number of applications have pointed out to structural problems in the Italian legal system which did not contain any remedy on national level. Italy created the legal possibility by the so called *legge Pinto* to claim for compensation in a special proceeding because of too long proceedings. Consequently, applications because of too long proceedings got inadmissible as the *legge Pinto* came into force according Article 35 para. 1 of the Convention (Keller/Bertschi 2005: 208). The Court carried out the second step in its judgement Kudla v. Poland (26.10.2000, 30210/96, CEDH 2000-XI, p. 197 et seq.). It changed its jurisdiction. Formerly, applications because of too long proceedings were just analysed with regard to Article 6 and 13 of the Conventions separately. Now, it is analysed as constituting a violation against Article 6 as well as against Article 13 of the Convention. The change of the Court's jurisdiction resulted from Article 35 para. 1 of the Convention's definition of the exhaustion of national remedies: it contains rights of appeals like actions for modifications of rights as well as declaratory actions. Consequently, a proceeding to claim for compensation had to be established on national level (Keller/Bertschi 2005: 208).

The Court's next step in developing its jurisdiction referred to structural problems in the member states and led to the so called "pilot-judgement" (Bronchiowski v. Poland, 08.04.2004, 71503/01) in 2004. The background is the following: The Court's judgements have declaratory character. All final judgments of the Court are binding on the respondent states concerned (Article 46) which also includes temporary orders (Oellers-Frahm 2003: 689; 2005: 347, Breuer 2004b: 257). On the one hand Article 46 of the Convention means that the Court has no right to dissolve national legislation, to reverse national jurisdiction or to repeal national administrative acts. But on the other hand, the member state is obliged to change national legislation or to annul of an administrative act. National judgements violating the Convention can not be quashed by the Court automatically. So, the decisions by the Court do not have any impact on the judicata effect of the national decision; the Court does not have any competence as a court of cassation (Laue 2005: 96). But the Court's jurisdiction pointed out that the member states are responsible to end violations of the Convention under the control of the CM. So, such a finding by the Court of a violation of the Convention has led the respondent state, and sometimes even other contracting states, to take general measures to comply with the decision in question and the higher domestic courts to adapt their case-law. In some cases, the reference of a case to the Court has of itself prompted or expedited amendments to legislation and regulations or changes in the case-law. Judgments have also resulted in the respondent state adopting concrete measures in relation to the person or persons concerned. This declaratory character of the Court's judgements are accompanied by the fact that around 60% of the cases which fulfilled the admissibility criteria were so called "repetitive cases", processing individual applications which derive from the same structural cause as an earlier application which has led to a judgment finding a breach of the Convention (CoE 2004: 2) and producing an overwhelming caseload. The Court gave in its judgement Assandidze v. Georgia (08.04.2004, 71503/01) concrete instructions to abolish the permanent Convention's violations according to Article 41 of the Convention in stating that the contracting state has no alternative in choosing other measures. On this base, the Court could develop its jurisdiction which led to the so called "pilot-decision" (Bronchiowski v. Poland, 08.04.2004, 71503/01). It stated a "inadmissible structural dysfunction" (Bronchiowski v. Poland, 08.04.2004, 71503/01, 189) so that the contracting state had to reassure that the applicant can claim to its property right or compensation. The Court adjourned the applications until the contracting state implemented the necessary and general measures terminating the violation. If the Court managed to balance the individual applicants' need to obtain a reasoned decision on the one hand and on the other hand to handle the caseload produced in particular by same structured cases was doubted (Breuer 2004c: 445). If it can reach this aim remains to be seen.

Whilst streamlining measures taken by the Court enabled no less than 1500 applications to be disposed of per month in 2003, this remains far below the nearly 2300 applications allocated to a decision body every month (CoE 2004: 2) As a result of the permanent and massive influx of individual applications, the effectiveness of the system, and thus the credibility and authority of the Court, were seriously endangered (CoE 2004: 2). As a follow, the Ministers' deputies, in February 2001, assigned a prominent "Evaluation Group"[3] in order to develop proposals on guaranteeing continued effectiveness of the Court. The Evaluation Group received additional input from a "Reflection Group on the Reinforcement of the Human Rights Protection" set up by the CoE's Steering Committee on Human Rights and submitted its report to the CM in November 2001. The Drafting Group on the Reinforcement of the Human Rights Protection Mechanism presented its final report in April 2004. The Protocol No. 14 was open for signature on 13th April 2004, all member states have to sign and if necessary to ratify it that it enters into force. Until now (March 2006) all member states except Russia signed it, 18 signatures were not followed by ratifications[4].

According to the explanatory report (CoE 2004: 7) Protocol No. 14 – unlike Protocol No. 11 - makes no radical changes to the control system established by

[3] The Group was composed of Justin Harman, Permanent Representative of Ireland to the CoE; Chairman of the Minster's Deputies Liaison Committee with the Court (in the Chair); Luzius Wildhaber, President of the Court, and Hans Christian Krüger, Deputy Secretary General of the CoE.

[4] See further details: http://conventions.coe.int.

the Convention. It previews several amendments which are introduced in three main areas:

- reinforcement of the Court's filtering capacity in respect of the mass of unmeritorious applications – in particular by making a single judge competent to declare inadmissible or strike out an individual application.,
- a new admissibility criterion concerning cases in which the applicant has not suffered a significant disadvantage; the new criterion contains two safeguard clauses,
- measures for dealing with repetitive cases and
- the possibility of European Union's accession to the ECHR.

Structure and functioning of the Court
At present, the Court's judges are elected by the PACE for a term of six years. Under Protocol No. 14 the judges' terms of office will change and increase to nine years; at the same time, the possibility of re-election will be excluded (Article 23 as amended by Art. 2 para. 1 and 2 of Protocol No. 14). These changes are intended to reinforce their independence and impartiality, as desired notably the by the PACE in its recommendation 1649/2004 (CoE 2004: 9). This amendment is criticised because the judges reintegration into the national system is questioned (Keller/Bertschi 2005: 216). There is no restriction on the number of judges of the same nationality although Article 20 provides that the number of judges is equal to that of the contracting parties. At the moment, the terms of office of one half of the judges elected at the first election expired after three years, so as to ensure that the terms of office of one half of the judges are renewed every three years. Under Protocol No. 14 (Article 23 as amended by Article 2, 3 and 4) this system will be abolished in order to ensure that the introduction of a non-renewable term of office will not threaten the continuity of the Court. Judges sit on the Court in their individual capacity and do not represent any State. They cannot engage in any activity which is incompatible with their independence or impartiality or with the demands of full-time office. At present, their terms of office expire when they reach the age of seventy. This will be amended by Protocol No. 14 that the terms of office of judges shall expire when they reach the age of 70 but the judges shall hold office until replaced (Article 2 para. 2 and 3).

At present, the Court sits in committees of three judges, in Chambers of seven judges and in a Grand Chamber of seventeen judges (Article 27 para. 1 of the Convention). The Court is divided in four sections. A considerable part of the Court's work is done by the registry which is responsible for the application from its incoming to its presentation before panel of judges. After the registration, the application is examined as preparatory "pre-judicial" (Laubner 2004: 699) by a registry case-lawyer under the formal control by judge-rapporteur

(Keller/Bertschi 2005: 214 et seq.). Article 7 of Protocol No. 14 contains new provisions defining the competence of the new single-judge formation. It is specified that the competence of the single judge is limited to taking decisions of admissibility or decisions to strike the case out of the list "where such decision can be taken without further examination" (Article 27 para. 1 as amended by Article 7 of Protocol No. 14). This amendment is strongly criticised: The final character of any such admissibility decision – which previously could only be effected by unanimous decision of three judges - combined with vagueness of the supposedly restricting criterion and that of the new admissibility provision introduced by Protocol No. 14, warrant special scrutiny as regards the Court's future practice. The filtering capacities released by introducing the single-judge formation will have to make up for the loss of confidence applicants so far could have in collegial decisions derived from different judicial and national perspectives. Whether this will be the case remains to be seen, given the fact that most of the work filtering applications currently is done by the registry rather than the judges (Laubner 2004: 699). In addition to the single-judge formation, Protocol No. 14 seeks to enhance the Court's filtering capabilities by introducing a new category of personnel called "rapporteurs": They will replace the legal secretaries introduced by the Protocol No. 11 under current Article 25 of the Convention. The purpose will be to assist the single-judge (Laubner 2004: 699).

Any contracting state (Inter-State application) or individual claiming to be a victim of a violation of the Convention (individual application) may lodge directly with the Court in Strasbourg an application alleging a breach by a contracting state of one of the Convention rights. The procedure before the Court is adversarial and public. Hearings, which are held only in a minority of cases, are public, unless the Chamber/Grand Chamber decides otherwise on account of exceptional circumstances. Memorials and other documents filed with the Court's registry by the parties are, in principle, accessible to the public.

Individual applicants may present their own cases, but legal representation is recommended, and indeed usually required once an application has been communicated to the respondent Government. The Council of Europe has set up a legal aid scheme for applicants who do not have sufficient means.

The official languages of the Court are English and French, but applications may be submitted in one of the official languages of the Contracting States. Once the application has been declared admissible, one of the Court's official languages must be used, unless the President of the Chamber/Grand Chamber authorises the continued use of the language of the application.

According to Article 33 and 35 admissibility criteria differs between

- Individual applications, Article 35 and
- Inter-State cases, Art. 33.

At present, individuals ("any person, non-governmental organisation or group of individuals") have to fulfil all of the following criteria:

- to be a victim of a violation of rights guaranteed by the Convention and its protocols by one of the High Contracting Parties (Article 34),
- all domestic remedies have been exhausted and the final decision is not longer than six month ago (Article 35 para. 1),
- application is not anonymous (Article 35 para. 2 lit. a) or manifestly ill-founded or an abuse of the right of application (Article 35 para. 3) and
- is not substantially the same as a matter that has already been examined by the Court or has already been submitted to another procedure of international investigation or settlement and contains no relevant new information (Article 35 para. lit.b).

Under Protocol No. 14, new and additional admissibility criterion will be inserted into the new Article 35 para. 3 lit. b that the Court shall declare inadmissible any individual application submitted under Article 34 if it considers that: "the applicant has not suffered a significant disadvantage, unless respect for human rights as defined in the Convention and the Protocols thereto requires an examination of the application on the merits and provided that no case may be rejected on this ground which has not been duly considered by a domestic tribunal". According to the interim provisions, this new admissibility criterion may only be applied by the Chambers and the Grand Chambers of the Court in the two years following the entry into force of the Protocol. What "significant disadvantage" means has to be developed by the Court's jurisdiction. It was suggested as a possible interpretation that application violating Article 2 (right to life" and 3 (torture, inhuman or degrading treatment or punishment), Article 5 (liberty and security of person) and 12 (right to marry and to found a family) of the Convention could fulfil this criterion (Keller/Bertschi 2005: 221). The new criterion received opposition from almost all sides including members of the CoE's Steering Committee on Human Rights itself, the Court, the PACE, State Parties and NGO's (see for further details Laubner 2004: 705). The opinion about the consequences of this new admissibility criterion varies: On the one hand, in regard of the current inadmissibility rate, a further reduction of these cases by 5% certainly would not qualify as a significant effect on the Court's work because it will neither affect the vast number of cases that already are inadmissible nor will it specifically affect repetitive cases. On the other hand, any curtailment of the right of individual application must be presumed to send a signal that despite all safe-guard clauses might be misconceived by some contracting states – probably even willingly so (Laubner 2004: 710). Namely in these cases, the Court offers the only possibility to claim for the own rights (Keller/Bertschi 2005: 211). Instead of new admissibility criterion better financial resources to increase in personnel in particular were recommended (Satzger 2005: 658).

Article 33 provides that states as "any High Contracting Party may refer to the Court any alleged breach of the provisions of the Convention and the protocols thereto by another High Contracting Party". Article 35 para. 1 (exhaustion of domestic remedies) also apply to Inter-State cases (Gomien 2000: 145) although the real practicability can be questioned.

At present, current Article 29 para. 3 of the Convention generally requires decisions on the admissibility of an individual to be taken separately from the judgment on the merits. Only in exceptional cases may the Court decide otherwise. This indicates the following procedure: Once the Chamber has decided to admit the application, it may invite the parties to submit further evidence and written observations, including any claims for "just satisfaction" by the applicant. If no hearing has taken place at the admissibility stage, it may decide to hold a hearing on the merits of the case. The President of the Chamber may, in the interests of the proper administration of justice, invite or grant leave to any contracting state which is not party to the proceedings, or any person concerned who is not the applicant, to submit written comments, and, in exceptional circumstances, to make representations at the hearing. A contracting state whose national is an applicant in the case is entitled to intervene as of right. Under Protocol No. 14, the current exception – no separate decision on the admissibility and the judgement on the merits – will become the rule in order to streamline the individual applications procedure considerably (Laubner 2004: 701 et seq.) and to promote friendly settlement agreements (Keller/Bertschi 2005: 216). Currently, during the procedure on the merits, negotiations aimed at securing a friendly settlement may be conducted through the Registrar. Protocol No. 14 seeks to facilitate the conclusion of friendly settlements in several ways. In a first step, the relevant procedure will be merged into a single consolidated provision (new Article 39 of Convention). Second, the Court's obligation to place itself at the disposal of the parties as a mediator will no longer be restricted to the post-admissibility stage but will extend to any stage of the proceedings. Third, future Article 39 para. 4 of Convention will expressly subject friendly settlement agreements to the supervision of the CM (Laubner 2004: 704 et seq.) which reflects the current practice and ought to make friendly settlement agreements more attractive (Keller/Bertschi 2005: 216). At the moment, the Court pronounce a judgement in the case of a friendly settlement agreement which leads to the supervision by the CM: This practice is in contradiction to current Article 39 which previews a decision which is out of the CM's control.

At present, Chambers decide by a majority vote. Any judge who has taken part in the consideration of the case is entitled to append to the judgment a separate opinion, either concurring or dissenting, or a bare statement of dissent. Within three months of delivery of the judgment of a Chamber, any party may request that the case be referred to the Grand Chamber if it raises a serious question of interpretation or application or a serious issue of general importance. Such requests are examined by a Grand Chamber panel of five judges composed of the President of the Court, the Section Presidents, with the exception of the Section President who presides over the Section to which the Chamber that gave judgment belongs, and another judge selected by rotation from judges who were not members of the original Chamber. A Chamber's judgment becomes final on expiry of the three-month period or earlier if the parties announce that they have no intention of requesting a referral or after a decision of the panel rejecting a request for referral. If the panel accepts the request, the Grand Chamber renders its decision on the case in the form of a judgment. The Grand Chamber decides by a majority vote and its judgments are final. All final judgments of the Court are binding on the respondent States concerned.

Responsibility for supervising the execution of judgments lies with the CoE's CM. The CM verifies whether states in respect of which a violation of the Convention is found have taken adequate remedial measures to comply with the specific or general obligations arising out of the Court's judgments. In order to strengthen this function Article 46 para. 3 as amended by Protocol No. 14 empower the CM to ask the Court to interpret a final judgement, for the purpose of facilitating the supervision of its execution.

Conflicts with regard to legislation and jurisdiction of the member states may arise from the national implementation and integration of the Convention into national law due to its nature as an international treaty. The form of the national implementation is not previewed by the Convention. Its status and in particular its position in the national hierarchy is due to national constitutions of the member States (Ehlers 2003: 23). From a conceptual point of view, there are distinct approaches to the manner in which European states give domestic legal effect to international treaties directly related to the tradition, monist or dualist. The status itself varies among constitutional law (Austria), above national law (e.g. Belgium, Netherlands, Luxembourg, and France), national law (e.g. Italy, Greece) and the Conventions binds the state internationally upon its ratification, but that act alone does not have the legal force of transforming the treaty's provisions into domestic law, until a separate legislative act is given, it has no domestic binding effect (e.g. Ireland, Norway). For example in Germany, according to Article 59 para. 2 of the German constitution (Grundgesetz), the Convention was ratified as act of assent. Formally, the Convention has the status as a regular act. Because of this status, conflicts with laws on the same level but in particular with law of higher hierarchy are foreseeable. This conflict can be easily solved if the national law guarantees higher standards because the Convention's aim is to establish a minimum standard (see Article 53). Problems arise if the national law has lower protection standards and the application of the Convention means to restrict constitutional (fundamental) rights. So, the national legal situation differs from the obligation by the international treaty. In consequence, the member state, e.g. Germany, would not fulfil its obligation previewed by the Convention and be liable for compensation. Until now, this consequence could be prevented by the German constitutional court's jurisdiction stated that the German constitution as be seen in the preamble is "international law friendly" and so the fundamental rights guaranteed in the constitution have to be interpreted in consideration of the Convention (BVerfGE 74, 358, 370; 82, 106, 120). The next conflict is related to the question how the decisions by the Court do have an impact on the national law. The Court is a court established by an international treaty. When the Court finds that there has been a violation of the Convention, and if the domestic law of the State concerned allows only partial reparation to be made, it may award the victim just satisfaction (Article 50 of the Convention). This generally involves the reimbursement of costs and expenses, and when appropriate, compensation for pecuniary and/or non-pecuniary damage. In 2004, the German constitutional court stated in the so called "Görgülü-judgement" (BVerfG NJW 2004: 3407) that – comparable to the "Maastricht-decision" which described the relation between the German constitutional court and the European Court of Justice from the German point of view – it acts in cooperation with the international courts. The German constitutional court stressed that it is not satisfied with a role as a court which is limited by the international obligation entered by the Federal State of Germany; it sees itself as a court with equal rights, in conflict situation with higher authority in regard of the application of the Grundgesetz and its fundamental rights (Kadelbach 2005: 486). But it also disagreed with the lower stage decision of the Oberlandesgericht Naumburg that only the Federal State of Germans as contracting party is bound by the Convention. The Constitutional Court held that all constitutional organs on federal and Laender level and all courts and authorities have to accept the general binding effect (see Cremer 2004: 699). In order to solve this problem caused by the individual implementation by the member states several improvement had been suggested within the context of Protocol No. 14, e.g. constitutional law status in all member states, implementation of a procedure of preliminary rulings at the request of national courts comparable to that before the European Court of Justice under Article 234 of the EC Treaty or constitutional complaint on national level (Laubner 2004: 697) and higher binding effect of the Court's decisions with regard to the member states by an erga omnes effect[5] (Keller/Bertschi 2005: 218). These suggestions were rejected because of the high degree of intervention in internal affaires and the loss of sovereign rights (Keller/Bertschi 2005: 218).

But besides conflicts related to the legal hierarchy, problems arise if the jurisdiction by the Court seems to enlarge its authority stated in Article 53 of the Convention to establish and protect a minimum standard: In 2004, the so called "Caroline-judgment" by the Court (Caroline von Hannover v. Germany, 24.06.2004, 593200/00) effected the national jurisdiction concerning the privacy

[5] The enforceable decisions / judgements are binding on all member states and not only the parties of the proceedings.

sphere of prominent figures in collision with the protection by the Convention. Although the German Medias were afraid of their own rights, the German government accepted the judgment, so that the German courts have to take this new jurisdiction by the Court into consideration interpreting German fundamental rights. This judgment was criticised because the Court seems not accept its own subsidiarity laid down in the Convention with regard to the national courts that the Court only guarantees a minimum standard according to Article 53. As a consequence, the national courts would lose the margin of appreciation and have to implement the higher standard without alternative (Bölke/Gostomzyk 2005: 336). In order to respondent this criticism, the judgement was described as a "fine-tuning" (Keller/Bertschi 2005: 212). In the conclusion, the Court has to cooperate with the national courts and its jurisdiction ought to be limited on its subsidiary competences in accepting national competencies (Jaeger 2005: 203). This implementation seems to be yet unsolved.

One criticism, the Court's lack of autonomy and personnel, was not solved by Protocol No. 14. In 2003, the Court had a budget about 34.9 million €. That means one quarter of the budget of the European Court of Justice in comparison. The Court's budget arose about one third in 2004 and 2005 (Engel 2003: 131). According to Article 50 and 54 of the Convention, the CM decides about the Court's budget which indicates that the Court's independence is questioned (Engel 2003: 131 et seq.; different opinion Boes-Boquicchio 2003: 562). Concerning the autonomy of the personnel, the Convention remains silent. According to the CoE's General Secretary, the Court's personnel are "its personnel" which is supported by the CM and criticised that this old tradition collides with the Convention (Engel 2003: 132).

Future of Court and the Convention

Answering the initial question *"intergovernmental or supranational: recipe for success or congenial defect?"* is directly linked with the Court's future perspectives. The European Union and the European Court of Justice claim for themselves the authority to protect fundamental rights in the European Community / Union since the so called "Stauder-judgement" (ECJ 29/69, 12/11/1969, Stauder v. Stadt Ulm). So, since the 1970ths the European Court of Justice in Luxemburg as one of the organs of the European Union recognises the existence of Human Rights as a general principle in the European Union although a legally binding catalogue of Human Rights lacks until now. In 1977, the European Parliament, the European Council and the European Commission recognised the protection of Human Rights in a joint declaration (see Official Journal C 103, 27/04/1977, 1 - 2). The Court's future is connected with questions about effectiveness and legitimacy of the Court itself.

The effectiveness of international law in general depends upon the willingness of States to surrender some of their sovereign powers to wider international control. In the context of treaty law, sovereign States will often ratify a treaty only on the understanding that all States parties to the same treaty have surrendered equivalent sovereign powers. The underlying principle of such treaties therefore is reciprocity, the understanding that each party will act in a certain way because the other will (Gomien 2000: 141). Because of the intergovernmental nature of the CoE, the Court has limited competencies and so a limited impact on the national jurisdiction compared to the European Court of Justice as one organ of the supranational European Community / Union. Haltern (2004: 182) explained that "juridical review in the Community is a tandem system of justice, one leg being located at the Community, the other at member state level". He focussed on preliminary references under Article 234 E.C which previews that the national court may suspend the proceedings and requests a preliminary ruling from the ECJ when a question concerning the interpretation of the treaty arises. Weiler describes that action as "the principle vehicle for imposition of judicially driven Community discipline" (Weiler 1993: 421). At first sight, because of the lack of supranational competencies, the Convention and the Court cannot be effective. But at the same time, international human right law and in particular the system created by the Convention has introduced two important new innovations to international law. First, it is largely based on a system of multilateral conventions that establish objective standards for state conduct, rather than reciprocal rights and obligations. And second, these conventions place duties on the states in relation to individuals within their jurisdiction rather than to the other state parties (Gomien 2000: 141) which is reflected in Protocol No. 14. The restrictions in regard of individual applications do not endanger the actual success by the Convention and the Court but reassure it. Concerning the often discussed competition between the European Court of Justice and the European Court of Human Rights the following can be stated:

The European Community / Union have twenty-five members, the CoE / Convention fourty-six. So, a lot of questions remain which have to be solved by the Court with regard to the other twenty-one members who are not members of the European Community / Union. Because of the fact, that before becoming members of the European Community / Union states have already been member of the CoE / Convention, the CoE is titled as a "flow heater". But in regard of this interpretation, the work of the CoE loses out and fails to notice that the Court is and will be occupied with a case-load produced by the members States of the European Community / Union. For example, in 2004, 2.470 cases were held against Germany in regard of the total case-load of 40.943 cases (BJMin: 2005: 449) and had a high impact on the national discussion (e.g. Görgülü and Caroline-decisions). Until now, the possibility of individual application in the system of the European Community / Union is very limited; the action of annulment under Article 230 E.C. is a direct challenge upon the validity of the Community act. But in most cases, the act comes from the member States implementing European law and so the action is not admissible. In comparison with other Human rights protection mechanism – regardless of whether to have an effect on international (e.g. Human Rights Convention by the United Nations) or regional level (e.g. American Convention of Human Rights) – the Convention guarantees a high standard to protect human rights by offering individuals to lodge directly with the Court an application alleging a breach by a contracting state of one of the Convention rights after using all remedies on national level. If the Court rules that one of the Convention rights was violated, the decision binds the member states. The interpretation of human rights by the Court enhanced human rights protection in Europe and in the member states in a successful way especially regarding the protection of human rights supranational system of the European Union. The European Court of Justice refers to the Convention mentioned in Article 6 E.U. and as a general principle. According to Article 17 of Protocol No 14 and within the amendment of Article 59 of the Convention, the European Union's accession to the CoE is possible. Article I-7 of the draft of the European Union's Constitution stated that the European Union endeavours to the CoE's accession. Although the future of the draft itself is unclear after the "no" of the French and Dutch referenda, the Charter of Fundamental Rights of the European Union is not questioned because it does not provides more competencies than the European Court of Justice already claims in its jurisdiction by now (Mahlmann 2000: 442). However, the procedure for coming into force has to be solved. The accession would provide a better coherence between the two courts which does not mean the subordination of the European Court of Justice under the jurisdiction of the Court (Pache 2004: 414) because the actual authority of the Court in regard of controlling the national jurisdiction remains and a complementary stages of appeal will not be added. But in conflict, the Convention will be better suited (Grabenwarter 2004: 567) because Article II – 53 provides that no rule by the Charter of Fundamental Rights in the European Union can limit the Convention. Additionally, it can balance lacks in the Convention because the protection of the Charter of Fundamental Rights in the European Union is more detailed (Ruffert 2004: 471). The accession would be the first step to a coherent system of fundamental rights' protection (Breuer 2005a: 234).

European Commissioner for Human Rights

The Office of the Commissioner for Human Rights was established in 1999 as an independent institution within the Council of Europe. In accordance with his mandate, and without excluding the possibility of complementary actions, the Commissioner focuses his activity on four main areas:

- The promotion of the education in and awareness of human rights,
- the encouragement for the establishment of national human rights structures,

- the identification of short-comings in the law and practice with regards to human rights and,
- the promotion of their effective respect and full enjoyment in all the member States of the Council of Europe.

The European Commissioner for Human Rights completes the CoE's mechanism to protect human rights by creating preventive measures and rapid crisis intervention in the case of human rights violations.

The instruments of the European Commissioner for Human Rights are to visit the member states officially and to be informed about the national situation of human rights legislation and its practical implementation by the authorities. Generally, it recommends legislative and executive improvements. Besides the official visits, he proposes further improvements e.g. new migration legislation in Finland. Furthermore, the European Commissioner for Human Rights organises roundtables with national and regional ombudsmen and seminars concerning "tolerance, education, religion", "Fight against child trade" and "Human rights and armed forces" (Roth 2004: 452).

Under the new Article 36 para. 3 of the Convention as amended by Article 12 of the Protocol No. 14, the European Commissioner for Human Rights will have the right "in all cases before a Chamber or the Grand Chamber, the Council of Europe Commissioner for Human Rights may submit written comments and take part in hearings" which could have a bad impact on the effectiveness rather than to promote a higher standard (Keller / Bertschi 2004: 216).

The European Commissioner for Human Rights fulfils through its work deficits in the human rights system of the Convention which White (1996: 239) described: "The lack of collective will on part of States in the most established human rights treaty is disappointing, but illustrates the need for implementation systems based on inter-State claims but on reporting and individual applications. Thus, the European Commissioner for Human Rights offers a reporting and monitoring system which seems to be more effective than the inter-State cases regulated in Article 33 of the European Convention on Human rights that "any High Contracting Party may refer to the Court any alleged breach of the provisions of the Convention and the protocols thereto by another High Contracting Party" which is used comparably seldom.

European Commission on Racism and Intolerance (ECRI)

In 2004, on the occasion of the ECRI's tenth anniversary, Walter Schwimmer, Secretary General of the Council of Europe, stated that the ECRI "represents on many levels an original and unique example of the development of an independent human rights monitoring mechanism in a practical and progressive way" (Kelly 2004: 11).

The ECRI was established through the Vienna Declaration in 1993 adopted by the first Summit of Heads of State and Government of Council of Europe member States of the CoE and considerably strengthened by the second summit in Strasbourg in 1997. The main function is to analyse and propose solutions to the problems of racism, xenophobia, anti-Semitism and intolerance faced by the member States of the CoE. So, its work on prevention of and solutions to problems related to racism and intolerance has always been firmly anchored to the protection and promotions of human rights simultaneously benefiting the existing CoE's framework and supporting the goals of the CoE.

ECRI consists of experts of all forty-six CoE's member states and works at both international and national level, co-operating with other international organisations active in the field and undertaking activities in respect of each of the CoE's member states. ECRI's experts are nominated by the national government as personality with individual responsibility without being subject of instructions by the member state outside the intergovernmental cooperation in the CoE.

ECRI exercises its mandate through its programme of activities which consists of three main strands:

- "Country-by-country" (CBC) work,
- relations to with civil society and
- work on general themes.

The need to establish besides the Court an institution which can react more flexible and deal more pragmatic with problems of discrimination can be seen in the fact that Court had to decide the first case violating Article 14 because of race discrimination in 2004 (Thürer/Dold 2005, 10). So, ECRI proposed in order to strengthen its position to include a more general prohibition of discrimination combined with further rights not guaranteed by the Convention e.g. economic, social and cultural rights. Further to this proposal and after four years of deliberations Protocol No. 12 to the Convention which is supposed to fulfil the existing lack of a broad range to prevent discrimination is open for signature since June 2000. On the first of April in 2004, the Protocol entered into force when ten CoE's member States have ratified it. Whether ECRI can strengthen its work to prevent racism and intolerance in assistance of Protocol No. 12 remains to be seen. So, Kelly (2004: 139) stated in his report analysing the success of ECRI's ten years work against racism and intolerance about one of ECRI's advantages: "the fact that it is not based on a convention has allowed it to enjoy a wider degree of autonomy and flexibility in its work than might otherwise have been possible. Given the ever-evolving nature and character of racism, such flexibility continues to be a valuable asset".

Conclusion

Due to the Statute of the CoE and of its conventions, the CoE is not a supranational organisation but has to act within its intergovernmental competencies. So, the CoE's main capacity to act is by monitoring. Under the periodic reporting system, member states are under the obligation to inform the European organ concerned at certain intervals of the legal and factual human rights situation within their territories. The outcome of the review is the adoption of recommendations which aim at guiding the future policy of states and / or at condemning them for actual violations. This mechanism has inherently a dual nature: preventive and repressive (Tardu 2003: 140). In contrast, the Convention does not preview a monitoring system; it is built on the obligation that the member state has to implement the convention's standard with limited binding effect. In principle, the parties are responsible vis-à-vis one another for the reciprocal implementation of treaty obligations. In the past, the PACE has made several attempts to establish a judicial organ which generally is competent for the interpretation of the CoE's treaties. None of the variants proposed (creation of a new judicial body or competence of the Court to give advisory opinions) has been taken up by the CM. The failure of the various attempts made by the PACE can be explained by a number of factors e.g. that a monitoring system is already established, that monitoring is more flexible, that there is a wide acceptance for friendly settlements (Polakiewicz 1999: 120). But the main reason besides an initial lack of enthusiasm for losing sovereign rights is quite simple: the system is functioning.

Table 2

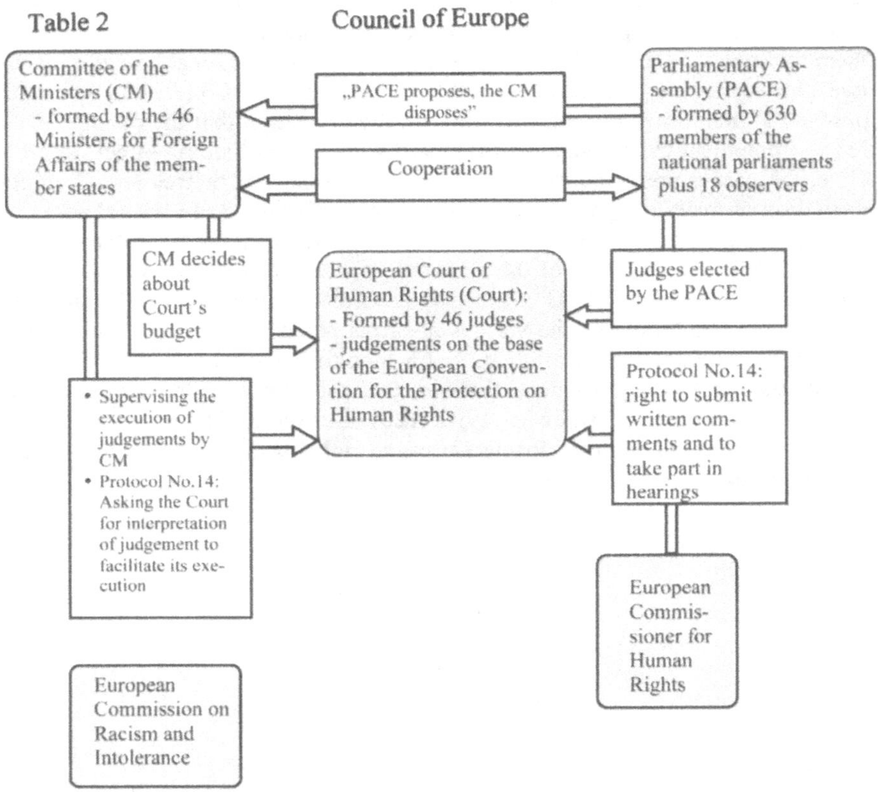
Council of Europe
Committee of the Ministers (CM) - formed by the 46 Ministers for Foreign Affairs of the member states
„PACE proposes, the CM disposes"
Parliamentary Assembly (PACE) - formed by 630 members of the national parliaments plus 18 observers
Cooperation
CM decides about Court's budget
European Court of Human Rights (Court): - Formed by 46 judges - judgements on the base of the European Convention for the Protection on Human Rights
Judges elected by the PACE
Supervising the execution of judgements by CM
Protocol No.14: Asking the Court for interpretation of judgement to facilitate its execution
Protocol No.14: right to submit written comments and to take part in hearings
European Commissioner for Human Rights
European Commission on Racism and Intolerance

Human rights before the courts: Concurrence or complementary protection by the European Court of Human Rights, the European Court of Justice and by national constitutional courts?

Hartmut Aden

The individual access to independent courts is an important precondition for an effective implementation of human rights. The right to have checked by a judicial authority intrusions on individual rights is a fundamental characteristic of the rule of law. At the national level, some European states have therefore opened the way for individual complaints before constitutional courts. Additionally human rights monitoring by courts has become an important feature in supranational and international arenas. The Council of Europe's member states have built up the European Court of Human Rights since the 1950s, located in Strasbourg. For the European Union's European Court of Justice (ECJ), located in Luxembourg, human rights are only a side topic in its fields of competence that are largely dominated by economic integration. But fundamental rights issues have nevertheless grown in importance in the ECJ's case law. In a way the fact that the Court of Human Rights, the ECJ and national Constitutional Courts deal with human rights case law is a product of the fragmented regime for human rights protection in Europe. In this paper I will show that the relationship between these courts is in some respects characterised by concurrence, but that their functions are in sum rather coherent and complementary.

The European Convention for the protection of human rights and fundamental freedoms as a common point of reference

Since it was signed in 1950, the European Convention for the protection of human rights and fundamental freedoms (in the remainder of this paper: Convention) has been a common point of reference for human rights protection in Europe. The Convention has defined a number of basic human rights and fundamental liberties as well as limits for state intrusions on these rights.

The Convention and the member states' constitutions

Article 1 requires from the member states to guarantee to all people submitted to their power the respect of the rights established by the Convention. How to implement this guarantee is left to the member states. Therefore, the normative relationship between the Convention and the member states' laws follows different models. In some member states the Convention has a normative position above the national constitution; in others it has only the status of a regular law, as in Germany (for an overview, see Peters 2003, 2-4 and Chryssogonos, 2001). In France, the Convention has, according to Article 55 of the French Constitution, a position above national laws, but below the Constitution (cf. Fromont 2005: 2). In most member states the rights established by the Convention have a complementary function for the fundamental rights guaranteed by the national constitution.

Fundamental rights such as the right to human dignity, life and physical integrity as well as the right to a fair trial are protected by the Convention and generally also by those national constitutions that contain a chapter on the protection of individual rights. The scope of these rights can, however, vary between different legal orders. The limits for state intrusions on individual rights also vary due to particularities of the national constitutional doctrine or to their interpretation established by constitutional or other high-ranking courts in case law. For member states that have fully ratified the Convention and its additional protocols, these documents establish a minimum standard for human rights protection in the fields covered by this legal regime. Therefore the Convention has become a core element of a formal rule of law in Europe (cf. Joubert/Bevers 1996: 17-19 *et passim*).

The way in which national courts and administrations adapt their practise to the requirements of the Convention as they are interpreted by the European Court of Human Rights is even more important for the practical implementation of the Convention than the formal relationship between the Convention and the national constitutions. Only if these actors are prepared to change legal doctrine and administrative practise where they do not conform to the Convention is this legal regime able to influence the level of human rights protection in Europe.

The Convention and EC/EU law

The relationship between EC/EU law and the Convention is ambiguous. In an opinion published in 1996,[1] the ECJ answered negatively to the question raised by the EC Council if the Community was entitled by the EC treaty to join the Convention. This legal position was not a rejection of the EC's further engagement for the protection of human rights, but rather of a further enlargement of the EC's fields of authority without a clear will expressed in a treaty.

At the same time, since the early 1990s, when difficulties in the ratification process for the Maastricht treaty revealed that it was no longer possible to legitimate the EC's and the EU's growing power only by the economic outcome of European integration, human rights protection became a major topic for the EU. The Convention therefore was a point of reference where the EU's authority was enlarged to policy areas where violations of human rights may occur, such as policing and immigration. Therefore, according to Article 6-II EU treaty, the Union respects fundamental rights as they are laid down in the Convention. The

[1] ECJ, opinion 2/94, coll. 1996, p. I-1759.

reference to the Convention was then complemented by the EU Charta on fundamental rights that is partly based on the Convention (cf. Zimmermann 2002).

The draft EU constitutional treaty brings to an end the conflict concerning the EU's adhesion to the Convention. It integrates the reference to the Convention as Article I-9-III and it clearly expresses the EU's will to accede to the Convention (Article I-9-II). If the Constitutional treaty enters into force in this or another form, the EU will very probably become a contracting party of the Convention.

Aspects of concurrence and possible conflicts between the courts

The fact that citizens can bring human rights cases before the European Court of Human Rights, the European Court of Justice and, in some cases, before national constitutional courts, opens the floor for situations of concurrence between these high-ranking judicial actors in different polities. Because of the uncontested position that these courts occupy in their jurisdictions, it is sometimes difficult for them to accept that high-ranking courts from other jurisdictions or polities might intervene in their fields of authority.

Concurrence between national Constitutional Courts and the European Court of Human Rights

Where member states do not have a constitutional court or where individuals do not have the right to bring a case before an existing constitutional court, the Court of Human Rights can take this function. Therefore in countries such as the Netherlands, the interpretation of fundamental rights is closely linked to the European Court's case law (cf. Joubert/Bevers 1996; Uerpmann 2003); in France this has developed since the 1980s, when the way for individual applications to the Court was opened (cf. Fromont 2005).

Where human rights cases can be brought before national constitutional courts, the question arises as to whether these courts are obliged to bring their jurisprudence in line with European fundamental rights and the relevant doctrine established by the Court of Human Rights or the Court of Justice. This question is particularly relevant for fundamental rights that are protected by the Convention as well as by national constitutions or by EC law.

Differences are especially probable where the European Court of Human Rights has established a specific interpretation of a right guaranteed by the Convention. The length of proceedings is the practically most relevant example for this. According to Article 6-1, "everyone is entitled to a fair and public hearing within a reasonable time." Based on this wording, the Court of Human Rights has stated in a large number of cases that the right to a fair trial includes that proceedings before national courts may not have an excessive length. These cases have opened a field of direct conflicts with national courts that are now forced to take more seriously the length of their proceedings (on the consequences for legislation and doctrine in France: Bouloc 2001; on Germany: Krehl/Eidam 2006). Some member states have even been convicted in cases of long-lasting proceedings before their constitutional courts.[2]

Another example is the line between legitimate force exerted by state institutions (e.g., police, prisons) and torture or ill-treatment (cf. Tulkens 2001). Opting for a dynamic interpretation of the Convention, the Court for example convicted France in 2003 for having violated Article 3 of the Convention in the case of a 75 year-old prisoner who was not especially dangerous. The prison personnel had attached one of his ankles to the bedpost during the night while he was treated in a hospital.[3] French Courts had not declared this treatment illegal before.

In other cases, the evolution of real life demands a dynamic interpretation of human rights. This is especially the case where new techniques open the field for new forms of state intrusions on individual rights. While French law, for example, did not clearly define the preconditions for using telephone tapping in criminal proceedings until the 1980s, the European Court of Human Rights stated in 1990 that telephone tapping constitutes an intrusion into the right to private life guaranteed by Article 8 of the Convention. The Court held that the French rules for telephone tapping were not in line with Article 8-2, which states that state interference in private life conforms to the Convention only if it is "in accordance to the law".[4] The outcome of these judgments was ambiguous: The French political-administrative system finally did not reduce its telephone-tapping activities but passed more detailed laws in order to legitimate them (cf. Aden 1998: 379-387).

Procedurally, these cases raise the question as to which of the courts has the authority to pronounce the last and definite decision. The procedural relationship between the European Court of Human Rights and national constitutional courts is rather clear since the 1990s, when all member states were obliged by the 11th additional protocol to the Convention to allow individuals to refer directly to the Court of Human Rights if all domestic remedies have been exhausted. Therefore member states such as the United Kingdom, which had previously refused to its citizens the right to bring individual applications before the Court, had to change their relevant legislation and practise in the 1990s. An individual who loses a case before a member states' highest-ranking court is entitled to bring the case

[2] For example the German Bundesverfassungsgericht, application no. 47169/99, Voggenreiter ./. Germany, judgment from 8 January 2004.
[3] Application no. 65436/01, Henaf ./. France, judgment from 17 November 2003.
[4] Applications no. 11105/84, Huvig ./. France and 11801/85, Kruslin ./. France, judgments from 24 April 1990.

before the Court of Human Rights if he or she argues that the judgment violates a right guaranteed by the Convention.

In a number of cases, Germany has been convicted by the Court of Human Rights for state intrusions onto rights guaranteed by the Convention even where the German Constitutional Court *(Bundesverfassungsgericht*, BVerfG) had declared a practise to conform to the fundamental rights as guaranteed by the German Constitution *(Grundgesetz)*. This happened, for example, in the case of a school teacher who had been suspended from her functions for being an active member of the communist party, which was officially suspected of opposing the Federal Republic of Germany's liberal constitutional order until the end of the Cold War. With a small majority of ten votes to nine, the Court held that there had been a violation of Articles 10 and 11 of the Convention that guarantee the freedom of expression and the freedom of assembly and association. The *Bundesverfassungsgericht*, which since the 1970s had declared constitutional the practise of eliminating members of the communist party from public services, had not accepted her case for a regular hearing before. As the BVerfG, for capacity reasons, only selects a few cases for in-depth consideration, applicants who have not passed this hurdle are more likely to bring their cases before the Strasbourg Human Rights Court (for more examples: Jaeger 2005: 199-200).

In countries such as Germany, where the Convention has the status of a parliamentary law and therefore ranks below the national constitution, national courts have to take into account the Court of Human Rights' interpretation of fundamental rights. If this interpretation is in conflict with fundamental rights guaranteed by the national constitution, then the latter takes precedence. The BVerfG has recently confirmed this doctrine for cases of child care after divorce[5] in which the Court of Human Rights' interpretation of Article 8 of the Convention may conflict with the relevant interpretation of Article 6-II of the German Constitution (cf. Meyer-Ladewig/Petzold, 2005).

In sum, the European Court of Human Right not only has the power to influence the interpretation of fundamental rights by high-ranking national courts, but also increasingly to encourage cooperation in situations of conflict and concurrence between courts (cf. Jaeger 2005).[6]

[5] BVerfG, case 1 BvR 1664/04, decision from 5 April 2005.

[6] The author of that article, *Renate Jaeger*, was a judge of the German *Bundesverfassungsgericht* from 1994 to 2004 before she became a judge of the European Court of Human Rights in November 2004. Her career therefore symbolises the trend towards a more cooperative relationship between these courts.

Concurrence between high-ranking national courts and the European Court of Justice

The relationship between the European Court of Justice and high-ranking national courts – especially constitutional courts – is even more complex. Generally speaking, the supremacy of EC law over the member states' laws also comprehends a supremacy of ECJ judgments over the doctrine developed by the member states' courts, including constitutional courts. High-ranking French courts, especially the powerful *Conseil d'État,* tried for a long time to prevent judges from referring cases to the ECJ and thus submitting French law to the supremacy of EC law (cf. Alter 2001: 135-157).

Cases in which citizens argued before national constitutional courts that EC measures violated their fundamental rights as they are guaranteed by a member states' constitution forced national courts to define their relationship to EC law and to the authority of ECJ rulings in fundamental rights issues. The long-standing conflict between the German *Bundesverfassungsgericht* and the ECJ is largely based on judgments in this kind of cases. The BVerfG repeatedly asked itself if the protection of fundamental rights through the judicial control exerted by the ECJ was sufficient for the level of protection required by the German Constitution *(Grundgesetz)*. Depending on the historical situation, the BVerfG came to different conclusions that are today known as the *solange* ("as long as") doctrine: Initially, in 1974, the BVerfG concluded that it would not be prepared to renounce its jurisdiction to hear cases in which the ECJ had already pronounced a judgment – *as long as* the protection of human rights in the E(E)C did not fulfil the requirements of the German Constitution in the BVerfG's perspective.[7] Later, in 1986, the Court renounced jurisdiction in cases related to the interpretation of EC law – *as long as* the protection of fundamental rights exerted by the ECJ's control is in line with the requirements established by the *Grundgesetz* (cf. Alter 2001: 71-118 for an extensive overview and analysis of this doctrine).[8] Since then the BVerfG has used further conflicts to develop its position concerning the relationship between the German Constitution and EC law, especially concerning the EU's democratic legitimacy in the phase of the ratification of the Maastricht treaty in the early 1990s[9] and – in 2005 – the protection of fundamental rights of citizens named in a European arrest warrant.[10] The fact that the ECJ has developed its own doctrine concerning the protection of individual rights can be interpreted as a reaction to the requirements formulated by the German BVerfG.

[7] BVerfGE 37, 271 („Solange I").
[8] BVerfGE 73, 339.
[9] BVerfGE 89, 155.
[10] BVerfG, case 2 BvR 2236/04, judgment from 18 July 2005.

Behind the legal arguments that high-ranking courts in the EU member states have developed to define their relationship to the ECJ, there is a second layer of conflicts over the future distribution of power between courts in the developing European multi-level polity. High-ranking national courts fear losing their traditional power if EC/EU law becomes more and more important. Where the doctrine that is protecting fundamental rights goes further at the national level than at the EC/EU level, national courts as the German BVerfG continue to feel legitimated to adopt legal positions conflicting with the ECJ or other European institutions. The field for this kind of conflict will be reduced if the EU Charta of fundamental rights becomes a part of a future EU constitution as is foreseen by the draft constitutional treaty. However, as the fundamental rights that are defined by the Charta differ in some respects from the rights as they are guaranteed by national constitutions – and in some cases from the doctrine developed by constitutional courts – potential fields of conflict will remain.

Concurrence between the European Court of Justice and the European Court of Human Rights

Situations of concurrence over the definite interpretation of human rights can also occur between the ECJ and the European Court of Human Rights. Since the ECJ started to develop a doctrine of EC fundamental rights, situations of conflicting interpretation have become possible.

In the initial period, there was a factual division of labour between these two European Courts. While the ECJ limited itself to the interpretation of EEC law and therefore basically to questions related to economic integration, human rights issues were reserved to the Court of Human Rights. This changed when the ECJ was more and more confronted with cases related to fundamental rights issues and to the pressure exerted by actors such as the German *Bundesverfassungsgericht* to take more seriously the protection of fundamental rights. Therefore, step by step, the ECJ developed its own fundamental rights doctrine (cf. Kühling 2003; Schwarze 2005 for an overview).

New conflicts are likely if the EU constitutional treaty enters into force, bringing with it the EU Charta of fundamental rights (cf. Zimmermann 2002; Kühling 2003). From then, the ECJ will have to apply in its judgments fundamental rights as they are guaranteed be the Charta. At the same time, if the EU becomes a contracting party of the Convention per the wish expressed in the draft constitutional treaty, individual litigants will have the right to bring their cases to the Court of Human Rights if they lose them before the ECJ. The ECJ then will have to accept that it does not have the right to pronounce the final decision concerning those fundamental rights that are guaranteed by the Charta *and* by the Convention. At the same time, accession to the Convention will open to the EU institutions the possibility of presenting their positions directly before the Court of Human Rights (cf. Krüger/Polakiewicz 2001: 97).

While representatives from the European Court of Human Rights and from the Council of Europe (see, for example, Council of Europe 2001) have been promoting the EU's accession to the Convention on a regular basis, the ECJ judges increasingly welcome it as well in recent years. The concurrence and conflicts between the two European courts more and more cede to new forms of "supranational judicial diplomacy" (Scheeck 2005: 43): The Courts' presidents and judges organise meetings and emphasize in pubic statements the complementary functions of their institutions.

Complementary functions of the courts

In sum, the case law of the European Court of Human Rights, the European Court of Justice and national constitutional courts shows that the level of human rights protection tends to be higher where individuals have the possibility to have checked by more than one high-ranking court an intrusion into their fundamental rights. In this respect, concurrence between these courts is a kind of productive interaction. In a number of cases, this interaction has led to a wider interpretation of human rights where the specific wording or legal interpretation had led to restrictions at the national level before. Again, the length of proceedings is among the most far-reaching examples of this kind of complementary functions.

A cooperative concurrence between courts also has a preventive aspect. When national courts have to hear a case related to fundamental rights that are protected by the Convention, they more and more tend to refer to the judgments produced by the Court of Human Rights in the relevant field. Only in rare cases do they then adopt an interpretation that openly conflicts with the doctrine established by the Strasbourg Court (cf. Jaeger 2005). If the EU becomes a member of the Convention, the division of labour and authority between the two European courts will be rather complementary than conflicting, because the European Court of Human Rights' authority will continue to be limited to cases related to fundamental rights, while the ECJ will keep the authority to pronounce the final decision in all other cases concerning EC/EU law (cf. Krüger/Polakiewicz 2001: 100 *et passim*). The Court of Human Rights will not become a court superior to the ECJ or the member states' constitutional courts, but will rather be a more specialised judicial body (cf. Pernice/Kanitz 2004: 11 *et passim*).

On the one hand, overlapping fields of authority between different courts make a dynamic interpretation of human rights more complicated. On the other hand, they open the field for a productive concurrence. In this respect, intercourt competition in a multi-level context is characterised by patterns that can also be observed for other international regimes, for example in the field of environmental protection: If different international regimes handle a problem at the same time, this may in some respect lead to confusion and uncoordinated parallel activities. At the same time, however, it accelerates the process of coming to results and policy outcomes, simply because a larger number of actors in different regimes tend to produce more results than a smaller number of actors in a single, homogeneous structure (for the example of environmental protection, see Aden 2002).

Conclusion: Towards a system of multi-level human rights monitoring in Europe

In conclusion, the fact that several high-ranking courts share the task of hearing human rights cases and developing human rights by differentiated case law contributes to improving the implementation and prevents those rights from staying pure theory as "law in the books". This is relevant not only for states with a short democratic tradition or failing judicial systems, but also in countries such as France, the United Kingdom and Germany with a longer tradition of fundamental rights protection and a differentiated, powerful judicial system; the dynamic interpretation of human rights by the European courts contributes to developing the protection of individual rights in fields such as policing or prisons where security considerations often predominate (cf. Tulkens 2001; Jobard 2002 and 2003; Aden 2001; European Court of Human Rights 2006, 36-37). Obligations established by European or international law and monitored by independent courts also contribute to preventing politicians from suspending or abolishing fundamental rights in situations of panic, for example after acts of terrorism.

With the Convention, the EU Charta on fundamental rights and the constitutionally guaranteed rights at the national level, a multi-level system of human rights documents has developed in Europe, complemented by other documents elaborated by international human rights regimes. The existence of different high-ranking courts that hear human rights cases reflects this multi-level system in the field of implementation and monitoring. As is typical for multi-level governance, the judicial interaction between the courts at different polity levels is neither hierarchical nor unilateral. Inter-court competition leads to forms of mutual influence through the adoption of rules and ideas that have been developed at other geographical levels or in other jurisdictions. In such a multi-level judicial system, the hierarchy of norms and judicial authority is not as clear as in monolithic political and judicial systems as they have been established in the national states since the 18th century. For the protection of human rights, this is no major problem as long as it is procedurally clear which court is entitled to pronounce the last and definite judgment in a specific case. This will be the minimum task for political decision makers in the field of multi-level judicial policy. One simple and clear principle should therefore be respected: A judgment in favour of an individual's rights at a "higher" geographical level cannot be overruled by judgments at "lower" geographical levels that handle the individual's rights in a more restrictive way.

The protection of fundamental rights in the European Union – selected aspects[1]

Katarzyna Cuadrat-Grzybowska

„*Morality always makes better citizens than law*"

Montesquieu „*Persian Letters*"

Communication from the Commission to the Council and the European Parliament on Article 7 of the Treaty on European Union. Respect for and promotion of the values on which the Union is based of 15 October 2003

> If Europe were once united in the sparing of its common inheritance, there would be no limit to the happiness, to the prosperity and the glory which its three or four hundred million people would enjoy.

Winston Churchill, 1946

The European Union is committed, under the provisions of its Treaties, to ensure full respect for human rights and fundamental freedoms in its policies as well as in each of its member states. Based upon the provision of Article 6 of the Treaty on European Union (hereafter TUE), the Union should be built upon such principles as democracy, respect for fundamental rights and freedoms and the rule of law. This commitment laid down in the Treaty is closely linked to the ongoing process of the creation of the Area of Freedom, Justice and Security, as originally envisaged by the Amsterdam Treaty.[2]

[1] The opinions expressed in this article are the author's own and do not represent the position of the institution to which she belongs.

[2] As stipulated in the Final Report of Working Group X of the European Convention[2], since the entry into force of the Amsterdam Treaty, the establishment of a coherent Area of Freedom, Security and

The current position of fundamental rights in the institutional and legal system of the European Union is the outcome of a lengthy historical, legal and political process, which can be summarised as a number of milestones or *dynamics*[3]. The first dynamic was the statement given by the Court of Justice of the European Communities (hereafter *Court*)[4] in 1969 that fundamental rights should be included in the general principles of Community law that the Court is to protect[5]. The Court took as a starting point the shared constitutional traditions of the member states and the international instruments on human rights which

Justice has formed one of the key objectives of the European Union, spelt out in the ambitious political agenda set by the European Council of Tampere of 1999 and further developed in the Treaty of Nice (CONV 426/02, WG X 14).

[3] See: O. De Schutter, Les droits fondamentaux dans le projet européen, Une Constitution pour l'Europe, sous la cordination de Olivier De Schutter et Paul Nihoul, Larcier 2004.

[4] The role of the Court of Justice in the process of considering fundamental rights as general principles of Community law, could never be overestimated. The Court's involvement, which can be mainly seen through the rich jurisprudence developed over the years, should be considered as one of the most important dynamics concerning the EU's policy on fundamental rights. This essay shall not however deal with the issue of the Court's jurisprudence with regard to the EU's competence in the field of the protection of fundamental rights. This wide topic should be subject to separate analyses.

[5] Stauder v Ulm (Case 29/69), 1969 ECR 419, ECJ. In this judgement the Court refers to "fundamental rights enshrined in the general principles of Community law and protected by the Court of Justice". See also the following judgements: Broadcasting, Entertainment, Cinematographic and Theatre Union (BECTU) v. Secretary of Satte for Trade and Industry, Case C-173/99 [2001] 3 CMLR 7. 194; Brunner v. European Union Treaty (2 BvR 2134/92 & 21549/92) [1994] 1 CMLR 57. 188; Casagrande v. Landeshauptstadt München, Case C – 9/74 ETS [1974] ECR 773; Cinéthèque S.A. and others v. Fédération nationale des cinémas français, Cases 60 i 61/84 [1996] ECR 2605; Costa v. ENEL, Case 6/64 [1964] ECR 585.181; Criminal Proceedings against L.E. Sanz de Lera, R. Díaz Jiménez and F. Kapanoglu, Joined Cases 163/94, 165/94, 250/94, Judgement of 14 December 1995, [1995] ECR I-4821; Defrenne v. Sabena, Case 43/75 [1976] ECR 455; Dow Benelux NV v. Commission of the European Communities, Case 85/87 [1989] ECR 03137; Elliniki Radiophonia Tileorassi AE v. Dimotili Etiria Pliroforisis i Sotirios Kouvelas, Case C-260/89 [1991] ECR I-4239; French Customs Authorities v. customs agents, Case C-368/92 [1994] ECR I-00605; Geitling and Nold, Cases 36-38 and 40/59 [1960] ECR 423. 182; Germany v. Consillium, Case C-280/93 [1994] ECR I-4973; Hauer v. Land Rheinland-Pfalz, Case 44/79 [1979] ECR 3727. 183; Internationale Handelsgesellschaft mbH v. Einfuhr-und Vorratsstelle fur Getreide und Futtermittel, Case 11/70 [1970] ECR 1125. 183; Johnston v. Chief Constable of the Royal Ulster Constabulary, Case 222/84 [1986] ECR 1561. 184; Kremzow v. Austria, Case C-299/95 [1997] ECR I-2629.Liselotte Hauer v. Land Nadrenia-Palatynat, Case 44/79 [1979] ECR 3727; National Panasonic UK Ltd. v. European Commission, Case 136/79, [1980] ECR 2033, s. 2056-2058; Nold v. Commission of European Communities, Case 4/73 [1974] ECR 491. 182, 183; Opinion 2/94 on Accession to the ECHR [1996] ECR I-1759; R. (on the application of Broadcasting, Entertainment, Cinematographic and Theatre Union) v. Secretary of State for Trade and Industry, Case 173/99 [2001] 3 CMLR 7. 194. Procuratori di Milano, Case 55/94 [1995] ECR I-4165; Sgarlata & others v. European Commission, Case 40/64 [1964] ECR 215;Society for the Protection of Unborn Children (Ireland)(SPUC) v. Grogan, Case 159/90 [1991] ECR I-4685. 188; Stork & Co. v. High Autority, Case 1/58 [1959] ECR 17;The Netherlands v. European Parliament and the Council of the European Union, Case C-377/98 ECJ 9.10.2001;Union Royale Belge des Sociétés de Football Association ASBL and Others v. Jean-Marc Bosman and Others, Case 415/93; Van Gend en Loos v. Nederlandse Tariefcommissie, Sprawa 26/62 [1963] ECR3. 181; Wachauf v. Germany, Sprawa 5/88 [1989] ECR 2609.

the member states had signed. The case-law was subsequently extended to the member states when they act in areas covered by Community law. The second essential development in this area consisted in the incorporation into the Treaties of provisions aimed at the protection of fundamental rights, the most important of them being the Articles 6 and 7 of the Treaty on European Union (hereafter *TEU*). However, before addressing the content and meaning of Article 6 and 7 TUE, one should mention that already in the European Single Act it was stipulated that the member states were "determined to work together to promote democracy on the basis of the fundamental rights recognised in the constitutions and laws of the Member States, in the Convention for the Protection of Human Rights and Fundamental Freedoms and the European Social Charter, notably freedom, equality and social justice."

Article 6 of the TUE lays down the principles on which the Union is founded, amongst them respect for human rights and fundamental freedoms. It also declares that the Union shall respect as general principles of Community law those fundamental rights which are guaranteed by the European Convention for the Protection of Human Rights and Fundamental Freedoms (hereafter ECHR) and as they result from the constitutional traditions common to the member states. Article 7 of the same Treaty requires each member state to respect the principles set out in Article 6.[6] This is in fact an obligation backed by a

[6] Article 7 TUE, as amended by Nice Treaty, reads as follows:
"On a reasoned proposal by one third of the Member States, by the European Parliament or by the Commission, the Council, acting by a majority of four fifths of its members after obtaining the assent of the European Parliament, may determine that there is a clear risk of a serious breach by a Member State of principles mentioned in Article 6(1), and address appropriate recommendations to that State. Before making such a determination, the Council shall hear the Member State in question and, acting in accordance with the same procedure, may call on independent persons to submit within a reasonable time limit a report on the situation in the Member State in question.
The Council shall regularly verify that the grounds on which such a determination was made continue to apply.
2. The Council, meeting in the composition of the Heads of State or Government and acting by unanimity on a proposal by one third of the Member States or by the Commission and after obtaining the assent of the European Parliament, may determine the existence of a serious and persistent breach by a Member State of principles mentioned in Article 6(1), after inviting the government of the Member State in question to submit its observations.
3. Where a determination under paragraph 2 has been made, the Council, acting by a qualified majority, may decide to suspend certain of the rights deriving from the application of this Treaty to the Member State in question, including the voting rights of the representative of the government of that Member State in the Council. In doing so, the Council shall take into account the possible consequences of such a suspension on the rights and obligations of natural and legal persons.
The obligations of the Member State in question under this Treaty shall in any case continue to be binding on that State.
4. The Council, acting by a qualified majority, may decide subsequently to vary or revoke measures taken under paragraph 3 in response to changes in the situation which led to their being imposed.
5. For the purposes of this Article, the Council shall act without taking into account the vote of the representative of the government of the Member State in question. Abstentions by members present

specific procedure which gives the Union the capacity to act preventively in the event of a *clear risk of a serious breach* of one of the principles or to take necessary measures in case of the existence of a *serious and persistent breach* of one of these principles by way of sanctions against the member state concerned. On 15 October 2003 the Commission adopted a Communication to the European Parliament and to the Council on Article 7 of the Treaty on European Union called "Respect for and promotion of the values on which the Union is based"[7]. The Communication offers a framework of analysis of the conditions of applicability of Article 7 TEU and spans over the aspect of prevention ("Morality always makes better citizens than law", Montesquieu "Persian Letters" - this famous passage has been chosen as motto to the Communication on Article 7). The Communication focuses on the monitoring of the respect of fundamental rights in the Union, the development of independent expertise, the interaction between the institutions and the member states, as well as on a dialogue with civil society and providing information to the public.

The introduction of the concept of citizenship of the European Union established by the Treaty on European Union could be easily considered as the third milestone in the creation of the EU's policy on fundamental rights. The second part of the Treaty Establishing the European Communities (hereafter *TEC*) deals with the above-mentioned concept[8] which is in fact based on the principle that every national of a member state is a citizen of the Union. Citizenship of the European Union does not, however, replace nationality; it rather confers additional rights on nationals of member states and gives them a sense of common belonging[9].

in person or represented shall not prevent the adoption of decisions referred to in paragraph 2. A qualified majority shall be defined as the same proportion of the weighted votes of the members of the Council concerned as laid down in Article 205(2) of the Treaty establishing the European Community.

This paragraph shall also apply in the event of voting rights being suspended pursuant to paragraph 3.

6. For the purposes of paragraphs 1 and 2, the European Parliament shall act by a two-thirds majority of the votes cast, representing a majority of its Members."

[7] COM(2003) 606 final.

[8] Articles 8 to 8e of the EEC Treaty, now Articles 17 to 22 TEC

[9] Under the TEC, a citizen of the Union:

- has the right to move and reside freely within the territory of the Member States;
- to vote and stand as a candidate at elections to the EP in the Member State in which she/he resides, under the same conditions as nationals of that State (corresponds to Art. 39 of the Charter);
- to vote and stand as a candidate at municipal elections in the Member State in which he/she resides under the same conditions as nationals of that State (corresponds to Art. 40 of the Charter);

The fight against discrimination provides an example of the specific policy linked to the process of ensuring full respect of fundamental rights in the EU. With the Amsterdam Treaty, a new Article 13 TEC was added, giving the Community the power to legislate against discrimination on a wide range of grounds. The Treaty of Rome of 25 March 1957 guaranteed men and women equal pay for equal work (Article 119 EEC, now Article 141(1) TEC, amended) and freedom for workers to seek employment in another member state, which entailed the abolition of nationality discrimination (Articles 7 and 48 EEC, now Articles 12 and 39 TEC, amended). Moreover, specific powers were conferred on the European Community to take action to combat discrimination based not only on sex but also on racial or ethnic origin, religion or belief, disability, age or sexual orientation by the Amsterdam Treaty (Article 13 EC). The Community has been quick to take action in this area, especially through two instruments: the Directive of 29 June 2000 implementing the principle of equal treatment on grounds of racial or ethnic origin and the Directive of 27 November 2000 establishing a general framework for equal treatment in employment and occupation. There is also the Community action programme against discrimination 2001-2007.

Another important dynamic is of institutional nature and is a result of a true political will on the part of the Union's institutions to promote and protect fundamental rights within the territory of the European Union. The Parliament, the Council and the Commission – acting within the legal framework established over the years by the jurisprudence of the Court of Justice – are the key players in the process of shaping the European Union's policy concerning the protection of fundamental rights. It goes without saying that each of the above-mentioned institutions intends to contribute, within its own field of competence, to the development of this dynamic area.

This essay, while only constituting a brief introduction to this wide subject concerning the developments in the field of the protection and promotion of fundamental rights in the Union, shall only mention a few aspects of the important role of the EU's institutions in the process of ensuring better and more efficient protection of human rights across Europe.

The European Parliament monitors from a political point of view the situation of the protection of human rights in both its internal and external dimensions. Two general reports are drafted each year by the Parliament. The first

- they are entitled to protection by the diplomatic or consular authorities of any Member State apart from their own, if they are in the territory of a third country in which the Member State of which they are a national is not represented;

- they have the right to petition the European Parliament, and they are entitled to refer to the Ombudsman of the Union cases of maladministration in the activities of the Community institutions or bodies (corresponds to Art. 43 of the Charter).

concerns the external dimension of the issue in question and is prepared by the Committee on Foreign Affairs (it should also be mentioned that a specific subcommittee dealing with human rights has been created within this committee reflecting the importance that the Parliament attaches to these matters). The second report is drafted by the Committee on Civil Liberties, Justice and Home Affairs (otherwise known as the LIBE Committee) and deals with the situation of fundamental rights on the territory of the European Union. Some reports have also been prepared on specific issues such as for example the situation in prisons in the EU. In this context one should note that in 2005 the LIBE Committee issued so called Kinga Gal's report which was adopted by the Parliament on 26 May 2005 as *European Parliament resolution on promotion and protection of fundamental rights: the role of national and European institutions, including the Fundamental Rights*[10]. The Parliament is also responsible for many other political initiatives whose main objective is to promote the culture of human rights and to encourage the fight for human rights all over the world. One of them is the Sakharov Prize for freedom of thought, which the European Parliament awards annually. In 2004, the prize was awarded to the Belarusian association of Journalists.

Since 1999 the Council of the European Union has produced an annual report on human rights, working closely with the Commission and the member states. The objective of this report is to provide a general overview of the most important developments in the sphere of human rights, both within the EU as well as in its relations with third countries. The report presents the legal and political foundations of the EU activities in this area as well as the initiatives developed by the EU with the most important regional and international groups (for example, the OSCE and the United Nations' Commission on Human Rights) and initiatives developed through dialogue with third countries. Furthermore, the report focuses on certain particularly important issues of human rights such as the prohibition of torture and inhuman and degrading treatment, prohibition of the death penalty, the fight against racism and xenophobia, and the fight for the rights of women and children. The Council has also recently established an *ad hoc* Group which deals with various issues concerning the EU policy on fundamental rights, such as the creation of the Fundamental Rights Agency (the Group is currently discussing the Commission proposals setting up the new Agency) and the financial programmes aimed to ensure the protection and promotion of fundamental rights in the EU.

Special attention should be paid to a significant number of initiatives undertaken by the Commission with the aim to ensure full respect for fundamental rights in all activities and proposals to be put forward or adopted by these institutions, especially as far as legislative powers are concerned. This is based upon

[10] 2005/2007 INI.

the concept of "mainstreaming of fundamental rights" in all policies of the Union. As often stressed by the new College, fundamental rights are to be at the very heart of all the actions and measures carried out by the Commission. This commitment, undertaken from the very beginning of the appointment by President Barroso and his Commission (in particular Vice President Franco Frattini, Commissioner responsible for the area of Freedom, Justice and Security), can been seen in particular through the establishment in December 2004 of a specific Group of Commissioners dealing with Fundamental Rights, Anti-discrimination and Equal Opportunities[11]. This Group, chaired by President Barroso and Vice President Frattini, deals with various issues related to the EU policy on fundamental rights. Based upon the decision of 2004, the following Commissioners are also taking part in the work of the Group: Commissioner for the Institutional Relations and Communication Strategy; Commissioner for Administration, Audit and Anti-fraud; Commissioner for Information Strategy and Media; Commissioner for Education, Training, Culture and Multilingualism; Commissioner for Enlargement; Commissioner for Development and Humanitarian Aid; Commissioner for External Relations and Neighbourhood Policy and Commissioner for Employment, Social Affairs and Equal Opportunities.

The Group will meet 3-4 times a year. Amongst other issues, it discusses such matters as the issue of accession of the European Union to the ECHR, the Rights of the Child and the Fundamental Rights Agency.

Another important example of Commission commitment in the area of protection of fundamental rights is the setting up of a very specific internal mechanism for ensuring that fundamental rights are fully and effectively observed in all legislative proposals to be adopted by the Commission. In 2002 the Commission introduced a new Impact Assessment procedure designed to contribute to a more coherent implementation of the Sustainable Development Strategy. The Commission is now involved in the implementation of the integrated impact assessment mechanism (based on so called *Revised Impact Assessment Guidelines*), which provides for useful guidance in actually carrying out the assessment of the potential economic, social and environmental impacts of the proposals. The new structure of this mechanism enables to ensure that fundamental rights impacts are identified comprehensively and that a proportionality analysis is carried out when drafting proposals in the Commission.

In the context of the general impact assessment procedure, one should mention the process of the application of the Charter of Fundamental Rights in the daily actions of the Commission.

[11] The decision to create the Group of Commissioners on Fundamental Rights, Anti-Discrimination and Equal Opportunities was announced in the Communication to the Members of the Commission, Functioning of the Commission and internal coordination, adopted by the College of the Commission on 22 December 2004. SEC (2004) 1617/4.

On 13 March 2001, the Commission issued a Communication on "the application of the Charter of Fundamental Rights of the European Union". The objective was to draw the concrete consequences of the proclamation of the Charter in the daily action of the Commission, as well in its relations with the citizens and the recipients of its decisions, as in its rules and internal procedures. Accordingly, any proposal of a legislative or regulatory act to be adopted by the Commission should be subject to an *a priori* control of compatibility with the Charter. Moreover, the legislative or regulatory proposals which present a specific link with the fundamental rights will be subject to a formal compatibility statement, by the insertion of an additional clause as follows: "This act respects the fundamental rights and observes the principles which are recognised in particular by the Charter of Fundamental Rights of the European Union".

The Commission has recently issued a Communication on the respect and application of the Charter of Fundamental Rights in legislative proposals of the Commission[12]. This Communication provides for a specific methodology aimed at ensuring full conformity of Commission initiatives with the Charter of Fundamental Rights. As mentioned in the Communication, the methodology has the following objectives:

1) to allow Commission departments to check systematically and thoroughly that all fundamental rights concerned have been respected in all draft proposals;
2) to enable the Members of the Commission, and the Group of Commissioners on Fundamental Rights, Anti-discrimination and Equal Opportunities in particular, to follow the results of the scrutiny and to promote a "fundamental rights culture"; and
3) to make the results of the Commission's monitoring of fundamental rights more visible to other institutions and the general public.

According to the methodology, the Legal Service of the Commission shall continue checking for compliance with the Charter of Fundamental Rights as an integral part of its verification of legality. Moreover, the lead department shall also ensure that the Directorate-General for Justice, Freedom and Security is involved in the interdepartmental consultation when a proposal is liable to raise issues relating to fundamental rights, notable in the light of the impact assessment. Likewise it will ensure that the relevant external relations Directorate-General is consulted where a proposal might affect the fundamental rights of third-country nationals outside the Union.

[12] Communication from the Commission "Compliance with the Charter of Fundamental Rights in Commission legislative proposals. Methodology for systematic and rigorous monitoring" of 27April 2005, COM (2005) 172 (final), www.europa.eu.int.

To reinforce the scrutiny at the stage of interdepartmental consultation within the Commission, two documents should accompany the draft legislative proposal subject to verification: the impact assessment (including the different impacts on individual rights) and the explanatory memorandum, which for certain legislative proposals should contain a section on the legal basis for compliance with fundamental rights. According to the Communication, a general appraisal of internal monitoring, prepared by the Legal Service in agreement with the Justice, Freedom and Security DG and the Secretariat-General, will be submitted in 2007 to the Group of Commissioners on Fundamental Rights, Non-discrimination and Equal Opportunities, accompanied as necessary by proposals to amend or supplement this methodology in the light of experience.

In the context of institutions in the field of the protection of fundamental rights, one should also mention the role of the EU Network of Independent Experts on Fundamental Rights, which was set up by the Commission in September 2002 upon a specific request of the European Parliament. Its objective is to ensure a high degree of expertise on the situation of fundamental rights in relation to each of the member states and the European Union as a whole. It is important to stress that all national experts who constitute the network are fully independent from the Commission and that their opinions do not in any way bind on either the Commission or the European Parliament. Moreover, they should also be independent from national authorities in order to be able to provide fully independent and objective information on the issue.

The network has three main tasks: 1) to draft an annual report on the state of fundamental rights in the European Union and its member states; 2) to provide the Commission with specific information and opinions on fundamental rights issues directly linked to matters falling within the scope of EU competence; 3) to assist the Commission and the Parliament in developing the European Union's policy on fundamental rights in their field of competence. The objectives of the annual report are the following:

1) to inform the institutions of the state of play regarding fundamental rights in all the member states;

2) to make recommendations to the institutions based on the information gathered to promote the safeguarding of fundamental rights;

3) to add to the pool of experience by producing a list of measures to be presented as good practice.

The reports are available in English and French on the Internet, on the website of DG Justice Freedom and Security.[13]

Each year, the thematic comment prepared by the network covers in greater depth a specific subject selected by the Commission and the European Parliament and relevant to their competence. For the first two years the subjects were

[13] http://europa.eu.int/comm/justice_home/cfr_cdf/index_en.htm.

"The balance between freedom and security in the response by the European Union and its Member states to the terrorist threat" and the issue of "Fundamental rights in the external activities of the European Union in the fields of justice and asylum and immigration in 2003". The thematic comment N° 3 of 25 April 2005 addressed "The protection of minorities in the European Union".

To sum up the brief analysis concerning the institutional framework of fundamental rights of the European Union, it should be stressed that the different institutions are indeed very active in the area in question. The institutions are striving for better coordination amongst themselves, in particular as far as the production of reports is concerned. One visible effect of this effort is the common page under the Europa website (http://europa.eu.int), which contains links to the human rights web pages of the relevant institutions.

The Charter of Fundamental Rights of the European Union

The Charter of Fundamental Rights, proclaimed in Nice on 7 December 2000 by the European Council, the European Commission and the European Parliament, reaffirms the rights arising out of the constitutional traditions and the international obligations common to the member states. The Charter focuses on the common values shared by the peoples of Europe and on the indivisible and universal values of human rights in recognition of "the spiritual and moral heritage". According to the Charter,

> (...) the Union contributes to the preservation and to the development of these common values while respecting the diversity of the cultures and traditions of the peoples of Europe as well as the national identities of the Member States and the organisation of their public authorities at national, regional and local levels; it seeks to promote balanced and sustainable development and ensures free movement of persons, goods and services and capital, and the freedom of establishment. To this end, it is necessary to strengthen the protection of fundamental rights in the light of changes in society, social progress and scientific and technological developments by making these rights more visible in a Charter.

As regards the process of drafting the Charter, it is important to note that the Charter is in fact the first document in the history of the Union to be drawn up by a Convention with representatives from the governments of the member states, national Parliaments, the European Commission and the European Parliament. The Court of Justice was also present as an observer during the work of the Convention.

The Charter provides a list of rights and liberties that are binding on the institutions, bodies and agencies of the Union, as well as on the member states in implementing Union law. Insofar as each of the Charter's 50 articles sets out individuals' rights or freedoms which already exist in other international texts, they are not new. In fact, the main reason for drafting the Charter which was to make these rights more visible for all EU citizens. This means that each citizen shall be better equipped to understand the extent of his or her rights, and therefore more able to defend him or herself against any violation of fundamental rights by EU institutions or by member states when they implement EU legislation.

The first part of the Treaty establishing a Constitution for Europe and signed on 29 October 2004 incorporates the Charter of Fundamental Rights. Although the Charter promulgated in 2000 is not legally binding, "it contains the fundamental principles which have been held to be binding in case-law as general principles of Community law[14] ". If the Charter receives legally binding effect in the future, individuals will be able to refer to the Charter to challenge any decision taken by the institutions of the Union and by member states when implementing EU law. The consequences of the latter would be the following: If, for example, an individual feels that a particular law in his or her country which derives from a Community Directive is not compatible with fundamental rights, he or she can bring the matter before a judge in his or her own country. If the judge is not convinced, he or she can request an interpretation or validation from the Court of Justice of the European Communities.

It is also important to stress that the Charter does not entail any transfer of powers to the European Union. On the contrary, the Charter is fully neutral in terms of legislative competence. Instead, it sets up an instrument with which to control the way the institutions of the Union and member states implement their existing powers with regard to fundamental rights whenever they act in the field of Union law.

As regards the meaning of the Charter, lawyers are increasingly referring to it and the Advocates-General at the European Court of Justice regularly quote it in their conclusions, although they emphasise that it is not mandatory. For the first time since its proclamation, the Charter was specifically cited by the Tribunal of First Instance in a judgement given on 30 January 2002 which was followed by two other judgments, the second of the 3rd May 2002.[15] These were the

[14] See: Communication from the Commission "Compliance with the Charter of Fundamental Rights in Commission legislative proposals. Methodology for systematic and rigorous monitoring" (...), page 2, footnote 2.

[15] Tribunal de première instance, arrêt du 30 janvier 2002, max.mobil Telekommunikation Service / Commission, T-54/99, Recueil de jurisprudence 2002; Tribunal de première instance, arrêt du 3 mai 2002, Jégo-Quéré / Commission, T-177/01, Recueil de jurisprudence 2002.

very important steps towards recognition of the Charter by the courts. The Court of Justice as such has never mentioned so far the Charter in its decisions.

Accession of the European Union to the European Convention for the Protection of Human Rights and Fundamental Freedoms (ECHR)

The possible future accession of the European Union to the ECHR is crucial for the consistent development of the protection of fundamental rights in Europe, especially as regards the introduction of an external judicial review of the Union's respect for fundamental rights.

The legal and political implications regarding accession to the ECHR have been discussed for years. The Commission has played a significant role in this discourse, advocating accession since 1979. In 1996 the Court of Justice of the European Communities rejected the possibility of accession to ECHR without a previous Treaty amendment and ruled that under the current Treaty provisions there was no legal basis for the European Union to accede to the European Convention (Opinion 2/94 on Accession to the ECHR [1996] ECR I-1759).

In order to allow for accession, the Constitutional Treaty[16] provides for the possibility of the European Union to accede to the ECHR. As envisaged by Article I-9, paragraph 2, of the Constitutional Treaty "The Union shall accede to the European Convention for the Protection of Human Rights and Fundamental Freedoms. Such accession shall not affect the Union's competences as defined in the Constitution". It is interesting to note that the previous version of this provision stated that "the Union shall seek accession to the European Convention for the Protection of Human Rights and Fundamental Freedoms."[17] Article III-325 of the Constitutional Treaty provides for a specific procedure under which agreements between the Union and international organisations shall be negotiated and concluded. According to this provision, the Council is entitled to

[16] As agreed on 17-18 June 2004 (CIG 81/04 Annex 47)

[17] According to Protocol relating to Article I-7(2) on the accession of the Union to the ECHR to the Constitutional Treaty, the agreement related to accession (...) shall make provision for preserving the specific characteristics of the Union and Union law, in particular with regard to:

1) the specific arrangements for the Union's possible participation in the control bodies of the ECHR;
2) the mechanisms necessary to ensure that proceedings by non-Member States and individual applications are correctly addressed to Member States and/or the Union as appropriate.

The Protocol further states that the above-mentioned agreement shall ensure that accession shall not affect the competences of the Union and the power of its institutions.

One should also mention that according to the Declaration for incorporation in the Final Act re Article I-7 (2), the Conference agrees that the Union's accession to the ECHR should be arranged in such a way as to preserve the specific features of Union law. Moreover, the Conference notes the existence of a regular dialogue between the Court of Justice of the European Union and the European Court of Human Rights. Such dialogue could be reinforced when the European Union accedes to the ECHR.

adopt a European decision authorising the opening of negotiations. The Council also adopts negotiating directives, authorises the signing of agreements and concludes them. The role of the Commission is to submit recommendations to the Council with respect to the matter in question and to negotiate the agreement on the basis of the Council's directives and agreement of the European Parliament. As stipulated in Art. III-325 (8) of the Constitutional Treaty, decisions to open negotiations and to accede require a qualified majority of member states. The consent of the European Parliament is also required.

In this context it is also important to mention the last reform of the European Court of Human Rights, as envisaged by Protocol 14 adopted by the Committee of Ministers on 13 May 2004. This Protocol contains a specific provision of the issue of accession of the European Union. According to Article 18 of Protocol 14, "The EU may accede to the Convention". This provision gives a political message and paves the way for future negotiations to that end. However, it does not oblige the EU to accede to the ECHR and further negotiations will be required for the Union to accede to the Convention.[18]

Were it to become reality, accession of the EU to the ECHR would constitute a very important step for the protection of human rights in Europe by providing a good tool to ensure a harmonious development of the case law in human rights matters of the two European Courts, in Strasbourg and in Luxembourg. It also goes without saying that accession would encourage closer cooperation between the European Commission and the Council of Europe in the field of the protection of human rights. Such cooperation is of particular importance for the entire process of building the long-term effectiveness and the credibility of the human rights' system in Europe. In this context it is essential to stress the complementarity, both legal and political, of the Charter of Fundamental Rights with a legally binding nature and accession of the Union to the ECHR.

When it comes to consequences for the national systems of the member states and allocation of competences between the Union and the member states, accession will not affect the national positions of the member states in Strasbourg. As regards the question of division of competencies between the Union and the member states, it should be stressed that accession would not have an influence on the scope and division of competences between the Union and its member states. The legal "scope" of the Union's accession to the ECHR would remain limited to issues in respect of which the Union has competence; it would thus not lead to any extension of the Union's competencies. Accordingly, "positive" obligations of the Union to take action to comply with the ECHR, in ac-

[18] The Steering Committee of Human Rights within the Council of Europe has already identified a significant number of legal and technical points concerning the possible accession of the EU to the Convention (CDDH Activity Report of 2 April 2002).

cordance with Article 1 of the ECHR, would arise only to the extent to which competencies of the Union permit such action under the Treaty.

As regards the issue of the future coexistence between the Charter and the ECHR after the accession, the Charter of Fundamental Rights answers this question when it refers to the meaning and scope of rights guaranteed by the European Convention of Human Rights, declaring in its Article 52 § 3 that so far as the Charter contains rights which correspond to rights guaranteed by the ECHR, the meaning and scope of those rights shall be the same as those laid down by the Convention. The coexistence of the Charter of Fundamental Rights and the European Convention on Human Rights should therefore be seen as a positive element aimed at enhancing the fundamental rights protection of the Union's citizens. Incorporation of the Charter into the Treaties and the Union's accession to the ECHR should be regarded as complementary steps for ensuring full respect of the fundamental rights within the EU. The existence of the Charter does not in any way diminish the benefits of extending the control of the European Court of Human Rights to cover the Union's acts. Moreover, accession to the ECHR does not reduce the significance of the Union's own catalogue of fundamental rights.

In this connection, mention should also be made of the problems resulting from the present non-participation of the Union in the Strasbourg judicial system in cases where the Strasbourg Court is led to rule indirectly on Union law without the Union being able to defend itself before that Court or to have a judge in the Court who would ensure the necessary expertise on Union law.

In the context of the ongoing discussions on the Constitutional Treaty, the positive attitude towards the Union's accession to the European Convention on Human Rights seems to be shared by all member states and by the Commission. Being conscious of the current difficulties with the ratification of the Constitutional Treaty which contains legal basis for the essential developments of fundamental rights in the EU, one could nevertheless believe that the future of fundamental rights in the European Union will receive a very positive impetus by the possible incorporation of the Charter of Fundamental Rights of the European Union in the Treaties as well as by the potential accession of the European Union to the European Convention of Human Rights. These two developments should be considered as "the fundamental rights' package". In the European Union of today, one must never perceive fundamental rights as external adjuncts or embellishments on the European integration process; they must remain at the heart of the discussion on the future of the European Union.

The creation of the Fundamental Rights Agency of the European Union

The representatives of the member states meeting within the European Council in Brussels on 12 and 13 December 2003 decided to extend the remit of the Vienna-based European Monitoring Centre on Racism and Xenophobia in order to convert it into a Fundamental Rights Agency. This decision was a logical and concrete consequence of the growing importance of fundamental rights issues within the European Union. Moreover, that decision ended a long debate in which support for setting up such an agency was widely expressed. The Commission fully supports the creation of such agency, as the latter is in line with the specific commitments of the Union to provide for full and effective respect for fundamental rights.

The Agency will complement the existing Community system of protection and promotion of the existing fundamental rights, characterised by different elements, for example:

- the judicial review by the Court of Justice, which will be reinforced by a future external review by the European Court of Human Rights following accession to the European Convention on Human Rights;
- the monitoring by the European Ombudsman to ensure that EU institutions respect the right to sound administration;
- the monitoring by the European Data Protection Supervisor with regard to the processing of personal data by a Community institution or body.

In this manner, the Agency will play an important role in the development of a fundamental rights culture at the European Union level.

Before drafting a Regulation to set up the Agency, the Commission launched a public consultation with the interested parties. As the result, a Communication was adopted in October 2004. The consultation process aimed to encourage public debate on the delicate questions related to the establishment of the Agency, such as the precise definition of its field of action, its missions, tasks and the relations it might develop with the Council of Europe and other international institutions, as well as national bodies. It also raised problems concerning the adaptation of the existing structure to ensure that the Agency was effective. Based upon the results of the consultation, the Commission took note of the fact that the solutions to these problems should be sought with an eye to the beneficiaries of the Agency's activities: the EU institutions, the member states and civil society in general. The Agency should be a crossroads facilitating contact between the different players in the field of fundamental rights, allowing synergies and increased dialogue between all concerned. This should benefit the holders of fundamental rights, citizens and all people within the EU. Furthermore, the national institutions for the protection and promotion of human rights set up by some member states on the basis of UN principles can serve as a source of inspiration when establishing the Agency, even though given the uniqueness of the EU care should be taken to avoid simply transposing these examples. According to those principles, the institutions must have consultative, informative and monitoring functions and be able in particular to formulate opinions and draw up studies, reports and education and information schemes.

In June 2005 the Commission adopted and presented to the Council a proposal for Regulation establishing a European Union Agency for Fundamental Rights. The proposal is currently subject to discussion in the Council. According to the Commission proposal, the objective of the Agency shall be to provide the relevant institutions and authorities of the Community and its member states when implementing the Community law with assistance and expertise relating to fundamental rights in order to help them when they take measures or formulate courses of action within their respective spheres of competence. The proposal for Regulation focuses on the first pillar (Article 308 TEC) and the competence of the Agency should be pursued within the competence of the Community. Nevertheless, the scope of the activities of the Agency is proposed to be extended to the third pillar matters relating to police and judicial co-operation in criminal matters with a Council Decision to be adopted under Articles 30 and 31 of the TUE.

Subject to the Council agreement on the Regulation, the Agency should start functioning in 2007. Its seat, as is the case with the European Monitoring Centre for Racism and Xenophobia, should be in Vienna.

Cooperation with the Council of Europe in the field of ensuring respect for human rights in Europe

The issue of cooperation between the EU and the Council of Europe is nowadays particularly important. This aspect of the creation of "the European culture of fundamental rights" has been mentioned both in the context of the issue of accession of the European Union to the ECHR as well as the creation of the Fundamental Rights Agency of the European Union. The Commission and the Council of Europe are constantly looking for synergies.

The financial programme for the promotion of fundamental rights

On 6 April 2005, the Commission adopted a package of legislative proposals concerning financial perspectives for 2007-2013. This package includes Communications to the Council and the European Parliament establishing 3 Framework Programs:

- Fundamental Rights and Justice;
- Security and Safeguarding Liberties,
- Solidarity and Migration Flows Regulations.

The "Fundamental Rights and Justice" Program is the response to all these political objectives which have been confirmed in the Hague Programme. Under the Programme, the Commission aims at funding actions to develop information tools enabling all persons to access fundamental rights-related information. This Programme has as the main objective to promote those rights and thus contributes to the development of a European culture based on common values enshrined in the Charter of Fundamental Rights by targeting specific groups of the population to ensure real added value.
The four detailed objectives are:

(1) To promote the development of a European society based on European Union citizenship and respectful of the fundamental rights provided for in the Charter of Fundamental Rights; to fight anti-semitism, racism and xenophobia and to strengthen civil society in the field of fundamental rights.
(2) To contribute to the setting up of an area of freedom, security and justice by combating violence and by providing information and preventing the use of drugs.
(3) To promote judicial cooperation with the aim of contributing to the creation of a genuine European area of justice in civil and commercial matters.
(4) To promote judicial cooperation with the aim of contributing to the creation of a genuine European area of justice in criminal matters.

Calls for proposals issued in 2005 solicited projects focusing on the following subjects:

1. Promotion of European Union citizenship;
2. Promotion of fundamental rights through sports and arts;
3. Organisation of seminars on the role of fundamental rights and rights relating to European citizenship in the future of the Union.

Conclusions
Based upon the above observations, one can arrive at the conclusion that even if the present European Treaties do not contain many provisions related to the protection and promotion of fundamental rights in the European Union, there exists a significant, consistent and well-built framework to deal with this issue.
The recent developments in the field in question have provided solid grounds for the belief that the European Union has been transforming itself from a structure with purely economic objectives into an organisation with more universal na-

ture, based upon such values as respect for human rights and fundamental freedoms, the rule of law and democracy.

However, the process of transformation has only started and its continuation will certainly require a great deal of legal and political efforts in the near future. The continuation of this process should be considered as one of the most important challenges currently standing before the Union.

Courts, Charters and Conventions: The Institutionalisation of Human Rights Protection in the European Union

Justus Schönlau

Introduction

The project of European integration has been inspired by the desire to preserve peace and avoid the abuses of human rights that Europe had seen in the first half of the 20th century, from its very beginnings. Even though some remark critically that at the level of the institutions set up in this process, which have come to form the European Union, the commitment to the preservation of human rights has been constructed with hindsight and might even be considered a consciously created 'myth' to legitimise the European Union (Williams 2004: 137), it seems fair that in several important ways the emerging human rights awareness has influenced moves towards creating European institutions from the 1940s onwards. Yet, for a number of political and historical reasons it has been a long and sometimes twisted road from this general inspiration to the development of an EU-level human rights regime, and some argue that we are still a long way off (Weiler 2002). This chapter will highlight some important recent steps on this way with a particular focus on the role of European institutions in this process and the changes which they have undergone. The gradual institutionalisation of human rights protection in the EU system is presented as both a product of, and an important condition for, the consolidation of the Union as a self-sustained political system in this perspective. The protection of fundamental rights, and the development of the policies and institutions to ensure it therefore fulfil two functions for the emerging EU polity: on the one hand, the respect of an core set of human rights is a minimum requirement for a legitimate democratic polity. At the same time, however, the definition of these fundamental rights and the development of the structures and practices to protect them, are in themselves important 'constituent' acts for the polity in question.[1]

In the case of the European Union, both aspects of human rights have become much more visible in recent years, in particular since the setting up, in 1999, of a 'Convention' to draft the EU's own Charter of Fundamental Rights. The decision to embark on such a project, despite the fact that highly developed systems of rights protection already existed in all EU member states and at the level of the Council of Europe, supports the argument that at least a substantial part of the EU's reason for institutionalising its own Fundamental Rights are due to a more or less self-conscious effort to 're-found' the Union as a fully fledged constitutional system. This impetus of course continued with the creation of the

[1] Following the use of the terminology of 'human rights' and 'fundamental rights' as interchangeable by the European institutions and by most analysts, the chapter will treat them as synonymous unless specified otherwise.

'Convention on the Future of the EU' in 2002, one of whose tasks it was to propose a solution to the open question of the legal status of the Charter of Fundamental Rights. The debates in the 'second' Convention, which eventually proposed the EU Constitutional Treaty (CT), quickly established that the overwhelming majority of Convention members wanted a full inclusion of the Charter into the new constitutional text, thus confirming both the Charter's legal value and the Convention's claim to produce a 'complete' constitution including a catalogue of basic rights. Despite the ensuing difficulties in ratifying the Constitution, it appears that the Charter of Rights is one of the least controversial elements of the Constitutional Treaty, and it is bound to take its place as a key document of the EU's constitutional structure sooner rather than later -if not as part of a constitutional settlement then in some other form. With this step, the chances for the gradual development of a more comprehensive and coherent human rights regime in and for the European Union are likely to improve, even though some analysts seem to pit the creation of an EU human rights policy and of an EU Constitution against each other in a zero-sum equation (Weiler 2002, see below).

The chapter therefore traces this most recent episode of the gradual institutionalisation of a fundamental rights regime and discourse in the European Union. The next section therefore looks at the developments which led up to the decision of the 1999 European Council in Cologne to issue a mandate for the drafting of a new document of fundamental rights for the EU. Previous decisions by the European Court of Justice and national constitutional courts had, of course, alerted the political actors to the fact that the progressive deepening of European integration would inevitably touch upon questions of fundamental rights, and might lead to conflicts between different systems for their protection. Yet the section will also highlight how the prospect of impending enlargement, but also the immediate backdrop to the decision with the NATO-led war on Kosovo inspired the German presidency at the time to push for the drafting of the EU's own catalogue of rights through a novel process in the Convention.

The following section will then take its cue from the somewhat curious statement of the Cologne mandate that 'protection of fundamental rights is a founding principle of the Union and an indispensable prerequisite for her legitimacy...[and] (t)here appears to be a need, at the present stage of the Union's development, to establish a Charter of fundamental rights in order to make their overriding importance and relevance more visible to the Union's citizens.' (European Council, 1999). This affirmation shows clearly the dual role ascribed to fundamental rights as a founding principle and important element of the Union's legitimacy. The expectation, apparently harboured by at least some members of the European Council, that the Convention would therefore merely list existing human rights and thus increase their visibility for the EU citizens was soon to be disproved by the Convention's work. A brief account of the drafting of the Charter in fact reveals, how the endeavour to define a set of fundamental rights in a given political context at a given moment in time immediately raised important questions about the 'constitution' of that political context. The Charter experience in this sense was a path-breaker and predecessor of the Constitutional Convention, despite the fact that the Charter Convention could not decide on the Charter's legal status and the Charter was eventually proclaimed in December 2000 only as a 'political declaration'.

In fact, the dynamic of the institutionalised debate about the fundamentals of European integration was such that the failure of institutional reform at the intergovernmental conference in Nice created the need for an even more profound debate about the future of the EU. The following section therefore continues the account of the institutionalisation of human rights protection in the EU system from the Laeken declaration to the draft Constitutional Treaty. It shows how the contents of the Charter had, by the time the second Convention started to work on it, already become an ingrained part of the *acquis communautaire* in the sense that changes to the substance of the Charter, though proposed by some, did not have a serious chance of approval in the Convention of the Future of the EU. Instead, the will to make the Charter an integral part of the emerging constitutional document was established quickly, even though the debate about its precise scope and legal force continued and continues to date. This latter fact shows indeed that beyond the constituent function of a catalogue of rights and the process of its realisation at the EU level, there are still disagreements about the EU's human rights protection regime itself, and its legal ramifications. The concluding part therefore draws together the account of the two Conventions to show how the progressive institutionalisation of a specific EU-system of fundamental rights is part and parcel of the ongoing development of the EU polity. Driven and torn by the parallel forces of widening and deepening, the EU's emergence as a political system with an independent claim to legitimacy has meant that the issue of human rights has become increasingly prominent. This process is, of course, by no means completed: on the one hand, at the time of writing the fate of the Constitutional Treaty itself, after it was rejected in two national referenda, is unclear. On the other hand, the institutionalisation of a catalogue and a discourse on human rights is at best one part of their realisation, and there are many areas in which the EU's policies on human rights are far from coherent. Yet, the fact that fundamental rights have not only taken their rightful place among the proclaimed core values of the integration project, but have also been spelled out in a comparatively open and comprehensive process, means that future developments in this area will have a suitable basis in a (legal) text, as well as in the political narrative of the European Union.

Towards an EU Charter of Rights

From early on in the history of the integrated Europe did it become clear that even an initially primarily economic project of integration could affect the fundamental rights of the member states' citizens. The creation of a single market with internal freedom of movement clearly raised the prospect of fundamental human rights protected in different member states coming into contact, and maybe even conflict with each other. At the same time, the emergence of new international systems for the protection of human rights in parallel with the process of European (economic) integration, notably the development of the European Convention on Human Rights and Fundamental Freedoms (ECHR), drew attention to the question whether supposedly universal human rights would be evenly protected in all member states and what their interaction would be with the new legal order that began to take shape among the member states of the EC. At the latest with the 1963 decision of the European Court of Justice that EC law had to have 'supremacy' over national law in order for the economic community to function properly[2], it became clear that all areas of national law, including the protection of fundamental rights under national constitutions, would be affected by integration. This situation of potential conflict was crystallised in the famous 1974 decision by the German constitutional court in its '*Solange*' judgment (and similar pronouncements by other national courts), that the supremacy of EC law as acceptable only 'as long as' the level of protection was at least the same as that guaranteed by the national constitutions.[3] Thus the issue of the protection of basic rights had become one of potentially existential dimensions for the new EC legal order - to the extent that Weiler referred to the balance between the different protection systems as an equilibrium of 'mutually assured destruction' (Weiler 1997).

Not least in response to this somewhat uneasy situation, the institutions of the European Community became more concerned with the issue of human rights. The 1970s saw a great number of ECJ judgements establishing particular rights within the EC law system. At the same time, the European Commission, the European Parliament and the Council of Ministers adopted a joint declaration on fundamental rights in 1977 in which they confirmed their commitment to uphold fundamental rights as derived from the national constitutions of the member states and from the ECHR (European Commission, Parliament and Council of Ministers, 1977). And while the legal development of an EC-internal human rights doctrine continued, the European Parliament after its first direct election in 1979 increasingly pushed also for a political-institutional initiative to highlight the centrality of human rights for European integration. The Parliament's first draft for a European Constitution, the 1984 Spinelli draft, already

[2] Case 26/62 [1963], Van Gend en Loos v. Nederlands Aministratie der Belastingen

[3] BVerfGE 37, 271ff, of 1974

contained a catalogue of fundamental rights as part of a fully-fledged constitutional framework for the Union (Schmuck 1987). While this document was too ambitious to ever be realised, it did find a resonance in the preamble to the 1986 Single European Act, which for the first time introduced the obligation of the EC to respect the fundamental rights enshrined in the ECHR. Also amidst mounting pressure to 'bring the EU closer to its people' and to re-launch the dynamics of the integration project which had flagged in the 1970s and 80s, the commitment to human rights was seen as a way to increase the legitimacy of the Community and to appeal to the citizens. Moreover, the 1985 Adonnino report had argued that, among other things, one way to improve the EC's standing with its people would be to give them a number of 'special' fundamental rights, to increase the visible benefits from membership (European Commission 1985:7). This dual approach, of binding the EC/EU more closely to the existing systems of rights protection (notably the ECHR) on the one hand, and of pursuing an additional strategy of creating new, 'special European' rights on the other, became a key element of the EC/EU's policy in the decades to follow, and is still visible in the Charter. Thus, in the late 1980s - early 90s the question of a possible signing up of the EC as a whole to the European Convention became increasingly topical. This was partly due to the continued fear that sooner or later conflicts would arise between the jurisdictions of the ECJ and the ECHR, and partly it was seen as a necessary proof that the EC/EU was applying the same standards to its own system as it was increasingly projecting outwards. In particular with the changes of 1989 and the subsequent support Europe gave to the new democracies of central and eastern Europe (who all signed the ECHR as one of the first steps of their 'return to Europe'), the charge of double standards against the EU became increasingly embarrassing (Williams 2004: 53). Yet, despite several expert groups and preparatory steps, the fact that the EU itself lacked legal personality meant that in 1996 the ECJ had to state that the Union could not become party to the European Convention itself.[4] Short of this, however, the Amsterdam Treaty of 1996 re-enforced the commitment to human rights (as in the ECHR) by making their respect a 'founding principle' of the Union (Art 6) and providing for sanctions in case of breaches of these principles by the member states (Art 7).

Meanwhile pressure was also building for a genuinely EU set of fundamental rights. Notably in Germany, where the concern with the protection of basic rights in the interplay between the national constitution and the European legal system was particularly prominent, the national Parliament had called for an EU catalogue of rights in 1995 (Deutscher Bundestag 2001: 93). Gradually this idea gathered pace, to the extent that an initiative for such a Charter during Germany's EU presidency in 1999 became part of the coalition agreement between

[4] European Court of Justice Opinion 2/94 on Accession to the ECHR [1996] ECR I-1759.

the victorious social democratic and Green parties in the fall of 1998. The idea then came to fruition during the Cologne summit at the end of the German presidency, in June 1999. In preparing the Council meeting, the Charter project had apparently turned out to be widely accepted by the other member states' leaders.[5] This might seem somewhat surprising, certainly in the case of the United Kingdom which had earlier on not been keen on anything so closely resembling a constitutional document, and which had just one year earlier adopted its own Human Rights Act based on the ECHR. Two factors have to be born in mind, however, which help to explain the particularly favourable climate for the German initiative in mid 1999: on the one hand, EU enlargement to include a substantial number of new democracies from Central and Eastern Europe (the precise number was not clear at the time, of course) was rapidly drawing closer. This created a widely shared feeling of the need for a symbolic re-confirmation of the common basis of Europe's values in the face of an expected increase in diversity. Moreover, since the 1993 Copenhagen summit the respect for the Union's principles (including human rights) had become a criterion for membership. A clarification what exactly human rights meant in the EU context was therefore seen as a useful strengthening of the Union's political framework.

Secondly, the Cologne summit came at the height of the Kosovo crisis. NATO had started to wage war on the EU's doorstep less than three months earlier. By this time, the EU's role as a guardian of democracy and human rights had become increasingly part of the self-image of the Union and its leaders. In this situation the proposal to launch a high-level 'body' to take stock of Europe's human rights assets 'to make their importance more visible to Europe's people' (see below) was widely welcome. In fact, as Merlingen, Mudde and Sedelmeier notice, "...by the end of the 1990s, the idea of protecting democracy and human rights in Europe became a central component of a common identity shared by key national and supranational decision-makers in the EU." (Merlingen, Mudde & Sedelmeier, 2001: 61). A strongly symbolic action, such as the creation of a body of high visibility, with the task to re-iterate the EU's commitment to fundamental rights, while granting an otherwise difficult German presidency (which had to struggle with the multi-annual budget negotiations) one of its pet projects, thus seemed a step easily taken.

The Charter Convention

The text of the Cologne mandate as it was adopted by the summit set out the task of the new body with the somewhat curious formula quoted above that there 'appears to be a need, at the present stage of the Union's development, to establish a Charter of fundamental rights...' to make their '...overriding importance and relevance more visible to the Union's citizens' (European Council, 1999).

[5] Author's interviews with officials from the Federal Ministry of Justice, Germany, 2000.

The mandate then provided an important list of documents from which these rights were to be drawn, thus suggesting that mainly (and some would argue exclusively) the Convention should collect these rights already formulated elsewhere, as opposed to drafting new ones. Most importantly, the Cologne text took up the phrase already contained in the EU treaties with reference to the rights "...guaranteed by the European Convention for the Protection of Human Rights and Fundamental Freedoms and derived from the constitutional traditions common to the Member States.' Significantly, however, the text also mentioned those fundamental rights 'that pertain only to the Union's citizens', as well as 'economic and social rights' from the European Social Charter and the EU's Charter of Fundamental Workers' Rights 'insofar as they do not merely establish objectives for action by the Union' (European Council 1999). This last provision turned out to be one of the most controversial issues in the Convention and a lot of debate focussed on the question which, if any, social rights could and should be included in the Charter.

Moreover, the Cologne mandate set out the completely new structure and method by which the Charter would be drafted: a 'body' consisting of representatives of the heads of national government, the Commission, the European Parliament and the national Parliaments, with observers from the Court of Justice, the Economic and Social Committee and the Committee of the Regions would draw up the Charter, which would then be 'solemnly proclaimed' by the three EU institutions. Only afterwards it would be decided, if and how the text could be integrated into the Treaties. This last opening proved to be very important because it prevented the Convention from getting bogged down in the controversial question of whether the rights in the Charter could and should be legally binding. At the following summit meeting in Tampere under Finnish presidency (October 1999), the provisions for the Charter drafting body were further specified: it would consist of a majority of parliamentary representatives (two from each national Parliament, 16 from the EP), one representative of each national head of government, one Commission representative and additional observers both from the ECJ and the European Court of Human Rights. It would have an elected president and four vice-presidents, representing the four constituent elements of the body (EP, Commission, national governments, national Parliaments). Consultations would be undertaken with civil society and with the applicant countries. The debates about the EU's fundamental rights regime would be held in public and would be concluded if and when a draft text could be agreed upon by 'all the parties'. This last provision is particularly important because it formed the basis for the Convention's decision making 'by consensus'.

The story of this first Convention has been told elsewhere (for example Schönlau, 2005) and marks an important episode both for the question of human rights in the EU, and for the Union's institutional and constitutional development. In fact, both aspects were always tangible in the Convention's debates and probably the most significant lesson to be drawn from the Charter experience is the degree to which fundamental rights had become, and were becoming, a constitutional issue for the Union. The Charter body quickly decided to call itself 'Convention' with clear constitutional overtones, and even though there was a substantial group of Convention members at the outset who maintained that the Convention could and should do nothing but 'just' compile a list of existing human rights which were already common to all member states, it is widely recognised that the Charter in the end became substantially more than that. For one, the Charter goes clearly beyond the ECHR in the sense that it contains not only those 'classical' human and civic rights that were already consensus in 1950, but more controversially lists a number of social and economic rights (like, for example, the 'right to collective bargaining and action' (Art 28 of the original Charter draft), the recognition of 'social security and social assistance' (Art 34) and 'health care' (Art 35), or the much-fought over right to 'access to services of general economic interest' (Art 36)). While the Convention has been criticised by some for raising false expectations and creating legal uncertainty by giving the impression that these 'rights' could be protected at the same level and to the same degree as the classical rights (for example Ewing, 2002), it is clear that the inclusion of such new rights is symbolically and politically important. As is, indeed, the fact that apart from these social and economic rights, and some significant 'new' rights like the 'right to the integrity of the person' (Art 3), including the prohibition of reproductive cloning, or the 'protection of personal data (Art 8), the Charter also has a separate chapter on 'citizens rights' (Arts 39-46). This part of the Charter takes up a number of rights (to participate in European and local elections in one's country of residence, consular protection by other member states' diplomatic missions, the rights to petition the European Ombudsman and the EP, the freedom of movement and residence within the Union, the right of access to documents and a right to 'good administration') which had been introduced by the Treaty of Maastricht in order to give substance to the idea of a 'European citizenship'.

While these rights in themselves are still limited, it has been argued convincingly that they form an important part of a developing 'citizenship practice' and thus of the EU's move towards becoming a self-sustained polity (Wiener 1998). At the same time, the fact that here, in a document otherwise containing supposedly 'universal' human rights, a category of rights is included which applies specifically to EU citizens only (like the voting rights, freedom of movement and consular protection) highlights once more the dual function of the Charter in the EU context: to show the Union's commitment and indebtedness to the global discourse of universal human rights, but at the same time the desire to create an EU-specific interpretation of these rights as an underpinning of a distinct (EU)-European identity. This duality is in fact part of the problem of 'incoherence' and the resulting charge against the EU's human rights 'irony' (or hypocrisy) (Williams 2004). These criticisms refer to differing attitudes to human rights issues across different parts of the EU system (such as more exigent human rights requirements in the Union's external relations, as opposed to its internal policies) and the lack of an overall coherent political and institutional framework for an EU human rights policy. Indeed, these problems have been highlighted by many observers (see for example contributions to Alston & Weiler 1999) in recent years. The above mentioned insertion of special EU-citizens rights in the Charter seems to confirm that the tension between the different spheres of human rights in the EU have not been resolved. Yet, a closer look at the debates in the Convention and the drafting of these rights in particular also shows that within the process of defining fundamental rights in Europe, an opening up of at least some rights occurred: for example, Art. 41, the 'right to good administration' was initially phrased as a rather restricted right of 'every citizen', but successive debates and re-drafts in the Convention meant that the article now grants this right to 'every person' (see Schönlau, 2005: 95).

The Charter Convention thus seems to have 'broadened' the EU's approach to human rights in some important respects: by including some new and innovative rights, by opening up the application of some significant rights and not least by debating extensively the relationship between the concept of a European community of values, certain rights or principles, and the consequences from this for a new political entity like the European Union. The Convention did this in a comparatively open process which helped to gauge the agreements and disagreements in the search for a body of rights that represented, at a particular moment in time in the process of integration, the level of common commitment. Instrumental in 'finding' and/ or 'constructing' this agreement was firstly the particular composition of the Convention bringing together actors from different institutional, political and cultural backgrounds with a comparatively clearly defined common purpose. Secondly, the decision by Roman Herzog, the Convention's president, to run the debates as a search for 'consensus' and avoid voting in the Convention, and to circumvent deadlock on the question of the legal status of the Charter by having the Convention work 'as if' the rights were to become legally binding, also contributed to the success of the mission.

Yet, this strategy also meant that some important disagreements were not resolved, but were 'trimmed off' the agenda, while others were merely papered over or put aside by 'segregation' (Bellamy and Schönlau 2004). This became particularly visible during the controversies, towards the end of the Convention's work, about the Charter's preamble and in particular about a reference to Europe's religious roots. In many respects, this struggle, which ended with a linguistic compromise which allowed one language version (German) to contain a reference to Europe's religious heritage whereas the other versions refer to Europe's 'spiritual heritage' (Schönlau, 2003), illustrates how the Convention had to run sooner or later into much larger 'constitutional' questions about Europe's identity and purpose, for which, however, it felt it had no mandate. The fact that the very same problem came back to haunt the Constitutional Convention obviously shows that the question had not been 'solved'.

The same was of course true for the question of the legal value of the Charter itself: following the Cologne mandate, the result of the Convention's deliberations was presented to the three European institutions and was then 'solemnly proclaimed' as a political declaration at the Nice summit in December 2000. The heads of state and government could not agree, however, at that stage and in the poisoned atmosphere of a less than successful intergovernmental conference, to go further and take any decision on whether to include the Charter in the Treaties. They put this matter off, and included the issue in the 'declaration on the future of the Union' (European Council, 2000) as one of four key questions to be debated in the next phase of European reform (the other three being the delimitation of competences between the EU and the member states, the simplification of the EU Treaties, and the role of national parliaments in European integration). The legal institutionalisation of the new EU catalogue of fundamental rights was not yet achieved. Nevertheless, both the European Parliament and the European Commission were quick to declare that they would feel bound by the rights in the Charter, whatever its legal status was going to be. In fact, the Charter soon became a core part of the informal legal acquis of the Union, with references being made to it both in new legislation and by different parties before the ECJ, including a number of advocates general and the court of first instance (Peers & Ward, 2004).

The Charter Convention in many ways set the stage for the following debate about the European Constitution and must therefore be considered a key part of this phase of the Union's constitutionalisation process. Not only did the Charter experience provide one of the key questions which still had to be resolved, but it also had shown that a debate about the EU's approach to human rights would inevitably raise many more profound questions about the kind of political entity which the Union is and wants to be. Moreover, it showed the potential (and some of the problems) of a new kind of process in which to tackle these questions. The Convention thus institutionalised not only a set of fundamental rights for the EU, but also a certain understanding of, and procedure for the constitutional development of Europe. Whether this two-fold impact of the Charter Convention on the EU's human rights regime detracts from the essence of developing a more coherent policy by providing a fundamental rights fig-leave (Weiler 2000), or whether it rather creates the conditions to finally make this move, remains open to debate - not least in the light of the uncertainty surrounding the result of the next round of constitutional development.

The Constitutional Convention and Fundamental Rights

The continuing pressure of impending enlargement meant that the failure to achieve substantive institutional reform with the Nice Treaty had to be remedied sooner rather than later. Moreover, the EU's popularity (and by extension its legitimacy) continued to be challenged, most visibly when the Irish referendum on the Nice Treaty failed in 2001. There was a sense of urgency among national leaders and the Union's political actors to try and resolve the outstanding issues. Among these, the legal status of the Charter was seen as one which had the potential to improve the EU's standing in the eyes of its citizens, and which had to be resolved in order to avoid the charge of double standards as the Union had pushed hard for its new members to fulfil its human rights requirements, but had failed to reach agreement on the internal rights dimension (Williams 2004). The Charter experience also served as a powerful precedent for those who argued that the next set of reforms should not be prepared by the classical IGC (which had failed to deliver results at Nice), but by a much more open and transparent process involving all levels of European governance (Norman 2003: 24-5).

The Laeken declaration of December 2001 thus set up a new Convention (this time calling it by this name from the beginning) to address a great number of questions on the future of the European Union, including '...whether the Charter of Fundamental Rights should be included in the basic treaty and [..] whether the European Community should accede to the European Convention on Human Rights' (European Council, 2001). Importantly, the Laeken declaration also raised the question whether the necessary simplification and reorganisation of the Union's primary legal texts "...might not lead in the long run to the adoption of a constitutional text in the Union." (European Council 2001). This phrase provided the opening through which the new Convention (under the guidance of its president) extracted a 'constitutional mandate' for itself.

As far as the Convention was concerned, it followed the model of the Charter Convention, but some significant changes were introduced: in a clear attempt to exercise more (political) control over the new Convention, the heads of state and government in the European Council appointed, after some quite bad-tempered wrangling, the Convention's president Giscard d'Estaing, and its two vice-presidents, Giuliano Amato and Jean-Luc Dehaene (Ludlow 2001). Moreover, the new Convention was significantly larger, due to the fact that the soon-to-be ten new member states, and three candidate countries (Romania, Bulgaria and Turkey) were all participating in the Convention with one government and two national Parliament representatives. Since the number of representatives from the European Parliament remained the same as in the Charter Convention (16), the balance shifted clearly in the favour of the 'national' representatives as opposed to the European ones. This was even more apparent in the initially twelve (later 13) member presidium of Convention II, where the president and his two vice-presidents were joined by three representatives of national governments holding the presidency during 2002-2003 (Spain, Denmark and Greece), and two representatives each of the European Parliament, the European Commission and the national Parliaments.

The larger size of the Convention, and of course its vastly broader mandate also meant that the presidium and the secretariat had an even bigger role to play in structuring the work than had been the case in the Charter Convention. The way that Giscard d'Estaing in particular used this prerogative has given rise to some criticism, even though the overall result of the Convention has been widely praised afterwards. This also meant that the body which soon became the 'constitutional Convention' did set up thematic working groups unlike the Charter body. One of these, under the leadership of Antonio Vitorino who had already represented the European Commission in the Charter Convention, was charged with proposing a solution for the question of the Charter's legal status. It turned out in the course of the debates that those working groups with clearly defined mandates, and which managed to reach broad agreement on a common proposal, were quite effective in preparing proposals which then were carried also by the Convention plenary.

The Charter working group was given the task, presumably at Vitorino's own request in the presidium, not so much to debate '… the major political questions (whether the Charter should be incorporated…)', but rather to find a solution 'how' this could be achieved, and additionally to answer the question of how the EU could accede to the European Convention of Human Rights, a question which was introduced as '…complementary and not alternative…'.(Convention II Conv. 72/02, 31.05.2002: 2). The debates in the working group therefore were rather focussed on a number of legal-technical possibilities and details, despite the fact that some members of the Convention did try to re-introduce the question if the Charter should be included at all, or if some rights should not be changed. In particular the British government representative was very actively pushing for a further limitation of the scope of application for the Charter because he feared that otherwise the Charter could be seen, or could be portrayed by the euro-sceptic opposition in Britain, as an instrument to extend EU competencies.

In response to this, and in order to avoid a re-opening of the entire Charter compromise, the second Convention did eventually apply some important changes to the so-called horizontal articles (Arts 51 (scope of the Charter) and 52 (scope of guaranteed rights)). Thus Art. 51 of the Charter (Art II-111 of the Constitutional Treaty) was re-enforced in stating that the Charter binds first and foremost the EU institutions, and the member states only if and when they are implementing Union law: i.e. Charter rights apply only within the '…limits of the powers of the Union as conferred on it in other parts of the Constitution' (Art. II-111.1). It also mentions explicitly that the Charter *does not* extend the field of application of Union law in any way (II-111.2). Moreover, four new paragraphs were added to Article 52 (Constitution Art. II-112): firstly a phrase to recognise explicitly the respect for the constitutional traditions of the member states (Art. II-112.4), secondly the limitations of the Charter rights to the EU's institutions and acts (Art. II-112.5) was emphasised, and thirdly (Art. II-112.6) stresses the importance of the references to national laws in certain articles of the Charter itself. Finally, a reference to the 'explanations' of the Charter presidium was included in Article II-112.7 during the final days of the Convention, at the insistence of the British government (Norman 2003: 296). These explanations had been drafted by the Charter Convention's presidium at the very end of the negotiations in 2000, without consulting the Convention as a whole. A number of Charter Convention members were outraged at this and suspected that some governments (notably the British) had already then tried to force a certain, more restrained interpretation of the rights contained in the Charter onto the Convention presidium. Due to this row in late September/ early October 2000, the explanations were eventually published with the Charter text but clearly marked as '...prepared at the instigation of the presidium' and as having '... no legal value...' at the time (Convention I Conv. 49, 11 October 2000). Despite these limitations on the explanations, they did become an important focus for the discussions in the Constitutional Convention's working group.

As for the actual inclusion of the Charter in the Constitutional Treaty, working group II discussed three alternatives (including the Charter's full text in the Constitution, annexing it to the text, or making an 'indirect reference' to the Charter in an article of the Constitutional Treaty), and its 'highly consensual report' made clear that there was the widest support for a legally binding Charter as an integral part of the draft Constitution (Convention II CONV 354/02, 22.10.2002). This option was also supported by the overwhelming majority of the Convention in its plenary debate on October 28/29 2002. Moreover, the working group recommended an accession of the European Union to the ECHR, and the Constitutional Treaty therefore duly includes a legal personality for the EU (Art. I-7) and states that the Union '...shall acceded to the European Convention for the Protection of Human Rights and Fundamental Freedoms' in Article I-9.

In this sense, the Constitutional Convention 'completed' the phase of the institutionalisation of fundamental human rights at the EU level that had begun with the first proposal, by the European Parliament, for a set of rights as part of an EU Constitution, in 1984. Given the inability, in 2000, to reach agreement on the key issue of the legal status, it is somewhat surprising that the question of including the Charter in the Constitutional Treaty did not meet more resistance in the second Convention. Despite strong reservations of the British government and some euro-sceptic Convention members, however, the Charter was seen by the vast majority as an already consolidated, consensus-based part of the European Union's institutional structure, and thus its inclusion in the Constitution as a natural development. The fact that the European Commission and Parliament had, after December 2000, quickly adopted the Charter as a key point of reference for the Union's human rights policy, and that it had been referred to before the European Court (and cited in some judgements of the Court of First instance), surely played an important role in this 'informal consolidation' that preceded the formal institutionalisation of the EU's own fundamental rights catalogue.

This consensus was further underlined by the intergovernmental conference (2003-04) which followed the Convention. The IGC which started under Italian presidency did, of course, introduce quite a few changes to the draft constitution put before it by the Convention, and it did re-open some of the compromises that had been reached (notably on the institutional questions), but it is important to note that the inclusion of the Charter itself was not a controversial issue. There were, however, some more attempts by the British government to make sure that the 'explanations' of the Charter rights mentioned above would be anchored even more visibly in the Constitutional Treaty. After the failure of the IGC in December 2003, and in the general climate of renewed calls from various member states for their particular concerns to be placated, the Irish presidency in spring 2004 agreed to the British demand by adding a new sentence to the Charter preamble (paragraph 5) mentioning that the Charter will be interpreted '...by the courts of the Union and the Member States with due regard to the explanations prepared under the authority of the Praesidium of the Convention which drafted the Charter and updated under the responsibility of the Preasidium of the European Convention' (Constitutional Treaty 2004). Moreover, the explanations were published as Declaration 12 annexed to the Constitutional Treaty. This declaration clarifies that they '...do not as such have the status of law, [but] they are a valuable tool of interpretation intended to clarify the provisions of the Charter'. Thus the explanations have clearly become part of the EU's human rights acquis, but their precise effect will become clear only through legal practice. In fact, some observers argue that the explanations in their 'updated form' (which includes references ECJ case law and EU legislation), contain a number of inconsistencies which the courts will have to resolve in due course (Schmitz 2004) if the Constitution enters into force.

With the agreement of the IGC and the subsequent signing ceremony of the constitutional Treaty in Rome on October 29th 2004, it seemed as if the EU had finally consolidated its constitutional structure in one single document, including one of the most comprehensive catalogues of fundamental rights currently available. Yet, the ratification of the Treaty, which was to be approved in ten member states by referenda, ran into somewhat unexpected difficulties with resoundingly negative votes on the Constitution in France and the Netherlands in 2005. At the time of writing, it is still unclear what this set-back means for the eventual fate of the EU Constitution. It is, however, noteworthy that during the ratification campaigns in different member states the Charter appeared as one of the more 'popular' parts of the Constitutional Treaty (see for example Incerti, Kurpas and Schönlau 2005). While the reasons that caused the Constitutional Treaty to be rejected in some countries are complex and are still awaiting full analysis, it seems fair to say that the idea of a catalogue of rights in itself was not the problem, but rather that it did appear as (at least part of) the solution in terms of the aim of a more legitimate EU which provides tangible benefits for its citizens. It is therefore likely that the Charter might be among those parts of the Constitution which could, in one way or another, be 'rescued' from the wreckage of the Constitutional package, if the latter is indeed definitely unravelled.

Conclusion

The European Union has had an ambiguous relation to the question of human rights since its beginnings because the notion of human rights has influenced the development of European integration in two quite distinct ways: on the one hand, human rights and their protection were (or were presented to be, see below) an underlying part of the European idea and the common tradition of the member states. In this sense, human rights are a key part of the social and cultural fabric that holds the European Union together. In fact, as such they have been actively used, and a specifically European 'narrative' or 'myth' of human rights has been constructed by actors in the integration process to 'authenticate' the existence of the European Union (Williams 2004: 128). On the other hand, human rights and their protection have become an increasingly important part of the policy output of the European Union, both externally and internally. Of course, also this dimension of human rights in the EU context is concerned with justifying and thus legitimising the EU as a new layer of political decision making. It remains thus to be seen whether the incoherence between the different dimensions and functions of human rights in the European Union project which many authors identify, should be understood as a structural and therefore more or less permanent 'bifurcation' (Williams 2004), or whether it is rather a product of the uneven development and the resulting 'in-betweenness' of the European Union as a new polity between supra-statism and international organisation.

The present chapter has sought to highlight some aspects of the most recent phase of human rights debate at the institutional level of the Union which, in my view, point towards the serious intent on the part of a large majority of forces in the process to move the Union towards a more unified human rights policy. Such a policy would have to be anchored to the constitutional 'myth' of human rights as a core underlying value on which the whole idea of a European Union is founded, but it would also have to be capable of realising these rights both within the Union and outside, through the necessary political and legal means. A pre-condition for the development of such an approach was the establishment of a defined set of (EU-specific) human rights. This has been provided with the drafting of the Charter of Fundamental Rights. This catalogue of rights, whatever its merits or demerits might be in concrete legal terms, can provides a basis for the further discussion of which rights can and should be protected how in the European Union. Of course the quality of the EU's human rights regime does depend on the concrete steps (policies, institutions, legal developments) to ensure that these rights are taken seriously and are not 'frozen' but continue to evolve and be developed (Bellamy and Castiglione 2001).

In this sense, the gradual building of a human rights discourse at the institutional level, and the eventual definition of a set of European fundamental rights in a political process in the first Convention were a necessary but not sufficient condition for the emergence of a genuine human rights regime. The subsequent debates in the Constitutional Convention showed on the one hand that there was overwhelming recognition of the important role which a catalogue of rights could and should play in a constitutional framework for the Union. The body of rights identified by the first Convention also seemed to have wide support. On the other hand, the persistent concerns of some member states about the possible interference of the Charter with domestic and international systems of human rights protection and the fear that the Charter rights could lead to an unwarranted expansion of EU competencies also showed, where the fault-lines lie for the debates in the years to come. A political balance has to be found at each stage in integration concerning what can, should and must be done at European level in order to respect the autonomy of the member states and other human rights protection system, while at the same time honouring the claims made to the foundational role of human rights for the European Union. In fact, by proposing *both* the inclusion of the Charter *and* the accession of the Union to the ECHR, the Convention on the Future of Europe clearly underlined that the European human rights regime is based on a number of sources. Overlap and interaction between them is therefore inevitable and has to be managed.

The European Union is thus a part of a larger network of interlocking human rights protection systems. The institutionalisation of its own internal system is necessary for the Union to find its place in the wider structures. The uncertain fate (at the time of writing) of the Constitutional Treaty does raise questions about the place of the Charter rights and their location in the constitutional fabric, but independently of the adoption of this particular draft Constitution, the Charter has already become a part of the Union's legal set-up and is there to stay. The mechanisms to streamline and improve the implementation of the rights contained in the Charter are currently under discussion, and the creation of a fundamental rights agency is yet another piece in the jig-saw. Naturally it raises the same questions about how precisely the Union can ensure certain rights to be protected, how it will interact with the member states in this endeavour, whether the agency will have an external as well as an internal mandate and so on (European Commission 2005). The debate about this next step in the institutionalisation of the European Union's human rights regime provides the platform for finding concrete political solutions for these questions, and through this kind of steps the Union has the possibility of moving closer to a coherent human rights regime for itself.

The Human Dimension: The OSCE's Approach to Human Rights

Jens Narten

The "Organization for Security and Co-operation in Europe" (OSCE) is the successor organisation to a series of conferences on security and co-operation, formerly known as the CSCE[1]. The CSCE aimed to link politico-military aspects of security, such as arms control, with economic co-operation and the so-called human dimension. The latter was highlighted in the third basket of the Helsinki Final Act in 1975 and was meant to reaffirm human rights standards and rule of law and democracy through politically binding commitments, especially in countries in the former Soviet sphere of influence. The end of the East-West confrontation provided an opportunity to further deepen the recognition of human rights principles in and among OSCE's participating states by adopting documents stressing human rights standards by establishing mechanisms and functional institutions for the promotion of various areas of human rights and by deploying OSCE field missions with a mandate dedicated to human rights monitoring and promotion. Focussing on these developments and following the logic of OSCE's contribution to human rights under the label *human dimension*, this article will first concentrate on different developmental phases of human rights commitments along with core documents of the OSCE/CSCE. In this respect, the Helsinki Final Act, the documents of the Vienna and Moscow conferences, the Copenhagen Document and the Paris Charter will serve as prominent examples that also provide for mechanisms of interference into internal affairs of participating states in support of the human dimension. Secondly, the function of specialised institutions of the OSCE for the promotion of specific human rights areas, such as the Office for Democratic Institutions and Human Rights, the High Commissioner on National Minorities and the Representative on the Freedom of the Media, will be discussed. Third, as long-term field missions represent a central element of OSCE's applied human rights work, the OSCE Mission to Kosovo with its comprehensive human rights mandate will serve as a practical case study. Finally, this article will conclude with a look at the future perspectives of the OSCE's human rights approach by considering the latest developments that put the human dimension at risk.

Phases of Human Dimension Commitments within the OSCE System

Human rights norms and standards have been of paramount importance to the entire development of the OSCE over the past 30 years. These can be divided into different phases with regard to their varying political importance for the

[1] The Conference on Security and Co-operation in Europe was renamed the Organization for Security and Co-operation in Europe in 1994. For practical reasons, the term OSCE will be used in the ongoing text of this article.

organisation. When the representatives of participating states to the Conference on Security and Co-operation in Europe met in 1975 to sign the guiding principles under the Helsinki Final Act, strong emphasis of their future relations was placed on the "respect for human rights and fundamental freedoms, including the freedom of thought, conscience, religion or belief" and the "effective exercise of civil, political, economic, social, cultural and other rights and freedoms all of which derive from the inherent dignity of the human person" (Helsinki Final Act 1975, Guiding Principle VII). Amidst the East-West confrontation of the Cold War and at the beginning of an era of *détente*, the participating Western states hoped to ease the position of political dissident groups and civil rights activists in the Soviet sphere. At the same time, Moscow tried to fix the geopolitical status quo in Europe following WWII by the inclusion of other principles such as state sovereignty, inviolability of borders, territorial integrity and non-intervention into the catalogue of principles. The first phase of human rights commitments of participant states from 1975 to 1990 was characterised by these strategic interests. This era came to an end after the Cold War and the process of opening up in the Soviet Union under Gorbachev gave momentum to a second phase of OSCE human rights-related commitments. Starting in 1989 with the Vienna Document and culminating in the Copenhagen Document and the Charter of Paris of 1990 as well as the Moscow Document of 1991, the early 1990s, in particular, saw a series of OSCE documents in which the participating states elaborated their comprehensive security approach. Elaborating on the term *human dimension,* they stressed the importance of individual human rights and minority rights under the principles of democracy and the rule of law, regarding them as the foundations of international order and of international concern, no longer exclusively considered internal affairs (Document of the Moscow Meeting 1991, preamble). With the emergence of ethnic violence and civil warfare following the collapse of Yugoslavia and the Soviet Union, a third phase of OSCE's engagement for human rights began. After the previous phase of standard-setting, the importance of field-based human rights monitoring and promotion through short- and long-term missions became clear throughout the 1990s. The biggest missions were established in Bosnia and Herzegovina and in Kosovo but there were also smaller presences in the Baltics, Eastern Europe, the Caucasus and Central Asia. Parallel to the intensive mission work, the OSCE continued, in a fourth phase, with its human rights standard-setting efforts elaborating, from the mid-1990s, specialised fields of human rights concerns. Particular focus was put on human rights protection of vulnerable groups such as children, trafficked persons, or ethnic minorities such as Roma or Sinti. Consequently, the more recent OSCE documents of Istanbul, Vienna, Maastricht and Sofia from 1999 to 2004 have concentrated on aspects of non-discrimination, gender equality, trafficking, crime prevention, etc. These four overlapping phases of continual development of human rights commitments of the OSCE participating states should be seen as mutually complementing and reinforcing processes that have led to a comprehensive system of human rights engagement and contributed significantly to what has been known as the OSCE human dimension *acquis* (OSCE/ODIHR 2001: XV, Evers 2005: 5). Whether the developments following the terrorist attacks in New York and Washington in 2001, Madrid in 2004 and London in 2005 - among other places affected by terrorism - will lead to a fifth developmental phase combining OSCE human rights commitments with the organisation's anti-terrorism efforts (Steinacker 2004: 89; Biering 2003: 31; Dekker 2003: 321), remains to be seen. In sum, the overall development of human dimension commitments within the OSCE system started with a reaffirmation of civil and political rights in the 1970s and 1980s, saw a phase of encompassing standard-setting in the early 1990s and has continued with a twofold approach involving human rights work of OSCE field missions since 1992 and a broadening of specialised fields of human rights-related commitments since the mid-1990s. All of this has contributed to the comprehensive security concept of the OSCE.

Human Rights within the OSCE Commitments and Standard-setting Process

The centre-piece of human rights commitments and normative standard-setting within the OSCE system is based on the concluding documents of the Third Follow-up Meeting in Vienna of 1989, the second Conference on the Human Dimension in Copenhagen of 1990, the CSCE summit in Paris with its Charter for a New Europe of 1990 and the Third Conference on the Human Dimension in Moscow of 1991. With reference to legally binding human rights norms under the United Nations and the Council of Europe system (OSCE/ODIHR 2003: 25), these OSCE documents further elaborated Principle VII and Basket III of the Helsinki Final Act on the human dimension, as politically binding commitments by which, in 1975, the participating states reaffirmed individual human rights and fundamental freedoms as essential components to the peace order in Europe. The Concluding Document of the Third Follow-up Meeting in Vienna committed the participating states to respect rule of law principles and to better incorporate existing human rights norms into their national legislation, especially with regard to fair trial rights and legal protection of individuals, freedom of assembly, freedom of movement, freedom of thought, conscience, religion or belief and prohibition of torture (Concluding Document of Vienna 1989, par. 11-27). It was at this conference that the decision was taken to call for series of three further conferences on the human dimension that led ultimately to the Copenhagen and Moscow Documents. The Copenhagen Document fine-tuned human dimension commitments such as freedom of expression, the right to free media and information, freedom of association and peaceful assembly and the right to property. Thus, it represents the most encompassing human dimension document in the OSCE system (Bloed 1991: 72). Remarkable is the fact that the Copenhagen Document, by strengthening the principle of non-discrimination and the right to use minority language in the public sphere and for religious and educational purposes, contains commitments that surpass provisions of international law with regard to protection for members of national minorities. (Document of the Copenhagen Meeting 1990, chap. IV, par. 30-40.7). It also elaborated provisions of political rights for the conduct of free and fair elections as well as for support of democratic oversight and human rights institutions, such as ombudsperson institutions or human rights defenders (Ibid, par. 3-8, 10-12 and 24-27). In 1990, the Paris summit of heads of participating states concluded with the Charta for a New Europe. With this proclamation, the state representatives committed themselves to accept democracy as the only form of government for their nations and reinforced the status of democratic institutions, of electoral and political rights and of NGOs (Charter of Paris: Human Rights, Democracy and Rule of Law, par. 1-4 and 9). The Moscow Document of 1991, concluding the Third Conference on the Human Dimension reiterated the previous commitments and stressed areas such as freedom from arbitrary arrest, the independence of the judiciary, the right to private and family life and the position of non-governmental organisations (Document of the Moscow Meeting 1991: par. 9, 19-20, 23-24 and 43). Marked by the impact of the failed *coup d'etat* in Moscow of August 1991, the document provides that all commitments under the human dimension are of concern to all participating states and prepared the ground for the human dimension mechanisms. The commitments included in the Vienna, Copenhagen and Moscow documents and the Paris Charter represent the central norms and standards of today's OSCE human dimension *acquis*. The documents of the following summits of Heads of States in Helsinki (1992), Budapest (1994), Lisbon (1996) and Istanbul (1999), as well as the meetings of the Ministerial Council in Vienna, Bucharest, Porto, Maastricht and Sofia from 2000 to 2004 resulted in only minor amendments to the existing *acquis* (table 3, appendix[2]). Regarding overall human rights standard-setting and its elaboration under the OSCE human dimension, it should be stressed that all the commitments are solely of a politically binding nature for the participating states and cannot be enforced by legal action of individuals in these states on the basis of the OSCE *acquis*. Nevertheless, the commitments represent such an elaborated set of human rights norms that they have effectively contributed to international norm- and standard-setting, especially in co-operation with the Council of Europe and the European Union (Pentikäinen/Scheinin 1993: 117). Consequently, the OSCE human dimension complements the often long-lasting

[2] Table 3 provides a comprehensive schematic overview on the main OSCE conferences and meetings and the corresponding human rights-related commitments of the OSCE human dimension *acquis*.

and - due to numerous legal reservations of signatory states – oftentimes deficient normative standard-setting process under international human rights conventions with OSCE's much faster and more flexible political approach based on its well-established culture of dialogue among the participating states and with non-governmental actors.

Monitoring and Promotion Instruments of the OSCE Human Dimension

Declaring human dimension commitments "matters of direct and legitimate concern of all participating states [that] do not belong exclusively to the internal affairs" under the Moscow Concluding Document of 1991 (cit. op., p.2), state compliance with these commitments, which include and exceed international human rights standards, is subject to a combination of political and institutional, as well as ad-hoc and long-term mission-based monitoring and promotion measures. The following chapter will describe this set of instruments.

The Vienna and Moscow Mechanisms: As all of the OSCE commitments are based on political consensus, they are immediately effective and politically mandatory to the participating states and do not have to undergo a lengthy ratification process (Heintze 2002: 222, Pentikäinen/Scheinin 1993: 110). Nevertheless, if a participating state feels that another OSCE member state is committing serious human rights violations, it may take action to start an investigative process on that matter by using the so-called Vienna or Moscow mechanism. The first, described in the Vienna Concluding Document of 1989, foresees the opportunity to invoke a four-step procedure. First, all participating states can request an exchange of information and are obliged to respond to requests made to them with regard to human dimension concerns through diplomatic channels or OSCE institutions (Concluding Document of Vienna 1989, par. 1). Second, a state can call for bilateral meetings with the respective state to examine the situation or specific cases with the aim of resolving them (ibid., par. 2). Third, any state may bring these situations or cases, including those raised at bilateral meetings, to the attention of other participating states through diplomatic channels (ibid., par. 3). Fourth, any state may provide information on these exchanges and responses to requests and on results of the bilateral meetings at the meetings of Human Dimension Conferences and Follow-up Meetings (ibid., par. 4). In 1990, the Copenhagen Document made important changes to the Vienna mechanism by making the mechanism compulsory for every participating state and requiring them to respond to requests for information on human dimension questions within four weeks, as well as to agree to hold bilateral meetings within three weeks of the date of enquiry (Document of the Copenhagen Meeting 1990, par. 42.1-2).

The so-called Moscow mechanism under the Moscow Concluding Document of 1991 takes these modifications further by shortening the time limit to ten days for written responses to requests and to one week for holding the bilateral meetings requested (Document of the Moscow Meeting 1991, par. 2). But most importantly, the Moscow mechanism provides the opportunity to send ad-hoc missions of human dimensions experts or rapporteurs to participating states under concern, following five independent procedures. First, any participating state may voluntarily invite a mission of up to three experts[3] to its territory to address or contribute to the resolution of questions related to the human dimension. The experts are allowed to travel freely in the country and to meet freely with officials, NGOs and any groups or persons to gather information. The experts submit a report of their observations via the inviting state to the OSCE Council of Senior Officials (CSO) (ibid., par. 3-7). Second, following the first two phases of the Vienna mechanism, an initiating state may request that the OSCE inquires another state to invite an experts' mission to address a particular and clearly defined human dimension question on its territory (ibid., par. 8). Third, should the other state refuse, the requesting state may initiate the establishment of a mission of up to three rapporteurs without the consent of the other state, as long as five other states support this initiative. The rapporteurs will establish facts, report on them and give advice on possible solutions to the OSCE within a period of three weeks. Once transmitted to the participating states, the report will be placed on the agenda of the next meeting of the CSO or of the Permanent Council to decide on follow-up action (ibid., par. 9-11). Fourth, in case a state considers that a particularly serious threat to the human dimension commitments has taken place, it may also initiate the establishment and the reporting procedure of a rapporteurs mission with the support of at least nine other states (ibid., par. 12). Fifth, upon request of a participating state, the CSO or the Permanent Council may decide on the establishment of and reporting by a mission of experts or of rapporteurs (ibid., par. 13).

Complemented by the Prague Ministerial Council Decision which, in case of gross violations of human dimension commitments, allows for political declarations and other steps without the consent of the state concerned - commonly known as the Consensus-Minus-One procedure (Prague Document 1992, chap. IV, par. 16; Evers 2005: 32), the monitoring and reporting measures of the Vienna and Moscow mechanisms provide a flexible and comprehensive set of measures to monitor and promote the compliance of the participating state with their OSCE human dimension commitments. However, the Moscow mechanism, in particular, has been used very rarely - only five times between 1992 to 2003. Nevertheless, the mere existence of these measures can contribute to produce commitment-compliant behaviour among participating states and helps to support state recognition of international human rights standards in the OSCE area.

[3] Each participating state committed itself to appoint six eminent persons as impartial experts in the field of the human dimension available for such missions for a period of three to six years. An updated resource list with the names of the current experts is published by the OSCE under www.osce/documents/odihr/2003/09/1807_en.pdf

OSCE Institutions as Special Actors on Human Rights Issues: The three main institutional bodies of the OSCE dealing with specific human rights issues are the Office for Democratic Institutions and Human Rights (ODIHR), the High Commissioner on National Minorities and the Representative on Freedom of the Media. The ODIHR is OSCE's principle institution for the human dimension and holds the most extensive mandate with respect to human rights (Oberschmidt 2002: 387; Merino 1999: 383). Its traditional expertise lies in the field of election monitoring, as it was originally established in Warsaw as the Office for Free Elections in 1992. Two years later it was transformed into the ODIHR under an enlarged mandate to cover a wider area of democracy and human rights in general. Its current mandate foresees helping OSCE participating states to "ensure full respect for human rights and fundamental freedoms, to abide by the rule of law, [...] and to build, strengthen and protect democratic institutions, as well as to promote tolerance throughout society" (Helsinki Concluding Document of 1992, chap. IV, par. 2). The ODIHR employs over one hundred staff members with an annual core budget of 9.6 million Euros. It is composed of three thematic departments for human rights, democratisation and elections, as well as a contact point on Roma and Sinti issues and a programme on tolerance and non-discrimination (ODIHR 2005a). With respect to human rights, the ODIHR performs monitoring and reporting tasks on compliance of OSCE participating states with their human dimension commitments, particularly in the areas of freedom of assembly and association, the right to liberty and a fair trial and the use of the death penalty. The Human Rights Department runs programmes on a broad range of interrelated issues such as promoting human rights in the fight on terrorism, public information campaigns on the death penalty, monitoring trials and conducting training, technical support and educational programmes for governments and civil society organisations, oftentimes in co-operation with long-term OSCE field missions. ODIHR programmes focus on both longer-lasting institutional and capacity-building engagement as well as shorter-term projects with a high-impact. The ODIHR also serves as a focal point for the organisation of regular meetings at high level such as the so-called Human Dimension Implementation Meetings, Human Dimension Supplementary Meetings and Human Dimension Seminars (Prague Document 1992, chap. III, par. 10), described in the following chapter. It also provides the forums to work on specialised fields of human rights concern, such as trafficking, migration, children and women rights, etc. In addition, the ODIHR acts as a contact point for interagency co-operation with other international organisations such as the Council of Europe, the European Union and the Office of the UN High Commissioner for Human Rights as well as with NGOs active in the field of human rights (Ibid., par. 11; Concluding Document of Budapest 1994, chap. VIII, par. 9). In sum, the ODIHR fulfils manifold functions that range from thematic monitoring and reporting, to programmatic human rights input, to technical organisation, and to overall elaboration of OSCE's human dimension.

With the eruption of ethnic violence and civil war in former Yugoslavia and the collapse of the Soviet Union, the need to protect individual human rights and minority rights became increasingly important to the OSCE participating states. In order to create an institution, which would function as an early warning and resolution instrument, the OSCE (then CSCE) established the post of the High Commissioner on National Minorities (HCNM) in 1992. The office of the HCNM, located in The Hague, comprises a team of twenty-five staff working for the High Commissioner on an annual budget of 2.5 million Euros (HCNM 2005a). Its mandate is to provide early warning and preventative action to reduce tensions involving national minorities, which could develop into a security concern in the OSCE area (Concluding Document of Helsinki 1992, chap. II). The practical work under this mandate includes the promotion of minority rights, such as the right to use of minority language in public, in the school system or for religious purposes, based on the OSCE commitments set out in the Copenhagen Concluding Document of 1990. The HCNM has been active in numerous participating states such as Albania, Croatia, Estonia, Hungary, Kazakhstan, Kyrgyzstan, Latvia, Romania, Slovakia, Macedonia, Ukraine, and now increasingly in the regions of the Caucasus and Central Asia (HCNM 2005b; Van der Stoel 1998: 64). Nevertheless, the HCNM does not serve as an ombudsperson for minority issues, but rather functions as a mediating body *on* minority-related issues using the principles of silent diplomacy and impartiality to resolve potential conflict between minority groups and governments that might endanger peace, stability or friendly relations among the participating states (Concluding Document of Helsinki 1992, chap. II, par. 3). The HCNM is authorised to conduct on-site missions for fact-finding in states under concern, to receive first-hand information, to apply preventative diplomacy at an early stage and to give detailed recommendations to states and the OSCE Permanent Council, based on personal and independent judgement. The recommendations of the HCNM have had a great impact on changing national policies and in clarifying international standards of minority rights. Most prominent are the recommendations of Hague in 1996, of Oslo in 1998, of Lund in 1999, giving detailed advice for better protection in the fields of minority education, language and participation in public life (Heintze 2001: 257). Together with the minority-related commitments under the Copenhagen Document, the recommendations of the HCNM have contributed to the further elaboration of legal standards and provisions on minority rights, especially in co-operation with the Council of Europe and the application of the Framework Convention for the Protection of National Minorities of 1995 (HCNM 2005a: 2). Although the HCNM is not allowed to focus on individual cases of minority rights concern and despite the mainly secret and confidential working style, the High Commissioner has succeeded in providing a remarkable value-added for the recognition of those human rights standards that benefit the protection and promotion of minority rights.

The Representative on Freedom of the Media (RFM), youngest of the three OSCE institutions, specialises in a particular field of human rights, the free media. The post was established in 1997, following the declaration of the OSCE summit in Lisbon in 1996 (Permanent Council Decision No.193, 1997). The representative, appointed for periods of three years, has the task of assisting governments in the promotion of free, independent and pluralist media and journalism, regarded as crucial to a democratic society and transparent political system. The RFM is authorised to observe media development in all participant states of the OSCE and to advocate its development in full compliance with human dimension commitments related to the freedom of expression, media and information. The RFM, based in Vienna with an office of six international staff and advisors, exercises a clear monitoring function with a threefold working task. First is an early-warning function, monitoring media development in the participating states. The RFM is asked to work closely with other OSCE bodies, such as the Permanent Council, the ODIHR and the HCNM to allow the forwarding of information about potential violations of media-related commitments to other relevant institution and decision-making bodies (Representative on Freedom of the Media 2005). Second, by seeking direct contact with participating states, the RFM may also concentrate on rapid response by states under concern to remedy obstruction of media activities or restrictions to the free work of journalists and to resolve such situations by forwarding recommendations. Third, the RFM may collect and receive information from all kinds of resources, including media representatives and NGOs, which may forward requests, suggestions and comments through this office, giving detailed information on alleged instances of media intolerance by participating states (ibid.). The mandate is only restricted with respect to meeting people who publicly practise or support terrorism or violence or engage in hate speech. With these activities, the representative can contribute significantly to the respect of media rights as a cornerstone for the protection of human rights and democracy in the OSCE participating states (Duve 2005; Möller 2004: 323; Reljic 2002: 385).

The Human Dimension Meetings

The human dimension of the OSCE is subject to a permanent process of programmatic elaboration, contributing to the monitoring and promotion of human rights-related commitments through a series of specialised meetings dedicated to the human dimension, the so-called Human Dimension Implementation Meetings (HDIM). According to the Helsinki Concluding Document of 1992, the HDIM take place in those years in which no regular Review Conferences in preparation of OSCE summits are held, and are complemented by the Supplementary Human Dimension Meetings and the Human Dimension Seminars (Martin Estebanez 1999: 340). The HDIM are organised and conducted annually by the ODIHR in Warsaw with the aim of reviewing the implementation of the state commitments including key human rights aspects. The meetings last for two weeks during which experts and representatives of OSCE participating states meet with other state officials and representatives of NGOs and international partner organisations to discuss the latest developments within the human dimension and to exchange views, all of which influences OSCE policy-making (Sandoval Villalba 2002: 30). The HDIM follow a standard pattern of agenda-setting composed of two plenary sessions and eight working groups dedicated to democratic institutions, the rule of law, tolerance and non-discrimination, humanitarian issues and other commitments. In the second part of the meetings, working sessions on concrete project work, human dimension activities and selected human dimension topics take place and conclude with a closing plenary meeting. Parallel to this standard procedure, all participants may propose side events to the agenda to elaborate detailed questions in continuation of previous discussions or additional concerns (ibid.: 12). Within two weeks after the closing session, the Director of the ODIHR compiles a report about the course, results and recommendations of the HDIM for submission to the OSCE Permanent Council[4] for its further review and follow-up on human dimension commitments.

In addition to these meetings, three Supplementary Human Dimension Meetings (SHDM), organised by the OSCE Chairmen-in-Office (CiO), are held every year. These are dedicated to specific issues of human dimension concerns determined at preceding implementation meetings or review conferences to be in need of further discussion. The SHDM, usually lasting for two days, cover topics decided by the CiO in co-operation with the ODIHR, other OSCE institutions and the OSCE delegations of participating states in Vienna. All SHDM are open to representatives of NGOs and other international organisations (ODIHR 2005c). A third kind of meeting regarding human dimension commitments is held in Warsaw each year in the spring in the form of Human Dimension Seminars (HDS) that also focus on specific human dimension concerns. The HDS, lasting four working days, provide an additional forum for the discussion and exchange of views and information among state officials and representatives of NGOs and co-operating international organisations (ibid.). In recent years, most of the human dimension meetings and seminars have been dedicated to topics such as fair trial, the role of defence lawyers, the fight against terrorism, migration and integration, election procedures, displaced persons, torture and inhumane treatment, freedom of religion, community policing, prison reform, the

[4] The Permanent Council approves the agenda of the HDIM and provides topics for the SHDM each year.

situation of Sinti and Roma, trafficking in human beings, violence against women, children in armed conflict, human rights defenders and asylum seekers (ODIHR 2005b). In sum, the human dimension meetings provide the basic platform for the permanent development of OSCE human dimension commitments and related decision-making of the organisation (Binder 2001: 431; Sandoval Villalba 2002: 12). With that approach, the human dimension meetings not only establish the necessary culture of constructive dialogue on the commitments of participating states, but also provide the indispensable link for reviewing and promoting the development of the human dimension between the political structures and institutional bodies of the OSCE and external co-operating organisations and NGOs and provide thematic input for OSCE missions in the field.

Human Rights Mandate of OSCE Field Missions: A Case Study on Kosovo

The OSCE is the international organisation with the most field missions operational in Eastern Europe, the Balkans, the Caucasus and Central Asia. Much of its personnel and financial resources are deployed into these regions. Important elements of the mandates of these missions are oftentimes the promotion and protection of human rights as a direct consequence of the OSCE human dimension commitments (OSCE Handbook 2000: 45). Kosovo provides an excellent case study of the intensive human rights engagement of an OSCE field mission. In the late 1990s, the conduct of the Serbian army, the militia, police units and other state institutions such as the judiciary or the public administration under the Milosevic regime led to an immense number of gross human rights violations ranging from executions of civilians, torture, rape and destruction of property to arbitrary arrest and denial of fair trial rights and of equal access to labour, education, social welfare and health care that mainly affected the Kosovo-Albanian and other non-Serb speaking communities in Kosovo. During the war in 1998/99, it also led to a mass exodus of refugees, a high number of internally displaced people and thousands of casualties and missing, abducted or evicted persons (OSCE/ODIHR 1999: 33). In order to verify the withdrawal of security units used for civilian repression as agreed for in UN Security Council Resolution 1199 and the so-called Holbrooke-Milosevic agreement, the OSCE Kosovo Verification Mission (KVM) was deployed from October 1998 to March 1999 with more than 1,350 mission members.[5] Their mandate included verifying the cease-fire between Serbian units and the Kosovo Liberation Army, monitoring their movements and promoting human rights and democracy. The task of the KVM Human Rights Division was to monitor, investigate, document and report allegations of human rights abuses committed by all parties to the conflict. The Division became operational in December 1998 and had deployed monitors throughout all regions of Kosovo by late-January 1999 (Mitchell 2001: 242 ff;

[5] Originally, the OSCE aimed at deploying about 2,000 mission members to the KVM.

Eiff 2000: 283). With the failure of the Rambouillet peace process, the intensification of the armed conflict and the start of the NATO bombing campaign, the entire KVM staff had to be withdrawn from Kosovo in March 1999. The Division continued with its work of collecting evidence of human rights violations in Kosovo by conducting interviews with victims and witnesses among refugees to Albania and Macedonia. The findings of the KVM monitors have been compiled by the ODIHR into a comprehensive report (OSCE/ODIHR 1999) and provide documentation of human rights violations that has been used by the International Criminal Tribunal for the former Yugoslavia (ICTY) in The Hague to bring perpetrators of war crimes, genocide and crimes against humanity to justice.[6]

Following the Decision No. 305 of the OSCE Permanent Council and the UN Security Council Resolution 1244 a new mission was deployed to Kosovo after the war in June 1999, the OSCE Mission in Kosovo (OMIK). OMIK is integrated into the mission structure of the United Nations in Kosovo as the so-called pillar III of the UN Interim Administration Mission (UNMIK). With more than one thousand mission members, it is responsible for institution- and democracy-building as well as for the monitoring, protection and promotion of human rights.[7] The mission is composed of different thematic departments, the Department of Elections, the Department for Democratisation and the Department of Human Rights and Rule of Law, and the Kosovo Police Service School (Everts 2002: 137; OMIK 2005a: 1). The work of the OSCE Department for Human Rights and Rule of Law (HRD) mainly covers four fields of engagement: 1) capacity building of state officials, legal professionals, civil society, and youth; 2) developing rule of law institutions; 3) monitoring cases of human rights violations and inadequate legal remedies; and 4) public reporting on human rights including detailed recommendations (OMIK 2005b: 1). Over the period from 1999 to date, the HRD has adapted its primary focus from merely monitoring and reporting to institutional capacity-building and advising local structures of self-government in Kosovo.

The immediate phase after the end of the war in June 1999 was marked by individual cases of human rights violations directed mainly against Slav-speaking minority communities[8] in revenge by Kosovo-Albanian groups or individuals. These cases were also documented in detail by the OSCE in a report similar to the KVM report (OMIK 1999). Grave cases of human rights violations such as killings, rapes, beatings, house-burnings, abductions, threats to physical integrity, intimidation and harassment in conjunction with bomb explosions, physical attacks, arson and destruction of property, that led to the dis-

[6] Former Serbian state officials such as ex-Yugoslav President Slobodan Milosevic but also former leaders of the Kosovo Liberation Army have or had been indicted under investigations by the Tribunal.

[7] OMIK personnel comprise around 310 international and 990 local staff.

[8] Such as the Roma, Bosniak and Gorani communities.

placement of numerous members of non-Albanian communities and to an increasing exodus of Kosovo-Serbs to Serbia and Montenegro, were documented and also used by the ICTY and for purposes of judicial prosecution in Kosovo.[9] At that time, the HRD also played a critical role in establishing an emergency judicial system in Kosovo by identifying and recruiting judges and prosecutors and equipping courtrooms through its Judicial Support Section (OMIK Human Rights Department 2003: 21). The main reports of the HRD in the period from 1999 to 2000 concentrated on the situation of ethnic minorities, the deficient justice system and prolonged detention periods (OSCE 2005c). By 2001, the field work of the HRD changed from monitoring individual cases of human rights concern to a concentration in selected fields such as legal system (court) monitoring, law enforcement and security issues, non-discrimination and minority issues, residential property issues, victims advocacy and anti-trafficking, and human rights education and awareness raising (OMIK Human Rights Department 2003: 4). Consequently, the HRD had reorganised itself by 2002 into different thematic sections covering each of the above-mentioned fields with special teams of human rights officers. At headquarters level this thematic structure has remained basically in place. During that period, the HRD issued comprehensive reports on areas of human rights concern such as trafficking, the criminal justice system, ethnic minorities, property, social services, and legal remedies (OSCE 2005c). With respect to further institutional capacity-building, the Rule of Law Division of the HRD established various institutions dedicated to the rule of law, such as the Kosovo Judicial Institute (2000) for the legal education of judges and prosecutors, the Kosovo Law Centre (2000) offering seminars and legal publications to law students and the general public, the Criminal Defence Resource Centre (2001) assisting lawyers in all areas of criminal law, and most significantly, the Ombudsperson Institution (2000) (OSCE 2005b: 4). The Ombudsperson is the first independent institution outside the UNMIK pillar structure with a mandate to deal with complaints, to initiate investigations and to give recommendations concerning alleged human rights violations or abuse of authority by UNMIK or the local Provisional Institution of Self-Government, the PISG (Ombudsperson Institution in Kosovo 2005: 1). Another important achievement that has helped turn the recommendations of the HRD reports into human rights-compliant legislation was the establishment in mid-2002 of the high level Human Rights Oversight Committee and its bi-weekly Inter-pillar Working Group on Human Rights (OMIK Human Rights Department 2003: 3). These bodies, in compliance with international human rights standards, aim to achieve greater transparency and accountability within the UNMIK structure

[9] In contrast to the human rights violations committed under the Milosevic regime the cases that took place after June 1999 did not indicate a systematic or strategically planned pattern of violations although former KLA members are suspected of being responsible for many of these cases.

with respect to the legislative process and to enhance overall human rights protection in Kosovo.[10] Participating institutions in this two-tiered structure of human rights oversight are the HRD of OMIK, that acts as its secretariat and provides the Chairperson, all UNMIK pillars including the EU presence and the Office of the UN Special Representative of the Secretary-General (SRSG), as the main (former) legislator with legislative veto power for Kosovo, and the Office of the UN High Commissioner for Human Rights. The Working Group reports directly to the Committee and provides the main forum for discussing relevant human rights issues at inter-agency level. By forming ad-hoc subgroups it has succeeded in reviewing and commenting on numerous pieces of draft legislation in compliance with international human rights standards (ibid.). A recent development in the applied human rights work of the HRD took place in summer 2003, in parallel with the substantial transfer of law-making authority from the SRSG to the PISG, when the Department initiated its Human Rights Experts Programme (OMIK 2005d). Currently these experts are attached to the offices of local chief executive officers in 16 municipalities to provide expertise and advice to local authorities on the compliance of their activities with human rights standards and to offer training sessions if needed. Similar expertise is provided to selected ministries of the PISG and to the regional and central police headquarters by the Senior Human Rights Experts of the HRD sections at headquarters level.

As renewed ethnic violence erupted throughout Kosovo in March 2004, leaving nineteen people dead, over 900 injured, hundreds of houses and Serb-Orthodox churches burnt down and over 3-4,000 members of ethnic minorities displaced from their homes, the HRD reactivated its cases-by-case monitoring capacities for fact-finding and reporting purposes (Buerstedde 2005; OMIK 2004; Human Rights Watch 2004; Schenker 2004). The latest reports of the HRD cover these findings as well as aspects like legal remedies, the review of criminal justice, the implementation of Kosovo laws by the PISG, informal settlements, parallel structures and trial cases (OSCE 2005c). With a possible transfer of all reserved powers from the UNMIK to local authorities following a decision on the future status of Kosovo, a reduced presence of the OSCE Mission to Kosovo is likely to remain deployed with a special mandate for further human rights monitoring and capacity-building in order to continue with its work of protecting and promoting human rights. In sum, the comprehensive working structure of the current OSCE mission in Kosovo represents the largest possible spectrum of human rights engagement of OSCE missions in general, ranging from the practical field work of monitoring individual cases and aware-

[10] This structure succeeded the previous Joint Advisory Council on Legislative Matters that was established in 1999 at the insistence of OMIK for legislative review and drafting and in which the HRD participated as an active member.

ness raising projects to high-level institution-building and recommendations for the drafting of laws.

The OSCE Human Dimension at Risk?

Considering the latest developments of the current OSCE reform debate that gives the impression of an organisation in crisis (Rupel 2005; Dunay 2005; Rotfeld 2004: 31), the OSCE's comprehensive approach to human rights within its human dimension runs the risk of being seriously affected by a policy of revised national interests among the participating states *vis-à-vis* new transnational threats and relatively weak institutional decision-making structures. Despite the wide recognition of the successes that the OSCE had achieved with respect to human rights promotion, as a leading actor of standard-setting, as an important human rights monitor and as the prime implementing agent of human dimension commitments, criticism has been expressed by the governments of Russia, Belarus and some Central Asian states about an unbalanced concentration of human dimension activities (Zellner 2005: 26). Transnational threats such as international terrorism, illegal migration or border security have reduced OSCE's efforts to further promote its human dimensions commitments in the recent years. In view of these new challenges, it continues to be important to maintain and secure the achievements of the human dimension *acquis* and its related efforts within the OSCE system. As the human dimension commitments were found to be of paramount importance in complementing the comprehensive security approach of the OSCE in the 1970s, 1980s and the 1990s, these commitments represent essential elements to be integrated into the approach of the participating states in respect to the new challenges. Anti-terrorism efforts, for example, are unlikely to achieve any sustainable effect without being grounded in civil society and based on principles of human rights standards, the rule of law and democracy. The same argument applies to additional threats and challenges such as organised crime, illegal border crossing or trafficking in human beings (Kemp 2004: 314; Zannier 2004: 225; Kartusch 2003: 259). However, new efforts are needed to combine human dimension commitments with the current organisational and thematic reform debate, without diminishing OSCE's capacities to monitor and assist the compliance of participating states with their commitments (OSCE Parliamentary Assembly 2005: 6). In that respect, a better geographic distribution of human dimension activities should be aimed at remedying a situation in which most of OSCE activities and missions took place east of Vienna, in countries of Eastern Central and South East Europe or the CIS, apart from Russia[11] (Haaland Matlary 2002: 163). Countries of Western Europe and North America were barely covered by any OSCE mission or monitoring activ-

[11] The OSCE Assistance Group to Chechnya, the only OSCE field activity on Russian territory, was closed in 2003

ity although these states are also facing problems with respect to the transparency of election procedures (US electronic voting) or national minorities and secessionist groups (Basque country, Northern Ireland, Corsica). A general monitoring and review process of human dimension commitments through a reporting and information procedure i.e. through an independent committee of human rights experts or at OSCE's Human Dimension Implementation Meetings, covering all participating states to determine adequate follow-up action, would be desirable and could give new momentum to human dimension commitments (Netherlands Helsinki Committee 2005: 3; Zellner 2005: 26). With regard to interagency co-operation, the OSCE has proved its distinct expertise with the elaboration of normative standard-setting and its high profile in the work of long-term field missions and, thus, represents an ideal counterpart to other European and international organisations, such as the Council of Europe, with its approach of adopting legally-binding human rights norms, the European Union, with its continuing association and integration process, or the United Nations, seeking stronger regional co-operation in the area of peace building or human rights promotion. In that respect, the OSCE has already prepared the ground by having signed co-operation agreements with other organisations that provide the potential for enhanced synergy effects on the organisations' efforts to deal with new global challenges and threats (ibid.: 27, Boden 2004: 48; Oberschmidt 2002: 395). Its comprehensive organisational and thematic expertise, the wide spectrum of norm-setting procedures, monitoring institutions, mechanisms, field operations and programmes in all fields of the human dimensions make the OSCE unique in its approach to protecting and promoting human rights in the entire Northern hemisphere, from Vancouver to Vladivostok. Its human rights achievements remain indispensable for the maintenance of peace, security and democracy in the participating states. Both its strengths and its weaknesses are based on OSCE's principle of consensus and its culture of dialogue. However, the effectiveness of the OSCE human rights approach can only be as strong as the willingness of participating states to further contribute to the comprehensive system of human dimension commitments.

Appendix - Table 3: Human Dimension Commitments of Selected OSCE Documents

Right to/ Freedom from:	H 75	Ma 83	Vi 89	C 90	Pa 90	Mo 91	H 92	B 94	Li 96	Is 99	Maa 03	S 04
Self-determination	●		○			○						
Capital Punishment			◉	●		◉	○	○				
Torture			◉	●		◉		◉		◉		
Trafficking						◉				◉	●	
Arbitrary Arrest			◉	◉		●						
Fair Trial			●	●								
Effective Remedy			●	●		◉						
Thought, Consc.Relig.	●	◉	●	●				◉		◉		
Expression MediaInform.	●	○	◉	●		●		◉		◉		
Association, Assembly				●								
Movement, Hum.Contact	●	○	◉	●		◉		◉				
Private and Family Life						●						
Children Rights				◉						●		◉
R of Disabled Persons						●						
Property Rights				●								
Nationality, Citizenship							●			●		
HumanRights Defenders			●	●				◉				
NGOs			◉	◉	◉	●				◉		
Rule of Law				●		◉		◉		◉		
Independent Judiciary				◉		●						
Ombudsman HR Institut.				●								
Economic/ Social Rights	◉	◉	●	◉			◉		◉	◉		
Workers Rights		◉	◉	●								
CulturalRight Heritage	◉	◉	●	◉	○	◉		◉				
Educational Rights	○	○	●	◉		●						
Democratic Institution				●	◉	◉	○	○	○	○		
Electoral R's				●	◉				◉	◉	◉	
Non-discrimination	◉		●	●	◉			◉	◉		●	●

Equality, Gender R's		◉	◉			●			◉			●
Racism, Anti-Semit.				●	◉		◉	◉	◉	◉		
National Minorities	◉	◉	◉	●	◉	◉	◉	◉	◉	◉		
Roma/Sinti Protect.				◉		◉	◉			●	●	
Indigenous Rights							●					
Migration, Refugees			◉				●	◉	◉	◉		
Migrant Workers R's	●	◉	◉	◉	◉	◉	◉	◉				
Humanitarian Law							●	●		◉		

● central commitments; ◉ main commitments; ○ other commitments (by J. Narten)
H – Helsinki, Ma – Madrid, Vi – Vienna, C – Copenhagen, Pa – Paris, Mo – Moscow, B – Budapest, Li – Lisbon, Is – Istanbul, Maa – Maastricht, S – Sofia.

CHAPTER III

MINORITIES AND MINORITY RIGHTS IN EUROPE

Minority Rights in Europe: an introduction into a fragmented regime
Carmen Thiele

Introduction
With the break down of socialist multiethnic states in Europe like the Soviet Union, Yugoslavia and Czechoslovakia as a result of ethnic and political conflicts at the beginning of the 1990s new states were created which inherited the ethnic composition of their territories. Homogeneous states became seldom. Apart from the majority population persons with different ethnic affiliation live on the territory of the states. The protection of their rights is an indicator for peace and security within the state which affect the whole region. The new states took the obligation to build up a democratic state based on the rule of law and the protection of human and especially minority rights, which are generally recognised as European values.

In answer of ethnic conflicts in the new European states the international community reinforced its efforts to protect minority rights. In Europe three regional organisations exist with different instruments and mechanisms for the protection of minority rights: the Organisation for Security and Co-operation in Europe (OSCE), the Council of Europe (CoE) and the European Community (EC), which belongs to the European Union (EU). The OSCE counts 55 states. The membership of the CoE increased to a total of 46 states. Since 1 May 2004 the EU consists of 25 member states, between them several new democratic states. All member states of the European Union are members of the Council of Europe and all member states of the Council of Europe are members of the OSCE. Consequently, to numerous European states apply norms for the protection of human rights and especially minority rights of three regional organisations with different main aims and to others only of two or one organisation. An example for the latter is Belarus as a member state only of the OSCE (it is only a state candidate for membership to the CoE).

European Organisations for the protection of minority rights

The Council of Europe

Because of severe and mass violations of human rights during Second World War 10 European states created on 5 May 1949 the Council of Europe with the aim to build a new democratic Europe protecting human rights. As on the universal level within the United Nations (UN) the European state community parted from the point of view that minority rights form a part of human rights. Subsequently, neither the UN-Charter nor the Statute of the CoE (ETS No. 1) refer to minorities. According to Article 1 of the CoE-Statute "the maintenance and further realisation of human rights and fundamental freedoms" is one of the aims of the organisation. European states willing to apply for the CoE "must accept the principles of the rule of law and of the enjoyment by all persons within its jurisdiction of human rights and fundamental freedoms" (Article 3 of the Statute). Any member of the Council which has seriously violated the provision in Article 3 may be suspended from its rights of representation and requested by the Committee of Ministers to withdraw (Article 8 of the Statute). The accession to the European Convention for the Protection of Human Rights and Fundamental Freedoms (ECHR) of 4 November 1950 (ETS No. 5) is an indispensable requirement for the membership of the CoE.

The European Community

Whilst the Council of Europe mainly pursues political aims the European Community as one part of the first pillar of the European Union, was created for a European integration in the economic field.

The Treaties of the EC and the EU still do not contain a catalogue of human rights and fundamental freedoms, but only single provisions. The protection of human rights was inserted in the preamble of the Single European Act (OJ 1987 L 169/1) and the Maastricht Treaty of the European Union of 7 February 1992 (OJ 1992 C 191/1). Article 6 of the Amsterdam EU-Treaty of 2 October 1997 (OJ 1997 C 340/145) and the Nice EU-Treaty of 26 February of 2001 (OJ 2001 C 80/1) explicitly refers to the European Convention of Human Rights of the Council of Europe and the common constitutional traditions of the member states. In case of violation of human rights and fundamental freedoms certain rights can be suspended (Article 7 EU).

The Organisation for Security and Co-operation in Europe

As the Council of Europe and the EU is open only for states which are based on the common values as democracy, the rule of law and human rights, the OSCE is open for all European states. One of the main aims of the Conference for Security and Co-operation in Europe as the largest regional security organisation in the world was directed towards peace and security in the region through an East-

West dialogue. Because human rights issues form a great part for the achievement of this aim they are included in basket III of the Final Act of Helsinki of 1975 CSCE (CSCE/OSCE documents at: http://www.osce.org/documents).

With the end of the East-West-conflict the institutional structure of the CSCE was developed and the Conference was renamed from 1 January 1995 in Organisation for Security and Co-operation in Europe.

European instruments for the protection of minority rights

The three European systems have elaborated a variety of documents for the protection of minority rights, which differ from the point of view of their content and legal character.

Documents of the CSCE/OSCE

The greatest achievement in minority protection sources can be seen in the field of the CSCE/OSCE which is on the political rather than on the international legal plain. The CSCE already stood up for the protection of minorities in the Final Act of Helsinki. The protection of rights of members of national minorities is assigned to principle VII, the respect for human rights and fundamental freedoms. A further reference to national minorities and regional cultures is made under chapter III section 3 "Co-operation and exchanges in the field of culture". The more important documents "could only be produced after the end of the East-West conflict at the end of the 1980s, beginning of the 1990s in the field of the so called human dimension.

The concept of human dimension was first introduced in the Concluding Document of the Vienna Meeting of 1989 as the need to improve the implementation of the CSCE commitments and the co-operation in the areas of human rights and fundamental freedoms, human contacts and other issues of a related humanitarian character, which includes the protection of persons, belonging to national minorities.

The most far reaching and outstanding document for the international protection of minorities is the Copenhagen Document on the Human Dimension of 29 June 1990, which contains a remarkable catalogue of rights for members of national minorities and duties for states. Members of national minorities are guaranteed rights for the maintenance and development of their ethnic, cultural, linguistic and religious identity as well as the participation in public affairs. The Copenhagen Document served as a main source of inspiration for the UN Declaration on the Rights of Persons Belonging to National or Ethnic, Religious and Linguistic Minorities of 18 December 1992 (General Assembly Resolution 47/135) and the Framework Convention for the Protection of National Minorities of 1 February 1995 (ETS No. 157) (Pentassuglia 2002: 142).

With the great changes in Europe the Helsinki Final Act needed to be adapted to the actual situation. The Charter of Paris for a New Europe of 21

November 1990 as a new "constitution" for Europe (Pentassuglia 2002: 143) reaffirmed the commitment to the protection of minority rights in the context of human rights on the basis of non-discrimination.

In the Moscow Document on the Human Dimension of 3 October 1991 the participating states agreed on the non-application of the principle of non-intervention does not apply to the human dimension and that human rights issues, democracy and the rule of law are of international concern. As a consequence they have priority over one of the most important principles of international law, the principle of state sovereignty.

Although the CSCE/OSCE commitments do not establish international legal obligations which are binding on participating states, they are of great importance for the development of a common European international law (Pentassuglia 2002: 139).

International treaties of the Council of Europe
Whilst the CSCE/OSCE documents have "only" a political binding character (*soft law*), the Council of Europe tries to create legally binding rules of human rights protection in Europe. The Council of Europe dedicated its work just at the beginning of the 1990s to the protection of minorities and now it is one of its most important tasks.

The European Convention on the Protection of Human Rights and Fundamental Freedoms and its Protocols
There are still no rules on the protection of minorities in the European Convention on the Protection of Human Rights and Fundamental Freedoms, due to its human rights character and is therefore restricted to the prohibition of discrimination in Article 14:

> The enjoyment of the rights and freedoms set forth in this Convention shall be secured without discrimination on any ground such as sex, race, colour, language, religion, political or other opinion, national or social origin, association with a national minority, property, birth or other status.

The notion of discrimination was defined in the Belgian Linguistic case by interpreting Article 14 ECHR (Judgement of 23 July 1968, Series A, Vol. 6).

As the incidents in former socialist multiethnic states, especially in the former Yugoslavia, sorrowful demonstrated there was a special need for the protection of minorities. For that reason the Council of Europe suggested a convention on the protection of minorities. The European Commission on the Development of Democracy through Law, the so called Venice Commission, presented a Proposal for a European Convention for the Protection of Minorities on 8 February

1991 (CDL/MIN (93) 6 and 7). The Preamble makes reference to the Copenhagen Document of the CSCE of 1990, Article 14 ECHR, and Article 27 ICCPR (UNTS, vol. 999, p. 171), which is up to now the only universal legal binding norm on minority protection. The new minority protection system and the establishment of a European Committee for the Protection of Minorities (Article 18), which does not follow the ECHR-system and is mentioned in chapter III needs to be emphasised. The Proposal was never opened for signature.

The future development in Europe is aimed at the drafting of an additional protocol to the ECHR concerning minorities. Austria presented a Proposal for an Additional Protocol to the ECHR for the Protection of Minorities to the Council of Europe on 26 November 1991 (798 CDDH (91) 46). Pursuant to Article 11 paragraph 1 of the Austrian Proposal, each state has the obligation to report to which minority this protocol applies. This would weaken the effectiveness of the protocol since each state could decide itself to which of their minorities it will apply. The Proposal also suggests the observation of the guarantees by the organs of the ECHR in Strasbourg (Article 13).

Another attempt was made by the Parliamentary Assembly of the Council of Europe by the Proposal for an Additional Protocol to the ECHR concerning Persons belonging to National Minorities of 1 February 1993 in its Recommendation 1201. The benefit of such an Additional Protocol would be, that the legal procedure of the ECHR could be used for the implementation of minority rights listed in the additional protocol, as it is proposed in Article 17. The Assembly reaffirmed in Recommendation 1492 of 2001 the need for an additional protocol to the ECHR on the rights of national minorities, inspired by Recommendation 1201. The work of the Council of Europe on an additional protocol to the ECHR on minority protection did not yet lead to a final outcome.

Protocol No. 12 to the ECHR of 4 November 2000 (ETS No. 177), which general prohibition of discrimination goes beyond the scope of application of Article 14 ECHR, unfortunately also does not regulate the protection of minority rights directly. Article 1 of Protocol No. 12 prohibits discrimination on any ground such as "association with a national minority" in the enjoyment of "any right set forth by law", whereas Article 14 ECHR only prohibits discrimination on any ground such as "association with a national minority" in the enjoyment of the rights and freedoms set forth in the ECHR (Pentassuglia 2002: 126 f.).

The European Charter for Regional or Minority Languages

A concrete result of the work of the Council of Europe is the European Charter for Regional or Minority Languages (ECRML) of 5 November 1992 (ETS No. 148) – an international treaty, which entered into force on 1 March 1998. In the preamble of the Charter reference is made to the Copenhagen Document of the CSCE-Meeting of 1990 (Thornberry / Martín Estébanez 2004: 140).

The Charter is characterised by its specific field of application – regional and minority languages – and by the wide latitude of states for its domestic implementation. The Charter adopts an intercultural and multilingual approach, which corresponds to the Council of Europe efforts "to promote closer relations between peoples, increased European co-operation and a better understanding between different population groups within the state on an intercultural basis" (Explanatory report, paragraph 14). The aim of the Charter is, according to the Explanatory Report (paragraph 10), not to protect minorities as such but to protect the cultural diversity in Europe (Spiliopoulou Åkermark 1997: 237). Consequently, the Charter does not include either dialects of the official language(s) of the State or the languages of migrants (Article 1 lit. a ii.) and does not establish individual or collective rights for the speakers of regional or minority languages (Explanatory report, paragraph 11).

The structure of the Charter consists of five parts: general provisions, objective and principles, measures to promote the use of regional or minority languages in public life, application of the Charter and final provisions. The states determine themselves to which of the regional- or minority- languages spoken on their territory they apply in part III mentioned "Measures to Promote the Use of Regional or Minority Languages in Public Life in accordance with the Undertakings entered into under article 2, Paragraph 2". Therefore part III is also called the "menu" of protection for minority languages" (Oeter 2004: 133).

Instead of the protection of speakers of regional or minority languages by individual and collective rights the Charter provides guarantees for the benefit of historical regional or minority languages in Europe and a multilingualism in general (Pentassuglia 2002: 130).

The European Framework Convention for the Protection of National Minorities

The European Framework Convention for the Protection of National Minorities (FCNM) of 1 February 1995, which entered into force on 1 February 1998, is the first legally binding multilateral instrument, exclusively concerning minorities. The term "framework" indicates that the Convention contains 'programme-type' provisions. Because of different situations and problems in the member states the drafters of the Convention did not include provisions with detailed rights for minorities, but general objectives and principles (Barnes/Olsthoorn 1999: 5).

The purpose of this Convention is to establish legal principles guaranteeing the protection of national minorities, committing the states to obey these principles. The Convention includes no directly applicable rules but disposition-programs and its provisions are weakened by vague clauses. The provisions leave the States concerned a measure of discretion in the implementation of the objectives which they have undertaken to achieve, thus enabling them to take particular circumstances into account." (Explanatory report, paragraph 11). The Council of Europe fulfils with this Convention the hope to transform political obligations of the CSCE/OSCE documents into legal obligations.

According to Article 1 FCNM the main purpose of the Convention consists in the protection of national minorities as an integral part of the protection of human rights, which does not fall within the reserved domain of States. Because of its human rights approach the Convention "does not imply the recognition of collective rights. The emphasis is placed on the protection of persons belonging to national minorities, who may exercise their rights individually and in community with others." (Explanatory report, paragraph 13).

Unfortunately, the Council of Europe was unable to define the term "minority", due to disagreement between the participating states. Therefore, "[i]t was decided to adopt a pragmatic approach, based on the recognition that at this stage, it is impossible to arrive at a definition capable of mustering general support of all Council of Europe member States." (Explanatory report, paragraph 12). One of the most disputed criteria for national minorities is citizenship with the consequence that those persons having the state's citizenship would be included and those without the state's citizenship would be excluded from the protection of national minorities. However, there are different indications which allow the conclusion that the Framework Convention does apply also to non-citizens. The wording in the Convention "every person belonging to a national minority" indicates the inclusion of every human being without discrimination. The fact that some state parties (Austria, Estonia, Germany, Luxembourg, Poland and Switzerland) provided unilateral declarations with their respective instruments of ratification concerning their understanding of whom the term 'national minority' applies to, restricting it to nationals of the state, indicates that "the States parties interpret the Framework Convention as applying to non-citizens" (Weissbrodt, D. 2003: paragraphs 41 ff.). The Advisory Committee on the Framework Convention, which assists the Committee of Ministers in the evaluation of measures taken by a state party to give effect to the principles set out in the Convention, has firmly expressed the view that the Convention applies to non-citizens as well (Thiele 2005: 281 f.).

The substantive provisions of the FCNM, Article 4 to 19, contain non-discrimination and positive measures; cultural, language and educational rights; communication rights; participation in cultural, social and economic life and in public affairs as well as transfrontier contacts (Thornberry / Martín Estébanez 2004: 100 ff.).

Despite some critical points, the Framework Convention remains to be one of the most important international binding instruments of the Council of Europe in the field of the protection of national minorities, which became a field of international concern.

Instruments of the European Union

In the past the EC/EU did not see the protection of minorities as one of their primary tasks. The Treaty on European Union does not mention the protection of minorities. The Treaty only calls in Article 6 paragraph 2 for the respect of fundamental rights, as guaranteed by the European Convention for the Protection of Human Rights. Attempts in the European Parliament to introduce a specific article regarding minorities into the Treaty were not successful.

In the framework of the anti-discrimination approach of the EC several provisions exist which are only a minimum standard for national minorities. In the Amsterdam EC Treaty was introduced a new Article 13, according to which the Council may take action to combat discrimination based also on racial or ethnic origin. On the basis of Treaty provisions were adopted different Council Directives implementing the principle of equal treatment between persons irrespective of racial or ethnic origin (2000/43/EC, OJ 2000 L 180/22) and establishing a Community action programme to combat discrimination (2001-2006) (2000/750/EC, OJ 2000 L 303/23).

The anti-discrimination approach was further developed in the Charter of Fundamental Rights of the EU – an integral part of the Treaty establishing a Constitution for Europe (OJ C 310 2004/1), which did not entered into force yet. The Constitutional Treaty, however, does not contain specific provisions for the protection of minority rights which could be enforced by the European Court or other competent body of the EU (Pentassuglia 2002: 150). It contains only a clause prohibiting discrimination (Article II-81) and a clause requiring respect of cultural, religious and linguistic diversity (Article II-82).

According to Article II-81 of the Constitutional Treaty, which draws on Article 13 EC, discrimination based on any ground such as for example membership of a national minority shall be prohibited. This provision does not create any power to enact anti-discrimination laws. It only addresses discriminations by the institutions and bodies of the Union themselves, when exercising powers conferred under other Articles of Parts I (The Constitution's fundamental provisions) and III (The Union's Policies) of the Constitutional Treaty, and by Member States only when they are implementing Union law (Explanations relating to the Charter of Fundamental Rights, Article 21).

European institutions for the protection of minority rights

Institutions of the OSCE

In the framework of the human dimension the Office of Democratic Institutions and Human Rights (ODIHR) is one of the most important institutions. The Office was established as the Office for Free Elections (OFE) under the Charter of Paris in 1990 to facilitate contacts and exchange of information on elections in OSCE participating States. The mandate of the Office was expanded at the Prague Ministerial Council Meeting in 1992 and it became the Office of Democratic Institutions and Human Rights. The mandate was further enlarged at the Helsinki (1992) and Budapest (1994) Summits.

The activities of the ODIHR are classified in four sections: election, democratisation, monitoring, and Roma and Sinti. The Election Section works on long-term election observation, technical assistance and training in the organisation of elections. The Democratisation Section is dedicated to practical projects to promote democracy, the rule of law and civil society. The Monitoring Section is responsible for monitoring the human dimension commitments. The Contact Point for Roma and Sinti issues acts as a clearing-house for the exchange of information on Roma and Sinti by providing advice on policy-making in this issue (OSCE 2002: 106).

An institution exclusively related to national minorities was created with the post of the High Commissioner on National Minorities (HCNM) pursuant to the Helsinki Document of 1992 as an instrument of conflict prevention in response to a large-scale violence in Europe because of tense ethnic conflicts. The mandate of the independent, impartial and confidential acting HCNM is described as early warning and early action "in regard to tensions involving national minority issues which have not yet developed beyond an early warning stage, but, in the judgement of the High Commissioner, have the potential to develop into a conflict within the OSCE area" (Helsinki Document of 1992: 8). The High Commissioner can not act on behalf of minorities. He is a Commissioner on but not for National Minorities (Neukirch/Simhandl/Zellner 2004: 164).

The High Commissioner is empowered to conduct on-site missions and to engage in preventing diplomacy at the earliest stage of tension. By this way he obtains first-hand information form the parties concerned and contributes to a dialogue between them. The High Commissioner may decide to bring before the government in question a report with recommendations. He has been involved in many OSCE participating States, contributing to minority protection (OSCE 2002: 94).

Institutions of the Council of Europe

The European Commission against Racism and Intolerance

Because combating racism and discrimination on grounds of race and national or ethnic origin is a precondition for the protection of national minorities, the activities of the European Commission against Racism and Intolerance (ECRI) have a great impact for national minorities too. The decision to establish ECRI as an independent human rights monitoring body on racism and racial discrimination was taken in 1993 in Vienna. The aim of ECRI is to combat racism, xenophobia, anti-Semitism and intolerance in Europe through necessary measures against violence, discrimination and prejudice faced by persons or groups of persons, notably on grounds especially of race and national or ethnic origin. In the framework of Country-by-country approach, ECRI monitors phenomena of racism and racial discrimination by examining the situation in each of the member states of the Council of Europe (http://www.coe.int/t/E/human_rights/ecri/).

Monitoring bodies of treaties on minority protection

The two mentioned treaties of the Council of Europe related to minority protection have established monitoring bodies for the supervision of the commitments taken by the State Parties. According to Article 17 ECRML it is the Committee of Experts. Pursuant to Article 26 FCNM the Advisory Committee assists the Committee of Ministers in this task.

The Committee of Experts of the ECRML, which is entitled to adopt the rules of procedure by itself, is composed of one member per Party (19), appointed by the Committee of Ministers for a period of six years. Pursuant to Article 26 paragraph 2 FCNM the composition of the Advisory Committee of the FCNM is determined by the Committee of Ministers Resolution (97) 10 adopted on 17 September 1997. The competence to decide upon the rules of procedure of the Advisory Committee is, unlike the Committee of Experts of the ECRLM, reserved to the Committee of Ministers (Oeter 2004: 137). The number of ordinary members of the Committee, elected by the Committee of Ministers for four years, shall be a minimum of twelve and a maximum of eighteen (actually 18). The members of both monitoring bodies serve in their individual capacity, they are independent and impartial.

The European Court of Human Rights

The European Court of Human Rights (ECtHR) is the judicial organ established according to Article 19 ECHR to ensure the observance of the engagements undertaken by the State Parties in the Convention and the Protocols thereto. The Court consists of a number of judges equal to that of the State Parties (46) (Article 20 ECHR). The judges are elected by the Parliamentary Assembly with respect to each State Party from a list of three candidates nominated by the State Party (Article 22 ECHR) for a period of six years. They sit on the Court in their individual capacity (Article 21 paragraph 2 ECHR).

That the European Convention on Human Rights and its Protocols do not contain special provisions for the protection of minority rights does not mean, that minorities can not make use of concrete human rights regulated by these treaties, which protect their interests, like rights related to language, religion and culture or freedom of association and freedom of expression (Varennes 2004: 87). Especially violations of non-discrimination based on national origin or association with a national minority (Article 14 ECHR in conjunction with other substantive rights and especially Protocol 12) can be brought before the Court against a State Party.

Institutions of the European Union

Unlike the previous two international organisations the EU does not dispose of a special body dealing with minority rights. Although the European Court of Justice (ECJ) as the judicial organ of the European Communities has made reference to the protection of human rights in several decisions, it is not an especial organ of supervision of human rights or minority rights.

As a permanent institution the European Union has established the European Monitoring Centre on Racism and Xenophobia (EUMC) by Council Regulation (EC) No 1035/97 of 2 June 1997 (OJ 1997 L 151/1), which was amended by Council Regulation (EC) No 1652/2003 of 18 June 2003. The primary task of the EUMC as an independent body of the EU is to provide the Union and its member states with objective information on racism, xenophobia, islamophobia and anti-Semitism at the European level in order to assist the EU and its member states to establish measures against racism and xenophobia. Although the Centre is not especially dedicated to national minority issues, they are of relevant concern.

The very core of the EUMC's activities is the European Information Network on Racism and Xenophobia (RAXEN). It is designed to collect data and information at national as well as at the European level. This is accomplished via 25 National Focal Points, contracted by the EUMC to collect, coordinate and disseminate national and EU information in close cooperation with the EUMC. Due to its mission, the EUMC has developed into an appropriate organ to deal with non-discrimination issues (Topidi 2004: 188).

In December 2003 human rights the European Council decided to extend the remit of the European Monitoring Centre on Racism and Xenophobia in order to convert it into a Fundamental Rights Agency.

European mechanisms for the protection of minority rights

Mechanisms of the OCSE

The human dimension mechanisms of the OSCE, which are frequently used to deal with minority protection issues, consists of the Vienna Mechanism (established in the Vienna Concluding Document of 1989, paragraphs 1 to 4) and the Moscow Mechanism (established at the last meeting of the Conference on the Human Dimension in Moscow in 1991, paragraphs 1 to 16, as amended by Rome 1993, chapter IV, paragraph 5), the latter partly constituting a further elaboration of the first.

According to the Vienna Mechanism participating States can raise questions relating to the human dimension situation in other OSCE States through an established set of procedures. The mechanism obliges participating States to respond to requests for information made by other participating States, and allows the States to bring situations in the human dimension to the attention of other participating states.

The Moscow Mechanism provides the possibility for participating States to establish *ad hoc* missions of independent experts to assist in the resolution of a specific human dimension problem on their own territory or in other OSCE participating States. The mission of experts can either be invited by the participating State concerned, or initiated by a group of six or more participating States.

The human dimension mechanisms consists of mandatory and formalised procedures for dialogue on human dimension issues between participating states, like requests for information, the holding of bilateral meetings, the invitation of missions of experts to address or contribute to the resolution of questions relating to the human dimension, and the sending of missions of rapporteurs to establish the facts, report on them and give advice on possible solutions to the question raised (Moscow Document on the Human Dimension: 1991: chapter I, paragraphs 5, 11). The mechanisms can be activated only by governments, not directly by individuals or NGOs (Neukirch/Simhandl/Zellner 2004: 163).

Nevertheless, the use of the Human Dimension Mechanism by another participating State tends to be perceived as an unfriendly act, rather than as a constructive one. The Moscow Mechanism was activated only a few times. Main examples are the expert missions to Moldova and Estonia (Neukirch/Simhandl/Zellner 2004: 167). Instead of inter-State procedures participating States prefer multilateral political bodies of collective decision-making (Martín Estébanez 1999: 36).

As an effective mechanism for the protection of minority rights are considered the long-term OSCE missions together with other field activities, which persist the aim to facilitate the political process that are intended to prevent or settle conflicts, and to ensure the information of the OSCE community about the developments in the states where missions are present. The composition and mandate of the missions and other field activities vary in dependency of the special situation, but all of them have as a main task human dimension issues, democracy and the rule of law (OSCE 2002: 45). Currently the OSCE has several long-term missions and other field activities in its participating States (OSCE 2005: 7 ff.), all of them Republics of the former Soviet Union and former Yugoslavia with tense ethnic problems which cause international security concerns. Long-term missions and other field activities ensure a continuous OSCE presence in the concerned areas. They occasionally comply the role of fact-finding related to minority right violations. Sometimes they provide legal assistance in drafting and implementing legislation on minority issues (Martín Estébanez 1999: 41).

Mechanisms of the Council of Europe
The instruments of the Council of Europe regulate different mechanisms for the protection of human and minority rights, which have either a binding character or a character of a recommendation.

Mechanisms within the European Convention on Human Rights
Within the European Convention on Human Rights exist two mechanisms having a legally binding character: individual complaints and state complaints.

Individual complaints
Individual complaints are an effective remedy for individuals to claim their rights. Persons belonging to national minorities can apply to the European Court of Human Rights relaying on the non-discrimination rule and/or substantive rights of the ECHR and its Protocols. According to Article 34 ECHR any person, non-governmental organisation or group of individuals claiming to be the victim of a violation by a member state can make an individual application. The applicants have to fulfil the admissibility requirements of Article 35 ECHR, such as the exhaustion of local remedies and the six months rule (from the date on which the final decision was taken). By using this effective judicial mechanism individuals may get a judgement where their rights were not guaranteed by their respective states through the national legal system (Varennes 2004: 103).

State complaints
Any alleged breach of the provisions of the ECHR and the Protocols by a member state may be referred to the European Court of Human Rights by another member state under Article 33 ECHR. It is not necessary that the applicant state demonstrate a bilateral interest in the protection of human rights.

In practise member states make use of this mechanism only in rare cases. States generally restrain from using it, because they are afraid of its political and diplomatic consequences. For instance, the possibility to refer a state complaint against the Russian Federation because of systematic human rights violations in Chechnya as proposed in Recommendation 1456 of 6 April 2002 by the Parliamentary Assembly of the Council of Europe was not made use of yet.

Mechanism of the European Charter for Regional or Minority Languages
The international monitoring of the national implementation of the Charter is carried out by the measures mentioned in Article 15 ECRML, which are a report on the policy of the states pursued in accordance with part II ECRML and on the measures taken in application of those provisions of part III which they have accepted.

Bodies or associations legally established in a member state may draw the attention of the Committee of Experts to matters relating to the undertakings entered into by that party under part III ECRML. They can furthermore submit statements concerning the policy pursued by a Party in accordance with part II (Article 16 paragraph 2). On the basis of the reports and the information given by the bodies or associations, the Committee of Experts prepares a report for the Committee of Ministers (Article 16 paragraph 3). The visits of the working group, consisting of the "country rapporteur", the national member from the state concerned and a third expert appointed by the Committee, have become a standard part of the monitoring system (Oeter 2004: 139). The prepared report contains in particular the proposals of the Committee of Experts to the Committee of Ministers for the preparation of such recommendations of the latter body to one or more of the Parties as may be required (Article 16 paragraph 4). The Committee of Ministers may make the report of the Committee of Experts public (Article 16 paragraph 3). The Secretary General of the Council of Europe makes a two-yearly detailed report to the Parliamentary Assembly on the application of the Charter (Article 16 paragraph 5).

The result of the reporting procedure is rather a legally not binding recommendation than the establishment of a treaty infringement, since the Charter establishes no rights which can be invoked by members belonging to regional- or minority languages but only the obligation of states to choose measures for the promotion of regional and minority languages. The enforcement of the obligations accepted by the states parties depends therefore on the political pressure of the member states of the Council of Europe (Spiliopoulou Åkermark 1997: 237).

Mechanism of the European Framework Convention for the Protection of National Minorities

The Framework Convention for the Protection of National Minorities as the European Charter for Regional or Minority Languages does not provide an individual or inter-state complaint procedure. The supervision is based on a state reporting system with a non-judicial character (Pentassuglia 2004: 22).

The Committee of Ministers of the Council of Europe is pursuant to Article 24 paragraph 1 FCNM responsible for monitoring the implementation of the Convention. It is a weakness of the Framework Convention that a political organ is in charge of the monitoring and not as in the case of the European Convention on Human Rights an independent judicial organ.

The Contracting Party transmits to the Secretary General of the Council of Europe full information on the legislative and other measures taken to give effect to the principles set out in this Framework Convention on a periodical basis (Article 25 paragraphs 1 and 2). In order to comply with the requirements of the reporting system the State parties have to inform about legal and non-legal measures taken by them. The provided information should give a correct picture of the status of minority rights.

Initial reports have to be transmitted within a period of twelve months following the entry into force of the Framework Convention in respect of a Contracting Party. The periodical basis for transmission of state-reports mentioned in Article 25 paragraph 2 FCNM is set at five years (Resolution (97) 10, paragraph 21). Despite of initial and periodical reports the Advisory Committee can invite the Committee of Ministers to request ad hoc reports in order to address situations which may arise between two periodic reports (Resolution (97) 10, paragraph 35).

The Committee of Ministers is assisted by an Advisory Committee in evaluating the adequacy of the measures taken by the Parties to give effect to the principles set out in the Convention (Article 26) (Klebes 1995: 97). The Committee of Ministers adopted an outline for reports to be submitted pursuant to Article 25 paragraph 1 FCNM in order to facilitate the work of the reporting state and of the Committee of Ministers and the Advisory Committee.

State reports are transmitted by the Party to the Secretary General who transmits them to the Committee of Ministers and are made public by the Council of Europe upon receipt by the Secretary General. The Committee of Ministers transmits the state reports to the Advisory Committee, which then considers the state reports and transmits its opinions to the Committee of Ministers. Following receipt of the opinion of the Advisory Committee, the Committee of Ministers considers and adopts its conclusions concerning the adequacy of the measures taken by the Contracting Party concerned to give effect to the principles of the Framework Convention. It may also adopt recommendations. The conclusions and recommendations of the Committee of Ministers, the comments of the Parties in relation to the opinion of the Advisory Committee and the opinion of the Advisory Committee are made public. The Advisory Committee may also receive information from sources other than state reports, for example from representatives of minorities, NGOs or specialised bodies. The Advisory Committee takes into account also information on the monitoring system of the European Charter for Regional or Minority Languages or the reports on states by the European Commission against Racism and Intolerance (Phillips 2004: 125).

Although visits to states are not regulated in the Council of Ministers Resolution (97) 10, it is already practice, that the Advisory Committee is invited by the member states. Theses visits as "a significant part in confidence-building" have become central in monitoring the Framework Convention and "transformed the methodology into a process of engagement of government and civil society, including national minorities" (Phillips 2004: 116). The Advisory Committee is involved in the monitoring of the follow-up to the conclusions and recommendations on an *ad hoc* basis, as instructed by the Committee of Ministers (Resolution (97) 10). As an outcome of the experience of the reporting system, it has been proposed to work on a commentary on each article of the Framework Convention as a guide for states and minorities, as it is known from different UN Conventions on human rights (Phillips 2004: 117).

A successful reporting system permits a constant evaluation of national approaches towards the protection of national minorities and may contribute to changes in law and practice of the State parties (Oberleitner 1999: 84).

Mechanisms of the European Union

Although the EC/EU documents do not pay special attention to minority rights, the "respect for and protection of minorities" was included as political criteria for EU membership at the Copenhagen European Council in 1993. For encouraging an independent monitoring of the EU accession process the EU Monitoring and Advocacy Programme (EUMAP) was initiated in 2000. Based on the Copenhagen declaration the candidate States are required to demonstrate that they guarantee the protection of minorities, while the requirement of minority protection is yet not regulated in EU documents binding upon member states. The monitoring reports on minority protection are prepared by independent experts in co-operation with NGOs in the respective states with the assistance of an international advisory board. Draft reports are discussed at meetings in the monitored state. Final reports may contain recommendations addressed to the national governments regarding legislation on minority protection and its enforcement (http://www.eumap.org).

According to an established practice for EU membership applications, EU organs relay the HCNM's advice on minority protection standards to the candidate States. For example, the HCNM recommendations on the citizenship issue were used as benchmarks for Estonia and Latvia in their EU accession process. By implementing the HCNM recommendations, a candidate State would fulfil the EU standards on minority protection. On the contrary, non-compliance with the OSCE standards in the sphere of minority protection could hinder the accession process (Thio 2003: 138).

In the 2001 reports it was recommended to apply this monitoring system on human rights standards, including minority protection, equally to all EU-member states and not only for candidate States.

Conclusion

There is no doubt that minority protection has developed into one of the European values. Consequently, European organisations can not avoid paying attention to the protection of minority rights. The greatest success in minority protection can be seen in the field of the OSCE. Occasionally, the non legal binding character of OSCE documents is seen as a disadvantage, but the political character allows the OSCE to take an active role in standard setting for the protection of national minorities and in contributing to their implementation.

The Council of Europe attempts to transform political obligations on minority protection of the OSCE documents into legally binding rules. Concrete results of the work of the Council of Europe were achieved with the European Charter for Regional or Minority Languages and the European Framework Convention for the Protection of National Minorities.

Because the protection of minorities was not seen as a main aim of the EC/EU, the Treaties and the Charter of Fundamental Rights of the EU as a part of a future European Constitution do not contain special clauses on minority rights. Nevertheless, minority protection is one of the Copenhagen criteria, required for political accession to the EU towards a European integration. The EU relay the OSCE minority protection standards to the candidate states.

Especially, the OSCE and the Council of Europe have developed their activities in the field of minority protection in a complementary way, to which the EC/EU refers to. No one of these organisations with different membership can take over the competence of the other. But there is a need for improving the coordination between the European organisations dealing with minority rights in order to transform a fragmented regime into an integrated one.

Diffusing Fragmented Human Rights Standards: Minority Rights in Estonia

Malte Brosig

Introduction

The article aims to develop applicable tools for studying processes of norm diffusion. Based on a growing literature on norm diffusion I will deliver a model that may explain the course through which an international norm diffuses to the domestic sphere. Five factors have been detected as centrally important for the adaptation of minority rights. They comprise the concept of resonance, the quality of norms, international supportive structures, domestic level actors, and consequences of norm compliance. Working through these five factors it will become more obvious that the international criticism which Estonia has to face regarding its minority policy cannot only be traced back to deliberate intentions to marginalise the Russian-speaking minority. The article argues that the highly fragmented character of European minority rights equally accounts for the sluggish integration process of the minority population in Estonia.

Diffusing the standard

In international relations IR scholarship a rich literature has emerged sketching out the influence international norms exert in global politics. Especially the constructivist school has inspired new research on norms. The process by which international norms flow into the nation-state and the conditions by which states implement these norms is one field of examination covered by this research. While many factors can be named to have influence in this process for practical reasons it makes sense to reduce the number and instead to concentrate on core variables. Accordingly norm diffusion is most likely to occur when

H1:	*The quality of norms is high, which means the norm should incorporate a high degree of specificity and clarity in content and application.*
H2:	*The norm resonates with domestic values, traditions, and practices.*
H3:	*International agents actively promote norm diffusion.*
H4:	*Domestic-level agents (government, civil society, individual) show willingness to adopt new standards.*
H5:	*The consequences of norm adoption point to a positive cost-benefit equilibrium.*

Quality of norms

The quality of a norm often bears in it the potential to increase or decrease norm diffusion. Actors compliance with norms depends in some parts on the character of a norm. Jeffrey Legro (1997: 34-35) states that those norms which integrate a high degree of specificity and durability are superior to those which do not. It matters if a norm is precise or ambiguous, if its implications are clear or if it contributes to discordance. A high standard of specificity facilitates norm promotion and compliance. Clarity has a positive impact on norm diffusion, whereas fragmentation and fuzziness is likely to slow down and delay the implementation process.

In the area of human rights, as well as in others, norms are not always legally binding. Some appear in political declarations, while others have been put into conventions. Commonly the former are called soft-law and the latter hard-law (Snidal 2000: 421- 456). It is not clear which has better prospects for diffusion. Legal norms are often more precise than political declarations. They are also more coercive because the legal option provides for litigation. On the other hand, although, political documents may lack the strong wording of legally binding conventions, they nonetheless have their own advantages. Because of the soft wording, consensus is easier to be reached. Furthermore, a legal norm is of almost no use if it is not backed by political support. Thus political declarations are more easily agreed upon but lack precession, whereas legal norms are more coercive but at the same time need highly developed enforcement structures which can be very bureaucratic.

Norm resonance

Resonance describes the degree to which international norms are "compatible" with domestic values (Wiener and Wobbe 2002). Resonance is not only measurable in terms of conformity to existing rules and laws. It asks for more than the embeddedness of norms in a legal framework, like its coherence with a constitution. A high value of resonance also encompasses compatibility with prior existing cultural habits and traditions. The extent to which a norm meets favourable conditions in domestic settings or is able to create such conditions influences its effectiveness in a crucial way. In more concrete terms, a new norm is expected to diffuse more easily when it resembles the dominant discourse, culture, or legal framework in a country or when it is able to attach its claims to current influential debates, political structures, habits, and traditions. A prerequisite of positive resonance is of course the existence of a coherent and qualitatively high (clear) set of norms. Fuzzy and fragmented norms are rather unsuitable to produced high degrees of resonance.

International organisations

For norm diffusion we need an international instrument or supportive structure which delivers the capabilities to distribute norms and ideas (Finnemore and Sikkink 1998: 899) and sets up a socialisation process. The UN, EU, Council of Europe (CE), and OSCE are examples for such a structure of norm-setting, distribution, and socialisation. They form an institutional environment by which shared beliefs or norms can spread. Often these institutional structures are the product of the norms they promote. Some conventions enhance the institutional framework by setting up new bodies that monitor or review norm adoption.

Norm promotion is more effective if it is carried out through an international body which can build up incentive structures or is able to sanction non-compliance through punishment. Furthermore, such an international body needs some positive record, credibility or competence in handling norms, their creation, distribution, and monitoring.

What makes international organisations (IOs) interesting is the fact that norm adoption reflects the ability of these organisations to create compliance through monitoring mechanisms and effective socialisation. As Johnston puts it "...the speed, uniformity, and effectiveness of norm diffusion in international relations ought to depend a great deal on what kind of institutional social environment leads to what kind of socialization..." (Johnston 2001: 496). Indeed, we have to focus on different institutional frames and their effects on norm diffusion to explain normative variances.

State actors and domestic level factors

In general, constructivists define norms as shared understandings of standards of action. Norms imply or prescribe certain behaviour but variation in norm adoption among states has often a connection to domestic structures, cultures, and rules. Internationally held norms are presumed to exert "influence through the filter of domestic structures and domestic norms can produce important variations in compliance and interpretation of these norms" (Finnemore and Sikkink 1998: 893). The interests of the economic elite, the human rights activist, or Member of Parliament do not directly form decisions. All these actors and their influence "are mediated by domestic structures that prevail during the policy process" (Davis and Cortell 1996:454). Variations in norm adoption and the sometimes selective success of norm socialisation can often be traced back to domestic-level factors.

It is hard to say which kind of political system directly triggers what kinds of action. At least two points remain of importance: access into the political machinery and utility demands. No matter how the political system is structured we should ask who promotes a norm or set of norms meaning what kinds of actors are the norm entrepreneurs (e.g., NGOs, states, international organisations, social movement, minority groups, church, companies, scientists, single activists) and how they have access to the decision-making process.

Domestic-level actors are of great importance because to a certain extent international norms must be reproduced at the domestic level to be effective and there is often room for interpretation and discretion. State authorities, not international agencies, execute the rules and procedures; domestic actors put norms into their pre-existing normative system. International norms often have to be adjusted to the national legal, cultural, and political system. Agents therefore engage in norm reconstruction to re-instantiate the internationally given norm.

Consequences of norm compliance and violation

Utility often refers to economic cost-benefit calculations. We can assume that actors whose cost-benefit balances are affected by a new norm are especially sensitive to a discourse about its adoption. They may either argue in favour of the norm if the norm fosters their interest or argue against it when they fear additional costs. Domestic political costs should not be marginalised. If they exceed the prospective benefits norm diffusion is unlikely to occur smoothly. Further, in cases where the adoption costs are positively related to future interaction of agents, the implementation process should encounter less resistance.

As rational actors, states are assumed to calculate consequences and respond positively to international norms in cases where benefits exceed costs. Costs and benefits may be material and ideational in kind. International organisations offer both material awards and reputational sanctions.

Norm diffusion can be influenced by IOs offering material rewards for norm compliance. But few IOs can do this. The EU with its budget of several billion Euro is an exception. The UN, CE, or OSCE have no material rewards to offer for norm compliance. Nonetheless, they can testify about states performance on human rights. Thus, compliance is tied to credibility. In cases where states' credibility is seriously endangered, reputational costs may be very high and norm adherence may be connected to the protection of a positive international image.

Estonia and Minority Rights

Any judgment of Estonia's performance on international minority standards has to consider history as an important backdrop. Estonia is a tiny country with 1.4 million people, less than a million of whom are ethnic Estonians. As a result fifty years of Soviet occupation, deportations, political and cultural suppression, the ethnic composition of Estonia changed dramatically. Whereas before WW II minorities made up around 10% of the population this number tripled under Soviet rule. After the USSR collapsed only a few thousands went back to their former home states. Thus, Estonia had to cope with a minority that had almost no cultural roots in the Baltics and in the early 1990s had nearly no knowledge of Estonian language, history and traditions.

The following qualitative examination tests the hypotheses formulated above through process tracing. A series of interviews has been conducted in February 2004 in Tallinn.

The quality of minority rights standards

Minority rights cannot be reduced to a single set of specific norms. Various international organisations have developed minority standards, but there is no common definition of what a minority is. As a consequence, minority standards are less than coherent and clear. Furthermore, minority rights draw on a mixture of hard and soft law. On one hand, minority standards can be deduced from international law based on a patchwork of international treaties. On the other hand, these standards draw on customary international law derived from political declarations and state practice. Some of the most influential documents, like the OSCE Copenhagen Document or the UN Declaration on Persons Belonging to National or Ethnic, Religious and Linguistic Minorities, have no legal force. Many other important documents are legally binding but have not been drafted in the first place for minority protection. Article 27 of the International Covenant on Civil and Political Rights (ICCPR), for example, promotes the only universally applicable standard of minority protection. The Convention of the Rights of the Child and International Convention on the Elimination of All Forms of Racial Discrimination (ICERD) comprise provisions that too enhance minority protection. Lastly, regional organisations such as the OSCE, CE, and EU have developed minority rights standards. Along with them the CE is the only one which has dedicated a whole convention to minorities, the Framework Convention on the Protection of National Minorities (FCNM).

Despite the fact that minority rights are fragmented they circle around some core values that reflect a minimal international consensus and belong either to international law or customary international law based on political declarations: First, non-discrimination, second, preservation of ethnic identity, third, protection of language, and fourth, political and societal participation (integration).

The CE has developed the most important instrument for the promotion of minority rights in Europe, the FCNM which sets minimum standards for minority protection. It is a clear sign of progress that European states have acknowledged the rights of millions of minority members. But consensus could only be reached by softening the wording of the Framework Convention. The explanatory report to the FCNM characterises the FCs provisions as "programme type provisions seeking out objectives which the Parties undertake to pursue". Much is left to the discretion of the contracting parties. In the FCNM numerous escape clauses water down the rights of minorities. Phrases like "where necessary", "as far as possible", or "where appropriate" open ways for arbitrary implementation and self-interested application. Realisation of the FCNM provisions left to the contracting parties (Pentassuglia 1999: 418-419) such that it depends on their decision how to interpret and implement the FCNM. A further shortcoming of the FCNM is the lack of a definition of the term 'national minority' leaving the contracting parties to decide to whom they grant the rights set out in the Convention. There is no international consensus on a single approach to a minority definition and it appears rather unlikely that such a consensus could be reached in the near future. The vague wording of the FCNM makes it almost impossible to go to the Strasbourg Court for Human Rights because the rights set up in the convention are not justiciable and no individual complaint mechanisms have been developed, litigation is largely ruled out as a further tool for norm promotion (Gilbert 1996: 175).

Minority rights standards are fragmented, incoherent and in many cases non-legally binding. Much is left to the discretion of states. Under these circumstances it is very likely that the implementation of these standards varies widely among states. Further, compliance is hard to measure because minority provisions lack clarity. Only programme type norms or political binding provisions are agreeable among states. No coherent approach has been developed. Effective minority protection can be hampered by a lack of quality in the minority rights area.

Estonia and international law

In principle, Estonia does not violate international minority standards and no severe human rights violations occurred since independence. However, a detailed picture of Estonia's minority performance reveals in which compliance is not fully reached. Furthermore, the rather poor quality of international minority standards helps Estonia to push through its own agenda which does not always foster minority integration.

Technically, non-citizens are regarded as immigrants irrespective of whether they came in 2002 from Afghanistan or 20 years earlier as Soviet citizens. Minority members without Estonian passports enjoy fundamental rights but struggle to benefit from minority standards. No universally valid minority definition exists and the FCNM contains no definition of the term 'minority'. Not surprisingly states have the last word. In 1997 Estonia declared that only citizens are eligible to enjoy the rights of the FCNM. This declaration is in line with the FCNM but contradicts the views of the UN Human Rights Committee[1] and the OSCE High Commissioner on National Minorities, both of which favour an inclusive approach that grants minority rights to everyone belonging to a minority without regard to citizenship. This situation illustrates how fragmented international minority standards are. Estonia's exclusion of non-citizens constitutes no breach of international law. Current trends tend to point in a different direction by favouring a more inclusive approach. While Estonia is not violating international law, its exclusion of non-citizens goes against this forceful international trend (Thiele 1999: 4) and the spirit of the FCNM which aims to prevent and solve ethnic tensions. Moreover, the exclusion of non-citizens is hardly adequate for a successful integration process.

[1] HRC general comment no 15, 22 July 1986 UN Doc. CCPR/C/21/Rev1.

The FCNM remains the most important legal instrument for promoting minority rights in Estonia. Unfortunately, it also contains many escape clauses and is imprecise in many areas. A striking example of how the meaning of certain articles can be overstretched is article 10 paragraph 2, which says that if minority members inhabit an area in "substantial" numbers they have the right to communicate in the minority language with state authorities. The term in "substantial" numbers is interpreted by the countries themselves. No specific threshold like 10% or 20% is mentioned in this article. Estonia decided to set the threshold at 50%, such that only a few cities with a minority population could benefit from article 10,2. This lack of specificity puts the whole Convention at risk. If central parts of the Convention can be distorted in the way described it is a weak instrument for minority protection and its coherence is questionable (Gál 2000: 12). Worse, FCNM allows for restrictive measures like those taken in Estonia.

Normative fit and resonance

For Estonians as a tiny group of less than a million people, the experience of five decades of occupation and the fear of assimilation through Russification was existential (Poletshuk and Semjonov 2000). Despite attempts from the Soviet side to russify the country through large-scale immigration, Estonians protected their cultural identity. An Estonian national culture was already existent in the mid nineteenth century (Raun 2003: 139). But Soviet dominance left a sense of vulnerability which remains influential even today (D.J. Smith 1998: 7). In 1993 67% of Estonians saw the Estonian nation at risk of extinction (Krich 1995: 83). Because Estonian national identity finds its strongest expression in language and culture, the nation's survival was tied to language and culture. When Estonians lost their state under the Soviet superpower, national survival was secured through practicing the Estonian language (Lagerspetz 2001: 407 and Hint 1995: 627-633).

What happened immediately after the USSR dissolved and the Estonian state re-appeared was a mystification of pre-war Estonia. In the eyes of the majority, the old state must be reinstalled in order to overcome the past tragedy. Restoration became the key concept in the early and mid 1990s. The idea to restore the former republic dominated the national discourse (Visek 1997: 315-373). On the basis of legal continuity the Estonian state never disappeared. The Soviet occupation was against international law and the presence of Russian troops was illegal, but Estonia did not cease to exist. Thus, when the Soviet Empire collapsed Estonia was liberated but not newly born. According to restorationist rhetoric , the status quo ante should be the benchmark for Estonia. Following this logic Soviet settlers are nothing more than the 'civil garrison of the Empire.' Granting them citizenship would legalise the Soviet injustice (Reinikainen 1999: 88). Moreover, restoration is viewed as a "delayed version of a war of self-defense"(Reinikainen 77) Thus, remigration could be described as a "delayed expulsion of illegal immigrants"(Reinikainen 91) Restorationism run directly counter to minority integration and minority protection because this logic denounces most Russians as immigrants and not as minority members.

One of the first and of course most important legal document that Estonia produced was the Constitution (1992). As the basic legal act it exerts influence on every other law and opens an access point for norm diffusion by creating resonance for European human rights standards. The Constitution guarantees fundamental rights and freedoms to everyone and minority protection to its citizens.

Part II of the Constitution which deals with basic rights and freedoms was modeled according to the European Convention for Protection of Human Rights and Fundamental Freedoms (Uibopuu 1998: 214,223). The Constitution also contains certain minority provisions. For instance, Article 49 states that "Everyone shall have the right to preserve his or her ethnic identity." The Constitution also provides for self-government of minority members in Article 50. These Articles belong to the core of European human rights standards and can be regarded as fruitful ground for resonance and norm promotion. These basic fundamental rights are guaranteed for everyone. Furthermore, they constitute a real commitment to European values.

Despite the positive resonance for norm diffusion which the Constitution might produce, there are several provisions that give indications to an other direction by restricting minority rights. First of all according to Article 6 there is only one official state language, Estonian. The Estonian language is granted a special status despite the fact that 30% of the population consists of non-Estonian speakers. Political participation seems to be a privilege of Estonian citizens, since non-Estonians are not allowed to join political parties (Art. 48,1) not to speak of voting in parliamentary elections. The Constitution grants the right to self-government for minorities but has no indications on how to realise this right. Subsequently, the law on cultural autonomy foresees only cultural self-government and even this limited autonomy can only be enjoyed be minority members with Estonian passports, excluding the vast majority of Russian-speakers are excluded. Moreover, Article 52,1 defines Estonian as the "official language of state and local government." Only in areas where at least half the population does not speak Estonian may a further language be used in official communication. In fact, this passage led to strange situations. In the capital Tallinn, where around 48% Russian-speakers live Russian cannot be used in local governments for internal communication or for giving information to the public. In sum, the Constitution may well account for restrictive legislation in the years after 1992. At the same time, it contains core European human rights norms, which should facilitate the diffusion of new standards such as minority rights. Estonia's self-perception is that of a parliamentary democracy rooted in Western values (Järve 2000: 6).

Normative fit or resonance is likely to have positive effects on norm diffusion as well as it probable is fostering a restrictive nationality policy. There is a tension between restoration and democracy building.

The restorationist view made it almost impossible to adopt an inclusive approach toward citizenship that would allow the Russian-speaking minority to participate and integrate over time into the new Estonia. Before the war Estonia had a small minority population of about 10% compared to 30% after 1989. To return to former times would have meant to expel hundreds of thousands of people. Restorationism resembles very much ethnocentrism and nationalism (Berg 1999: 128).

Estonia's attitude toward its large minority group has changed tremendously, from exclusion to integration. This change reflects the positive and negative degree of resonance. The restorationist approach accounts for a rather restrictive language policy, whereas Estonia's commitment to western values made an incremental change toward integration more likely.

International supportive structures

According to hypothesis three norm diffusion is most likely when international agents actively promote the norms under consideration. Although Estonia never witnessed violent ethnic clashes like in Yugoslavia, international attention to this tiny country has been impressive. The UN, EU, CE, and OSCE are among the most influential organisations that deal with minority protection. However, each of these organisations follows its own agenda and applies different criteria to assess compliance. Each organisation has different monitoring mechanisms that vary in their effectiveness. Moreover, in different phases different actors have played a predominant role in diffusing minority rights standards. Despite this obvious fragmentation synergy effects have become visible. If positively interpreted, fragmentation is of less concern because it draws on specialisation. The best example is the CE, which has built up a high reputation as a special agency for protecting European human rights. The OSCE, on the other hand, is not a human rights organisation as such, but its emphasis on conflict prevention is helpful and approaches human rights and minority issues from a broader perspective. The EU is the least engaged organisation but it draws heavily on OSCE opinions and recommendations. The UN as the world's prime protector of human rights takes a universal perspective. In sum, all these organisations constitute a loose minority rights regime, which is indispensable for proper norm diffusion.

Before Estonia could join the CE in 1993 it had to sign at least the ECHR and the CE statute. Despite the fact that Estonia had excluded nearly the entire minority population in the first parliamentary elections the CE basically approved the principle of *ius sanguinis* in citizenship law. Joining the Council was seen by Estonians as a confirmation of their nationality policy and legal restorationism (D.J. Simth 2003: 30). Thus no substantial change occurred. However, the CE soon pleaded for an inclusive citizenship law. In summer 1993 Estonian President Meri refused to promulgate the law on aliens until the CE and OSCE had commented on the act which put Estonia at the brink of civil unrest in Russian-speaking parts of the country. CE experts were hardly satisfied with the law on aliens, which forced non-citizens to clarify their status within 12 months, or risk deportation. According to CE experts this practice should only be applied for new immigrants. The draft law on cultural autonomy was also criticised for excluding non-citizens (Geistlicher and Krich 1995:109). The Parliament reviewed the law on aliens and amended 27 passages (Reinikainen 1999: 17). The CE continued to issue its concern about the low degree of naturalisation.[2]

In recent years the CE has continued to press for a more liberal posture against minorities. The CE scrutinised language requirements for election candidates which restrict the right to stand for election for people with poor Estonian language capabilities.[3] In its regular monitoring of the FCNM, the Advisory Committee (AC) mentions a whole series of laws and provisions that should be amended.[4] Language requirements in the private sector, the law on cultural autonomy, the absence of anti-discrimination provisions, a shortage of legal guarantees to use minority languages, language requirements for candidates standing for election, a decreasing naturalisation rate, and high unemployment rates among non-Estonia's are areas of concern.

Among international organisations the OSCE had the most direct effect on Estonian ethnopolitics. As the only organisation the OSCE set up a special agency that monitors minority relations. The High Commissioner on National Minorities as a norm-entrepreneur has demonstrated his influence in Estonia at several occasions. The HCNM can operate independently and raise any issue and monitor any situation he thinks is necessary. He is not tied to bureaucratic monitoring procedures which often only allow for reviewing legislation every two or three years. The HCNM's comments and recommendations can be issued at any time. In the case of Estonia the HCNM engaged in shuttle diplomacy as necessary to make his points. The HCNM can follow law-making processes and intervene if necessary. While other organisations comment on already implemented laws, the HCNM seeks to have direct access to decision-makers. A long-term OSCE Mission to Estonia (1993-2001) functioned as an information platform for the HCNM office in The Hague and OSCE member states. The OSCE was monitoring minority relations closely and intensively.

[2] CoE Res. 1117 (1997).
[3] CoE Recommendation 81 (2000) on the Situation of Local Democracy in Estonia.
[4] Advisory Committee on the FCNM, opinion on Estonia, 14.09.2001.

With the start of EU accession negotiations the influence of the EU increased considerably at the partial expense of the OSCE. However, the EU's approach to minority rights is far from being coherent. Eastern European countries experienced more pressure to regulate their ethnic relations than did western countries (Johns 2003). Furthermore, the EU has been unwilling to develop special minority standards or even to harmonise national legislation dealing with minority issues (Toggenburg 2000). Nonetheless, the European Commission sponsors important integration programmes that could not be run by accession countries because of their limited financial resources.

One should keep in mind that the EU has almost no capacities to monitor human rights activities of the accession countries; such that it has to rely on the CE and OSCE. As a result, joining the CE and compliance to OSCE recommendations has become a precondition to EU accession. Since 1997/98 the OSCE remained important for Estonia because following the HCNM comments secures EU accession.

The European Commission decided to measure progress toward accession in annually published reports. The Commission drew heavily on OSCE data for compiling the reports on minority issues. For each candidate state the Commission compiled reports between the years 1998 and 2003. In the case of Estonia only a very short section (not more than four pages) was dedicated to minority relations. The quality of these reports is questionable. The lack of efficient monitoring by the EU was partly remedied by the willingness of Estonia to join the Union and to comply with its minority standards and conditions of enlargement. The progress reports were not designed as an instrument for sanctions rather to encourage accession states to carry on their reforms. Criticism was mildly formulated.

In the 2000 report Estonia was determined to have fulfilled all of the OSCE recommendations. The EU itself has not developed its own minority standards but it could create new momentum and stabilised the positive process Estonia had started. The EU supported integration by encouraging Estonia to complete the reform process.

Estonia and international influence

With regard to international influence one can draw different pictures. On one hand Estonia hardly changed its citizenship law substantially but on the other hand international influence provided the basis for incremental steps toward minority integration. In the end, international agencies played a role in Estonian nationality politics by promoting liberal standards that aimed to integrate minority members into society. The international arena played a positive role by encouraging Estonia to review its restrictive and in some cases discriminatory policy. However, the final word on integration remains a domestic one.

Domestic-level actors

The actual implementation of international minority standards is mostly left to the contracting parties. Many obligations as contained in the FCNM give room for discretion. It is for this reason that domestic-level actors have a decisive impact on how minority rights are instantiated. The domestic sphere encompasses various actors that can be grouped in three categories; macro-level agents (government), meso-level agents (civil society), and micro-level agents (individual attitudes).

In 2003 the Riigikogu (parliament), a macro-level agent, elected Estonia's seventh prime minister in eleven years. Interestingly, this volatility in voting has only minor effects on Estonia's nationality policy. Despite frequent changes in government the party system appears as relatively stable. Three quarters of the 101 seats in parliament belong to parties that were present since 1992, only the Res Publica party which won the 2003 elections by surprise is a genuine new party (Sikk 2003). No government questioned in principle the concept of legal continuity eased the language test for naturalisation substantially or privileged *ius soli* over *ius sanguinis* for granting citizenship. On the governmental side international engagement in Estonia was seen with scepticism and even today, after the OSCE Mission to Estonia has been closed and the country has joined the EU some politicians describe Europe as obsessed with conflict prevention and Estonia's minority policy.[5] However, Estonians are well aware of the need to integrate the country into European organisations to secure its independence. The EU, OSCE, CE and NATO to varying degrees satisfy the very security needs which rank high on any government's agenda. This fact does not make integration a self-engendered process but it makes any prime minister sensitive to international opinion.

President Lennart Meri who stood in close contact with High Commissioner on National Minorities Max van der Stoel was a central figure from 1992-2002. Van der Stoel was able to convince President Meri to refuse promulgation of the law on aliens in 1993 forcing the Riigikogu to amend the law.

Until 1998 Estonia had no coherent concept for minority integration. Since then a state integration programme comprised all efforts to integrate the Russian-speaking population. This key document is primarily a result of domestic politics. While international pressure led Estonia to reconsider its nationality policy the development of the state integration programme and its implementation through the Integration Foundation in Tallinn are domestic events. The theoretical basis for integration was developed by Raivo Vetik a professor at the Pedagogical University of Tallinn. He could follow his work independently as an expert on integration.[6]

[5] Interview Katrin Saks, former Minister for Ethnic and Population Affairs, Feb 2004, Tallinn.
[6] Interview with Raivo Vetik , Feb. 2004, Tallinn.

At the meso-level civil society forces appear as rather weak. Regarding Russian-speakers in Estonia, those forces did not manage to develop political parties or strong civil society actors that could lobby effectively for their interest (D.J. Smith 1998: 9). This can be reduced to several reasons. First, non-citizens are not allowed to join political parties.[7] Second, the Russian community is less homogenous in its ethnic constitution than is the ethnic Estonian community. Since the Soviet immigrant came from all parts of the Soviet Union they are a mixture of many ethnicities and cultures. Nonetheless, ethnic Russians make up the biggest part of Russian-speakers. Even today no Russian party of influence exists. On one hand Russians vote for Estonian parties which can be interpreted as a sign of political integration, while on the other hand structural conditions to form minority parties are unfavourable which marginalising Russian influence in politics.

Civil society actors in Estonia are clearly underdeveloped. As a consequence, a further tool for conflict prevention, solution and integration cannot be used adequately. NGO influence in Estonia from outside and more so from inside is marginal and has almost no measurable impact. Even the world's biggest human rights organisation Amnesty International has no office in Estonia. Only one organisation, the Legal Information Centre for Human Rights, is functioning as a mouthpiece for Russian interests and fulfils ombudsman like tasks.[8]

In a study conducted for the Open Society Institute Estonia Iris Pettai compiled a typology of tolerance for analysing the attitudes of Estonians and non-Estonians. According to her, around 20% of Estonians have developed a degree of active tolerance. 28% are indifferent towards Russian-speakers and 20% distrust other ethnic groups. One third of Estonians have taken a pragmatic arrangement with Russian people. Integration which is based on a two-way process may be slowed down by the nearly 50% of Estonians who are either against integration or are indifferent toward the process.

Following Pettai's typology non-Estonians are divided in five groups

1. Strongly assimilated	13%
2. Emphatic	33%
3. Pragmatic	19%
4. Less-tolerant	21%
5. Exclusionary	14%

[7] Estonian Constitution Article 48,1.

[8] Interview Alexei Semjonov, LICHR, Feb. 2004, Tallinn.

Among the Russian-speakers, willingness to integrate can be found in group one and two. Both groups account for nearly half of the Estonian minority population. Integration finds more resonance among non-Estonians than among ethnic Estonians. At the same time, one third of the minority population shows no signs to integrate which may explain the low number of naturalised minority members.

To sum up, analysing domestic-level agents does not deliver clear outcomes that point only in one direction. We have found evidence for and against integration. Nonetheless, the cautious path Estonia chose with regard to minority integration reflects very much on those domestic actors mentioned above. Incremental improvements in the domestic sphere always found their way to the surface and affected receptiveness to implementing international minority standards.

Consequences of norm violation and compliance

A rationalist assumption is that states calculate consequences responding positively to international norms in cases where the benefits exceed the costs of compliance. States are supposed to calculate costs and benefits. Costs as well as benefits may be material or ideational kinds. International organisations offer both material awards and reputational sanctions. Estonia continuously calculates these effects and acts accordingly.

As a consequence, after fifty years of occupation and suppression the main concern for this tiny country was survival. A high number of Red Army soldiers remained in Estonia until the mid 1990s and a huge non-Estonian minority with almost no historic ties to the country and minimal language knowledge was perceived as threatening to Estonian integrity and stability. National security ranked first on the political agenda. Russia's fragile political constitution, nationalistic rhetoric, and accusations of human rights violations in Estonia increased the pressure on Estonian politicians to stand firm on minority questions. Furthermore, Estonians feared that those who had lost power in Estonia would undermine independence (Geistlicher and Kirch 1995: 42). Ethnocentrism and restrictive legislation regarding minority issues were the result. Russia and its minority members in Estonia were perceived as a security threat. Hence, granting Russian-speakers full political participation was weighed against security needs and regarded as too costly.

Since Russian troops left Estonia, NATO has enlarged enlarging and US-Russian relations have improved, such that security concerns appear less eminent. Despite this objective improvement in security issues, Estonia's self-perception is one of defence, which justifies the special protection of their culture and language that remains deeply ingrained in the Estonian collective psychology. Nonetheless, without improved national security, ethnic relations and norm diffusion would have been less successful.

Immediately after regaining independence Estonia turned to European organisations and joined the CE, and OSCE, later also becoming a member of the EU and NATO. By joining these organisations Estonia committed itself to human rights, democracy, the rule of law, and western style market reforms. In the first years after independence Estonia hold a pragmatic posture toward international organisations. IOs were of special value because they recognised Estonia as a sovereign state and reduced security threats. This becomes clearest in the case of OSCE-Estonian relations. Estonia used the OSCE as an instrument for securing independence and to build up pressure for a quick Russian troop withdrawal (Birkenbach 2000: 7). Integration into western organisations was the first foreign policy goal because it guaranteed Estonia security and independence from Russia (Park 1995: 27). In contrast to the EU the OSCE could not offer any material rewards for norm compliance. Nonetheless, its reports found interested readers in Brussels. The EU Commission drew on the OSCE reports by compiling its progress reports over enlargement. Estonians took heed of the OSCE because they knew that EU accession is partly dependent on positive OSCE opinion about Estonia. Norm diffusion is made more likely because EU accession satisfies Estonia's security needs and expectations for economic welfare. From 1991 to 2004, Estonia received 460.4 Million Euro in assistance. Between 2004 and 2006 Estonia receives 1020.4 Million Euro from the EU budget and contribute to the budget 230.3 Million.[9] These figures show that Estonia was risking millions of Euros by not fulfilling the EU accession criteria, including the implementation of minority rights standards. No other international organisation other than the EU could offer a comparable amount of money and economic rewards.

In Estonia the realisation of key integration programmes would not be possible without EU support. In implementing the state integration programme the integration foundation spent 38.090.392 EEK[10] for all its projects in 2002. 15.684.000 EEK of this sum came from the PHARE programme run by the EU. As regards integration material costs are reduced through international support which poses no extra burden for the Estonian tax-payers. Progress in the implementation of minority standards is facilitated first through material incentives as a consequence of EU membership, and second through direct assistance for integration. Norm following is rewarded with economic benefits. Estonia complied with international minority standards in order to receive these material rewards. Norm compliance is reinforced by positive material incentives that coincide with norm promotion.

[9] These numbers have been calculated by the Delegation of the European Commission in Estonia, authors interview Feb. 2004. One Euro has a value of 15,65 Eesti Krooni.

[10] 2002 Integratsiooni Aastaraamet, Integration Yearbook, published by the Integration foundation, Tallinn. 1 € = 15,65 EEK.

While norm adherence is rewarded, norm violation can seldom be punished effectively. The UN recommendations on Estonia have almost no effect on norm compliance. In Estonia OSCE and EU opinions on the country are well known and given influence whereas UN documents are widely ignored or considered as unimportant. The UN's rather poor performance compared with those of the OSCE and EU can be explained easily from the point of rational calculations. Violating UN standards is not costly and norm following brings minor benefits. Only in cases of severe human rights violations with a systematic pattern and long-lasting abuses of fundamental rights would the UN and other IOs be able to create some leverage, and then only because such a situation would undermine Estonia's reputation as a democratic and peaceful country. But at no time could Estonia be accused of severe human rights violations. Lower-scale violations or using tactics to circumvent or delay the implementation of some minority standards do not suffice to challenge Estonia's international reputation or damage its credibility substantively. Put simply, lower-scale non-compliance is cheap and creates minimal costs. Nonetheless, Estonia committed itself to European values, which at least demand a substantial degree of pro-norm behaviour.

On the whole a cost-benefit calculation has to highlight material benefits resulting from norm compliance and minor costs for lower-scale norm violations. Taking a pragmatic view, Estonia has implemented minority standards to benefit from the economic rewards offered by the EU, while application of minority standards remains selective because punishment is exceptional.

Summary

In the end, a mixed picture emerges. Estonia surely has made visible progress in implementing European minority standards. However, the fragmented and in parts fuzzy content of minority norms has fostered a conservative interpretation of the Framework Convention. Pressure from international organisations and economic incentives as a consequence of EU enlargement had a positive effect on the norm diffusion process. Analysing domestic level-agents and resonance did not lead to clear statements. In future they can be a source or progress or regress alike.

Minority Rights in Europe: Roms in Slovakia and the Czech Republic

Eben Friedman[1]

Introduction

From the Communists' rise to power in 1948 until the Velvet Revolution of 1989, policy toward Roms ('Gypsies')[2] in Czechoslovakia was designed primarily in Prague. Since the fall of the Communist regime, however, Czech and Slovak policies toward Roms have differed significantly from one another. Addressing the integration of Roms in the context of the European Union (EU) accession process, this chapter provides an overview of Czech and Slovak treatments of Roms and of two factors underlying the differences between them.

Treating the Slovak and Czech Republics in turn, the section on each republic begins with a brief discussion of the size of the Romani population. Next, I present what are in my view the most important policy documents aimed at the Romani populations of each country in the post-Communist period. In conjunction with this documentary analysis, I also offer a summary examination of trends in state practice. Finally, I attempt to explain the divergence between Czech and Slovak treatments of Roms in terms of policies of the previous common Czechoslovak regime on the one hand and differences in international orientation between post-Communist Czech and Slovak governments on the other.

The Slovak Republic

The Romani Population

The results of the census conducted in the Slovak Republic in 2001 indicate the size of the country's Romani population to be 89,920, or 1.7 per cent of the total population.[3] In 1989, however, the official estimate stood at 253,943, with the sharp drop between 1989 and the 1991 census figure of 75,801 attributable primarily to a change in the way the census was conducted: Whereas the determi-

[1] This chapter draws heavily on the author's doctoral thesis, "Explaining the Political Integration of Minorities: Roms as a Hard Case" (Department of Political Science, University of California, San Diego, 2002), the completion of which was made possible by support from the American Councils for International Education (through the US Department of State, Program for Research and Training on Eastern Europe and the Independent States of the Former Soviet Union); the American Council of Learned Societies (Fellowship for East European Studies); the Center for German and European Studies; the J. William Fulbright Foreign Scholarship Board; the Institute on Global Conflict and Cooperation; the University of California, Berkeley; the University of California, San Diego; and the University of Pittsburgh.

[2] Whereas 'Rom' is neutral, 'Gypsy' often has a pejorative connotation. I therefore use the latter term only in presenting policies and statements the declared targets of which are "Gypsies." In using the plural 'Roms' rather than 'Roma', I accept Victor Friedman's (1999: 319-320 fn **) assertion that "'*Roma*' exoticizes and marginalizes rather than emphasizing the fact that the group in question is an ethnic group" equal to all others, the names for which end in 's' in the English plural.

[3] Data provided by the Statistical Office of the Slovak Republic.

nation of "Gypsy ancestry" was left to local authorities between 1945 and 1989, the 1991 census included the nationality category "Rom." While Romani activists have estimated the number of Roms in the Slovak Republic at over 500,000 (see, for example, Druker 1997: 23), the Slovak demographer Boris Vaňo gives a range of 360,000 to 365,000 for the year 2000 (Vaňo 2001: 12).

Policy Documents

Policy toward Roms in post-Communist Slovakia has been marked by considerable discontinuity not only between successive governments, but also within the terms of the various governments formed since 1989. Rather than apply a program consistently, until mid-2000 Slovak authorities repeatedly drafted what they presented as new policy priorities and called for new pilot projects to reflect those priorities. Moreover, although constructive attention to Roms has generally increased under the governments led by Mikuláš Dzurinda, the parliamentary elections of 2002 (which gave Dzurinda a second term as Premier) resulted in reshuffling as officials attempted to avoid responsibility for the problems of the Romani population (Vašečka 2003). As a result of these changes of direction, the number of policy documents requiring discussion is high for the relatively short time period covered.

Czecho-Slovakia

Post-Communist Slovakia's first policy document aimed at its Romani population, Resolution 153 of 9 April 1991 "Principles of the Policy of the Slovak Republic towards the Roms" recognises the Roms as a nationality (*národnosť*) and promises political and legal equality (Vláda Slovenskej republiky 1991). The first article of Resolution 153 establishes the Council of the Government of the Slovak Republic for Nationalities and Ethnic Groups, as well as the Committee for Nationalities, Ethnic Groups and Human Rights. Article 2 promises to resolve the problems of Roms who require special assistance within the framework of a set of social policies directed "at all citizens without regard to their ethnic membership," emphasising that programs directed at "all unsocialized [...] groups of the population" must not be called 'Romani programs'. The third and final article of Resolution 153 takes stock of the social climate resulting from decades of Communist policy and accordingly recommends that future policy target only at-risk social groups, "including a portion of the Roms." In this manner, Resolution 153 promises an ethnically neutral approach to the problems of Slovakia's Romani population.

Although approved in 1991, Resolution 153 was not implemented until the period leading up to the parliamentary elections of the following year which brought Vladimír Mečiar to power. The document was also not elaborated in the period following the elections (Sobotka 2001; Vašečka and Džambazovič 2000: 26). In the meantime, Slovakia drafted its own Constitution, Articles 33 and 34 of which guarantee "national minorities" and "ethnic groups" various rights including the use of their own languages. However, nowhere in the 1992 Constitution or in any other Slovak official document are the terms 'national minority' and 'ethnic group' defined or the members of the categories enumerated (Kľučka 1995: 43; Mann 1995: 38; Trifunovska 2001: 566). As a result, it is unclear which groups fall into which category and on what grounds. Further, common usage of the term 'ethnic group' to distinguish the Roms from other ethnic minorities (i.e., "national minorities," such as Magyars) in Slovakia suggests that even the *de jure* equality of Roms with other ethnic minorities is highly tenuous (Davidová 1995: 224; Mann 1995: 38-39). In so doing, the distinction between national minorities on the one hand and ethnic groups on the other calls into question the applicability to Roms of the *Framework Convention for the Protection of National Minorities*, which does not contain the term 'ethnic group' (Council of Europe 1995).

The Mečiar Years

The Slovak government's next piece of policy aimed at the Romani population came only in 1998. Resolution 668 created the "Office of the Government Plenipotentiary for Solving the Problems of Citizens Who Need Special Care" under the Ministry of Labour, Social Affairs and Family (Vláda Slovenskej republiky 1995). Drafted in the month following Slovakia's first officially recognised racially motivated murder, Resolution 668 was an attempt to quell agitation by human rights organisations and the Romani population (Vašečka 1999b: 292). Whereas Romani activists had demanded the creation of a government office for Roms headed by a Rom, the office created by Resolution 668 was in theory ethnically neutral and the person chosen to fill it, Branislav Baláž, was an ethnic Slovak and a member of the ruling Movement for a Democratic Slovakia (HZDS).

In the report accompanying Resolution 668, "citizens who need special care" were defined as the unemployed, the socially and culturally "backward," ex-convicts, alcoholics, drug addicts, former inhabitants of orphanages and children's group homes and persons awaiting housing. The resolution which created the Office of the Government Plenipotentiary for Solving the Problems of Citizens Who Need Special Care was followed in 1996 by Resolution 310 "On the Proposal of Activities and Measures for Solving the Problems of Citizens Who Need Special Care" (Vláda Slovenskej republiky 1996). While the objects of Resolution 668/1995 and the office created by it are defined in ethnically neutral terms, the text of Resolution 310/1996 deals primarily with the Romani population. While much of the time this concern is explicit, the resolution also contains language where the reference to Roms is implicit yet clear (e.g., "un-adapted citizens").

The materials accompanying Resolution 310/1996 recommend measures under seven headings (not all of which will be discussed here): formal education; employment; living conditions; practical and occupational education; healthcare; "negative social phenomena"; and "organizational, material and personal procurement of a solution." In the area of formal education, the resolution recommends preparatory "zero grades" to ease entry into primary schools. Also recommended are other alternative programs with an emphasis on the Slovak language, as well as experimental projects focusing on teaching Romani children traditional Romani crafts. Making note of "the devastation of apartments by citizens," widespread delinquency on rental payments and "the frequent migration of a part of the citizens and problems with registering for permanent residence," the section on living conditions recommends "a solution for [...] unadapted [*neprispôsobení*] citizens" and support for the renovation of Romani settlements. Additionally, the section of Resolution 310/1996 on practical and occupational education calls for a project to prepare adult Roms in the professions and traditional crafts, also recommending courses in home economics and other living skills. In order to put an end to "negative social phenomena," the resolution recommends supporting the "natural authority" of traditional leaders (*vajdovia*) in Romani settlements, encourages cooperation between the police and organisations active in raising Roms' knowledge of the law and suggests a review of the mass media's practice of emphasising Romani ethnicity in its crime reports. Finally, in the section entitled "organizational, material and personal procurement of a solution," the Slovak government promises to present its approach to the problems of the Roms in international forums, to compile information on other European states' solutions to these same problems and to commission research on the effects of the social and economic transformation "on some groups of citizens, especially Roms."

While Resolution 310 On the Proposal of Activities and Measures for Solving the Problems of Citizens Who Need Special Care identifies problem areas and lists possible remedies, it neither assigns duties nor allots funds for the measures outlined in the text of the Resolution. In similar fashion, the May 1997 "Report on the Fulfilment of the Functions and Measures for Solving the Problems of Citizens Who Need Special Care in the Year 1996 and Proposal of Measures for Solving the Problems of Citizens Who Need Special Care in the Year 1997" states that "the results which were attained in the year 1996 fulfilled the functions assigned for the year 1996 and are a good starting point for securing the functions approved in the year 1997 with an outlook to the year 2000," while noting that "[t]he proposal of measures for the year 1997 does not contain a quantification of the requirements on the state budget of the Slovak Republic for the year 1997" (Vláda Slovenskej republiky 1997b).

Rather than take steps toward the implementation of Resolution 310, however, on 3 November 1997 the Slovak government issued Resolution 796, better known as "Conceptual Intentions of the Government of the Slovak Republic for Solving the Problems of Roms in the Current Social-Economic Conditions" (Vláda Slovenskej republiky 1997a). Among the "fundamental theses" of the new resolution are that the education of Romani children constitutes a necessary condition for successful solution of the problems of the Romani population and that the funds and materials used to solve the Roms' problems should not be distributed on the basis of ethnicity but rather for "concrete projects in the context of aid to citizens who need help" as well as for regional development projects. Despite commonalities in approach with Resolution 153 of six years earlier, Resolution 796 devotes several pages to criticising the earlier document on the grounds that "[i]n the current conditions the problematic of the Roms is not characterised by membership in a national minority, but as a problematic of social position and social aid."

The priorities of Resolution 796 are organised into the categories of education and culture, employment, living conditions, social aid, healthcare and "the prevention of antisocial activity." In this last area, the government plans "to register, analyse and explain the criminality of the Romani population" in order to gather information for the prevention of such criminality. Good or bad intentions of Resolution 796 notwithstanding, it (unlike Resolution 310) both assigns roles to specific governmental bodies for the realisation of specific measures and outlines sources of funding for these measures. As Eva Sobotka (2001) puts it, however, Resolution 796 became a dead letter with Mečiar's removal from office as a result of the 1998 parliamentary elections.

Overall, policy toward Roms under the Mečiar governments varied between ineffectiveness and outright subterfuge (cf. Barany 2002: 293). Also worth noting is that the considerations grounding policy in this period seem to have been connected less to a concern with Slovakia's image abroad than to constituencies within Slovakia. With the parliamentary elections of 1998 came a change in government priorities, eventually resulting in a more consistent approach to the situation of the Romani population.

Policy under the Dzurinda Governments

Less than a month after taking power in November of 1998, the explicitly pro-EU government under Mikuláš Dzurinda fired Branislav Baláž from his post as Government Plenipotentiary for Solving the Problems of Citizens Who Need Special Care and abolished the office (Vláda Slovenskej republiky 1998). Government Resolution 127 of 1999, however, created a similar office with an ethnically specific name, the "Office of the Government Plenipotentiary for Solving the Problems of Citizens Belonging to the Romani Minority," which was now filled by a Rom, Vincent Danihel (Vláda Slovenskej republiky 1999b). In much the same way as previous policy documents, Article 1 of the Statute of the new Government Plenipotentiary states that the most fundamental problems to be addressed by the Office are unemployment and living conditions, as well as health problems, social problems, educational problems and problems of hygiene. Article 3 of the Statute breaks new ground in listing among the tasks of the Government Plenipotentiary the compilation of proposals for programs to improve the enjoyment of civil rights by members of the Romani population. Article 4 of the Statute places the Government Plenipotentiary for Solving the Problems of Citizens Belonging to the Romani Minority under the (newly created) Deputy Prime Minister for Human Rights, Minorities and Regional Development, while Article 6 makes the Government Plenipotentiary a member of the Government Council for the Fight against Anti-Social Activity.

On 27 September 1999, the Dzurinda government adopted the "Strategy of the Government of the Slovak Republic for Solving the Problems of the Romani National Minority and the Set of Measures for its Implementation – Stage I" (Vláda Slovenskej republiky 1999a). Declaring Resolution 796/97 ("Conceptual Intentions") null and void "in the interest of legislative purity," the new resolution lambastes the Mečiar government for working against the spirit of its own resolution by refusing to draft a law on the use of minority languages, lowering subsidies for the development of minority cultures and languages and failing to create a government office for solving the problems of the Romani minority. Stage I of the Strategy also observes that the philosophy of equality promulgated in Resolution 153/1991 ("Principles") conflicts with the realisation of such equality, but leaves the Principles in force as "historically valuable material." In similar fashion to the policy instruments which preceded it, Stage I divides the solution of the problems of the Romani population into seven domains, including education, living conditions, social policy, healthcare and employment. Unlike previous measures, however, Resolution 821 also contains sections on human rights and Romani culture. Another departure from previous measures is that Resolution 821 takes note of the international environment, stating that foreign democracies will not only accept but will also provide material support for concrete projects designed to solve specific problems. Still, while Stage I promises much, its proposals are for the most part vague and the document fails to allocate funds to specific bodies for the realisation of the measures outlined in the resolution (cf. Open Society Institute 2001b: 431-432; Sobotka 2001; Vašečka and Džambazovič 2000: 26).

Stage II of the Dzurinda government's program for Slovakia's Romani population, called the "Elaborated Strategy of the Government of the Slovak Republic for Solving the Problems of the Romani National Minority," was approved on 3 May 2000 as Resolution 294 (Vláda Slovenskej republiky 2000). In the area of human rights (Stage II uses the same categories as Stage I), Roms are characterised as a "specific national minority" subject to discrimination "mainly in the past" and calls for the Roms' active engagement in the solution of their own problems. In the area of education, Stage II presents multicultural training as a necessity for improving relations between Roms and the majority population and calls for the creation of conditions conducive to preparing Romani children for school. Additionally, "the Government of the Slovak Republic recognises the culture and language of the Roms as undeniable cultural values of the Slovak Republic," with the Ministry of Culture promising to commission social-historical research on the Romani population of Slovakia and to expand broadcast offerings for Roms. The section on living conditions promises another research project, this one concerning the state of Romani settlements throughout the country. Finally, the government promises to make room for nongovernmental organisations to participate in the distribution of social assistance to the Romani community. On the whole, Stage II deals with the implementation of the measures outlined in the text of the resolution in considerably more detail than does Stage I, but the allocation of funds to concrete tasks remains unclear and some tasks require funding which cannot be secured from the state budget (see European Commission against Racism and Intolerance 2004: 6, 26; Open Society Institute 2002b: 530; Vašečka and Džambazovič 2000: 27-28; Vláda Slovenskej republiky 2002; 2003).

Shortcomings of Stage II notwithstanding, the third Government Plenipotentiary for Romani Communities (as the post has been called since September 2001), Klára Orgovánová, has been consistent in working to bring about implementation of the Strategy. Initial steps in this direction under Orgovánová's leadership included the formation of an advisory board to the Government Plenipotentiary to aid in preparing appropriate projects, the opening of a branch of the Office of the Government Plenipotentiary in Eastern Slovakia (where most of the country's Romani population lives) and the establishment of the "Inter-ministerial Commission for the Affairs of Romani Communities" as an advisory body to the Cabinet. Further, in April of 2002, Orgovánová's office took the step – unprecedented in Slovakia – of publishing a critical appraisal of implementation of the Strategy, noting that fulfilment of government priorities requires sufficient resource allocations (Vláda Slovenskej republiky 2002).

Following the parliamentary elections of September 2002, the Office of the Government Plenipotentiary was transferred from the authority of the Deputy Prime Minister for Human Rights, Minorities and Regional Development to that of the Prime Minister. Additionally, the new Cabinet redefined the Office's areas of responsibility in relationship to other government bodies at both state and regional levels. Later that year, political wrangling over the institutional framework within which the Office of the Government Plenipotentiary should operate led the World Bank to withdraw its funding for the Office, with this funding not replaced from within the state budget (European Commission against Racism and Intolerance 2004: 12; Vašečka 2003: 175).

Slovak policy documents on Roms published since the 2002 elections suggest continuing tensions between the Office of the Government Plenipotentiary for Romani Communities and the Cabinet. A case in point are the "Fundamental Theses of the Concept of the Government of the Slovak Republic's Policy in the Integration of Romani Communities" (Vláda Slovenskej republiky 2003), which combine the constructive-critical approach characteristic of Orgovánová's work with an introductory text reminiscent of policy documents issued under the Mečiar governments. Whereas the substantive sections of the document contain frank analysis of policy implemented to date and provides lists of concrete measures to be undertaken in the medium and long terms, the introductory section contains claims that "the essence of the problematic of the Roms has a socio-economic character" and that "Roms in a uniting Europe face similar challenges to other ethnic groups." Combined with the extremely limited resources of the Office of the Government Plenipotentiary, the presence of similar incongruities in the "Evaluation of the Fundamental Theses of the Concept of the Government of the Slovak Republic's Policy in the Integration of Romani Communities" and in the "Priorities of the Government of the Slovak Republic in the Integration of Romani Communities for the Year 2004" bodes ill for the coherence of Slovak government policy toward Roms in the aftermath of EU accession (Vláda Slovenskej republiky 2004a; 2004b).

Support for Romani Culture

The fall of the Communist regime in Czechoslovakia saw an initial blossoming of institutions connected to Romani culture. Among the first was the Department of Romani Studies, which opened at the University of Constantine the Philosopher in Nitra in 1990. The following year, Slovakia's first Romani newspaper began publication. These developments were followed in 1992 by the establishment of the Secondary School of the Arts in Košice. A year later, the Romani professional theatre *Romathan* opened in the same city.

Whatever the initial euphoria, state support for Romani culture decreased over the course of the next several years. From 1992 to 1995, subsidies for minority publications decreased by 44.8 per cent overall, with subsidies for Romani publications in particular decreasing by 65.1 per cent (the most of any minority) (Dostál 1998: 164). Although some relief came under the first Dzurinda government, the overall record of the two Dzurinda governments in supporting Romani culture has been mixed, with increases in some areas counterbalanced by cuts in others (e.g., publications).

Although the Romani population has often been an object of Slovak media, it has been consistently underrepresented in its ranks. The country's first weekly radio broadcast for Roms was aired in Hungarian in June 1998, while the first radio program in Romani was broadcast in December of the same year (Vašečka 1999a: 774). Whereas the television magazine *Romale* ("Roms") has never been broadcast with any regularity, Slovak Radio now airs approximately 68 hours of Romani programming per year, including a weekly 30-minute news and cultural program for Hungarian-speaking Roms (Vláda Slovenskej republiky 2004b). Among the Romani periodicals financed by the Ministry of Culture, the most successful is *Romano nevo ľil* ("Romani New Letter"), which has been published sporadically since 1991. Also financed by the Ministry of Culture are the educational monthlies *Štvorlístok* ("Four-Leaf Clover") and *Ternipen* ("Youth"), as well as the bimonthly *Rómsky list* ("Romani Letter"), which appears as a supplement to the Slovak weekly *Domino Fórum*.

In the domain of education, the first half of the 1990s saw the publication of a Romani-Slovak spelling book (*Romano hangoro*) and a Romani-Slovak reader (*Genibarica*) to be used in the first and second years of primary school (with the former to be used also in special education), as well as a Romani-Slovak textbook (*Amari alphabet* ("Our Alphabet")) for use in the third and fourth years of primary school (Council of Europe 1999b: 27; Radičová 2001: 149; Trifunovska 2001: 568). None of these publications, however, has been distributed systematically to schools with large Romani student populations. Additionally, the Romani language is neither taught as a subject nor used as the language of instruction in any school, with its occasional use in a single secondary school at most a gesture toward Romani students who must already have become proficient in Slovak in order to complete primary education. At the level of post-secondary education, Romani students have been given preferential admission to university since 1989 (Vašečka 1999a: 769). However, few Roms get as far as post-secondary education, such that Romani students constitute a small minority even in Nitra's Department of Romani studies. Nonetheless, the University of Prešov offers a post-graduate degree in Romani studies (Mann 1995: 39).

The Czech Republic

The Romani Population

If census figures concerning the size of the Romani population of Slovakia are of questionable use, the corresponding numbers from the Czech Republic are more problematic still. According to the most recent census, conducted in 2001, Roms account for 0.1 per cent of the total population, or 11,746 persons.[4] The previous census, however, conducted a decade earlier, indicated a Romani population approximately three times larger (i.e., 32,903), with the radical decline pointing to the failure of the Czech government's scheme of employing Romani assistants to census takers in areas with a relatively large Romani population, if not also to "a massive loss of confidence in the last decade" (Open Society Institute 2001a: 173). Estimates from the Czech government, on the other hand, put the country's Romani population at 145,711 in 1989 and give a range of 166,000 to 206,000 for June of 2000, according to which Roms would account for be-

[4] Data provided by the Czech Statistical Office.

tween 1.6 per cent and 1.99 per cent of the total population (Council of Europe 1999a: 7; European Roma Rights Center 1999: 6; Sobotka 2001; cf. Open Society Institute 2002a: 172). Even assuming the correctness of the higher estimate, the Romani population of the Czech Republic is much smaller than is the Romani population of the Slovak Republic in absolute as well as in relative terms.

Policy Documents

Roms as National Minority

Although the day-to-day problems of Roms in the Czech Republic are generally similar to those experienced by their counterparts in the Slovak Republic, since 1994 Czech policy toward the Romani population has exhibited a degree of consistency lacking in Slovakia. Further, even before 1994 there were some indications that Czech authorities had taken a more positive view of Roms than had Slovak authorities. Among the most significant of these earlier indications is the fact that Czech official documents do not include "ethnic group" as a category distinct from "national minority," leaving no question as to whether the *Framework Convention for the Protection of National Minorities* applies to the Romani population. Also distinguishing the Czech Republic from the Slovak Republic is the former's definition of national minorities as communities of citizens and permanent residents of the Czech Republic who share "ethnic, cultural and language characteristics" which differentiate them from the majority population; who express a desire to be considered a national minority in order to preserve their identity, customs and language; and who "have a long-term, solid and permanent relationship [with] Czech society" (Secretariat of the Council for National Minorities of the Government of the Czech Republic 1999: 2; Vláda České republiky 1994).

Official recognition of Roms as a national minority and inclusion of Roms in the Council for National Minorities are indicative of a broader legislative trend in the Czech Republic's treatment of its minorities which begins with the Czech Constitution. Unlike the Slovak Constitution, which opens with a reference to "the Slovak nation" and proceeds immediately to an undefined terminological distinction between national minorities and ethnic groups, the Czech Constitution mentions only "the citizens of the Czech Republic" (Zbierka zákonov Slovenskej republiky 1992; Sbírka zákonů České republiky 1993a). While these early measures serve to distinguish the Czech Republic from the Slovak Republic, it is important to note that little in the way of concrete policy toward Roms was enacted before 1995. Moreover, the Czech citizenship law of 1993 seems to have been designed in order to prevent Roms with Slovak citizenship resident in the Czech Republic from becoming Czech citizens following the division of Czecho-Slovakia into its constituent republics.

The Czech Citizenship Law

Although the "Law on the Acquisition and Loss of Citizenship of the Czech Republic" did not affect persons with Czech citizenship, it required Slovak citisens to apply for citizenship (Sbírka zákonů České republiky 1993b). In light of the practical irrelevance of republican citizenship under Communism and of the fact that the Romani population of the Czech lands was composed almost entirely of Roms from Slovakia and their descendants,[5] most Roms in the Czech Republic were technically Slovak citizens. In order to apply for Czech citizenship, Slovak citizens first had to obtain a release from their Slovak citizenship at a cost of approximately $120 (3,000 crowns) before filing for Czech citizenship at an additional cost of approximately $180 (5,000 crowns) (Human Rights Watch 1996: 20). Also problematic for many Roms was the Law's requirement of a clean criminal record for the five years preceding application for citizenship (Guy 2001: 297; Human Rights Watch 1996: 16).[6]

While statistical information is not available on the number of Roms affected by the Czech citizenship law, it is clear that the law's application resulted in deportations to Slovakia and, in rarer instances, statelessness (see, for example, Human Rights Watch 1996: 18, 26-27). Affecting Roms disproportionately, the citizenship law's discriminatory provisions were tempered by amendments in 1996 and (especially) 1999 (Guy 2001: 298, 302; Human Rights Watch 1996: 29; Sbírka zákonů České republiky 1996; 1999). Perhaps more significant than the amendments themselves, however, is their place in a broader pattern of official measures to improve the situation of the Czech Republic's Romani population. The first manifestation of this trend came in 1995 with the handling of the killing of a Rom by skinheads.

Criminal Law

Responding to a growing problem with racially motivated violence, on 1 September 1995 Czech authorities passed an amendment to the Criminal Code providing an additional one to two years imprisonment for criminal offences committed "due to a person's race, national identity, political orientation, religion or the fact that such a person has no religion" (Sbírka zákonů České republiky 1995; cf. Sbírka zákonů České republiky 2002). These new provisions to the Criminal Code were first applied in May 1996, when an appeals court over-

[5] See the next section of this chapter, "Explaining Differences between Czech and Slovak Republics."

[6] The Slovak citizenship law imposed requirements similarly restrictive to its Czech counterpart, including five years of uninterrupted legal residence on the territory of the Slovak republic, mastery of the Slovak language and a clean criminal record for the five years preceding the application for citizenship (Zbierka zákonov Slovenskej republiky 1993). Consequently, were Roms with Czech citizenship to apply for Slovak citizenship under this law, they would likely run into problems similar to those encountered by Roms with Slovak citizenship applying for Czech citizenship.

turned a lower court's December 1995 decision that the murder of a Rom by four skinheads who had never met their victim prior to breaking into his house and beating him with a baseball bat was not racially motivated (Human Rights Watch 1996: 9). Following a retrial spurred by protests from the Prime Minister (Václav Klaus), the ringleader of the skinheads was sentenced to a thirteen-year prison term.

Government Strategy
Another important piece of policy affecting the Romani population of the Czech Republic was the creation of the "Inter-ministerial Commission for the Affairs of the Romani Community" in 1997 (Vláda České republiky 1997b; 1998). Created as an advising body, the Commission consists of fourteen Roms (including two Vlach Roms) and twelve deputy ministers, and works in cooperation with the Council for National Minorities and the Council for Human Rights, the Commissioner of which is also chairman of the Inter-ministerial Commission for the Affairs of the Romani Community. Among the concrete tasks of the Commission is the compilation of at least yearly reports on the state and development of the Romani population of the Czech Republic. The first "Report on the Situation of the Romani Community in the Czech Republic and on the Current Situation in the Romani Community" was released in October of 1997 and hailed even by critics of Czech policy toward Roms as a significant accomplishment (Guy 2001: 301; Open Society Institute 2001a: 123, 128; Sobotka 2001; Vláda České republiky 1997a).

Although the Inter-ministerial Commission for the Affairs of the Romani Community has been criticised for lacking sufficient authority, some of the Commission's critics have also noted that its existence has increased the Czech government's attention to Romani issues in the years since the Commission was created (see, for example, Open Society Institute 2001a: 165-166; Sobotka 2001). Further, unlike its Slovak counterpart at the time of the Commission's creation (i.e., the Office of the Government Plenipotentiary for Solving the Problems of Citizens Who Need Special Care), the Inter-ministerial Commission has played a consistently active role in the design of government policy. Thus, in June of 2000, the Commission released its "Concept of Government Policy Toward Members of the Romani Community, Aiding Their Integration into Society" (Vláda České republiky 2000). Outlining measures to be taken in the course of the next twenty years in the areas of discrimination, education, unemployment, housing, health conditions, political participation, language, culture and interethnic relations, the Concept also proposes an affirmative action program of tax credits and direct subsidies to firms with a Romani employee base of over 60 per cent. Overall, the Concept places responsibility for bringing about significant change in the situation of the Czech Republic's Romani population in the hands of the Czech government (rather than calling on nongovernmental organisations, as the Slovak government has sometimes done).

In January of 2002, the government of the Czech Republic issued Resolution 87, a 148-page report on the fulfilment of measures outlined in previous policy documents to bring about the integration of the Romani population (Vláda České republiky 2002). In addition to providing a detailed account of the use of funds from the 2000 and 2001 state budgets, the Resolution notes areas in which the goals set in previous documents have been met, not met, partially met and met without bringing about the desired effects, as well as areas in which evaluation proved impossible. Noteworthy features of the documents which accompany the Resolution are a plan to transform special schools (in which Roms are disproportionately represented) into standard primary schools and a report on Roms' housing conditions. In this manner, Government Resolution 87/2002 provides a frank evaluation of previous policy toward the Romani population of the Czech Republic and proposes appropriate modifications to the Government Policy Concept.

Following on Government Resolution 87/2002, Government Resolution 243 of 2003 carries this practice of regular, critical reporting on implementation of the Government Policy Concept through the end of 2002 (Vláda České republiky 2003). Government Resolution 607 of 2004, however, seems to suggest that this ostensible example of a best practice in the region has lost momentum as a result of EU accession (Vláda České republiky 2004a; 2004b). Consisting of a 57-page report on the fulfilment of previously approved measures and a second minor revision of the Government Policy Concept, Resolution 607 notes that most of the goals set in previous documents are in the process of being met and promises a fundamental revision of the Government Policy Concept in 2005 which takes into account the "objective circumstances [which] fundamentally alter the possibilities of practical implementation of the Concept." Providing additional support for the view that the Czech government's constructive attention to Roms may be on the downswing following EU accession is the statement in the 2004 "Report on the Situation of Romani Communities in the Czech Republic" that "with the expansion of the EU, the Romani problematic increasingly enters into consideration for the operations of EU organs" (Vláda České republiky 2004c).

Support for Romani Culture

Although the Romani population of the Czech Republic is much smaller than the Romani population of Slovakia, the Czech government provides more support for Romani culture than does its Slovak counterpart in absolute as well as relative terms. In the domain of broadcast media, Czech Radio's independent Romani department produces the weekly hour-long program *O Roma vakheren* ("The Roms Speak"), while Czech Television produces programs for the Romani population in both Romani and Czech languages. As for print media, in 2003 the Czech Ministry of Culture funded three periodicals, the most popular of which is the biweekly *Romano hangos* ("Romani Voice"), with approximately 3 500 subscribers (Open Society Institute 2001a: 160). The other Romani periodicals funded by the Ministry of Culture in that year were the biweekly *Romano voďi* ("Romani Soul") and the monthly *Amaro gendaros* ("Our Mirror") (Vláda České republiky 2004a).[7] The Ministry of Education, Youth and Sports also funds publication of a Romani children's monthly *Kereka* ("Circle"), which is distributed in many primary schools.

Responding to the high proportion of Roms channelled into special education as a result of language barriers and psychological tests not suited to children brought up in a non-Czech cultural environment, Czech authorities established preparatory classes for primary schools in 1993 (Secretariat of the Council for National Minorities of the Government of the Czech Republic 1999: 10). Since their initial implementation, the number of such classes reached 137 with 1,824 children in the 2003-2004 academic year, with the numbers falling to 126 classes and 1,779 children in the 2004-2005 academic year (Vláda České republiky 2004a; 2004c). Additionally, since 1997 the state has certified Romani pedagogical assistants to serve as mediators between schools, children and the children's families in addition to assisting with the teaching of Czech to the mostly Romani-speaking children. By April of 2000, there were 180 Romani pedagogical assistants employed in 114 preparatory classes for 1,425 Romani pupils in nursery schools, primary schools and special schools, with the number of assistants reaching 230 by the end of 2001 (Open Society Institute 2001a: 159; Vláda České republiky 2002).[8] More recently, the Czech government has introduced optional programs on Romani history and culture for use in primary education (Open Society Institute 2001a: 159). At the secondary level, two schools offer instruction in the Romani language, with a private secondary school for Roms in Kolín also receiving funding from the Ministry of Education, Youth and Sports (Council of Europe 1999a: 39). Finally, three post-secondary institutions in the Czech Republic offer degrees in Romani studies as well as instruction in the Romani language, with East Slovak Romani taught at Charles University in Prague (Vláda České republiky 2000; 2004c).

Explaining Differences between Czech and Slovak Republics

To the extent that the exposition in the preceding sections of this chapter has been successful, it should by now be clear that policies and state practices concerning Roms in the Czech Republic have on balance been more productive as

[7] Government funding of *Amaro gendalos* ceased in 2004 (Vláda České republiky 2004c).

[8] As of late 2003, the total number of specially trained teachers and pedagogical assistants was 400 (Vláda České republiky 2004a).

well as more consistent than have their Slovak counterparts. Given that policy toward Roms in Czechoslovakia was largely uniform, the observed Czech-Slovak divergence in such policy over the past fifteen years requires explanation. I here propose to account for these differences in terms of two factors: the Czechoslovak Communist regime's attempt to equalise the distribution of Gypsies throughout the country and differences between post-Communist Czech and Slovak governments' relations with the EU (prior to accession). Whereas most of Slovakia's Romani population survived the Second World War, at the conclusion of hostilities there were fewer than 500 Roms left in the Czech lands (Crowe 1996: 54; 1998: 29; Kenrick and Puxon 1972: 135). In an attempt to move Roms from areas of high concentration and unemployment to areas of low concentration and labour shortage, the Communist regime pursued a policy of dispersal and transfer in the 1960s and 1970s (Davidová 1995: 205; Jurová 1993: 93; Vláda Československé socialistické republiky 1996). Insofar as the dispersal and transfer program tended to draw the most capable Roms out of rural Slovak settlements and into Czech cities, the Czech Republic found itself with a better integrated Romani population at the dissolution of the federal state (Council of Europe 1999a: 7 fn 8; Žáček 1997: 22).

In the aftermath of the Velvet Divorce, the Czech and Slovak Republics took divergent approaches in foreign policy. While Czech governments since 1993 consistently expressed their desire to participate in hitherto West European political and economic structures, the relationship of the Mečiar governments in Slovakia to these structures was less straightforward (see, for example, Commission on Security and Cooperation in Europe 1997; Krivý and Mesežnikov 2001: 58; Wlachovský 1998: 65, 70; cf. Wolchik 1997: 236). In light of the attention given to the treatment of minorities in the EU accession process, from the mid 1990s Czech authorities seem to have found themselves compelled to adopt measures for the integration of Roms which their Slovak counterparts did not have to consider until after the parliamentary elections of 1998 which brought to power an unequivocally pro-Western coalition. Thus, to take a concrete example, whereas the Czech government responded to a wave of asylum applications (mostly to Canada) by Roms in 1997 with the creation of the Inter-ministerial Commission for the Affairs of the Romani Community, the Mečiar government simply ignored larger waves of asylum applications by Roms from Slovakia (European Roma Rights Center 1999: 9; Guy 2001: 300; Open Society Institute 2001a: 128; Sobotka 2001).

Conclusion

In the end, the differences between Czech and Slovak treatments of Roms in the post-Communist period seem to have more to do with the two countries' divergent responses to EU conditionality than with the nature of the European minority rights regime. Moreover, although post-Communist policy and state practice toward Roms have thus far exhibited a degree of consistency in the Czech lands lacking in Slovakia, Roms remain the most disadvantaged population in both republics of the former federation. Finally, to the extent that the conclusion of the EU accession process in the two countries removes pressure on their respective governments to implement measures designed to better the situation of Roms, there is little reason to expect significant improvement in the near future in the absence of a European human rights policy revamped in such a way as to apply not only to EU accession candidates, but also to EU members.

Teaching Human Rights in Europe and its role for minority movements

Claudia Mahler and Anja Mihr and Reetta Toivanen

Introduction

This contribution is based on the interdisciplinary research project "Teaching Human Rights in Europe".[1] The study focuses on human rights education (HRE) during the United Nations' Decade for Human Rights Education and national minorities in six European countries: Armenia, Estonia, Finland, Germany, Slovakia, and Spain. The aim of this research project is to analyse the existing local, national and international legal frameworks of human rights education and for the protection of human rights in general, and to examine the frameworks introduced to protect and foster minority rights and to combat discrimination of minority groups through human rights education in particular. Simultaneously, the aim is to identify governmental, non-governmental and individual actors who have contributed to human rights education in the focus countries. The third research area is in scrutinising how these human rights instruments and institutions contribute and affect the lives of members of national minorities. This involves an assessment of how human rights education programmes and projects reach minorities, and in which ways minority members themselves can contribute to the contents of the programmes. The consequences and impact of human rights education for minorities, and European societies in general, constitute the focal point of this study.[2] In this article, we elaborate ways in which human rights education can provide the necessary tools in order to guarantee equal access to power and non-discriminatory treatment in European societies for the members of national minorities.

In this article, our aim is to introduce efforts by the United Nations (UN) and its sub-organisations to make human rights accessible to everyone regardless of cultural or societal backgrounds. The first part of the article defines human rights education and presents the aim of the Decade for Human Rights Education (1995-2004), proclaimed by the UN General Assembly in 1994. In the second part of this contribution, we consider the issues and target groups of the Decade and examine the UN evaluation of the Decade and other further steps taken by the UN and UNESCO after the Decade. The next part of the paper discusses our own research project and explains why we think focussing on minorities reveals interesting information on the societies in their entirety. Finally, we elaborate on the material we have analysed so far and show some of

[1] This research project is conducted by Dr. Claudia Mahler, lawyer (Centre for Human Rights, University of Potsdam), Dr. Anja Mihr, political scientist, and Dr. Reetta Toivanen, anthropologist (both Department for European Ethnology, Humboldt University of Berlin). The research assignment is financed by Volkswagen Foundation, Germany and will run from 2003 to 2006.

[2] The results of the study will be published in 2007.

the progress and short-comings in the actions undertaken by the European states, which claimed to have given human rights education a high priority in their educational systems in the course of the Decade.

Human rights education -- A priority for all?

Human rights education means that people learn about the human rights which they are entitled to and discover how to use this knowledge. Some authors have divided human rights education into three different interdependent levels. The first level consists of knowledge transfer about legal and universal human rights standards, the second with awareness-raising, and the third level with active empowerment (Müller 2002; Mihr 2004: 5).[3] In these models human rights education is perceived as something that aims at establishing a "culture" where human rights are understood, respected, and defended (Human Security Network 2003: 14-16).[4] The UN organisations have repeatedly stated that it is a priority aim of the UN to educate every single person on the rights they have. The UN has also stressed the importance of paying specific attention to the needs of the most vulnerable groups (i.e. minorities, women and children). Based on Article 26 of the 1948 Universal Declaration of Human Rights (UDHR), the general definition of human rights education aims at strengthening respect for human rights: "It shall promote understanding, tolerance and friendship among all nations, racial or religious groups, and shall further the activities of the United Nations for the maintenance of peace".[5] As outlined by the UDHR, these educational efforts call upon every individual and every institution in the society to promote respect for human rights and to strive for their universal and effective recognition. On the basis of several other human rights conventions, for example in Article 13 of the International Covenant on Economic, Social and Cultural Rights (ICESCR), Article 29 of the Convention of the Rights of the Child (CRC), and in Article 10 of the Convention on the Elimination of all Forms of Racial Discrimination (CERD), human rights education can be seen as a fundamental human right itself (Lohrenscheit 2002; Lehnhart 2003: 89-95).

The call for human rights education was reiterated during the World Conference on Human Rights in 1993 in Vienna where the idea of the world Decade for Human Rights Education was first institutionalised. After this conference, the General Assembly decided to create the post of the United Nations High

[3] Lothar Müller has an interesting categorisation which is based on empirical findings: "explicit HRE", "implicit HRE" and "education with human rights approach" (orig. Menschenrechtliche Erziehung), in Müller 2002: 7-9.

[4] In this publication Shulamith Koenig emphasises especially the goal of evoking critical thinking among people, see p. 15.

[5] Art. 26 of the UDHR adopted and proclaimed by the UN General Assembly Resolution 217 A (III), 10 December, 1948. http://www.unhchr.ch/udhr/lang/eng.htm. For background information see Claude 2005: 38ff.

Commissioner for Human Rights.[6] Mary Robinson was nominated as the first person to hold this position. The High Commissioner was requested to report annually on her activities, in accordance with her mandate, to the Commission on Human Rights and, through the Economic and Social Council (ECOSOC), to the General Assembly. In December 1994, the UN Secretary General proclaimed the UN Decade for Human Rights Education.[7] This proclamation was accepted unanimously by the governments. According to Mary Robinson, the proclamation of the Decade reaffirmed that the education in and of human rights is a human right in itself, the right of all to learn about the rights and dignity of all and about the means to ensure their respect (Robinson 1998). It was stressed that the tasks during the Decade would be first of all the dissemination of information and knowledge about human rights as formulated in the UDHR. Second, the member states and other partners should promote the further development of human rights values and attitudes. Third, the Decade should actively promote and defend human rights wherever and whenever human rights abuses occur. However, the UN Decade had a purely declaratory status: the member states had only been asked to report twice on their fulfilment of the tasks of the Decade before its end in 2004. An International Plan of Action for Human Rights Education was established to guide the governments in fulfilling their responsibility. It defines HRE as training, dissemination and information efforts aimed at building a universal culture of human rights through imparting knowledge and skills, and moulding attitudes (see also Mihr 2005: 190-195). The Council of Europe (CoE) as a regional human rights system in Europe actively took part in the preparation for the Decade. The CoE defines HRE as "educational programmes and activities which focus on promoting equality in human dignity, in conjunction with other programmes such as those promoting intercultural learning, participation and empowerment of minorities" (Council of Europe 2003: 17). It should, however, be noted that the CoE has been focussing more on establishing the rules of law in its member states according to human rights standards and hence pays more attention to "Education for Democratic Citizenship" than on HRE as its primary task (Mahler 2004: 105-117).

During the UN Decade governments, international organisations, national institutions, non-governmental organisations, professional associations, all sectors of civil society and individuals were asked by the UN bodies to establish partnerships and to concentrate their efforts on promoting a universal culture of human rights through human rights education. General guiding principles of the Decade included a comprehensive approach to human rights education, including civil, cultural, economic, political and social rights and recognising the indi-

[6] UN Resolution 48/141, 20 December, 1993.

[7] UN Document: General Assembly A/51/506/Add.1, 12 December, 1994; UN Resolution, Decade for Human Rights Education, UN Doc A/RES/49/184, 23 December, 1994.

visibility and interdependence of all rights. The International Plan of Action for the UN Decade for HRE outlined objectives for the international community. These objectives included an assessment of needs and formulation of effective strategies; the building and strengthening of programmes and capacities for human rights education at the international, regional, national and local levels; the co-ordinated development of effective materials; the strengthening of the role and capacity of the mass media; and the global dissemination of the Universal Declaration of Human Rights.

The UN evaluation of the Decade for HRE

The Office of the UN High Commissioner for Human Rights (OHCHR) had been responsible for co-ordinating all UN education and public information programmes in the field of Human Rights Education.[8] In 1998, Mary Robinson, pronounced that HRE was her highest priority because she believes in the fundamental role of HRE in empowering individuals to defend their rights and those of others. "This empowerment can also make a critical contribution to the prevention of human rights violations", she emphasised (Robinson 1998: iii). The Decade was conceptualised as an instrument which would provide a common framework to develop HRE. During the Decade, the comprehensive, effective and sustainable educational programmes at the local, national, regional and international levels should be developed and strengthened (Lehnhart 2003: 89-95). In order to co-ordinate the common goal, the OHCHR published "Guidelines for National Plans of Action for Human Rights Education". Thus, the OHCHR in Geneva was the institution which was asked to monitor and follow the progress of the UN Decade. The personnel of the OHCHR was aware that it would not be enough to motivate the states to meet the unanimously agreed upon engagement, it would have to encourage civil society and NGOs to call upon the state representatives in order to guarantee broader support for the Decade. However, the OHCHR did not establish any formal reporting obligation and monitoring mechanism for assessing the compliance of states in their undertakings to implement the UN Decade for HRE. This was nothing special as UN Decades in general have an open character.[9]

Other international organisations with experience in the field of education and human rights such as UNESCO[10] were called upon to co-operate closely with the OHCHR in the implementation of the HRE Action Plan. In 1997 UNESCO organised the first regional conference together with the Finnish Na-

[8] UN General Assembly Resolution 48/141, 20 December, 1993.

[9] UN Decades are designed to draw attention to issues of global significance and encourage co-operation and international action, see http://portal.unesco.org/education/en/ev.php-URL_ID=33167&URL_DO=DO_TOPIC&URL_SECTION=201.html, Visited on 6 September, 2005.

[10] United Nations Educational, Scientific and Cultural Organisation.

tional Commission for UNESCO and the Institute for Human Rights at Åbo Akademi University. Four other regional conferences were held in different parts of the world between 1997 and 2001.[11] The purpose of the meetings was to identify the regional needs in the field of HRE. For the European region, the conference drew the conclusion that even though only a few European countries had developed a national plan of action for human rights education, a vast amount of work had been done, especially at the level of regional and intergovernmental organisations as well as by non-governmental organisations (Spiliopoulou Åkermark 1998: V).

In the year 2000, the UN together with UNESCO commissioned a mid-term evaluation of the progress of the UN Decade for HRE.[12] In her report, Mary Robinson stated that the willingness of the states to provide any information had been weak and thus the report was to be seen as a more general description of the status of the HRE globally. The evaluation revealed that in fact very little had been done in Europe or elsewhere. Only 12 of the more than 200 member states and individual governmental representatives had reported to the OHCHR in Geneva about their efforts to promote or implement the Decade in their countries. In Spain, for example, only human rights NGOs and foundations reported to the OHCHR. For example, the UNESCO Chair on Peace and Human Rights at the Autonomous University in Barcelona reported in 2000 that research and teaching in human rights were conducted during the period of the UN Decade. This, however, was only available for a limited number of students (OHCHR 2000a). In Estonia, the Ministry of Education reported that human rights education was fully incorporated into the school curricula starting at the pre-school level and "we do not see any obstacles for human rights education in Estonia. The human rights education is a natural part of the curriculum" (OHCHR 2000b). However, no National Action Plan was adopted, and in practice human rights education in Estonia actually means for most teachers citizenship education.

When the Decade ended in 2004 major shortcomings were identified by the UN Office for the High Commissioner for Human Rights.[13] There was little political will but also reluctance and insecurity on what human rights education really means and how one should implement it (Müller 1999; Rosemann 2002). In 2004, only 24 countries had established a National Action Plan for human rights education. Simultaneously very few governments had implemented hu-

[11] For Africa in December 1998 in Dakar, Senegal, for Asia and the Pacific in November, 1998 in Pune, India, for the Arab region in Morocco in February, 1998 and for Latin America and the Caribbean in Mexico November / December, 2001.

[12] UN Document: A/55/360, 7 September, 2000.

[13] For report see UN Press Release GA/ 1037, 10 December, 2004 and UN Document E/CN.4/2003/100, 3 January, 2003. For the Follow up study by the High Commissioner see UN Document E/CN.4/2003/101, 28 February, 2003.

man rights education into their national school curricula (UN Press Release GA/10317, 10 December 2004). Finland, for example, included human rights education in the curricula as a basic value. This means that every teacher in every subject should include human rights education in his or her teaching (Finnish National Board of Education 2004a: 12; Finnish National Board of Education 2004b: 12.). Similarly, in Estonia, human rights are not taught as a separate subject but every teacher should be able to teach human rights. Both countries have the same problems. Most teachers are not trained to include human rights in their teaching and there are no monitoring mechanisms to control what the teachers really practice. This lack of monitoring was also criticised by the UN Committee of the Rights of the Child in its recent concluding observations on Finland (CRC 2005: para. 44, 45).

In March 2004, the Organisation for Security and Co-operation in Europe (OSCE) organised a supplementary meeting on HRE in Vienna. The objective of the meeting was to consolidate ongoing efforts to promote human rights education and training in the OSCE region. The participants shared best practices and discussed persisting difficulties that undermine initiatives in the field of HRE. The OSCE recommendation at the end of the meeting stressed that members of vulnerable groups such as Roma and Sinti, migrants, refugees, and asylum-seekers should receive equal access to education (and this means also to human rights education). Moreover, the OSCE participating states should give more attention to the specific needs of minority communities as part and parcel of the promotion of common international values and standards (OSCE 2004: 5). However, the critical conclusion by the participants was that the objectives of the Decade had remained rather far away from priorities of the 55 OSCE states' politics throughout Europe and North-America (OSCE 2004, 1). It was also discussed whether the Decade should be followed by a second decade, as for example lobbied by the Armenian NGO Armenian Constitutional Rights Protective Centre and by the delegates from Costa Rica at the meeting.

Instead, the idea of a second decade for human rights education was replaced with a follow-up procedure. The resolution by the UN Commission on Human Rights which was called "Follow-up to the United Nations Decade on Human Rights Education" was adopted on the 21 April, 2004.[14] The document states that the UN Commission on Human Rights takes note of the reports which explain about the achievements and shortcomings of the Decade as well as suggestions for its follow up. Consequently, it admits the need to continue a global framework for human rights education.

[14] UN Resolution 204/71, 21 April, 2004.

The World Programme for Human Rights Education

Even though there were several efforts to continue the first Decade with another Decade[15], experts agreed that a Decade at that time might not be the best way of enhancing HRE. In April 2004, the Human Rights Commission of the UN Economic and Social Council (ECOSOC) proclaimed a World Programme for Human Rights Education that was supposed to start in January 2005. The UN General Assembly had adopted the revised Draft Plan of Action[16] in its resolution on the World Programme for Human Rights Education.[17] Nevertheless since 2005, neither the UN High Commissioner's Office in Geneva and New York nor the UNESCO Commission for Education has been able to secure more resources for their work than they had during the UN Decade for HRE.

The first phase of the World Programme (2005-2007) will focus on the primary and secondary school systems and the implementation of human rights education. The goal of the action is not only to try to transmit pure knowledge-based content on human rights but also to promote respect for human rights in the teaching environment itself, with a variety of methodologies. The definition of human rights education is almost the same as for the Decade for Human Rights Education.[18] The World Programme is somewhat more concrete than the proclamation of the UN Decade. It aims to get more support by governments and civil society movements. National minorities are mentioned also in this document as a special target group.

Minorities and human rights

Every society consists of different religious, cultural, ethnic and national groups: All societies are heterogeneous. Various documents and declarations by the United Nations and Council of Europe define national and ethnic minority groups as the most vulnerable groups (together with women and children) which need special attention in any political system. This wording was also used in the documents of the UN Decade for Human Rights Education. For the purposes of our research, we decided to focus only on national minorities. In contrast to the so-called ethnic or immigrant minorities, national minorities are expected to be autochthonous to the territories of the states in which they reside, they have the citizenship of the state and enjoy in most cases a specific legal protection. We chose for our research project only countries which had ratified the Framework Convention on National Minorities of the Council of Europe. This gave a clear

[15] In August 2003 the Commission for Human Rights recommended to the Economic and Social Council that it recommends to the General Assembly the proclamation of a second decade to begin in 2005, E/CN.4/2003/C.14, 7 August, 2003. Next April, the same Commission recommended the World Programme to be adopted, see E/CN.4/2004/L.109, 15 April, 2004.

[16] A/59/525.Rev.1, 2 March 2005.

[17] A/RES/59/113b, 5 August 2005.

[18] UN Doc. A/59/525/Rev.1, p. 3, 2 March, 2005.

similarity as a starting point for the legal and policy analysis in Armenia, Estonia, Finland, Germany, Slovakia and Spain. We assumed that if any minority enjoyed a special status in human rights educational programmes and projects, then it would be the national minority groups, which are protected under international and national law.

The question that needs some further elaboration here is who actually forms a national minority group? We refer to treaties and documents by the UN and especially by the Council of Europe which use the concept of national minority (Toivanen 2005: 185-193). Lacking, however, is an international-legal definition of the term 'minority'. Consequently, many different approaches to defining minorities exist, depending on the political will and specific legal framework of a particular state. One of the best-known efforts at a legal definition on minorities is that of Francesco Capotorti, included in his study for the UN Sub-commission on Prevention of Discrimination and Protection of Minorities in 1979. He defines minorities as "(…) a group numerically inferior to the rest of the population of a state, in a non-dominant position, whose members being nationals of the state and possess ethnic, religious, or linguistic characteristics that differ from those of the rest of the population and show, if only implicitly, a sense of solidarity, directed towards preserving their culture traditions, religion, or language" (Capotorti 1979).

Minority rights are an essential part of general human rights, or in other terms, the universal catalogue of human rights includes the promotion and protection of minority rights. In the UN system, the key specific clause stating this is Article 27 of the International Covenant of Civil and Political Rights (UN ICCPR 1966). According to this article (and Capotorti's definition) minorities shall enjoy their culture without the fear of assimilation to the culture of the majority. It says: "In those States in which ethnic, religious or linguistic minorities exist, persons belonging to such minorities shall not be denied the right, in community with the other members of their group, to enjoy their own culture, to profess and practice their own religion, or to use their own language." This article is wide in its scope and addresses the majority populations as well the minority populations, placing responsibility for the protection of minorities in the hands of the state authorities.[19]

One can also find some special treaties on the protection of minorities which are particularly relevant for any research dealing with national minorities such as Roma, Basques, Frisians, Sorbs, Russian-speakers etc. at the level of the European regional human rights regime. The 1949 European Convention on Human

[19] In December, 1992 the UN General Assembly adopted a Declaration which sets international standards for the rights of national, ethnic, religious and linguistic minorities. Until today it has not reached the status of being legally binding treaty. See Declaration on the Rights of Persons Belonging to National or Ethnic, Religious and Linguistic Minorities, GA. Res. 47/135, 18 December, 1992.

Rights only includes a non-discrimination clause. The state parties to the convention were not able to agree on a special protocol on minority rights. Instead of a protocol, the Council of Europe drafted the Charter on Regional and Minority Languages in 1992 (Council of Europe 1992) and three years later the Framework Convention on National Minorities in 1995 (Council of Europe 1995). The European Union (EU) started its own human rights policy after the treaty of Maastricht and tried to implement minority rights and other human rights standards for the new member states during the accession process in the 1990s which cumulated in the accession of ten new EU member states in 2004. Human rights and minority rights were included in the political chapter of the Copenhagen Criteria in 1993, which the candidate countries had to fulfil to qualify as members of the EU (Mahler and Toivanen 2004). Recently, the protection of minority rights was even added in the draft of the European Union Constitutional Treaty (EU 2004).[20]

In order to fulfil international legal commitments, it is not sufficient for a state just to guarantee protection by law for the minorities inhabiting its territory, as the above mentioned conventions require that states offer active support and measures for their minority members (Weiß 2004). These efforts should also include HRE programmes and projects to empower and enable minority group members to become aware of their human rights and to realise these rights, for example in the area of housing, language courses, political participation rights and the right to work.

In Europe minority issues gathered more attention in international political discourses after the conflict in Yugoslavia and the founding of new CIS countries of the former Soviet Union since the beginning of the 1990s. This is one reason why minority rights have gained a stronger legal focus. There is an ongoing discussion on whether minority rights are integrated in the general concept of human rights or whether they constitute an added value. Some see minority rights as added human rights for specific groups (Eide 1998). In our view, the protection of human rights is applicable for every person without any distinction: Minority rights – whether ethnic, linguistic, sexual or other – attempt to protect the specific quality of the members of a particular group. In principle, these specific rights are not privileges, but rather aim to grant members of minorities in different status positions the opportunity to attain the same living conditions as other groups of society (Scheinin 2003: 487; Strauß 2002: 375).

There are some special groups in every society which need protection and additional support to have the same opportunities as the majority. As a member of minority group, one can make an effective rights-based argument for equality and recognition only if one knows about human rights. At the same time it is equally essential that the majority population knows and understands the special

[20] However, today there is uncertainty if it will ever come into force.

needs of the minority members. A crucial question is therefore whether human rights education for minorities differs from human rights education for majorities. The answer has to be both "yes" and "no": "Yes" because any human rights education course or project must be adjusted in content as well as form to the needs of the target group, but "no" insofar as the goals of human rights education (aimed towards equality, mutual respect and active participation for human rights) remain the same regardless of the target group.

Why focus on human rights education on and for minorities?
The overall goal of HRE is to educate members of the entire society to respect one another - including minorities. This is the basis for any anti-bias, peace, tolerance or anti-discrimination education, and it sets the grounds for a culture of human rights as outlined in the UDHR. Hence, one of the core elements of human rights education is to refer specifically to human rights standards. It is based on the assumptions that if people are not able to state precisely their own human rights and those of others, they will be able neither to claim human rights nor to fight for them (Mihr 2004: 8-10).

It would certainly be challenging enough to contribute to the assessment of the HRE programmes in general at the end of the UN Decade. Our interest, however, was to concentrate specifically on the study of national minorities. We were convinced that by looking at the situation of the persons who are defined in many of the previously mentioned documents as the vulnerable persons in European societies (national minorities), we would gain a better overview of the general situation of human rights in the given context. In this respect minorities and human rights education can be approached from two, complementary perspectives: first, education for minorities about human rights in general and minority rights in particular, and second, education for majorities about human and minority rights. Our research project strives for a holistic approach in which education about minorities and education for minorities are both vitally important. The third aim has been to examine how the development of self-identification and empowerment of minority groups have been informed by the HRE programmes.

The duties held by individual states vis-à-vis their own minorities and collectively by the international community of states are in some cases positive, such as in providing services like education. In other cases the obligations aim to combat negative effects of a minority status for example by protecting members of minorities from discrimination and disadvantages in the job market or housing. Adopting the human rights-based approach opens the door for the use of a rich and growing pool of information, analysis, jurisprudence and empowerment developed in recent years by treaty bodies and other human rights specialists and agencies. The transformation of these human rights norms and entitlements to human rights education for minorities can take many different forms. It can mean for example empowering members of minority groups to know and use their human rights and simultaneously training majority members to know that minorities enjoy the same universal human rights. One way of living together without discrimination is to enable political participation of minority members, respecting and allowing the use of the language of minorities and recognising the history as well as religious and cultural particularity of minorities. In addition, specific economic aid and support in accessing education in the formal and non-formal sector are in some cases a necessity in promoting equal treatment.

Human rights education can thus empower minority groups and their community to seek equality with other groups of society. It can also support the fostering of equality between the minority members in their own community. This is the case, for example, if some underprivileged persons belonging to a minority such as the Roma in Slovakia, with the help of human rights education, develop more self-esteem and begin demanding more economic or educational freedoms within their community.

During the UN Decade for Human Rights Education, very few state authorities became convinced that it is for the benefit of the society as a whole to implement minority issues in human rights education, particularly in the formal education sector. In Armenia a revision of all school books took place in 2001 and new school books were published. According to the plan, pupils in the formal education sector receive one hour per week education on human and civic rights. One of the chapters of the school book deals with the situation and problems of the Yezidi community in Armenia as a national minority (Khazinyan et al 2001). Although this can be considered as a major effort for implementing minority rights in the formal education sector, it should be noted that this approach can only be considered as a start, since most children of the Yezidi community never finish the eighth grade in school. Other programmes and methods will be necessary if the specific problems faced by Yezidi community are to be taken seriously in the Armenian context.[21] Very similar criticism can be raised against all the research countries.[22]

Main actors of human rights education with minorities

State authorities such as governmental representatives, local school authorities and cultural institutions are formally responsible for protecting and promoting

[21] In 2005 the Armenian government published a special school book for 1st and 2nd grade for Yezidi children. Yezidis are the biggest and most underprivileged minority of the country. The authors were two elderly political and spiritual leaders of the Yezidi community, who considered teaching on "Yezidi war heros" in the book to be essential. The lack of cooperation with human rights groups lead to the fact that such a book for Yezidi children was distributed as a human rights educational publication (Ministry of Education of Armenia, Tamoyan et al (Eds.), 2005).

[22] Likewise one has to emphasise that most of these school book reforms come through external pressure.

the human rights of minorities. This means that those governments and their agents who have ratified and signed international declarations and treaties for the protection and promotion of minorities are accountable for fulfilling such obligations. Our research showed that many government representatives simply think that it is enough when various NGOs are active in the field of human rights education and see it as the task of the NGOs to fulfil these governmental obligations. In all European states NGOs publish HRE material because they get financial grants and support from the EU, the CoE or from other international organisations. It also became obvious that governments were driven to undertake changes in the educational field because of pressure from international organisations. For example it is correct to state that the school book reforms as well as other educational reforms were carried out in post-Soviet Armenia because the country wanted to become a member of the Council of Europe in 2001 (Mihr, Mkrtichyan, Mahler, Toivanen (eds) 2005).

The low priority placed on promoting human rights and the rights of the most vulnerable in all of the countries included in our study has had tangible consequences for non-state actors' potential to act. The EU generally only finances programmes, projects or NGOs which work together with the state apparatus, with the support in most cases redirected by state authorities. Smaller NGOs have difficulties in accessing the governmental funding for their HRE work. Also, minority organisations which are critical of state policies sometimes fall completely outside of EU or UN supporting structures because governments ultimately decide which groups are eligible for funding. For example, in Estonia, where the government has defined the Russian-speakers as posing the biggest challenge for integration in Estonian society, the very small Roma organisations are constantly struggling for the recognition of their agenda in the state funding structures (Wilson 2002: 18-33; Toivanen 2006).

It is also true that minority groups often have very little of their own financial resources, such that they often lack the basic funding necessary to allow them to apply for large projects. As a result, minorities can easily become dependent on other bigger organisations or foundations such as the US-based Soros or Ford Foundations in Eastern Europe. Throughout Europe we find many short-term projects that are financed and granted by the EU or the Council of Europe. Other NGOs which are successful with their applications easily get fully or semi-professionalised in applying for funds without necessarily having a focus in HRE. It is also an assent that someone in the applying organisation has good English skills in order to be able to write good funding proposals for international donors and foundations. In this matter, representatives of underprivileged minority groups have often the problem that they lack the needed language skills.

Hence, smaller NGOs will need to cooperate with bigger NGOs and foundations in order to be included in the international support structures, but may also end up paying a high price for this inclusion in terms of defining the contents of the HRE programmes. There are other concerns to be taken into consideration, for instance difficult topics such as "oppression of minority groups", "denial of minority language policy" or "schooling policy for minorities". These may be avoided by NGOs in order to create consensus among applicants. Our research further revealed the presence of old and unpredictable connections between different actors in one country which may cause conflicts among the people sitting in the ministries and representatives of NGOs. It was also interesting to note that in countries such as Armenia or Estonia many people initiate their own NGO for the purposes of a single project application, creating a new organisation for the next application. On the other hand, in countries such as Finland or Slovakia, some representatives changed the roles back and forth, in the first instance, they are representing the NGO sector and then, later, the same people are representatives of some national ministry.

Teaching human rights – not the first priority

The question was posed in the beginning of this paper whether human rights education can provide the necessary tools in order to guarantee equal access to power and non-discriminatory treatment in European societies for the members of national minorities. We are convinced that in order to foster equality and participatory parity among minority groups and majorities in the European context, a specific minority rights system is necessary. This system of minority protection exists in Europe, but it remains on the one hand exclusive and elitist as long as the minority population does not know about and learn to use it, and on the other hand toothless as long as the majority population does not know about, recognise and respect it. This is why minority rights must be taught as pat of any successful human rights education programme. Many other questions still remain to be answered in the course of the research, one of the alarming ones being why human rights education and especially human rights education on and for minorities tends to be ignored by governments?

According to our interviews, media-analysis data, and other analyses, the UN Decade for HRE did not have significant impact in empowering national minorities in Armenia, Finland, Estonia, Germany, Spain or Slovakia. At the same time other processes of internationalisation of human rights standards through globalisation - as a side-effect - supported the empowerment of some minority groups, for instance increasing access to information about human rights standards and the situation of other minority groups elsewhere via the internet. In the course of the research it became apparent that there are varied and even unlikely HRE programmes for minorities: some of them have the aim of maintenance of peace, some aim at ensuring societal richness while others pursue the control or domination of minority members.[23] Some projects are launched because of the internal need to bridge social differences and inequalities while others come in to being only due to international pressure. This pressure can come from internationally active NGOs, intervention by another state's government or from international organisations such as the UN or the OSCE, for instance, for security reasons. There are also HRE projects that are based on academic research showing the lack of equality and participatory parity. This diversity of projects and actors has posed one of the biggest challenges for this research project: How can we select only those actors and programmes which are truly devoted to HRE?

It is always easy to raise criticism towards governments and towards international organisations of not fulfilling their obligations, but without NGOs and other actors in civil society – including but not limited to minority representatives – the necessary means for HRE can never be utilised effectively. We shall mention here only a few factors that have contributed to the weakness of the action during the UN Decade. First, there has been a lack of cooperation between different actors, for example the UN, Council of Europe, OSCE, governments, local authorities and NGOs promoting HRE in each country. This lack of cooperation has led on one side to contradictory support for certain issues and certain groups. On the other side, important human rights issues have received much attention, such as the right to work or the right to citizenship for members of minority groups in Spain. In the best cases the intergovernmental organisations such as the Council of Europe, European Union and the UN work together with other international organisations and funding sources such as the British Council or Soros Foundation, embassies, ministries and international NGOs. But even then there has been a tendency to support rather short-term projects, the longer-term impact of which is doubtful.

It is generally known that all projects have a beginning and an end, but the substance and meaningfulness of the HRE projects suffer under this short-term 'easy come, easy go' philosophy. We could often observe how the resources that were directed to certain issues came and suddenly vanished again. It has been very difficult to get financial support for what the Decade was actually calling for: the mainstreaming of human rights in the formal, informal and non-formal education sectors and for every single person. This should have included the reflection of minority rights in the general school curricula as well as specific HRE programmes for minority groups, but has been treated as a priority by the majority of UN member states and the European countries mentioned in this research project.

[23] This domination can be 'well-intended'; when a national NGO takes the opportunity to receive international finances i.e. for Roma participation projects, it may take the money but end up realising the project without any Roma consultation and participation.

Human rights education may be "misused" for citizenship education purposes which sometimes means to "obey" the state constitution regardless of whether the constitution and the national laws derived from it conform fully to human rights standards. Consequently, the most problematic issue, especially when doing research with national minorities, is that HRE is often interpreted as a means to produce loyal citizens contributing to a common goal in the societies they live in. But the challenging question remains "what is the purpose of human rights education?" As Katarina Tomasevski, the former independent UN Special Rapporteur on the Right to Education of the UN Commission on Human Rights answered, for many governments, this is "to produce useful citizens" (Tomasevski 2001; 2003). She poses in several of her critical reports the on-going question which still remains to be answered: Useful to whom?[24] The answer should, in our opinion, not be "to governments only", regardless of whether they respect human and minority rights as it was once intended by the UDHR. A will for human rights education is an asset for the on-going development of democratisation even in European societies.

[24] Her reports can be found under http://www.ohchr.org/english/issues/eduction/rapporteur/annual.htm, visited on 21 March, 2006.

CHAPTER IV

THE EU'S EXTERNAL RELATIONS AND HUMAN RIGHTS

EU External Relations and Human Rights[1]

Wolfgang S. Heinz

Since the beginning of the 90s, the European Union has developed first slowly, then more energetically an impressive framework for defining its international policy goals, especially in the area of external and development policies. For the outsider, the special mix of EU institutions, EU member states' interests and the wealth of documents produced are not easy to keep track of, let alone understand decision-making processes.

The purpose of this contribution is modest: it is to give a brief overview of major processes and potential weaknesses of EU human rights policy-making that have to be eliminated in order to make way for a consistent, coherent and effective human rights policy. This should be of some importance given the gap of credibility between EU institutions and policies in quite a number of EU member countries (recall only the failed plebiscites on the European constitution in France and the Netherlands). However, the focus of this contribution will be on explaining processes and activities, rather than presenting golden bullets that appear to solve problems.

In the first two sections I offer a brief introduction into relevant EU institutions and decision-making as well as major recent political decision-making. In sections three I address Common Foreign and Security Policy issues (CFSP) and Development Cooperation, the two arenas where most of the work on the promotion of human rights is being undertaken (election observation and assistance, however, cannot be addressed here). Finally, I present a number of critical evaluative remarks.

EU Institutions and decision-making

On the EU-level, there are many different players and institutions that influence the area of human rights. For a long time, the EU has not succeeded in creating lead institutions with a clear human rights mandate.

[1] I am grateful to Nursemin Sönmez, intern at the German Institute for Human Rights, for research assistance.

The Commission and the Council of the European Union lay down the political guidelines on human rights and control their implementation. In the Council, the working group on human rights, COHOM, coordinates EU policies. The Directorate-General for External Relations is responsible for human rights in its field. Its section on human rights is responsible for human rights questions worldwide and for coordination within the Commission. The Directorate-General for Development is responsible for the cooperation with the ACP States (Cotonou Treaty, see below). Other directorates-generals that deal with external relations are the External Trade, European Neighbourhood Policy and Enlargement.

The European Parliament, especially the Committee on Citizens' Freedoms and Rights, Justice and Home Affairs and the Petition Committee, the European Court of Justice (ECJ) and the European Ombudsman are monitoring the respect for human rights at the EU level (In the near future, a EU human rights agency will be created). They have a special responsibility to control of the executive. In the area of foreign relations, the parliament must agree to international treaties, e.g. accession of new member countries and association treaties with third countries. In these cases, the parliament can introduce human rights concerns. Institutionally, a sub-committee on human rights to the EP committee on foreign affairs has been created (DROI)[2].

In article 6 (2) of the Treaty of the European Union (Amsterdam Treaty) of 1997 (TEU) the jurisdiction of the European Court of Justice was extended to the observance of human rights "with regard to action of the institutions, insofar as the Court has jurisdiction under the Treaties establishing the European Communities and under this Treaty". What does this cover precisely? It would certainly include the rights and freedoms of the European Convention on Human Rights, though the Additional Protocols to the Convention have not been ratified by all EU member states. The same is true of the European Social Charter of 1961 and especially of the Revised European Social Charter of 1996, which has received only a limited number of ratifications from Council of Europe member states. Consequently, the protection of economic and social rights is much weaker than the protection of civil and political rights. Ratification of the two Council of Europe instruments on minorities is even more limited (The European Charter for Regional and Minority Languages of 1992 and the European Framework Convention for the Protection of National Minorities of 1995).

[2] http://www.europarl.eu.int/committees/droi_home.htm.

The place of human rights in EU political and legal documents – A brief overview

Box 1: Development of EU Human Rights' Policy[3]

- 1977: Joint declaration of the European Council, Parliament and the Commission in which the Community declared its protection of human rights
- 1978: Declaration on democracy
- 1986: Joint declaration against racism and xenophobia
- 1986: Joint declaration on human rights by the foreign ministers of the twelve member countries
- 1989: Declaration by the European Parliament on founding rights and fundamental freedoms of the European Parliament
- 1993: Treaty of the European Union comes into force, Article F (EUT Maastricht)
- 2000: Passing of the EU Charter on Fundamental Rights
- 2001: Commission Communication on the EU's Role in Promoting Human Rights and Democratisation in Third Countries (No. 252 final)
- 2004: Review of the implementation of Commission Communication No. 252

The Treaty of Amsterdam, which came into force on 1 May 1999, marked a significant step forward in integrating human rights into the legal order of the European Union. This treaty inserts article 6, a new article reaffirming that the European Union "is founded on the principles of liberty, democracy, respect for human rights and fundamental freedoms, and the rule of law, principles which are common to the Member States". Member states violating these principles in a "serious and persistent" way run the risk of having their rights deriving from the application of the Union Treaty suspended[4]. The Treaty of Amsterdam also brought to the "First Pillar," a general clause on combating discrimination, a provision on measures concerning asylum, refugees and immigration and certain competences in the field of employment, working conditions and social protection.

[3] According to Lippert 1995:263, supplemented by the author.

[4] Art 7 states: (2) The Council, meeting in the composition of the Heads of State or Government and acting by unanimity on a proposal by one third of the Member States or by the Commission and after obtaining the assent of the European Parliament, may determine the existence of a serious and persistent breach by a Member State of principles mentioned in Article 6(1), after inviting the government of the Member State in question to submit its observations.
(3) Where a determination under paragraph 2 has been made, the Council, acting by a qualified majority, may decide to suspend certain of the rights deriving from the application of this Treaty to the Member State in question, including the voting rights of the representative of the government of that Member State in the Council. In doing so, the Council shall take into account the possible consequences of such a suspension on the rights and obligations of natural and legal persons." (http://europa.eu.int/eurlex/lex/en/treaties/dat/12002M/htm/C_2002325EN.000501.html).

The Commission's action in the field of external relations will be guided by compliance with the rights and principles contained in the EU Charter of Fundamental Rights that was officially proclaimed at the Nice Summit in December 2000 for its promotion of coherence between the EU's internal and external approaches. The Charter makes the overriding importance and relevance of fundamental rights more visible to the EU's citizens by codifying material from various sources of inspiration, such as the European Convention on Human Rights, common constitutional traditions, and international instruments[5].
Today, the EU sets out its human rights goals as follows:

> The European Union respects and promotes the universal principles as laid down in the UN Universal Declaration on Human Rights and its complementary International Covenant on Civil and Political Rights and International Covenant on Economic, Social and Cultural Rights. The Union's activities are also based on the main international and regional instruments for the protection of human rights, including the European Convention on Human Rights. These instruments enshrine common values regarding fundamental freedoms and democratic principles, which are universal, indivisible and interdependent. Respect for these values is a condition for efficient development in any society. Other important sources with regard to defining the priorities of the EU are the declaration and the programme of action of the World Conference on Human Rights (Vienna, 1993), the declarations of the International Conference on Population and Development (Cairo, 1994), of the World Summit for Social Development (Copenhagen, 1995) and of the Fourth World Conference on Women (Beijing 1995)[6].

Regarding the relative balance between civil and political rights as opposed to economic, social and cultural rights -, there is a clear priority on the former in official policies and practical activities[7]. However, some activities have been developed to strengthen core labour standards and the Generalised System of Preferences[8].

[5] http://europa.eu.int/comm/justice_home/unit/charte/index_en.html. Generally, on human rights in foreign policy see Schmidt 1999, Clapham 1999, Alston 1999, Aschenbrenner 2000, Brimmer 2002, Lerch 2004, Williams 2004, on development policies cf. Simma et al. 1999, Pippan 2002, Windmeißer 2002, Fierro 2003, and Heinz 2003, 2004.
[6] http://europa.eu.int/comm/external_relations/human_rights/intro/.
[7] See Windmeisser 2002 on EU development policies.
[8] Cf. EU 2001b, EU 2004b:8f.

Commission Communications on Human Rights

In order to present a framework for all European Union activities in the area of human rights, the Commission, since 1995, has issued a series of communications to the Council and the Parliament. Strategies aimed at enhancing the consistency and effectiveness of the human rights and democratisation approach of the European Union are set up.

A key communication by the Commission on the EU Role in Promoting Human Rights & Democratisation in Third Countries (May 2001) concentrated mainly on developing a coherent strategy in this field for EU external assistance. Rather than seeking to rewrite the fundamental policy, the Commission aims to set this policy in the context of its overall strategic approach to external relations for the coming years. The document takes into account recent developments in the legal and political framework for the EU activities including the Amsterdam and Nice Treaties and the Charter of Fundamental Rights, which foresees in particular more coherence between the EU internal and external approaches to human rights.

Human Rights guidelines

The EU has developed guidelines on
- The Death Penalty (1998)[9]
- Torture and other cruel, inhuman or degrading treatment (2001)[10]
- Human Rights dialogues with third countries (2001)[11]
- Children in armed conflict (2003)[12]
- Protection of Human Rights defenders (2004)[13]

The instruments engaged are political dialogue, petitions to the government concerned (démarche), and bi- and multilateral cooperation. A trade regulation, moreover, is now being developed for equipment that could be employed for torture or for other humiliating treatment or punishment - including the implementation of the death penalty.

In 2004, in a comprehensive effort, the Council evaluated the implementation of EU guidelines on the prevention of torture. COHOM studied guidelines on children and armed conflict, on the death penalty, as well as human rights dialogues and issued recommendations for follow up measures[14].

[9] Cf. EU 2002a:245ff.
[10] Cf. EU 2002a: 249ff.
[11] Cf. EU 2002a: 257ff.
[12] http://europa.eu.int/comm/external_relations/human_rights/child/caafguidelines.pdf.
[13] http://ue.eu.int/uedocs/cmsUpload/GuidelinesDefenders.pdf.
[14] Draft Council Conclusions on the implementation of EU human rights policy, 23.11.2004, http://register.consilium.eu.int/pdf/en/04/st15/st15817-re02.en04.pdf.

EU External Relations:
Common Foreign and Security Policy (CFSP)
The EU describes its foreign and security policy goals as follows:
"Created with the entry into force of the Treaty on European Union (EU Treaty) in 1993, Title V replaced EPC with an intergovernmental pillar in the Community structure. Article 11 sets out its five main principles:

- To safeguard the common values and fundamental interests of the Union;
- To strengthen the security of the Union;
- To preserve peace and strengthen international security;
- To promote international co-operation;
- To develop democracy and the rule of law, including human rights.

The CFSP is also mentioned in Article 2 of the common provisions of the EU Treaty, which stipulates that one of the Union's objectives is 'to assert its identity on the international scene, in particular through the implementation of a common foreign and security policy including the progressive framing of a common defence policy, which might lead to a common defence…"[15].

Guidelines, common strategies, common actions and standpoints are the most important instruments of the CFSP (Art. 12 TEU).

Common strategies define goals and seek to establish better coherence between EU policy areas. They are decided by the European Council and implemented in areas in where EU member states pursue important common interests. The Commission formulates its recommendations on the strategies. Three strategies have been adopted so far on Russia, Ukraine and the Mediterranean[16]. Before, during and after the war in Iraq, problems of *common* CFSP have become very evident. France, German and Belgium took positions against the war; Great Britain, Spain and Poland actively supported the war, although Spain changed its position after a new government was elected. Both the EU member states and candidate members were unable to adopt a common position regarding the question of participation in the Iraq war. Apart from the issue of the alleged possession of weapons of mass destruction, the war in Iraq posed important questions with human rights and humanitarian aspects

Instruments of EU human rights policy
Essential instruments of the EU human rights policy are[17]:

- Confidential and public assessment of the human rights situation in a third country
- Political dialogue

[15] http://europa.eu.int/scadplus/leg/en/lvb/r00001.htm.
[16] http://europa.eu.int/scadplus/leg/de/lvb/r10112.htm.
[17] Cf. Tannous 2002:293.

- Human rights and democracy clauses in agreements with third parties
- Delay, suspension and abandonment of contractual commitments and agreements
- Coordinated procedure of the EU States in international organisations
- Imposition of economic sanctions (Art. 301 EUT)
- Human rights dialogues

Only a few of these instruments can be briefly addressed in the following sections.

Human Rights clauses in EU treaties with third countries

Even before 1995 the European Community had included in more than 30 agreements respect for human rights in the EC member states, ACP cooperation States and other countries - nevertheless using different formulations.

In the treaties with the Andean Pact and Brazil, for example, human rights were referred to as an essential element of cooperation, whereas cooperation with Argentina, Chile, Macao, Mongolia, Paraguay and Uruguay was agreed upon on the basis of respect for democracy and human rights that should inspire the domestic and international policy of the contracting partner. In the treaties with 13 Arab States, however, there was only a reference to respect for the United Nations Charter.

In 1995, the European Council decided to include a human rights' clause in all agreements with third States. In doing so, it was distinguished among countries, e.g. whether a suspension notice was included or not. In the standard clause, this means that human rights and democracy are "essential elements" of this agreement; meanwhile they have been adopted in treaties with more than 120 countries.

Reactions of partner countries to the EU's desire for a specific human rights' clause in the agreement differed widely. Whereas the African and Latin American States agreed to it, the ASEAN States, China and the Arab countries refused it. In the rest of Asia, only a minority of states were in agreement with it. By the end of 1995, however, 70 ACP States, 15 Latin American, 20 OSZE, 2 Mediterranean, 6 Asian States and South Africa have all adopted human rights and democracy clauses.

The EU at the United Nations

At the United Nations, the annual spring conference of the Commission on Human Rights (CHR) is of particular importance. For months, the EU tries to harmonise its positions, which infrequently means that the "common denominator" finds expression in a rather restrained position. Nevertheless, the EU point of view is often the most comprehensive one because it offers detailed criticism of human rights' situations in some 30 countries. It also proposes most of the resolutions to countries - one of the Commission's most powerful instruments, which has no sanction mechanism at its disposal. Government representatives from a fair number of countries from the South regard this rather critically, while others reject this criticism "of the South" by Northern industrialised countries. With reference to its present dominance in world politics and its past as a colonial power, the "North" is reproached for playing the part of an arrogant schoolmaster. The effect of this in the debate is to distract from the substance of human rights criticism, which is mostly rejected by the governments concerned as being false or exaggerated. The intense politisation of the CHR for all sorts of reasons, however, cannot be ignored. The discussions and decisions are increasingly along the lines of the North-South conflict and influenced by regional group identities rather than on an objective analysis of human rights' situations. They can only be mitigated in the medium to long term by patient consensus building efforts across regions of the world.

On 22 March 2004, the European Council adopted the following conclusions for the preparations for the 60th session of the United Nations Commission on Human Rights, being held in Geneva until 23 April.

> "At the start of the 60th session of the UN Commission on the Human Rights (CHR), the Council examined and endorsed the EU's position regarding action in that forum. The EU is determined to continue to play, in cooperation with other participants, a major role at the CHR, which it considers to be the primary UN body for the promotion and protection of human rights around the world. The EU will contribute to ensuring that the CHR acts as effectively as possible in the pursuit of those goals. …
> - The Council noted that the EU will present a significant number of geographic and thematic initiatives at the CHR. The European Union will table resolutions on the issue of death penalty, on the rights of the child and on religious intolerance. It will also put forward resolutions addressing the human rights situation in Burma/Myanmar, Democratic People's Republic of Korea, Democratic Republic of Congo, the Russian Federation (Chechnya), Sudan, and Zimbabwe, as well as the question of Israeli settlements in the Occupied Territories. In addition, it will propose initiatives on Turkmenistan and Belarus jointly with the United States. The EU will work with the governments of Colombia and Timor Leste to secure the adoption of Chair's statements in relation to human rights in those countries. The Presidency, on behalf of the European Union, will moreover make a general statement to convey its serious concerns about the situation in certain countries and welcome signs of progress, as well as statements on many of the different thematic human rights issues under consideration.

> - The Council stressed the importance it attaches to dialogue with third countries in the human rights field generally, and most particularly in the context of the CHR. It recalls that is has engaged in dialogue with the governments of China and Iran on human rights issues. In the view of the European Union, such dialogues do not preclude appropriate consideration by the CHR of the human rights situation in those countries"[18].

In 2004, EU submitted resolutions on Chechnya/Russia, North Korea, DR Congo, Israeli settlements in the occupied Arab territories, Burma/Myanmar and Zimbabwe. Jointly with the United States the EU introduced resolutions on the human rights situation in Belarus und Turkmenistan. Thematically the EU introduced resolutions on religious intolerance and the death penalty[19].

Human Rights Dialogues

In a difficult human rights situation within a partner country, it is the proclaimed aim of the European human rights' policy to seek a dialogue with the government, opposition, elites, and civil society for constructive solutions.

The EU conducts a special human rights' dialogue with partner countries, such as the USA, Canada, Japan, New Zealand, Russia and associated countries. These are supplemented by a gathering of experts before the meeting of the UN Human Rights Commission and the annual meeting of the UN General Assembly.

In addition to the large group of ACP states in Africa and the Caribbean with more than 70 countries, the EU conducts discussions with the Mediterranean, Asian and Latin American countries (the so-called Barcelona, ASEAN/ASEM and San José processes).

At present, the EU is only carrying on human rights' discussions, in the strict sense, with two countries: China and Iran, where the dialogue was interrupted for a long time but recommenced in December 2002. During these exchanges, human rights' topics are discussed at the governmental level and with NGOs, as well as with representatives of civil society.

The human rights dialogue with China

In the Council Conclusions from 18 March 2003, the Council reaffirmed that this dialogue

> "is an acceptable option only if enough progress is achieved and reflected on the ground. The EU will continue to evaluate the re-

[18] http://register.consilium.eu.int/pdf/en/04/st07/st07698.en04.pdf.

[19] EU 2004a: 53f.

sults of the dialogue at regular intervals, to determine to what extent its expectations have been met. The Union will also continue to express publicly its concerns about human rights in China and to raise them in meetings with China at all levels.
The Council decided that the EU at the UN Commission on Human Rights would convey its deep concern over the serious violations of human rights in China and the lack of progress in a number of areas. The Union will urge China to take the following steps to improve the situation: early ratification of the ICCPR and full implementation of both the ICCPR and the ICESCR, ratification of the OP/ CAT, enhanced cooperation with the UN human rights mechanisms, limitations on the use of the death penalty, with a view to its abolition, putting an end to the "strike-hard" campaign, addressing the systemic root causes of physical and psychological torture, abolition of restrictions on the formation and activities of independent labour unions, reform of the system of administrative detention, respect of the human rights of all prisoners, including the right to stay silent and not to be tortured, respect of the freedom of expression, religion and belief, reform of the judicial system in order to guarantee individuals the right to fair and open trial, release of political, labour and cyber activists and respect for the cultural and religious rights and freedoms in Tibet and Xinjiang"[20].

After an evaluation of this human rights dialogue, the General Affairs and External Relations Council (GAERC) concluded on 11 October 2004:

1. The Council welcomes the evaluation of the EU-China Human Rights Dialogue, which was prepared in accordance with the EU Guidelines on Human Rights dialogues, and based on a wide range of reports and contributions, including from civil society.
2. The Council recalls the objectives it has set for the EU-China Human Rights Dialogue in its Conclusions of January 2001. It acknowledges that China has made considerable progress over the last decade in its social-economic development and economic freedom for ordinary citizens. It welcomes steps towards strengthening the rule of law and urges China to ensure effective implementation of such measures. It also welcomes moves to enhance cooperation with UN human rights mechanisms and China's work thus far towards the ratification of the International Covenant on Civil and Political Rights (ICCPR). The EU looks forward to further work in

[20] http://europa.eu.int/comm/external_relations/human_rights/gac.htm#hr180303b.

this area and would welcome early ratification. It also calls for the early reform of the re-education through labour system.
3. Despite these developments, the Council expresses its concern about continuing violations of human rights, such as the freedom of expression (including press freedom and internet), freedom of religion and freedom of assembly and association. It also concludes that there has been no progress in the respect for the rights of persons belonging to minorities, in particular as regards religious freedom, and a continued erosion of minority culture, in particular in Tibet and Xinjiang. The Council deplores the continued widespread application of the death penalty as well as the persistence of torture, despite acknowledgement of this problem by the Chinese authorities. The overall assessment of developments shows a mixed picture of progress in some areas and continuing concerns in others.
4. On balance, however, and from a long-term perspective, a positive trend can be seen, with improvements in the rule of law and respect for economic rights and decline in the influence of the state on citizens' daily life. The Council is convinced that the dialogue, notably by providing a channel of communication and a forum for the candid expression of concerns, by exposing Chinese decision-makers to international human rights standards and practices, and by generating concrete human rights cooperation projects, remains a valuable process and has the potential to impact positively on the human rights situation in China.
5. At the same time, the Council notes that there is ample scope for improving and encouraging concrete outcomes of the dialogue and tangible results on the ground. It therefore endorses the operational conclusions made in the evaluation as regards the modalities of the dialogue, such as enlarging the scope of participation, increasing transparency by public debriefings, better preparation and follow-up of the dialogue, increasing coherence between dialogue and seminars and improved management of the list of individual cases.
6. The Council concludes that it considers the human rights dialogue a valuable instrument and an important element of overall EU-China relations. It will therefore pursue the human rights dialogue, the cooperation programmes and the seminars, taking into account the abovementioned recommendations. The EU will continue to raise human rights issues with China in bilateral and multilateral exchanges at all levels. As foreseen in the EU Guidelines on

> Human Rights Dialogues, the EU will continue to evaluate this dialogue on an annual basis.[21]

The human rights dialogue with Iran

Four dialogue meetings took place between Iran and the EU between 2002 and 2004[22]. Political relations with Iran have deteriorated significantly after the last parliamentary elections in February 2004 due to the exclusion of pro-reform candidates by the guardian's council, and more recently, the standstill of negotiations between the EU und Iran on the nuclear question.

After an evaluation in autumn 2004, the General and External Affairs Council concluded on 11 October 2004:

> (…) 4. The evaluation clearly establishes that with regard to the issues that this Council has designated as its priorities, although there seemed to be hopeful signs at some point, little overall progress has been achieved since the start of the dialogue in December 2002. These key areas of concern, which have been used as benchmarks to appraise the human rights situation in Iran and to measure the results of the dialogue, relate to Iran's cooperation with human rights mechanisms and implementation of their recommendations, ratification and implementation of key conventions; unhindered access for international observers and international NGOs; civil rights and political freedoms; reform of the judicial system; prevention and eradication of torture; criminal punishment; discrimination and the prison system.
> 5. The evaluation concluded that while Iran has extended a standing invitation for visits by UN Special Human Rights mechanisms and several such visits actually took place, little progress has been made on implementing the recommendations arising from them. With regard to the other priority issues, however, there has either been very little or no progress on the ground. …
> 7. The Council reaffirmed that the human rights dialogue with Iran remains one of the means by which the EU can make a contribution to improving the human rights situation. While welcoming the efforts that Iran has so far put into its dialogue with the European Union, it reiterated that this dialogue is an effective instrument in human rights policy only if sufficient progress is achieved on the ground, both in the short and the long term. The dialogue itself should be able to make a positive contribution to EU-Iran relations

[21] http://europa.eu.int/comm/external_relations/china/gac.htm.
[22] For information on these meeting see Danish Institute for Human Rights 2003a, b, 2004a, and b.

> in this regard. The EU remains committed to pursue the human rights dialogue, while however annually reviewing its modalities with the aim of improving its effectiveness in key areas of concern. Taking into account the outcome of the evaluation, the Council supported the need to attain a renewed commitment from the Iranian authorities to improve respect for human rights and promote the rule of law in the country and also supported the need to adjust the modalities of the dialogue with a view to enhancing its effectiveness.
> 8. The Council wishes to discuss with Iran a number of practical recommendations aimed at enhancing the effectiveness of the dialogue, such as early agreement on themes and regular dates before each UN Commission on Human Rights and UN General Assembly, a more thorough preparation for both the round table meetings and the government-only meetings, and more transparency towards the public. This dialogue has generated great expectations within the civil society in Iran. The EU and Iran should do their best to meet these expectations (…)[23].

Accession of new EU Member States

It has already been mentioned earlier that Article 6 (1) of the Treaty of the European Union states:

"The Union is founded on the principles of liberty, democracy, respect for human rights and fundamental freedoms, and the rule of law, principles which are common to Member States".

Accession of new member states requires the unanimous approval of the European Council and an absolute majority of the European Parliament (Nowak 1999, 691). In addition to the acceptance of the *aquis communitaire*, new members have to meet the so-called Copenhagen political criteria approved in June 1993. They are divided in three parts, "Democracy and the rule of law", "Human Rights and the Protection of Minorities" and "General Evaluation". Country analysis usually covers civilian and political rights as well as economic, social and cultural rights.

Evaluation of aspiring member states by the Commission was and is a fairly open process[24]. Evaluation reports are posted on the EU website. According to Nowak, the brief analyses on Human Rights and the Protection of Minorities in acceding states seem "rather superficial and relates more to the *de jure* than the *de facto* situation. Only the chapters on the protection of minorities contain a

[23] http://europa.eu.int/comm/external_relations/iran/intro/gac.htm.

[24] For reports on acceding as well as candidate and potential candidate countries, see http://europa.eu.int/comm/enlargement/report_2005/index.htm

more comprehensive and critical assessment" (ibid., 691). Especially in the case of Turkey, doubts were expressed as to the real progress under way, especially when assessing the practice of torture, the role of the national security council dominated by the military, and the treatment of the Kurdish population. Nowak criticised that the "competence of the European Court of Justice to review the human rights 'conditionality' in the accession and sanctions procedures is currently very limited and unclear", and "the actual practice of the Union in applying a policy of human rights 'conditionality' towards third countries seems to be somewhat selective and is often based on economic and political, rather than on purely legal grounds" (ibid, 698).

Other countries

Euro-Mediterranean-Partnership (Barcelona Process)

Regarding the Mediterranean, the EU has started a structured dialogue in the fields of human rights, democracy, rule of law and good governance[25].

The working program of the Euro-Mediterranean-Partnership for the next five years includes areas such as education, human rights and democracy as well as sustainable economic growth and reform. Other issues are social reforms, migration, struggle against terrorism and non-proliferation of weapons of mass destruction[26].

European Neighbourhood Policy (ENP)

European Neighbourhood Policy is addressed towards Eastern and Southern neighbours of the EU. It serves to enhance cooperation in the economical, political and cultural field. An action plan serves to address the strengthening of democracy, good governance, rule of law and human rights as well as economic modernisation. In the EU general strategy paper of 12 May 2004 and the action plan of 9 December 2004, however, human rights are not specifically mentioned- with the exception of a reference to the necessity of intensive cooperation to prevent the trade of human beings[27].

Démarches und public declarations on country situations

Démarches und public declarations have been used by the EU on a broad scale to address human rights' concerns. They were issued most frequently in cases of illegal detention, forced disappearances, the death penalty, torture, refugee and asylum issues, assessment of the fairness of elections, extrajudicial executions,

[25] EU 2004a, p. 38; http://europa.eu.int/scadplus/leg/de/lvb/r15009.htm.

[26] Cf. EU 2003b; „Commission launches 5-year work programme to reinforce Euro-Mediterranean Partnership"IP/05/419 - Brussels, 12 April 2005; http://europa.eu.int/comm/external_relations/euromed/news/ip05_419.htm.

[27] http://europa.eu.int/comm/world/enp/pdf/strategy/Strategy_Paper_EN.pdf.

right to freedom of opinion and assembly and the right to a fair trial. They were addressed in 2003/04 to a large number of countries[28].

Moreover, common standpoints were adopted on human rights issues on the Western Balkan, Burma/Myanmar, Africa, Rwanda, Somalia, Zimbabwe, DR Congo, Nigeria, Liberia, Angola and Cuba[29].

The EU as a military actor

In light of the newly arising - and somewhat open - international power architecture following the Iraq war and on-going UN reform discussions, it remains an open question as to what extent a stronger profile of the EU as a leading power and an emerging military player might lead to changes in the importance attributed to human rights. The new security strategy, "A Secure Europe in a Better World," from December 2003 and the follow-up discussions offer the hints towards these changes[30].

The new security strategy "A Secure Europe in a Better World" of December 2003 might offer the first leads. It states, among other key points:

> Our traditional concept of self- defence – up to and including the Cold War – was based on the threat of invasion. With the new threats, the first line of defence will often be abroad. The new threats are dynamic. The risks of proliferation grow over time; left alone, terrorist networks will become ever more dangerous. State failure and organised crime spread if they are neglected – as we have seen in West Africa. This implies that we should be ready to act before a crisis occurs. Conflict prevention and threat prevention cannot start too early[31].

[28] Countries covered were Afghanistan, Albania, Angola, Australia, Azerbaijan, Bangladesh, Belarus, Benin, Bhutan, Bolivia, Bosnia Herzegovina, Burkina Faso, Burma/Myanmar, Burundi, Cambodia, China, Colombia, Croatia, Côte d'Ivoire, Cuba, Democratic Republic of Congo, Democratic People's Republic of Korea, Dominica, Dominican Republic, Egypt, El Salvador, Eritrea, Ethiopia, Former Yugoslav Republic of Macedonia, Guatemala, Guyana, Honduras, Indonesia, Iran, Israel, Japan, Jordan, Kazakhstan, Kenya, Kyrgyzstan, Lebanon, Lesotho, Liberia, Madagascar, Malaysia, Mali, Mauritania, Morocco, Mozambique, Namibia, Nepal, Nigeria, Pakistan, Paraguay, Peru, Philippines, the Russian Federation, Serbia und Montenegro, Somalia, Sri Lanka, Sudan, Swaziland, Syria, Tanzania, Tunisia, Turkmenistan, Turkey, Ukraine, Uganda, the USA, Uzbekistan, Vietnam, Yemen, Zambia und Zimbabwe (according to EU 2004a:43).

[29] Ibid: 40-42.

[30] The Nice European Council in December 2000 approved the establishment of the following new permanent political and military bodies: The Political and Security Committee (PSC) (Council Decision of 22.1.2001, OJ L 27 of 30.1.2001, p. 1), the European Union Military Committee (EUMC) (Council Decision of 22.1.2001, OJ L 27 of 30.1.2001, p. 4) and the European Union Military Staff (EUMS) (Council Decision of 22.1.2001, OJ L 27 of 30.1.2001, p. 7).

[31] EU 2003b:7.

> "We are committed to upholding and developing International Law. The fundamental framework for international relations is the United Nations Charter. The United Nations Security Council has the primary responsibility for the maintenance of international peace and security. Strengthening the United Nations, equipping it to fulfil its responsibilities and to act effectively, is a European priority"[32].

Under policy implications for Europe, the strategy notes:

> More active in pursuing our strategic objectives. This applies to the full spectrum of instruments for crisis management and conflict prevention at our disposal, including political, diplomatic, military and civilian, trade and development activities. Active policies are needed to counter the new dynamic threats. We need to develop a strategic culture that fosters early, rapid, and when necessary, robust intervention.[33]

At present, military operations under the European Security and Defence Policy (ESDP) take place in:

- Bosnia Herzegovina EUFOR (ALTHEA)
- EU Military Operation in Former Yugoslav Republic of Macedonia (CONCORDIA)
- EU Military Operation in Democratic Republic of Congo (ARTEMIS)

There are also EU police operations underway in Georgia (Rule of Law mission/THEMIS), Macedonia (PROXIMA), DR Congo (EUPOL Kinshasa) and Bosnia and Herzegovina (EUPM), as well as a EU supporting action to the African Union mission in Darfur and EU mission to provide advice and assistance for security sector reform in the Democratic Republic of the Congo.

The four human rights guidelines on torture, death penalty, human rights defenders and children in armed conflict are valid for all EU operations under ESDP. In addition, so-called Generic Standards of Behaviour for ESDP Operations were requested by the Political and Security Committee and were noted by the external relations Council in May 2005:

[32] EU 2003b:9.
[33] EU 2003:11.

> **"Generic Standards of Behaviour for ESDP Operations**
> 17. The Council noted the generic document on standards of behaviour to be adhered to by all categories of personnel, whether military or civilian, involved in ESDP operations. This document is based on provisions already in force and applied to ESDP operations under way, and it could be adapted, in particular, according to the lessons drawn from ESDP operations and in the light of work currently being "conducted by the United Nations and in other international organisations. This living" document will be used in planning forthcoming ESDP operations in order to ensure that the personnel involved in ESDP operations comply with the highest standards of behaviour.
>
> 18. The Council considers that these standards of behaviour should also be applied, as appropriate, to personnel involved in other types of EU presence in areas of operations, in order to ensure consistency in the EU's approach. The Council would also encourage its relevant bodies to carry out further work in areas related to standards of behaviour and in the implementation of other specific aspects of UN Security Council Resolution 1325 on women, peace and security."[34]

Standards require, among other points, the establishment of a fair and unbiased complaints procedure and of a reporting mechanism about serious incidents to be reported directly to the EU Chain of Command. Special issues raised include organised crime, corruption, human trafficking and child abuse[35]. They were first annexed to the ALTHEA operation plan. Apart from these standards, for every mission rules of engagement (ROE) are adopted and kept confidential. However, penal law and disciplinary issues are still the responsibility of the sending state. The EU personnel heading the mission can only ask the sending state to withdraw personnel.

The UN Human Rights Committee has asked states which have ratified the UN Covenant on Civil and Political Rights whether they accept extraterritorial application of the Pact, for example, during military and police operations[36].

[34] http://europa-eu-un.org/articles/en/article_4735_en.htm (2.9.2005). The full ext can be found at http://register.consilium.eu.int/pdf/en/05/st08/st08373-re03.en05.pdf.

[35] http://register.consilium.eu.int/pdf/en/05/st08/st08373-re03.en05.pdf

[36] Germany has given the following response: "Statement by the Federal Government: Pursuant to Article 2, paragraph 1, Germany ensures the rights recognized in the Covenant to all individuals within its territory and subject to its jurisdiction. Wherever its police or armed forces are deployed abroad, in particular when participating in peace missions, Germany ensures to all persons that they will be granted the rights recognized in the Covenant, insofar as they are subject to its jurisdiction. Germany's international duties and obligations, in particular those assumed in fulfilment of obliga-

Responses clear differ among EU member states. Hence, which legal norms are valid when various countries are involved in a multinational military or police mission and some have accepted the extraterritorial application of human rights norms, others only to a limited extent and some not at all?

Interestingly, in the area of CFSP, the post of a Personal Representative for Human Rights was created. On 16 January 2005, High Representative Javier Solana appointed Danish diplomat Michael Matthiessen to this post. He receives invitations to meetings of the Political and Security Committee (PSC) and may present proposals at such meetings[37]. He may mention this and other pertinent issues.

Voluntary guidelines for arms exports

Between 2000-2004, EU member countries France, Germany and Great Britain ranked among top exporters of major conventional arms and third, fourth and fifth after Russia and the United States[38]. The EU has included respect for human rights concerning arms exports from EU member countries to third countries. In 1998, a voluntary European Union Code of Conduct on Arms Exports was adopted. EU member states committed themselves to refuse granting an export license if there is a risk that the weapons could be used for internal repression within the countries concerned[39]. This applies particularly if the UN, the Council of Europe and the European Union have established serious human rights' violations.

With regard to the export of arms, a cooperative effort with the USA exists. The collaboration resulted in the EU-US, "Declaration on the Responsibility of States and Transparency regarding Arms Exports" in 2000. Both the EU and the US have committed themselves to strengthen public accountability of weapons exports, professed their support for the promotion of democracy and respect for human rights, and promised not to export weapons to countries in where they could be used for internal repression and violation of internationally recognised human rights. In addition, the intensification of inner-state and interstate conflicts, excessive arms races, and regional instability are decisive factors to be considered. Surprisingly, on a well-published occasion at the end of 2004, French President Chirac and German Chancellor Schröder argued for ending arms export sanctions on China, but failed to receive sufficient support amongst EU member states.

tions stemming from the Charter of the United Nations, remain unaffected. The training it gives its security forces for international missions includes tailor-made instruction in the provisions of the Covenant."
(http://www.unhchr.ch/tbs/doc.nsf/(Symbol)/5b9311d84c20e497c1257006004c6485?Opendocumen)

[37] http://ue.eu.int/uedocs/cmsUpload/Appointment.pdf.

[38] SIPRI 2005:418ff.

[39] Cf. SIPRI 2005:444ff.

EU Development Cooperation: The Cotonou Agreement and Conditionality
In the 2000 Cotonou Agreement between the EU and ACP-countries, freedom and security and the promotion of a stable and democratic political environment are indicated as objectives of the partnership (art. 1). The respect for human rights and fundamental freedoms - together with the establishment of and reference to the European Human Rights' Convention - democratic principles and the rule of law (art. 9, para 2 of the Cotonou Agreement) are stressed as essential elements in article 9. These are equally applicable to both the domestic and foreign policy of the contracting parties. The EC undertakes support for the political, institutional and legal reforms, as well as for the capacity building of the State and private players (art. 9, para 4). The decisive instrument for the discussion and evaluation of the progress achieved between the ACP and EU member states is the regular political dialogue.

Art. 96 of the Cotonou Agreement regulates the procedure in the case where a state party - in spite of regular political consultations - fails to comply with its undertaking to respect human rights, fundamental freedoms, democratic principles and respect for the law, the "essential elements" according to article 9, paragraph 2. The State that has ratified the agreement must then inform the other signatories thereof, in order to permit a comprehensive examination of the situation and introduce consultations with the aim of remedying the deficiencies.

In the case where the consultations do not reach an acceptable solution for all the parties, or in a situation of special urgency, the EU may take "suitable measures", which can be rescinded as soon as the grounds for them are removed. Accordingly, suspension of the agreement is the most extreme measure.

Box 2: EU Negative Measures: 1998 – 2005[40]

Burma/Myanmar	**since 1997 EU sanctions on account of forced labour**
Comoros	1999 suspended
Congo, Dem. Rep.	since 1992 assistance limited to emergency aid and rehabilitations; 1997 resumption of development cooperation made dependant upon democracy and human rights. New development cooperation sought.
Congo, Dem. Rep.	1997 suspension of development cooperation on grounds of security, 2000 National Indicative Programme concluded; full resumption made dependant on political progress

[40] Windmeisser 2002:377-387, EU 2004a: 40-42 and own research on EU measures since 2003.

Cuba	In 2003, measures were adopted on 5.03.2003. In 2004, the14th evaluation of the EU common position took place.
Equatorial Guinea	1992 suspension following the abandonment of the democratic process, 1996 consultations, resumption of development co-operation
Gambia	1994 military coup, suspension of development cooperation, 1997 and especially 2000 normalisation
Guinea-Bissau	1999 suspended
Ivory Coast	consultation after military coup and popular uprising of 1999, no interruption of development cooperation
Liberia	since 1989 de facto suspension, 1997 confirmed; measures were amended and extended to include sanctions stipulated by UN Security Council resolution 1478 (2003)
Malawi	at first resistance with the abolition of the single party State 1991/92, which was then overcome; resumption of development cooperation
Niger	1999 after military coup, consultations, normalisation
Nigeria	1993 first sanctions, 1997, more severe after hanging of Ken Saro-Wiwa, 1999 lifted. In 2002, a new common position was adopted which should strengthen relations between the EU and Nigeria.
Rwanda	1994 development cooperation suspended, 1999 normalised
Sierra Leone	1992 suspended
Somalia	suspended since early 90s, support for rehabilitation measures. UN embargo according to UN Security Council resolution 1425 (2002) should be observed.
Sudan	suspended since early 90s
Togo	1992 development cooperation suspended until now, 1998 consultations, EU again expressed "serious worries" over the course of the elections
Uganda	1976-79 under President Idi Amin development cooperation suspended; even today many and serious human rights′ violations. EU development cooperation primarily directed towards fighting poverty and Poverty Reduction Strategy papers.

Uzbekistan	October 2005: Arms embargo on Uzbekistan after the violent suppression of anti-government protests in the city of Andijan in May; denial of visas to top Uzbek officials. (EU bans arms sales to Uzbekistan, 3.10.2005, http://news.bbc.co.uk/1/hi/world/asia-pacific/4306700.stm).
Zimbabwe:	In February 2002, the EU announced sanctions for Zimbabwe: travel restrictions and freezing of the accounts of more than 70 members of the leadership. Since the situation had not improved a year later, the sanctions were extended and continue until today.

In general, the EU lacks a systematic and transparent procedure for human rights violations. Clear criteria for the measures are hardly discernable. Almost without exception, the sanctioned countries concern small African states - apart from Nigeria and Cuba, and a small state in Southeast Asia, Burma/Myanmar. Sanctions are mostly applied for reasons of undemocratic change of government, coups d'etat. As Windmeißer pointed out in her study from 2003, everyday human rights' violations - especially those of an economic, social and cultural nature - do not lead to the introduction of consultation procedures by the EU[41].

In the recent past, a coherent foreign policy was lacking. Thus Algeria, despite the implementation of questionable methods in combating terrorism during the 80s, continued to receive support through the EU, despite the existence of a human rights' clause in the agreement between Algeria and the EU. Between 1991 and 1994, the Ethiopian dictatorship received EU financial support. The repressive regime of Sali Berisha in Albania was supported from 1990 onwards as well. Even Yugoslavia was able to count on a financial aid packet in the spring of 1997[42].

The European Initiative for Democracy and Human Rights (EIDHR): Funding Activities to Promote Human Rights and Democratisation

The European Council adopted two Regulations on 29 April 1999 (975/1999 and 976/1999) on the development and consolidation of democracy and the rule of law and respect for human rights and fundamental freedoms. The "European Initiative for Democracy and Human Rights", was created by an initiative of the European Parliament in 1994, which brought together a series of budget headings specifically dealing with the promotion of human rights[43]. This budget, B7-

[41] Windmeißer 2003: 385.
[42] Examples taken from Simma/Aschenbrenner/Schulte 1999: 581.
[43] http://europa.eu.int/comm/external_relations/human_rights/index.htm.

70, is aimed specifically at NGOs. The Union "values both the expertise which many organisations working to implement human rights possess, as well as their visibly high impact in the field of human rights"[44].
Since 1st January 2001, EuropeAid Co-operation Office has been responsible for the project cycle, from identification to implementation. The Directorate-General for External Relations and the Directorate-General for Development continue to be responsible for the programming of external assistance. EuropeAid has a separate website for the European Initiative for Democracy and Human Rights.

In June 2004, the Commission announced a budget increase. It had revised the EIDHR programming and the annual work programme for 2004 to reflect an increase in the budget of Euro 26,625 million, and to amend some of the priorities contained in the earlier programme as well as adding new ones[45]. The EIDHR budget increased to a total of Euro 132,625 million. The distribution of this increase is as follows: Two new themes have been added, support measures for victims of human rights abuses, Euro 7 million, and a pilot project for an expert network for conflict prevention, Euro 1,125 million.

Two themes have received an extra budget, support to development and consolidation of democracy and the rule of law, and respect for human rights and fundamental freedoms (increased from Euro 93 million to Euro 110.5 million), and support for the activities of the international criminal tribunals and the setting-up of the International Criminal Court (increased from Euro 6 million to Euro 7 million).

Regarding regional participation during 2002, Eastern Europe/MIS countries received 27,63% of the EIDHR funds, ACP 22,50%, Latin America 15,24%, Middle East 13,81%, Asia 11,01%, and the global level/N. America 9,81%. Concerning themes, in 2003 the areas most strongly supported were strengthening civil society, rule of law and institutions, strengthening elections and EU elections observer missions[46].

For 2005, the original budget for projects was set at Euro 118, 63 Mio. Applications were to be submitted by regional and international organisations, non-governmental organisations, national, regional and local authorities, public entities, community organisations and institutions as well as public and private actors[47]. Campaigns will focus on the promotion of justice and rule of law, fostering a culture of human rights, promotion of the democratic process and advancing equality, tolerance and peace.

[44] Ibid.

[45] Commission increases budget for democracy and human rights activities in 2004: € 26.625 extra million available (IP/04/708, Brussels, 03 June 2004).

[46] EU 2004b: 22.

[47] http://europa.eu.int/comm/europeaid/projects/eidhr/pdf/eidhr-annual-work-programme-2005_de.pdf.

Conclusions

It should have become clear by now that the European Union has indeed developed an impressive framework for defining its international policy goals, especially in the area of external and development policies. Instruments that exist to encourage positive developments in third countries through cooperation and criticism have been refined and have become increasingly differentiated.

Notwithstanding, so far the EU lacks a systematic and transparent procedure to address and manage human rights violations in third countries. Clear criteria for the selection of EU measures (country strategies and trigger points), e.g. when to engage in a formal human rights dialogue or when to use negative sanctions under the Cotonou Agreement, are hardly clear and discernible. Issues of coherence and consistency remain a major problem, even if the implementation process in 2004 (EU 2004b) has signaled these admittedly difficult challenges as priorities.

Although the claim that human rights policy be realised as a cross-sectoral task - in other words: human rights mainstreaming - is repeatedly raised in political decision-making, there is a long way to go in terms of its overall implementation.

The theme of human rights seems to be increasingly integrated in the CFSP of the EU, but realistically countries tend to be treated according to their political and economic relevance. Working toward more coherence and consistency, in other words to pursue a courageous human rights policy, is a constant challenge. Also, it must be kept in mind that the promotion of human rights and democracy is only effective when linked to internal social and political processes, and that these do not always permit enforcement or even decisive influence from the outside. Counter-tendencies might be present. This is especially true in the case of larger countries. Last, but not least, other EU policy interests might be of comparative weight or even stronger, such as trade interests or cooperation in the international fight against terrorism.

With this, a simple, but fundamental truth has to be recognised: EU external relations are political relations. There is no overwhelming human rights framework directing external relations exclusively. In other words human rights is only one of several central political objectives of the European Union including trade, the non-proliferation of weapons of mass destruction, crisis prevention, and combating terrorism to cite only a few.

Concerning the newly arising - and somewhat open - international power architecture following the Iraq war and on-going UN reform discussions, the extent to which a stronger profile of the EU, as a leading power and an emerging military player, may influence and lead to changes in the importance attributed to human rights and humanitarian law in ESDP operations remains questionable. Some developments were outlined in an earlier section.

The importance of human rights in EU development cooperation has considerably increased from being rather marginal in the Lomé III Agreement to being one of significance in the Cotonou Agreement of 2000. In this treaty, human rights along with fundamental freedoms, democratic principles and the rule of law have become essential criteria for cooperation.

The option to seek a political dialogue with "difficult countries" concerning measures such as the suspension or termination of development cooperation, depends in practice upon relevant foreign policy criteria such as the size of a country, its security policy, economic importance and other similar factors.

Clearly, value-based reactions to authoritarian regimes sometimes represent special challenges in foreign policy practice, but it's remains most important to ensure that a consistent, coherent and effective policy is being accepted.

'Exporting' values: Tracing the EU's human rights policy towards Russia[1]

Regina Heller

Introduction: Human rights 'export' as a post-modern security strategy

One of the major security interests of the European Union (EU) is the 'transformation of the political landscape' into an area of peace and stability (Tomaševski 2000: 325). Whereas traditionally, security was reinforced through the application of force, the EU clearly pursues a post-modern security approach (King 1999), putting the emphasis on soft power and means of non-military influence and persuasion. The soft power of the EU has in recent times been labelled a 'normative power' (Manners 2002: 235), since it aims at the transfer to third countries and the 'socialisation' (Risse and Sikkink 1999; Schimmelfennig 2003) of norms and values, including democratic principles, the rule of law and human rights (Börzel and Risse 2004).

This security objective applies especially for the European continent where the EU is 'exporting' (Petitville 2003: 127) its constitutive norms and values to both the new 'insiders' and to its neighbouring countries in order to (fully or partially) 'include' (Smith 1996) them into a 'security community' (Deutsch 1957) of democratic states. The Russian Federation is no exception to this post-modern security strategy of the EU. From the beginning of Russia's transformation in the early 1990s, it has been in the EU's interest to stabilise the country through democratisation and market liberalisation and to bring Russia closer to the West.

The full adaptation and implementation of the normative templates and sets of rules of the international and European human rights treaties was and still is understood as a precondition for a stable Russia and European security. This becomes even more imperative as the political importance of the Russian Federation as a strategic partner to the EU is growing and, consequently, so is the need for a stable and predictable partner, whose policies rest on the same policy rules, normative values and governance principles.

However, despite its increasing normative power in the European context, the human rights compliance level in Russia, compared to international human rights standards, is still far from satisfactory. Hence it remains an issue of concern to the EU. The key question that needs to be answered here is how the EU unfolds its 'normative power' vis-à-vis the Russian Federation. In order to shed light on this question, the following article will discuss the EU's human rights policy vis-à-vis the Russian Federation in the context of its general external policy approach towards the country. It traces the EU's human rights policy

[1] The findings of this article are drawn from parts of my dissertation project entitled "Norms socialisation in Russia – chances and limits for EU human rights policy vis-à-vis the Russian Federation". The PhD project is supported by the *Deutsche Stiftung Friedensforschung* (DSF).

since 1991 by exploring the socialisation strategy, the instruments applied and the different stages and characteristics of engagement. Defining the EU human rights policy towards Russia as an *external governance strategy*, it will also examine the relevance of direct, i.e. 'quasi'-vertical (such as conditionality)[2] in comparison to indirect an more horizontal (through functional co-operation) mechanisms of rule transfer in non-hierarchical governance structures. The article closes with a number of general observations about the EU's human rights policy vis-à-vis the Russian Federation.

The 'shared values' approach in the EU's relations with Russia: normative references and human rights instruments

The norms of the international and European human rights system play a vital role in the EU's relations towards the Russian Federation. The contractual foundation of intergovernmental relations – the 'Partnership and Co-operation Agreement' (PCA) (Communities of the European Union and its Member States 1997)[3] – rests on and is bound to a set of 'shared values', to which the parties commit themselves and which serve as normative 'points of orientation' (Timmermann 2000a: 167). These values embrace democratic principles, the rule of law and compliance with international and European human rights standards, as they are set out in the UN treaties, in the European Charta of Human Rights (ECHR) and in the 'Charter of Paris for a New Europe', adopted by the members of the Conference on Security and Cooperation in Europe (CSCE) in 1990. The PCA defines democracy, human rights and the rule of law as 'essential elements' of bilateral relations (PCA general provisions, art. 2) Thus, these normative principles represent common points of departure and, at the same time, common objectives in the bilateral relationship. As Hiski Haukala has put it, they are 'prerequisites on which the relationship rests in the first place' and 'benchmarks against which the future breadth and depth of interaction is measured.' (Haukkala 2005: 7)

Since 1991, the full adoption of these values including compliance with international and European human rights standards has been a key objective in the EU's overall external policy approach vis-à-vis Russia. In order to bring these values to life, the EU developed a human rights policy vis-à-vis the Russian Federation, drawing upon a number of standardised instruments which are applied by the EU globally, yet customised to regional requirements (Börzel and Risse 2004). Three main instruments form this human rights policy towards Russia:

[2] I use the term 'quasi'-vertical rule transfer at this point as to delineate norms and rule transfer in non-hierarchical governance structures from similar processes in hierarchical governance structures.
[3] The 'Partnership and Co-operation Agreement' (PCA) was signed in 1994 and is still the only legally binding contractual agreement for the relations between the EU and Russia. The PCA went into force in 1997 and expires in 2007.

a) *Changes in cost-benefit calculations of Russian domestic actors through a system of 'positive rewards':* the EU tries to change cost-benefit calculations of domestic actors by setting a number of incentives for Russian domestic actors to comply with and/or a number of disincentives to prevent them from violating human rights norms. With respect to Russia, the EU follows a positive approach, applying a positive 'reward system' (Light 2001: 21) or strategy of 'reinforcement by reward' (Schimmelfennig, et al. 2003: 495) as a mechanism to stimulate rule-consistent behaviour in the domestic context.[4] Within this positive system of rewards, the EU sets mainly economic and social incentives linked to the substance and prospect of strengthening interstate relations. Conversely, economic or social rewards are held back in the case of retreat in compliance. Instruments of behavioural adaptation through changes in cost-benefit calculations are underpinned by a number of diplomatic and policy instruments, used in bilateral as well as in multilateral contexts in to put social pressure on Russia or to provide positive social support for rule-consistent behaviour.

b) *Learning and persuasion through political dialogue*: political dialogue is another important instrument in the EU's human rights policy towards Russia. It is applied within the first pillar, but has been also developed as a policy instrument within the second pillar. Political dialogue is meant as a platform for discourse and harmonisation of positions with respect to controversial issues essential to the bilateral relations. Human rights issues represent a vital part here. Similar to the so called 'Europe Agreements' concluded with the Eastern European accession states in the early 1990s, the PCA foresees an intensified political dialogue with Russia at all levels of interaction – from the summit to the working level, including inter-parliamentarian forms of communication as well. Since the PCA was only ratified in 1997, regular political dialogue on the working level first started after a significant delay - in 1999.

c) *Democracy building through financial aid*: Third, the EU supports democratic capacity building in Russia through the provision of large-scale financial aid. EU democracy aid aims at supporting modernisation and democratic institution building as well as vitalising civil society in Russia. Technical aid to Russia is provided through the Technical Assistance

[4] The EU also knows the instrument of negative, mostly economic sanctions. However, such measures are only applied vis-à-vis developing countries (Aschenbrenner 2000: 75; see also: Börzel and Risse 2004).

Programme of the EU for the former CIS and Mongolia (TACIS).[5] Today, TACIS remains the EU's main aid instrument for Russia. Between 1991, when TACIS started, and 2004, the EU granted about 2,64 billion Euros in technical aid to the Russian Federation. More than 1,500 projects have been implemented in the country so far.[6] TACIS is a non-autonomous instrument, meaning that all activities must be agreed upon with the partner state. TACIS and its sub-programmes have been complemented by non-autonomous aid instruments, like the 'European Initiative for Democracy and Human Rights' (EIDHR), especially targeted at the support of domestic grass-root initiatives and non-governmental organisations (NGOs).

The substance and practical implementation of these three human rights instruments have undergone a number of adjustments during the last 15 years of the EU's human rights engagement in Russia. The adjustments came along with and were subordinated to general strategic re-orientations in the EU's overall external policy approach vis-à-vis Russia. In the period since 1991, three phases can be identified in the human rights policy towards Russia, within which such adjustments have taken place.

The early strategy: quick adaptation through direct incentives and disincentives

After Russia's democratic opening in 1990, following the first free elections and the declaration of Russian independence, the EU decided to bolster and manage the democratic reforms from outside in order to quickly stabilise the country economically and politically and to 'irreversibly' tie Russia to Western values and governance principles (Timmermann 1996: 200). Economically, the EU wanted to ensure stability with the development of a market economy (Herrberg 1998: 91). Politically, the institutionalisation and consolidation of democracy, including the implementation of European human rights norms and the rule of law, were seen as key components of that stability.

In order to achieve these ambitious goals, the EU had to put its relationship with Russia on a new contractual basis. Until then, bilateral relations with Russia had rested on the Technical and Co-operation Agreement (TCA), a purely economic instrument, originally signed with the Former Soviet Union and transferred to the Russian Federation in 1991. As such, the TCA had the potential to support the early transformation in Russia economically. However, it lacked the political instruments to control and manage the reform process in Russia from

[5] Initially, TACIS had been designed as a pure 'basic needs' instrument (Tomaševski 2000: 361). However, under the PCA, it was quickly extended to comprehensive democracy aid.

[6] For more details see also the homepage of the Delegation of the European Commission in Russia: http://www.delrus.cec.eu.int/en/p_260.htm.

the outside (Gower 2000: 72). Therefore, the European Commission worked out the PCA as a new contractual instrument that included political mechanisms able to support market opening and to manage Russia's democratic transformation (Timmermann 1996: 200).

While leaving out the prospect of membership, the PCA follows the same logic of norms transfer as do the Europe Agreements. The PCA 'serves primarily as an ambitious normative framework, designed to bring Russia closer to EU legislative, economic and trading standards.' (Gowan 2001: 9). It particularly makes intensified co-operation between the EU and Russia as well as continuing support for Russia's integration into Western co-operation structures conditional upon the progress of domestic democratic reform in the country, including achievements with regard to the implementation of European and international human rights standards and the rule of law.

Although the PCA was ratified, but had not yet entered into force by 1994, the EU made early use of the democratic conditionality. Conditionality was mainly oriented towards the positive reward system, but it also integrated aspects of light negative conditionality. A 'soft' suspension clause (Börzel and Risse 2004: 15), enables the contract partners to unilaterally suspend the provisions of the PCA in case essential elements of it are disregarded by one party (art. 107). However, such a step has to adhere to the principle of 'proportionality' and should not substantially disturb interstate relations (art. 107,2).[7]

(i) Direct material and social rewards for human rights compliance and norms adaptation

The EU openly supported Russia's early economic and political reform endeavours and tried to spur reform progress in these areas by underpinning them with material and social rewards and incentives to follow the path of reforms. Material rewards came in the form of direct intensification of bilateral trade relations as well as prospects for long-term strengthening of the economic relations. Social rewards were offered by supporting Russia's integration into European cooperative structures.

Intensification of economic co-operation as a material reward: Following the collapse of Russia's economy after the breakdown of the state trading system in the early 1990s, Russia very much depended on the EU as a remaining major trading and financial partner in its economic relations. The EU tried to make use of these extremely asymmetric economic and trade relations so as to trigger quick adaptation to free market rules and related democratic policy standards in Russia. The PCA provided for both short-term and long-term incentives for market liberalisation in Russia. In the short-term, the countries granted each other a 'most favoured nation' trading status in order to ease trade relations

[7] See also: Haukkala 2005: 16.

immediately. Over the long run, the PCA envisages the prospect of a free trade area with Russia. Given the very asymmetric economic relations, it can be concluded 'that mostly political reasons prompted the EU to conclude this treaty, so as to associate Russia with the Western mechanisms of integration and to raise Russian self-esteem by opening the European market.' (Timmermann 1996: 206).

Support for CoE membership as a social reward: In the beginning of Russia's democratic transformation, there was a strong demand from the Russian leadership for integration into Western, especially European political co-operation structures. This demand was manifested in Russia's application for membership in the Council of Europe (CoE) in 1992. Although the normative standards in Russia were far from equivalent to the prescriptions of the ECHR, the Western European countries strongly supported Russia's quick accession to the CoE as a tool to bind the country to a 'common European space of norms and identity' (Holtz 2000: 9) and as an additional instrument to control and manage democratic reforms and human rights compliance from the outside. Compliance was mainly managed through assistance in the institutionalisation of rule of law and through regular CoE compliance monitoring mechanisms. As some commentators have put it, the implementation of fundamental freedom rights had 'apparently become not a precondition for membership in the CoE any more, but its goal.' (Hutterer, et al. 1998: 14)

(ii) Modernisation and democracy-building through technical aid

The PCA also provided the prospect of substantial technical aid for modernisation and institution building in the economic as well as in the public sector. In the early 1990s, TACIS activities focused on socio-economic contexts for modernisation as well as on democratic institution building as a means to enhance the regulation capacity of the state structures. Legal adaptation to international and European standards, including the adaptation to human rights standards, was an especially key element in the aid strategy (Timmermann 1996: 209). TACIS projects were typically designed with a short-term perspective and targeted at know-how transfer from the West to the East, displaying a top-down approach in the EU's aid strategy (United States General Accounting Office 2000: 188). Training and know-how transfer were targeted at official actors and agencies, such as the courts, the procuracies as well as bureaucratic agents. Such activities in legal reform and institution-building were implemented in close co-operation with the CoE (Charities Aid Foundation 2000: 24).

While top-down activities were dominant in this phase of democracy building, the non-state sector was broadly ignored. This obvious deficit in democracy building was filled in 1993 by the European Parliament's 'PHARE and TACIS Democracy Programme' (PTDP), aiming to prompt democratisation from below (bottom-up), especially through the vitalisation of civil society initiatives. The programme focused especially on setting up an effective network of non-governmental actors and groups in the fields of parliamentarism, transparency in public administration, independent media, human rights supervision and protection of minority groups 'who lobby for democratic change and who constitute an ongoing form of public discussion and education.' (ISA Consult 1997: 5-6)

(iii) The EU's reaction to the first Chechen war: Suspending the rewards

Beginning in late 1993, domestic politics in Russia began to experience quite strong regressive tendencies, intensified in autumn 1994 when the first Chechen war broke out. Although the PCA had not yet been ratified, the EU, in reaction to these developments, decided to make use of the possibility of holding back the rewards connected with the agreement. The reaction reflected the EU's concern that the reform process in Russia was in serious danger and the judgment that domestic actors had to be brought in line with the 'common values' again.

First of all, the EU put the PCA ratification process on hold. As a means of economic pressure, the EU cancelled a planned signing of an 'interim agreement' between the EU and Russia, which was meant to activate the trade dimension of the PCA early (Cornell 1999: 91; Tomaševski 2000: 354). Secondly, the admission's process with respect to Russia's membership in the Council of Europe was postponed until a settlement of the conflict could be reached (Council of Europe Parliamentary Assembly 1995). While economic and social rewards were withheld, the EU decided not to touch financial aid within TACIS. Apparently, European politicians were afraid that the overall reform process in Russia could be significantly interrupted if technical aid was reduced or deferred (Timmermann 1996: 219; Trautmann 1995: 264; Vogel 1995: 64).

The EU then tied a reopening of the PCA ratification process to a number of requirements, which would require Russian politicians to bring the war in Chechnya to a peaceful end. These claims consisted of (Timmermann 1996: 220):

1. The adoption of an armistice agreement;
2. The immediate initiation of peace negotiations;
3. Free access for humanitarian aid; and
4. The appointment of a permanent OSCE assistance group and monitoring mission to Chechnya.

The Russian government reacted to the European requirements, although not entirely consistently. On 11 April, the OSCE Permanent Council decided to send an observation and assistance group to Chechnya and the Russian government promised to open peace negotiations with the Chechen rebels. Despite the fact that it took more than a year until an armistice agreement was fixed and another year until a peaceful settlement was reached, the European governments lifted their withdrawal of rewards promptly: in July 1995, the interim agreement was signed in Cannes and the CoE admission process was again taken up (Timmermann 1996: 220; Tomaševski 2000: 354).

Democracy and human rights as a source of friction in the emerging 'strategic partnership'

The regressive tendencies and the outbreak of the first Chechen war seriously challenged the EU's stabilisation objectives vis-à-vis Russia (Haukkala 2000: 22). At the same time, the importance of Russia as a political partner of the EU was growing. Following Finland's accession in 1995, Russia became a direct neighbour to the EU. The wars in the Balkans moreover showed that there was an urgent need for security co-operation, giving also Russia a say in European conflict settlement. It, thus, became clear that the EU had to seek stronger political relations with the Russian Federation in the future (Gower 2000: 79). However, such a political partnership would; in the eyes of the EU, only be stable if it rested reliably on compatible democratic rules and values (Timmermann 2002: 299). Thus, the realisation of 'common values' in EU-Russia relations became even more urgent.

In the light of these developments, the EU re-evaluated its overall policy approach towards the Russian Federation, which led to the adoption of the 'Common Strategy on Russia' in 1999 (Council of the European Union 1999a). The 'Common Strategy' tried to 'refine the political dimension of [the PCA], both conceptually and in its content.' (Malfliet 2001: 163). Compared to the policy strategy under the PCA, the 'Common Strategy' followed a stronger integrationist logic, putting more emphasis on immediate strengthening of political and economic relations as a means of security (DeSpiegeleire 2001: 86). On the basis of the PCA, the 'Common Strategy' offered a 'strategic partnership' to Russia through an intensification of bilateral co-operation in a number of security-relevant areas. The ,Common Strategy' set out three principle goals: the consolidation of democracy and the rule of law in Russia as a precondition for the development of a market economy, Russia's integration into a common economic and social space and security co-operation in and beyond Europe (Council of the European Union 1999a).

The EU's new approach vis-à-vis Russia also altered the substance of its human rights policy. In the PCA, the 'common values' were again highlighted as an essential part of the emerging 'strategic partnership'. However, the means by which they were supposed to come into being, changed. Here, the EU adopted a 'twin-track policy' (Lynch 2005b: 125): On the one hand, it followed the prior principle not to apply negative sanctions, but sought to increase interstate co-operation. As a result, the inclusionary strategy of the EU put more emphasis on horizontal, i.e. co-operative mechanisms and indirect incentives through co-operation than on conditionality or direct rewards, although not fully eliminating the conditionality element. On the other hand, the EU tried to make more use of discursive practises in bilateral relations, especially using political dialogue to discuss human rights issues. However, this dual approach caused a number of irritations in EU-Russia relations, especially following the outbreak of the second Chechen war in winter 1999 and the issue of human rights became a major source of friction within the emerging 'strategic partnership'.

(i) Indirect incentives and hidden conditionality: Democratisation, rule of law and human rights as an 'area of strategic action'?

With respect to changes in cost-benefit-calculations under the 'Common Strategy', the EU applied a mix of indirect incentives and rewards on the one hand and hidden conditionality on the other. The 'Common Strategy' formulated democracy, rule of law and human rights compliance as one of its principled objectives for the 'strategic partnership'. It especially emphasized, that a stable market economy in Russia could only develop on the basis of democratic order and the rule of law (Royen 1999: 82; Spanger 2004: 34). Therefore the EU saw as a strategic goal, creating the political conditions for economic development, consisting of 'the consolidation of democracy and the rule of law in Russia as well as Russia's compliance with its international human rights obligations, especially those fixed in the ECHR', (Council of the European Union 1999a). In the document, the EU made clear that the realisation of 'common values' was still a precondition for a further enhancement of the bilateral relations. Once the political conditions were established, the EU would offer the prospect of implementing a free trade area with Russia. Russia's accession to the World Trade Organisation (WTO) was set as a benchmark, upon which the success of the norms adaptation was to be measured.

While the political and economic areas were linked to more fundamental questions of democracy and human rights, the area of security co-operation lacked this linkage. Security co-operation in the European context mainly identified homeland and border security issues such as combating illegal migration and organised crime as relevant to the co-operation (Kahl 2004). With respect to international co-operation, joint action in international organisations as well as joint action within the European Security and Defence Policy, were considered. As Stephan DeSpiegeleire notes '[M]ember states appear to have been driven more by the new opportunities opened up by the Amsterdam Treaty, than with any logic that would be inherent to the developing EU-Russia relationship.' (DeSpiegeleire 2001: 87).

In its response document, the Russian government gave a positive answer to the EU's proposal to establish a 'strategic partnership' and signalled its willingness to intensify interstate relations (Pravitel'stvo Rossijskoj Federacii 2000). The Russian 'Mid-Term strategy on the EU', covering the years 2000-2010, reflected a significant foreign policy shift towards the EU as a modernisation and political partner (Borko 2001: 117; Malfliet 2001: 163; Mommsen 2002:

678f; Timmermann 2000b: 887). However, the strategy document did not make any reference to normative objectives, such as democratisation or human rights. Instead, the document emphasised economic and security co-operation, revealing substantial divergence from the status and the role of the 'common values' in the 'strategic partnership'. The discrepancies in the two strategic documents show that while the EU sought domestic reform in Russia as a precondition for a ,strategic partnership', for Russia, interstate co-operation was a possibility to fulfill its strategic interests without viewing human rights and democratic norms as part of these interests (Borko 2001: 132; Timmermann 2004: 345-6).

(i) Towards full-fledged democracy assistance

Financial aid for Russia was re-shaped according to the strategic goals of the 'Common Strategy', too. The new aid approach and aid objectives vis-à-vis Russia were set out in the Russia Country Strategy Paper for the period 2000-2006 (European Commission 2001a). The revised aid strategy also integrated a number of new objectives formulated in the re-authorised TACIS regulation from 1999 (Council of the European Union 1999b). The new direction of the aid strategy vis-à-vis Russia mainly highlighted the following two modifications:

- *From aid to assistance*: in order to underline the new co-operative approach in EU-Russia relations, the EU made efforts to put a stronger emphasis on the 'assistance' aspect of financial aid to Russia (European Parliament 2000: 12). In practice this meant that the EU intended to allocate financial aid more on the basis of dialogue-driven processes, helping Russia to find its own solutions for structural adaptation. In its new assistance strategy towards Russia the EU pointed out that it needed to engage more thoroughly in such areas where the commitment of the Russian government to reform and adaptation was already very high (European Commission 2001a).

- *Addressing the contexts of democratisation:* The strategic objective formulated in the 'Common Strategy' to create the basic political conditions for a market economy coincided with the insight formulated in the new TACIS regulation that the impact of external democracy aid was sustainable only in such contexts where a reform-conducive environment existed (Council of the European Union 1999b: Abs. 5).[8] Consequently, financial aid was broadened in scope and re-oriented towards the elimination of the causes of instability. Financial aid should target all contexts of democratisation in order to ensure 'long-term sustainability' of the democratic reform efforts (Council of the European

[8] See also: Development Researchers' Network 2000: 27.

> Union 1999b: Abs. 16). Human rights were defined as a key contextual aspect here and as a 'cross-area' issue relevant to all assistance areas in the new assistance strategy towards Russia (European Commission 2001a).

Accordingly, the Country Strategy Paper emphasised two focus areas of assistance: first, assistance should target the development of a political and legal culture in the public sphere. This should include the development of political responsibility and good governance, as well as the promotion of an active civil society and the development of a free media. Second, assistance should be targeted at the elimination of the social consequences of the transformation process. Capacity-building in municipal services as well as health care were defined as two major objectives in this sector (European Commission 2001a: 2). Special attention was given to the support of the current domestic political efforts under the new Putin administration for administrative and judicial reform as well as social development.

In TACIS, more technical assistance projects were designed according to the partnership model, stimulating both state-to-state assistance to key government organisations and civil society partnership on the local level. Here, such instruments like city twinning or co-operation between higher education facilities were integrated into the technical assistance programme. In general, the projects in TACIS were designed to enhance long-term structural democratisation rather than as a means for immediate reaction to current political developments. This applies also to the projects implemented under the special portfolio for 'democracy and human rights', added to the TACIS assistance programme for Russia after the outbreak of the second Chechen war. This special portfolio was set up as a political reaction to the serious disregard of international human rights principles by the Russian government (European Union 2000). However, due to the complicated organisational structure and project allocation practice in TACIS, the projects only started in 2002/2003 and were not able to contribute to immediate changes in domestic policies.

Instead, the autonomous EIDHR became the more important instrument for immediate reaction to political developments. In particular the EIDHR's 'micro projects' appeared to be flexible tools for responding to deteriorating policy practices in human rights performance and democratic governance in Russia. Micro-projects are small-scale projects with a budget of up to 50,000 Euro and a maximum duration of one year. In the first years of the Putin government, EIDHR made extensive use of the 'micro-project' tool for *bottom-up* support of democratisation, good governance and the development of the rule of law (European Commission 2001b). In this sector, EIDHR mainly financed human rights projects of Russian grass-root initiatives and NGOs, serving not least as a 'moral' backing of domestic non-state human rights entrepreneurs.

(ii) 'Chechnya irritations'

Despite substantial violations of human rights after the outbreak of the second war in Chechnya, EU politicians stuck to their 'twin-track policy' (Patten 1999). The year 2000 experienced a substantial 'dynamisation' of EU-Russia relations with a number of common initiatives put forward in the political dialogue, especially in the economic and security area.[9] At the same time, the EU tried to bring up the Chechnya issue in the dialogue (Splidsboel-Hansen 2002: 413), but Russian politicians were reluctant to make 'common values' an issue here. Alternatively, the EU increased public statements of concern about the human rights violations in Chechnya, insisting on a 'peaceful and political solution' to the conflict (General Affairs Council 1999). In addition, the EU announced a number of steps to show European concern about Russian non-compliant behaviour. However, these measures were 'symbolic' rather than targeted at a substantial change in the bilateral relations (Timmermann 2000a: 173). The EU announced a formal review of the 'Common Strategy', stricter control of Russian trade practices in the area of steel and textiles and a partial freeze on economic aid, loans, and tariff reductions if Russia would not give international observers access to the conflict area and keep its commitments arising from its membership in the CoE. EU policy-makers again reminded Russia that human rights compliance was a precondition for intensified relations with the EU (Council of the European Union 1999c).

Spring 2000 saw the frictions increasing. Russia protested against a UN-resolution, which was put forward by the EU member states in the April UN Human Rights Commission Session. The EU continued to issue public statements about the situation in Chechnya, which the Russian side perceived as a 'tone of condescension and hubris in the EU's approach to Russia [...].' (Gowan 2001: 11), not least as the Russian government had started to make efforts to find a 'political solution' in Chechnya. Although these efforts were highly questionable, the situation cleared up, when European politicians rejected a request to suspend the Russian delegation from the Parliamentary Assembly of the CoE. The European ministers argued that Russia had just fulfilled one of the main requirements, namely to give international observers access to Chechnya (Council of Europe Parliamentary Assembly 2000). This finally led both sides to adopt a more 'pragmatic' approach in bilateral relations by summer 2000 (Browning 2005; Danilov 2005: 89; Haukkala 2005: 16), with the EU reducing its open criticism against Russia step by step.

[9] Such as the energy dialogue initiated by President Putin and started in summer 2000, the Common Action Plan on Organised Crime adopted in April 2000, as well as intensified activity with regard to a security dialogue.

Re-linking interests and values in the 'Four Common Spaces'

Despite the 'pragmatisation' of bilateral relations, the 'gap between values and interests' in the EU-Russian partnership had widened by the year 2002 (Timmermann 2004: 359). The more the co-operation between the EU and Russia intensified, the more obvious became the policy differences between the two partners (Lynch 2005a: 18),[10] especially because the Russian government under Putin made no apparent moves to increase respect for international human rights standards and democratic principles within its domestic politics. Instead, domestic compliance made a considerable step backwards (Simon 2002: 57) as Russia showed more and more discriminatory legal practices and human rights violations in its domestic policies (European Commission 2004a: 4).

The policy differences have become even more extreme since the EU adopted its New Neighbourhood Policy (NNP), aiming at the stabilisation of the outer reaches of Europe including the Russian Federation (European Commission 2003).[11] The NNP aims to bring these countries closer to the EU normative standards by integrating them into the four freedoms of the European Common Market. The NNP very much relies on principles of democratic and human rights conditionality as a means of norms and values transfer (Wallace 2003: 18). This fact made Russia refuse the application of the NNP to the country at an early stage. Instead, the Russian government insisted on intensifying more horizontal relations, built upon principles of policy convergence rather than one-sided 'policy taking' (Lynch 2005b: 126). The EU and Russia apparently found a way out of this interest dilemma by adopting the 'Four Common Spaces' in 2005 – a 'jointly owned' (ibid.) co-operation agreement, which seeks to intensify co-operation in four selected areas of high mutual interest.[12] Detailed 'road maps' define common action, paving the way to achieving the four freedoms of the European Common Market (European Union 2005).

Yet, given Russia's resistance to open or hidden conditionality, the EU was faced with the question of how to 'invisibly' (Simon 2002: 64) enhance value transfer to Russia. Although the 'Four Common Spaces' do not constitute any democratic or human rights conditionality, the partners declare their shared acceptance as well as adherence to the 'common values' as they are laid down in the PCA (European Union 2003). Such a commitment from both sides was only possible, because the values were now defined as functional parts of the co-operation, rather than ends in themselves. In practice, the EU decided to use policy linkages, i.e. to link value issues to the profit and gains expectations on

[10] See also: Timmermann 2004: 359.

[11] The 'Wider Europe' concept was initially introduced by European Commission President Romano Prodi in 2002 (Prodi 2002).

[12] The 'Four Common Spaces' which are to be created are: a Common Economic Space, Common Space of Freedom, Security and Justice, Common Space of External Security, Common space on research, education and culture (European Union 2003)

the Russian side to spur norms transfer. Using its full bargaining power, the EU achieved a number of human rights linkages in the 'Four Common Spaces'. Financial aid and the political dialogue are both employed as additional instruments to keep up the value-interest linkage and to enable gradual diffusion and internalisation of human rights.

(i) Human rights as a functional part of the 'Common Spaces'

Human rights linkages can be identified mainly in the 'Common Economic Space' and in the 'Common Space of Freedom, Security and Justice'. With respect to the 'Common Economic Space', the EU falls back on the economic and trade asymmetries and on Russia's considerable economic dependency on Europe.[13] The road map for the 'Common Economic Space' sets out the objective of 'enhanc[ing] the competitiveness of the EU and Russian economies, based on the principles of non-discrimination, transparency and good governance' as a precondition for creating an open and integrated market between the EU and Russia (European Union 2005: Annex).

While the security co-operation under the Common Strategy lacked any normative linkages, the road map for the 'Common Space of Freedom, Security and Justice' makes extensive linkages to the rule of law. Under the primary goal – the securing of common borders – sub-issues like counter-terrorism and mutual assistance in law enforcement are linked to compliance requirements with respect to international human rights standards. The EU was also able to introduce regular human rights consultations, linking them to the common interest in fighting international terrorism (European Union 2005: Annex).

(ii) Financial aid: 'scaling down' on target

Financial aid under the EU's NNP is currently experiencing another conceptual modification. The main features of these modifications are twofold: First, the EU is about to abandon the concept of full-fledged democracy assistance in the Russia. This tendency coincides with the awareness that external democracy assistance has not been able to prevent the re-emergence of regressive trends, which have became visible all around post-Soviet space. Donors' expectations about the impact of external democracy assistance had apparently been excessive. Assessments of the impact of EU aid in TACIS have therefore come to the conclusion that aid contributions must be 'scaled down' in the future and with respect to the re-authorisation of the TACIS regulation in 2006, must be adjusted to the domestic modernisation progress and in particular to the individual dy-

[13] According to statistical data, 57 per cent of all Russian exports in the first two months of the year 2005 were sold to the European Union; 44 per cent of all imports to Russia currently come from EU countries, see: Russland und die EU auf Integrationskurs. Definition der Marschroute –unklares Endziel, in: Neue Zürcher Zeitung, 7.5.2005: 14.

namics of the inter-state relations of these countries with the EU (European Commission 2004b).

With respect to the Russian Federation, such a 'scaling down' strategy implies a more targeted aid approach, which is in line with the identified co-operation areas within the 'Four Common Spaces'. Aid for human rights internalisation again becomes relevant in the 'Common Economic Space' and in the 'Common Space of Freedom, Security and Justice'. While under the former co-operation area, aid commitments will most likely be linked to those areas of activity that were already relevant under the 'Common Strategy' objectives, substantial change in the areas of activity should be expected under the latter. These are expected to come in the form of shifts from rather technical issues in cross-border regulation towards a bigger focus on the development of substantial policy regulation standards within legal co-operation and common law enforcement, entailing the requirement to improve domestic legislative instruments and procedures according to European principles. Issues of civil society development, which do not fit within the four co-operation areas, will be outsourced to autonomous instruments or to EIDHR respectively.

(ii) Trust-building through 'open and frank' dialogue

In the political dialogue with Russia, the EU tries to balance out Russian interests with democratic and human rights values in order to achieve an 'indirect and stable effect' on Russian compliance behaviour.[14] This approach is double-sided: on the one hand, it requires an 'open and frank dialogue' with Russia (Patten 2002), pushing the human rights issue back into the bilateral relations (European Commission 2004a: 6). On the other hand, the EU is trying to stabilise Russian orientation towards the EU through trust-building in the new quality of bilateral relations. Two features are characteristic here: First, EU representatives more often publicly acclaim Russia's democratisation progress and achievements, instead of pointing to the existing policy differences between the two countries. Accordingly, Romano Prodi emphasised in 2004 that the EU 'should not over-dramatise [the] differences; [...]', but highlight the common grounds on which the partnership rests (Prodi 2004). While treating Russia as a *good European*, the EU can publicly and with a positive connotation call attention to Russia's commitment to the 'shared values' (European Union/Russian Federation 2003). Second, substantial differences on value issues are transferred to less public spaces and conventional dialogue mechanisms. EU officials point at means of discrete diplomacy, either through traditional diplomatic steps or through inter-personal dialogue, especially on the summit level, as promising instruments to trigger effects on Russian policy-makers at the moment.

[14] See: Markus Winter: Europas Strategie, in: Frankfurter Rundschau, 10.03.2005: 2.

Conclusion: 'Exporting' human rights to Russia – from quasi-vertical to horizontal value transfer

Tracing fifteen years of EU human rights policy vis-à-vis Russia, the study shows that the 'export' of human rights norms and democratic values represents a substantial part of the EU's security strategy, aiming at long-term stability through norms transfer and normative compatibility. The EU's human rights policy vis-à-vis Russia reflects an attempt to impose a set of values, including international and European human rights norms, on the country from outside by stimulating Russia to take over the norms-templates of the EU and those upon which the EU rests. As such, it can be termed an external governance strategy.

This general policy approach towards Russia has stayed the same over the last fifteen years of engagement, as has the set of human rights instruments applied by the EU – positive rewards, democracy aid, and political dialogue. However, the substance of these instruments has changed considerably over time. The conceptual adjustments carried out in the human rights policy vis-à-vis the Russian Federation since 1991 display an incremental shift from direct and 'quasi'-vertical to more indirect and horizontal mechanisms in order to trigger norms adaptation and human rights compliance. These shifts resulted from the need to optimise the overall policy approach towards Russia in the light of regressive domestic developments that run counter to the EU's own security goals.

In its initial phase, the EU pursued a strategy of immediate human rights transfer through direct rewards and conditionality, starting from the assumption that Russia itself was striving for democracy and human rights compliance. Therefore, a set of 'shared values', democracy, human rights and the rule of law, was made the normative reference point for bilateral relations. However, in this first phase domestic human rights compliance remained more formal than substantial. In a second phase from 1999 onwards, the EU has tried to trigger more substantial norms adaptation and has pursued a double-sided approach, applying vertical as well as horizontal mechanisms of norms transfer. While one major objective in the EU's policy strategy was to strengthen and intensify the relations with Russia through a 'strategic partnership', stable co-operation within this partnership has remained conditional upon the implementation of and compliance with the 'common values', especially democratic principles and international human rights standards.

Realising that by 2002 human rights norms still had not been internalised in Russia in a way satisfactory to the EU and its security goals and that normative principles like democracy and human rights were less and less in the primary interests of Russian policy-makers, the EU has now put indirect means of rule and norms transfer at the centre of its export strategy. At present, the requirement to comply with international and European human rights standards has been made an integral part of the inter-state partnership. Instead of applying direct conditionality, the EU today links the 'common values' to the primary interests and profit calculations of the domestic actors, thus ensuring an 'invisible' value transfer to Russia and prompting sustainable human rights compliance in the long-term in the country.

Turkey's Compliance with EU Human Rights Norms

Birsen Erdogan

Introduction

Turkey's long-lasting adventure on the path to the European Union has been marked most of the time by effects of human rights violations in Turkey. Turkey's poor record on the protection of human rights has, from time to time, caused serious problems both within Turkey and in Turkey's relations with the Union. There are many reasons behind those crises. Yet, maybe the most obvious reason is closely related to the construction of the Turkish identity throughout history.

When the modern Turkish Republic was founded by Mustafa Kemal and his friends, it was aimed at establishing a new Turkish identity, which was an alternative to the Ottoman past. The roots of this new identity can be found in modernisation and Westernisation movements that were active in the last decades of the Ottoman Empire. The new identity was based on a couple of principles. One of them was that the new state should be a modern and Western-oriented establishment with its institutions and its foreign policy objectives. This principle has been one of the unchanged policies of all governments in (modern) Turkish history, aimed at making Turkey an indivisible part of the Western world. Introduction of certain political reforms and freedoms such as woman's rights and reforming the education system back in the 1930s did not meet with public outcry or major difficulty. These kinds of reforms were seen as the symbol of breaking with the country's monarchical past. Rumford with a quotation from a Turkish scholar states "Kemalism is premised on the equation of modernity with progress, that is, on the making of a modern nation through the introduction and the dissemination of Western reason and rationality into what was regarded as traditional and backward social relations" (2003: 382).

However, the reformation did not facilitate a full-scale democratisation, which brings us to the question of other dimensions of the Turkish state identity.

According to Yavuz,

> These centralizing and homogenizing reforms divided Turkey into zones of prosperity and zones of conflict. The zones of prosperity are concentrated around the "white Turks," or governing political elite, who are at the centre of state power, while the zones of conflict are centred around the poor and marginalized sectors of the population--"the black Turks." Religion, as a residual variable of the category of the black Turks and Kurds, became the basis for the exclusion of the majority of the population by the hegemonic Kemalist discourse of the white Turks. Islam has become the op-

> positional identity for the excluded sectors of Turkish society (2000: 21).

The new republic was based on the undeniable, indivisible territorial and national integrity of the state. As a result of this, the new state emerged as a unitary and centralised body with strong and politicised armed forces and with no officially recognised minorities other than non-Muslims, whose rights had been recognised in the Lausanne Treaty of 1923. Impressed by the French model of state, founders of the new republic preferred to unite all peoples living on the Turkish territory under the umbrella of 'citizenship.' "The civic culture induced by Ataturk's reforms incorporated a nationalist ideology of Jacoben inspiration that emphasised the unity and indivisibility, not only of the state and its territory, but also of the people" (Rumford 2003: 383).[1] Although the Turkish model of citizenship was not based on any racial categorisation and exclusionary policies, it led to the politics of official denial and low tolerance, as far as diverse opinions and identities in society are concerned. Kurds were considered citizens of the Turkish Republic with no minority privileges and forced 'to see themselves as Turks' (Hale 2003: 116).

The lines of official state discourse and policies have been drawn by a deep-rooted and strong class in the form of the Turkish state elite. This elite is composed of the secular civil state bureaucracy, some components of the social democratic movement and members of the armed forces.[2] From the establishment of the new state in 1923 until today, the elite policies in Turkey have caused the emergence of a paradox that has been the main dilemma of the Western world in dealing with Turkey. This paradox can be defined by the different and confusing attitudes of the Turkish policy makers at home and abroad. While the main lines of Turkish foreign policy are grounded on the Westernisation ideal, policies of interior affairs are marked by slow democratisation and uncompleted liberalisation. Two ideals, a modern and Western style of state on one

[1] Also see Resat Kasaba and Sibel Bozdogan, "Turkey at a Crossroad," *Journal of International Affairs*, 2000, Vol. 54, No. 1, pp. 1-20; Yavuz M. Hakan, "Cleansing Islam From the Public Sphere," *Journal of International Affairs*, 2000, Vol. 54, No. 1, pp. 21-43; Dogu Ergil, "Identity Crises and Political Instability in Turkey," *Journal of International Affairs*, 2000, Vol. 54, No. 1, pp. 43-63; Muhittin Ataman "Ozal Leadership and Restructuring of Turkish Ethnic Policy in the 1980s," *Middle Eastern Studies*, 2002, Vol. 38, No. 4, pp.123-142.

[2] For more detailed analysis of the Turkish state elite, see Metin Heper and Aylin Guney, "The Military and Democracy in the Third Turkish Republic," *Armed Forces and Society*, 1996, Vol. 22, No. 4, pp. 619-643; Metin Heper and Aylin Guney, "The Military and the Consolidation of Democracy: the Recent Turkish Experience," *Armed Forces and Society*, 2000, Vol. 26, No. 4, pp.635-658; Metin Heper, *The State Tradition in Turkey*, 1985, London: Eothen Press; Metin Heper, "The Ottoman Legacy and Turkish Politics," *Journal of International Affairs*, 2000, Vol. 54, No. 1, pp. 63-83; Henri J. Barkey, "The Struggles of a 'Strong' State," *Journal of International Affairs*, 2000, Vol. 54, No. 1, pp. 87-106.

hand and a centralised, sovereign, independent, unitary, security-oriented nation-state on the other have caused the major crises of the modern Turkish history both at home and abroad. The roots of the identity crises of modern Turkey can be found in the tension, strain and lack of consensus between those two ideals.

According to Karaosmanoğlu, since the 18th century the process of Westernisation "has given rise to an identity problem that has in turn, complicated the understanding of Turkey's foreign and security behaviour" (2000: 199).

Although the mainstream Turkish foreign policy has never given up the ideal of being a Western state and a member of prestigious Western institutions, the Westernisation movements in Turkey went rather slow especially until 2002 and met with serious challenges at home. Critiques directed from Brussels at Turkish human rights policies did not always meet with appreciation and compliance in Turkey. It was obvious that the traditional state elite was not ready to transform its identity from a state-centric and security-oriented one to a tolerant and completely democratic one during the 1980s and the 1990s, as this would at the end mean the 'loss of sovereignty' in some areas (Onis 2003: 9). In spite of minor initiatives taken to protect human rights, the overall human rights record of Turkey was overshadowed by its problems with its Kurdish people and its low tolerance towards the recognition of fundamental freedoms such as manifestation of religious beliefs, expression and association.

From time to time, the European efforts to democratise Turkey have been considered a tool to intervene in Turkish domestic affairs and Brussels was blamed for not understanding the 'Turkish reality' which has its unique problems rooted in the geographical area that it is located and require unique ways of solving. As a result of this, the Turkish mainstream elite victimised themselves for living in a country surrounded by instable neighbours in its region, being weakened by the Kurdish terrorist organisation PKK which received support from the Western states and being left all alone by its Western allies to deal with their problems. Due to absence of democratic culture and tolerance, there was no widespread open discussion and internal consensus on questions like 'who we are' and 'what kind of state we want'. The critiques coming from Europe met with reactions of nationalist and Kemalist groups whose national pride was hurt. In addition to this, the image of Europe in Turkey was nothing more than a false generalisation, as if there was one single Europe outside which was not fair to Turkey and always asking too much.

Unfortunately, the Turkish identity has not been constructed by and over a consensus between internal dynamics of the country so far. The influence of the European Union on the reconstruction of the Turkish state structure has been greater than the imprints of internal dynamics. The compliance process with the European Union's conditions moved the controversies between mainstream elite and other social forces to the surface of the daily politics. The general picture of Turkish politics has been reshaped and main actors have changed due to efforts of either reactionary forces against democratisation or empowerment of long - silenced groups longing for freedoms.

The rigid model of civic nationalism adopted by the secular state elite not only carries the risk of completely abolishing Turkey's dreams in Europe, but also it makes it impossible to establish a peace, harmony and conciliation with members of its own society. Policies born out of the passion to be liked and accepted as well as out of victimisation and disappointment could only fail and be short-lived. As a consequence, the Turkish ambition to be a European Union state will require a transformation of state and even national identity on democratic and pluralist grounds.

This study will highlight the legislative achievements of Turkey in human rights, as consequences of the European Union's political conditionality. It will also discuss the political atmosphere of the times when these legislative reforms have taken place with a special emphasis on the role of political actors as proponents or initiators and as opponents of these changes.

1980s and 1990s: Beginning of Economic Liberalisation and Turkey's Candidacy Process

The most important event that marked the 1980s in Turkey was the military intervention which took place in 1980. Although the military rule did not take more than two years and civilian elections were held in 1982, the undemocratic Constitution brought by the military regime and approved by the majority of the people's votes established a system of restrictions in freedoms and rights. However, the reactions coming from European Community bodies were largely limited to the resolutions of the European parliament, which criticised the violations of fundamental freedoms. The effect of the parliament on the democratisation of the Turkish state structure was not significant. Turkish leaders of the time such as Turgut Özal employed economic and security-oriented policies. Although there were attempts to restore the civilian regime and democracy (such as lifting the ban on former politicians, partial amnesties granted to prisoners, lifting of the state of emergency except for some cities in south eastern and eastern Turkey and ceasing to carry out the death penalty), they were still far from being satisfactory.

Turkey's application for full membership came in 1987, almost at the same time with Turkey's acceptance of the individual petition system to the European Court of Human Rights in Strasbourg. Since then, it has been proven that the European Court was very influential on evaluating and interpreting major drawbacks of the human rights protection in Turkey. In 1987, the European parliament issued more resolutions on Turkey with special emphasis given to the protection of minorities and the Armenian genocide. The reaction to this resolution in Turkey was highly critical (Krauss 2000: 225). Although Özal himself was a liberal leader and mentioned several times that the Kurdish people and people with Islamic affiliations should live freely in Turkey far from fears of being convicted or blamed (Aral 2001: 80), he gave priority to economic development rather than social and political reforms, thinking that economic liberalisation would bring political liberalisation as well.

In 1989, the European Commission issued a report on Turkey's application for membership. The report focussed mostly on economic issues and recommended that the European Union was not ready for a new enlargement. In the report the only statement related to the human rights in Turkey was about insufficient attempts for democratisation, human rights protection and respect for minorities.

By the beginning of the 1990s, Turkey pursued a more active and security-oriented foreign policy, especially due to developments such as the independence of the Turkic language states in the former Soviet Union and the war in Iraq. One of the aims behind these policies was to show the European Union countries that Turkey still had geopolitical importance for Europe,. On the other hand, the European Union entered into a new era, where the traditional security policies were replaced by increasing desecuritisation of foreign and domestic affairs. However, Turkish leaders did not notice this change in European politics and they continued to look at Europe with their conventional glasses, focussed on geopolitics, strategic and material gains and threat analysis of the armed forces (Jung 2001).

Özal's liberal ideas were reflected in some positive developments in the country's legislation. The decree that regulates the use of the Turkish language was changed and the use of the Kurdish language in cultural life and written media was allowed. However, the use of native languages other than Turkish in radio and television broadcasting was still not allowed. Moreover, the pressure on political publications in Kurdish continued. Another important development was the abolition in 1991 of the controversial three articles of the Penal Code, which seriously restrict communist and Islamic ideas, expression and association. Unfortunately, the conflict in south eastern and eastern Turkey between the PKK and the armed forces resulted in restriction of basic rights and fundamental freedoms for many years. In 1991, the Law on the Fight against Terrorism was accepted by the parliament. The law not only promulgated a very general definition of terrorism, which could include almost everybody with certain political opinions, but also limited freedoms such as association, expression, assembly and press in the context of the fight against terrorism. According to the law, the detention period would be extended to thirty days and trials were held only in the State Security Courts within the context of the law. In the following years, the European Court of Justice has found that the establishment and composition of the State Security Courts was a violation of right to fair trial on many occasions. As a result of the anti-terror legislation, many people were held in custody for days, torture claims and disappearances increased to a serious level and many intellectuals and journalists went to jail.

By the beginning of the 1990s, the social and economic structure of Turkey underwent a radical change due to liberal policies introduced by Özal and to migration from the Kurdish-populated areas to bigger cities. Especially in big cities, economic and social differences between income and ethnic groups became visible. As a result of this, the new social picture was the marginalisation of income groups both in their life styles and political choices. Hundreds of thousands of Kurdish people emigrated to more developed areas, where they could find more security and save themselves from the conflict between the PKK and Turkish armed forces.[3] In addition to this, thousands of villagers were evacuated by the armed forces on grounds of security. In the 1990s, Turkey had an increasing report of unemployment and decreasing standard of living. The conflict in the eastern and south eastern areas did not only cost the lives of thousands from both sides and the restriction of freedoms in the name of the fight against terrorism, but it also cost an enormous amount of money, the effect of which was worsened by the general recession of the economy.

In Europe, the picture of Turkey was dreadful. Reports of human rights organisations on Turkey's serious violations of human rights, propaganda led by Kurdish migrants and refugees that moved to Europe in the 1980s and the beginning of the 1990s, and worries of European Union countries pursuing human rights-oriented foreign policies doubled the number and intensity of European parliament resolutions and decisions or embargos of single countries against Turkey. Unfortunately, leaders after Turgut Özal used the fight against terrorism as a legitimisation for their restrictive policies and could not dare to adopt alternative domestic or minority policies other than partial attempts for restructuring the Kurdish regions economically. It was almost clear that as long as terrorism threatened the country, there would be no hope for finalising democratic consolidation. Nonetheless, there were some small but significant attempts. The coalition government of the right-wing True Path Party and social democrats in 1992 managed to make important changes in the law of pre-trial procedures. The length of the custody period was reduced,[4] while the right to a lawyer and the right to information during custody was strengthened. A protection for possible torture victims was also introduced. However, these changes did not include people that were held in custody under the Law on the Fight against Terrorism. Another interesting development was the merger of the social democrats with a

[3] According to the American Department of State report for 1999, the official figures of displaced persons were between 300,000 and 560,000, whereas NGOs claimed them to be between 800,000 and 2 million. U.S. Department of State, "Country Reports on Human Rights Practices: Turkey" 1999, http://www.state.gov/g/drl/rls/hrrpt/1999/365.htm (12 May 2003).

[4] It was reduced to twenty-four hours in most cases, to four days in exceptional cases and to eight days with the decision of a judge.

political party focussed on the Kurdish question. As a result of 1991 elections, twenty-two people from the so-called Kurdish party gained seats in the parliament. This was the only and last chance for representing a Kurdish party in parliament since 1980. Unfortunately, it did not last long and in 1993 the Constitutional Court ordered the closure of this party on grounds of its close connections with the terrorist organisation PKK. In 1994, six MPs from the party, including the well-known Leyla Zana, were detained and sentence to fifteen years imprisonment for their alleged membership in the PKK. While there have also been other Kurdish parties, they have never managed to cross the 10 per cent national threshold in elections. Unfortunately, the political representation of the Kurdish parties has always been weak in Turkish society and political system. Although in the parliament there have been Kurdish MPs under the roof of other parties elected from their region, they were usually passive as far as the Kurdish question is concerned. The so-called Kurdish parties, on the other hand, did not find mass support and did not help reconciling the conflict between the armed forces and the PKK. Those parties were accused of being insensitive to the feelings of the majority of the people, who disliked the PKK.

Meanwhile, in 1993 there were two important developments in the European Union. On the one hand, the human rights clauses of the Maastricht Treaty entered into force.[5] On the other hand, the Copenhagen criteria for membership were accepted by leaders of member states. These two developments opened a new path for the European Union, not only as an economic integration model but also as a union of states which agreed on certain political values and norms. The Copenhagen criteria are very influential on the relations between Turkey and the European Union. In accepting the admission criteria, the candidate countries also accepted the EU political conditionality. According to these criteria, candidates have to respect human rights, rule of law, democracy and minority rights. The Copenhagen criteria are heavily criticised in Turkey. According to Turkish authorities, Turkey had made its application long ago and it was not fair to be bound by a new set of criteria. They also claimed that provisions like minority rights were ambiguous and not generally accepted even by all member states. After the Copenhagen criteria were accepted, Turkish authorities noticed that Turkey had no special place among applicant countries, which included

[5] According to Maastricht Treaty Title I, Section F and Paragraph 2, "The Union shall respect fundamental rights, as guaranteed by the European Convention for the Protection of Human Rights and Fundamental Freedoms signed in Rome on 4 November 1950 and as they result from the constitutional traditions common to the member states, and general principles of community law." The Maastricht Treaty considers as one of the objectives of the Common Foreign and Security policy of the European Union, the development and consolidation of 'democracy, rule of law and respect for human rights and fundamental freedoms.' Later in 1999, Amsterdam Treaty established procedures indented to secure the protection of human rights and reaffirmed that the EU is founded on principles of democracy and human rights. Visit http://europa.eu.int/comm./external _relations/human_rights/intro/ (15 November 2005).

states that had adopted democratic rules only a couple of years before. In addition to this, the Turkish government was well aware of the fact that as long as there is human and minority rights conditionality, Turkey's membership could be in question and even postponed for decades. Turkish authorities had always relied on their security card in the game, but suddenly the rules had changed.

As Uzun puts it,

> The term of 'political criteria' is perceived in a very distinctive way in Turkey and it almost rebels masses against the European Union. Even some of MPs who are representatives of the political will, in certain occasions qualify it as if it is coercion created against Turkey or it is one of the component of the European Union's rejection mechanisms and they influence people in this manner. However, political criteria are concrete principles of positive law, which are based on a completely legal ground and which represent the system of common values within the European Union. While the European Union does not hesitate to enter into any kind of harmonisation process for the achievement of the integration movement, to claim that the request for the preparation of the substructure which is necessary for the new members in order to be a part of the system is a conspiracy means not to know the past and the future mission of the European Union.(...) The Copenhagen Criteria is a package for democratisation proposed in order to prepare the substructures of candidate states in these subjects and to provide their integration into the system, whenever they are in the same level with the Union (2002: 77).

In 1995, the most important step on the way to economic integration into the European Union was taken, with Turkey and the European Union Association Council agreeing that the Customs Union would enter into force by 1 January 1996. However, prior to the acceptance of the decision, some members of the European parliament hesitated on the grounds of human rights violations in Turkey and the parliament adopted several resolutions against Turkey.[6] Afraid

[6] parliament in its resolutions before the Customs Union Agreement was confirmed strongly criticized Turkey for its operations in Iraqi territory, for the imprisonment of six former MPs and pressures on intellectuals before expressing their opinions. "Resolution on the draft agreement on the conclusion of a customs union between the EU and Turkey," *The European parliament*, B4-0171, 0175, 0179, 0180, 0204 and 0259/95.
At the end of 1994, the parliament even frozen relations between Turkey and called the Council not to sign the Agreement. However, when we come to 1995, the members of the parliament were softer and more cautious and at the end the agreement was confirmed by votes of 343 against votes of 149.

of a possible veto by the European parliament, the government made some amendments in the Constitution in July and in the Law against Terrorism in October. Although the Constitutional amendments did not entail an overall modernisation of the Constitution, they helped to liberalise the political culture.[7] The controversial Article 8 of the Law against Terrorism was changed on 27 October. The clause which had criminalised actions directed against the territorial and national integrity 'regardless of aim and method' was replaced by the phrase 'with the aim of destroying the national and territorial integrity.' The effect of the amendments in Europe was positive. In the end, due to the influence of the Commission and state leaders, a majority of the parliament voted in favour in December 1995. Immediately after confirming the Customs Union, parliament adopted a resolution calling all bodies of the European Union to develop a dialogue with Turkey to promote human and minority rights there. The acceptance of the Customs Union was an indicator that the Union states offered a reward to Turkey, instead of a punishment or a possible isolation. According to Krauss, the most important concern for the European Union states to conclude the Customs Union was their economic and geostrategic interests and *realpolitik* (2000: 225). By the Customs Union, the priority of human rights had been subordinated to the economic concerns. This is in fact a natural outcome of the complex structure of the European Union, where the Council was represented by leaders of member states and the parliament is composed of different political parties. According to Hale, "... even if there was no dramatic reduction in the military's actual role in Turkish politics in the near future, it seemed unlikely that the EU would use this as an explicit reason for not starting accession negotiations," since Turkey's role in NATO is still important for some EU leaders (2003: 122).

The outcomes of the 1995 general elections were interesting as far as the rise in the votes for marginal parties is concerned (Onis 2000: 284). The Kurdish party could not get more than 10 per cent of all votes, but it became the biggest party in five eastern cities. The nationalist party (Nationalist Action Party, MHP) increased its votes to 8 per cent, whereas the religious-oriented party (Welfare Party, RP) became the first party, obtaining the majority of nationwide votes. After the election, when the results were announced, the armed forces as the guardian of secularism in the republic were particularly alarmed. In the agenda of the armed forces, there were at least two priorities visible: first, smashing the Kurdish insurgency in the south east of the country, and second, controlling the new rise of Islamic fundamentalism. The growing dissent against the RP was

[7] Fifteen articles and Preamble of the Constitution were amended in 23 July 1995. Among those articles, there were amendments which lifted the obstacles before the students, university academicians, associations and labour unions to be members of political parties or organizations; the reduction of the voting age from 21 to 18 and the extraction of sentences in the Preamble which praised the 1980 military coup.

reflected in the decision of the Constitutional Court in 1998, which ordered closure of the party. The fate of the Kurdish people who were not happy with the system strangely intersected with those of Islamists. The Turkish state and social project would never be completed, unless there were peace and consensus between those groups and the state elite.

Although the RP coalition did not last long, there were some positive developments in the area of human rights. The length of custody in the areas of the state of emergency was reduced from thirty days to ten days. In other regions, those who are detained under the framework of the Law against Terrorism were to be brought before a judge within 48 hours (to be extended to seven days in collective crimes with a judge's permission). Moreover, an office open 24 hours per day was established under the authority of the Ministry of Interior Affairs to deal with disappeared people. The State Ministry of Human Rights, which was established in 1991, became quite influential especially in its struggle against torture. However, torture claims were still widespread and the ministry's power and influence were limited, especially in areas where the state of emergency remained in force. In 1997, a Human Rights Coordination Committee under the ministry was established. The Committee welcomed NGOs to its meetings and was able to advise the government on human rights issues.

However, these reforms were not sufficient to guarantee basic freedoms and rights. The overall situation on Turkey was still far from being democratic. Main problems addressed by the European parliament were limited religious freedoms, the conditions of Leyla Zana and her friends in jail, limitations on freedom of press and expression, forced evacuation of Kurdish areas and repression of minorities. The number of individual applications against Turkey before the European Court of Human Rights from 1991 to 1996 was more than 800. International NGOs issued detailed reports on Turkey's human rights violations. However, the most important actor for the Turkish authorities on issues of human rights was about to be the European Commission, which was to start issuing progress reports on applicant countries from 1998 onwards. But before that, the shocking decision of the European Union leaders came up in December 1997 in Luxembourg. Turkey was not recognised as a candidate state, since it did not meet the Copenhagen criteria. As then-Prime Minister of Luxembourg Jean Claude Juncker summarised, a country where torture was still practiced could not have any seat at the European table.[8] The conclusive remarks of the Luxem-

[8] These remarks met with reactions of the state authorities. Foreign Ministry Spokesman Necati Utkan said that Juncker's humiliating and unfounded style against Turkey is regretful. Utkan said Turkey has always taken into account just criticism concerning human rights issue, and extends sincere efforts to prevent discrepancies in this issue. Stating that Juncker's words are unacceptable, Utkan said "if human rights issue is forwarded as a disguise to keep Turkey out of EU, this situation will be evaluated separately." See http://www.hri.org/news/turkey/anadolu/1997/97-12-13.anadolu.html#02 (15 October 2005).

bourg summit also included provisions on the resolution of Cyprus and the Aegean Sea conflicts with Greece. The reaction of the Turkish side to the summit decisions was fierce and Prime Minister Mesut Yılmaz declared that there was a double standard and new criteria for Turkey to meet. He defined the situation as unacceptable and Turkey froze relations with the European Union unilaterally.

In 1998, the Commission issued Turkey's First Progress Report.[9] In the report, Turkey was advised to find political and democratic solutions to the terrorism problem. The high number of people who disappeared or claimed to have been tortured was emphasised. Article 7 and 8 of the Law against Terrorism and Articles 158, 159, 311 and 312 of the Penal Code which seriously restricted freedom of expression, opinion, association, assembly and press were called to be amended. As far as the Kurdish question is concerned, the Turkish government was called to respect cultural rights, such as the right to education and broadcast in minority languages. Although the Turkish side was not willing to continue normal relations with the Union, the Union bodies underlined the importance of the normalisation of relations in their 1998 summit decision. The Commission reports of the coming years were going to follow the same lines as the first one. In addition to the issues stated above, reports scrutinised problems related to torture, prison conditions, prohibition of discrimination especially based on sex and cultural and religious rights of ethnic minorities and non-Muslim and non-Sunni groups.

In 1999, Abdullah Öcalan, leader of the PKK was caught in Kenya and brought back to Turkey to be tried in the State Security Court. The capture of Öcalan brought the dissolution of the PKK for some time until it started its activities again in 2004. The normalisation of the former strained atmosphere – especially in south eastern regions – had reflections in the whole country and contributed to further democratisation and full-implementation of human rights. Obviously, this was also a chance to send the armed forces back to their barracks and minimise their influence on daily politics. However, the uproar of nationalist groups after the capture of Öcalan and possibility of his execution increased support for the nationalist party, MHP, in elections in April. The MHP became the second biggest party after the nationalist left party (DSP) of Ecevit. The nationalist movement was gaining more support from people by the second half of the 1990s. According to Ergil, this was a new kind of nationalism, which is

> (...) quite different from the nationalism of the founding Republic. It is not Western-oriented, but rather traditionalist, isolationist and

[9] For Commission reports since 1998, visit ttp://europa.eu.int/comm/enlargement/turkey/docs.htm (15 November 2005).

> supports a role for religion in public life. It has nothing to do with the modernizing bourgeois culture that the Republican elite revered and adopted. What it shares with the construct of the founding elite is its statist character; it puts the state in the centre of social life as the provider and protector as well as the source of political power" (2000: 58).

Gathering of the nationalists under the roof of the MHP brought a considerable power to the MHP. Behind the election results, the fury towards the European Union states for their decision at Luxembourg summit played an important role. Proponents of the European Union and further democratisation in Turkey were not feeling easy for possible obstructions of the MHP. However, the government program of the new coalition government of DSP, MHP and the Motherland Party (ANAP) was quite promising contrary to the fears. According to the program, the reforms for the European Union membership should commence immediately, as the membership was one of ultimate goals of the new government. The Kurdish Party, HADEP, could not pass the 10 per cent threshold, but had thirty-six mayors in eastern and south eastern regions, including seven provinces.

In December 1999, the Union leaders affirmed Turkey's official candidacy status on an equal footing with other states at the Helsinki summit. Excited by this decision and relieved by the capture of the terrorist leader, the new coalition government was aware of the importance and necessity of the democratisation. Although the State Security Court found Öcalan guilty and decided his execution, the coalition government issued a memorandum not to execute him. This was an interesting policy as far as the MHP was concerned, which came to the power through votes of millions of nationalists who believed in the execution of Öcalan as a punishment he deserved. However, the Öcalan trial has not been found fair by the European Court of Human Rights.

2000s: Transformation Years

The motivation from the European Union's Helsinki decision, the liberal policies of Mesut Yılmaz (the leader of the ANAP) and the optimism that arose by the appointment of the well-known academician and economist Kemal Derviş to the ministry responsible for economic issues created an atmosphere that was missed for years under the tension of terrorism and economic recession. The new government immediately decided on the replacement of the military judges from the State Security Courts. Öcalan himself was affected by this reform in his trial. The Chairperson of the Human Rights Commission in parliament, Sema Pişkinsüt, became very influential with her determined stance against torture practices. Torture reports prepared by her found great interest and attention among the public and for the first time, the Turkish people were informed about the widespread torture practices. Starting from 1999, many judges, public prosecutors and police were subjected to human rights training in the framework of projects funded by the European Union and governmental policies. In 2000, the Turkish government signed the Covenant on Civil and Political Rights and the Covenant on Economic, Social and Cultural Rights of the United Nations (hereinafter referred to as the 'Twin Covenants'). In 2000, the state of emergency was lifted in two eastern cities and the terror attacks in Kurdish areas were significantly reduced.

The Association Council between Turkey and the European Union finally met in April 2000, for the first time since 1997. The Commission issued its report on Turkey's Progress in November 2000, praising the government's attempts to eliminate torture and to give human rights training to civil servants, as well as its decision not to execute Öcalan.[10] However, the report mentioned serious problems with the implementation of human rights as they were mentioned above.

On the 8th of March 2001, the European Union Council confirmed and published the Accession Partnership, to become one of the most important guidelines for candidate states.[11] The document highlighted priority short- and medium-term policy areas in which the Turkish government has been encouraged to make further reforms.

On the 19th of March, the Turkish government introduced the National Program for the Adoption of the Acquis.[12] In the Program, priority issues that would be settled in the short and medium terms were summarised. The government promised to make necessary reforms in the areas of freedom of expression, assembly, association, and religion; for the elimination of discrimination and torture; improvement of detention conditions and the limitation of the role of the National Security Council.

In a section titled 'Strengthening Opportunities to Redress the Consequences of Human Rights Violations,' it was stated that the draft law on Indemnification of Losses Resulting from Terrorism and the Fight against Terrorism would be enacted in the medium term. However, on the issue of cultural life and individual freedoms, the Program reminded that the official language of Turkey is Turkish. At the same time, the document concluded that this did not prohibit the use of different languages, dialects and tongues of the Turkish citizens in their daily lives.

[10] For the report visit http://europa.eu.int/comm/enlargement/report_11_00/pdf/en/tu_en.pdf (12 October 2005).

[11] For the text visit http://europa.eu.int/eur-lex/pri/en/oj/dat/2001/l_085/l_08520010324 en00130023 .pdf (12 October 2005).

[12] For the text visit http://europa.eu.int/comm/enlargement/turkey/pdf/npaa_full.pdf (12 October 2005).

The reactions to the adoption of the National Program were positive in many circles. However, the restrictive policies stated in the program on the use of minority languages other than Turkish were far from the demands of the European Union organs. By 1999, the restructuring of Turkish politics toward harmonisation with the European Union gained considerable momentum. Mesut Yılmaz was appointed as the responsible minister for European affairs and the General Secretariat for European Union Affairs was established in 2000. Meanwhile, many other ministries reformed their internal structures and established offices for harmonisation with the European Union acquis.

On 3 October 2001, the Turkish Grand National Assembly voted in favour of the amendment of thirty-four Constitutional articles, including the Preamble to the Constitution.[13] This was the most important reformation of the Constitution so far. Articles which restricted human rights and freedom of expression have been either amended or completely lifted. The length of the detention period with collective crimes has been reduced from fifteen days to four days. The right to compensation for those held in custody in a way even contradicted existing law. Moreover, freedoms like property, movement, gathering data, communication and the protection of private life have been brought in line with the European Convention of Human Rights. Most limitations to the right of association have been lifted and the only remaining restrictions were in accordance with the European Convention. The right to fair trial has been introduced into the Constitution. By these changes, the execution of the death penalty was limited to times of war, imminent threat of war and crimes of terrorism. Through another change, the use of evidence gathered by illegal means was outlawed. The criteria for closing down political parties were tightened and alternatives were introduced, such as reducing state aid and funding. The structure of the National Security Council was reformed and a civilian majority was achieved by including the vice Prime Minister and Minister of Justice. The former provision stating that the decisions of the Council would be given attention by the government was replaced by a new phrase saying that decisions of the Council will be reconsidered by the government. Moreover, through a change to Article 26, the provision stating that a language forbidden by law could not be used to express and spread opinions has been lifted completely. Nonetheless, the use of other languages remained restricted with the aim of protecting national security, public order, public security, basic foundations of the Republic and the territorial and national integrity of state.

The Commission report for 2001 came just after the Constitutional reform in October.[14] Although the report praised the reforms and works of the human rights bodies, there were still fundamental problems with Turkey's compliance

[13] For constitutional reform, visit www.abgs.gov.tr (10 October 2005)
[14] For the report visit http://europa.eu.int/comm/enlargement/report2001/tu_en.pdf (12 October 2005)

with the Copenhagen criteria. According to the report these problems were basically about the protection of non-Sunni and non-Muslim minorities, the right to retrial in accordance with decisions of the European Court of Human Rights, freedom of expression and freedom of assembly. According to the report, the implementation of democratic changes in the fight against torture, judicial reform, prison conditions, effect of the armed forces on civil politics and cultural rights were still far from sufficient. The report called the government to take the necessary steps for the use of minority languages in education and in TV-radio broadcasting. The report also criticised harassment of members of the Kurdish party HADEP and continuation of the rule of emergency in some cities. But the government was praised for its detailed reform program for the elimination of poverty and economic problems in south east Turkey and for its attempts to normalise the situation there.

After the report was issued, the leader of the nationalist party Devlet Bahçeli criticised it for not being impartial and neutral. On the other hand Mesut Yılmaz claimed that the report was based on objective data and that Turkey was criticised on very relevant and well chosen issues.[15] These two different approaches in the government were indicators of big differences between these two parties and signals of increasing cracks within the coalition. According to Hale, "within Ecevit's government,(…), opposition to reform of the human rights regime came almost exclusively from the MHP, which regarded any constitutional liberalisation – especially on the Kurdish issue- as an insult to those who had died during the long struggle against the militants of the Kurdish Workers' Party (PKK)" (2003: 109).

2002 can be accepted as one of the most active years of Turkey as far as compliance with the Copenhagen criteria is concerned. Through documents like the Accession Partnership and the Commission reports on progress, the Turkish decision-makers became aware of the problem issues. In February 2002, parliament passed a comprehensive package of democratic reforms, which is known as the 'First Harmonisation Package'.[16] In spite of tensions between MPs of the MHP and other coalition parties, the majority voted in favour of changes to the controversial Article 312 of the Penal Code.[17] Through these changes, the criminalisation of an idea or opinion became more complex and difficult. In addition to this, through other changes, punishment for some crimes such as propaganda for the destruction of the state and insults to the state institutions have been

[15]http://haber.mynet.com/detail_news/?type=flash&id=A003BCD7&ref=haberdetail&date=09Ekim2002 (12 October 2005)
[16]http://www.euturkey.org.tr/abportal/category.asp?TreeID=246&VisitID={6CBEB806-4B3D4C8D-8BE8-868FEC3A02DC}&Time=131 (10 October 2005)
[17]http://www.hurriyetim.com.tr/haber/0,,sid~1@w~3@tarih~2002-02-06-m@nvid~92576,00.asp (10 October 2005)

reduced. Some of the MPs of the MHP criticised these changes as preparing the ground for the politicisation of the PKK.

Also in February, the Civil Code was reformed.[18] Among the changed provisions, there were articles to strengthen gender equality and the position of women both in family and in society, to extend the rights of foundations,[19] vulnerable people and children.

In March 2002, the second reform package was treated in parliament.[20] The second package included changes to the Civil Law, Press Law, Law on Meetings and Demonstrations and Law on Associations, parallel to the changes to the Constitution of October 2001. Although there were many positive changes in the relevant laws and legislation including deterrent regulations against torture, increasing freedoms for the assembly, association and foundations, TV and radio broadcasting in minority languages was still not included in this package. However, a provision in the Press Law on the restriction of languages other than Turkish was lifted.

In August 2002, the majority of the Turkish Assembly voted in favour of the most extensive and sophisticated reform package of modern Turkish history.[21] This development was applauded by the press.[22] According to the third package, capital punishment was abolished except for times of war, imminent threat of war and crimes of terrorism. Limitations on minority and religious foundations and the use of minority languages in education and broadcasting were lifted. The freedom of expression was brought in line with Article 10 of the European

[18] Visit http://www.euturkey.org.tr/abportal/uploads/files/Medeni%20Kanun%20Analizi% 2004.02.2002.doc (10 October 2005).

[19] Issue of procedural, property and organization rights of foundations established in Turkey had been subject to the Commission reports, since they were highly restricted. This issue was also stated in the National Program as one of medium term objectives. According to changes in Civil Law, everybody has the right to establish a foundation or association. Associations received the right to act in international arena, to open an office abroad and to be member of global organizations. International non-governmental foundations and associations will be given the opportunity to open branches in Turkey. Foreigners legally resided in Turkey have also given the right to establish and be member to an association. Regarding foundations, the former phrase banning to establish political foundations based on political ideologies has been abolished. However according to the changes, foundations cannot be established against qualifications of the republic stated in the Constitution, law, morals, national unity and national objectives. Accordingly, a foundation, which defends members of a specific race or community cannot be established. The foundations are given similar rights as associations.

[20]http://www.euturkey.org.tr/abportal/category.asp?TreeID=246&VisitID={6CBEB806-4B3D-4C8D-8BE8-868FEC3A02DC}&Time=131 (10 October 2005).

[21]Visit http://www.euturkey.org.tr/abportal/category.asp?TreeID=246&VisitID={6CBEB806-4B3D-4C8D-8BE8-868FEC3A02DC}&Time=131 (10 October 2005).

[22] Headlines from some Turkish newspapers were as follows: "Verheugen: I Congratulate the Turkish parliament," *Zaman*, 3 August 2002; "EU: We Greet Turkey," *Hürriyet*, 3 August 2002; "Giants made History!" *Hürriyet*, 3 August 2002; "406 Brave Men opened the Door to the EU," *Sabah*, 3 August 2002; "We have not missed the Train to Europe yet!" *Radikal*, 3 August 2002.

Convention of Human Rights. Laws on associations and assembly were liberalised. Retrial in compliance with judgements of the European Court of Human Rights was recognised. Rights of press were extended by lifting existing limitations. However, the differences between coalition parties became apparent at the vote and the MHP did not vote in favour of the abolition of the death penalty. As a result of these tensions between the coalition partners, early general elections were held at the end of 2002.

The third reform package constituted Turkey's determination and seriousness toward the membership to the European Union. More importantly, the Turkish people finally received rewards for democratic consolidation, which would help them live in a more equal and democratic manner. This was the most significant civilian response to those who interrupted the democratic process with the excuse of terrorism for many years.

The result of the general elections of 3 November 2002 was a big surprise to many people both in Turkey and in Europe. The AKP won the majority of seats in parliament.[23] All parties that had been represented in the previous parliament did not receive enough votes to return. The only political party which managed to reach the threshold was the Republican People's Party (CHP), which became the only opposition to the AKP in parliament.

As a result of this, the AKP has not only been a party that ended era of coalitions in Turkey but it was also Turkey's first ruling party with a religious and conservative background. For the first time, Turkey's first lady wears a headscarf. The AKP immediately committed itself to the cause of European Union membership. It did not take much time for the Turkish and European public to realise that the leaders of the AKP were traditional in their life-styles, but progressive and in some respects even revolutionary in their foreign and domestic policies. According to Hale, "in effect there seemed to be a rapprochement between Islamists and secularist liberals on this point, since both wished to widen civil liberties, albeit with different motives" (2003: 109-110).

On 30 November 2002, immediately after the AKP government took office, the state of emergency in the last two south eastern cities was lifted. The first signals of radical change were given just before the referendum on Cyprus in which the two communities were going to vote the United Nations plan in April 2004. The AKP, contrary to conventional Turkish state policies, pursued a policy of reconciliation and consensus. On 3 March 2004, parliament voted against aiding the American forces in Iraq. Although Prime Minister Erdoğan himself did not openly support this, the decision was applauded by the masses which were in vast majority against the US intervention. The AKP strengthened its position after local elections in 2004, in which it received 44 per cent of the

[23] According to election results, the AKP received 34.3 per cent of all votes and occupied 363 seats out of 550. The CHP received 19.4 per cent of all votes and had 178 seats in the parliament.

votes. Inflation was reduced to the single digits for the first time in recent history. Erdogan received strong support from different social groups, ranging from the economically poor to conventional business people. Although the Prime Minister and his party were criticised by secular groups, especially for their approach to religious schools and head covering for women, their rule generally represents an opportunity to overcome the traditional tension between religious groups and the majority of people in Turkey. The Turkish state for the first time is being run by an 'Other,' which had been repressed and controlled for many years.

In January 2003, parliament passed the fourth and fifth reform packages.[24] According to these reforms, torture allegations could not be postponed or lightened, procedures for the pre-detention period were regulated by including medical examination of the detainee, the division between crimes under the Fight against Terrorism and others was bridged on behalf of detainees held in custody under the former, rights of associations and right to association have been extended, eligibility criteria for election to parliament were softened, rights of political parties and foundations were increased and the possibility of retrial was regulated.

On 15 July 2003, there was another session in parliament to discuss the sixth package.[25] According to this package, the controversial Article 8 of the Law on the Fight against Terrorism would be lifted completely. The article was a serious breach of the freedoms of expression and speech. Article 1 of the same law, which had defined 'terrorism and terrorist organisations' in broad terms, was narrowed. On 30 July, the seventh package was accepted. Most important reform provisions included the priority of torture cases in the courts, the limitation of the competence of military courts to try civilians in times of peace, broadening of the rights of children, freedom of assembly and association, learning other languages and freedom of speech and criticism. In addition to these, the competence of the Secretariat of the National Security Council was limited. By these changes, debatable articles of the Law on the Fight against Terrorism and Penal Code were reformed. Moreover, in procedures like the appointment of the Secretariat to the National Security Council, responsibilities of the National Security Council and some budgetary affairs of the armed forces, the role of the civilian bodies was increased. Concerning the use of languages other than Turkish in education, it was stated that language courses can be given by private schools and establishments, while preserving Turkish as the only instruction language in state schools.

[24]http://www.euturkey.org.tr/abportal/category.asp?TreeID=246&VisitID={6CBEB8064B3 D4C8D8 BE8868FEC3A02DC}&Time=131 (10 October 2005).

[25] http://www.euturkey.org.tr/abportal/category.asp?TreeID=246&VisitID={6CBEB806-4B3D4C8D 8BE8-868FEC3A02DC}&Time=131 (10 October 2005).

On 7 May 2004, ten articles of the Constitution were amended by a nearly unanimous vote.[26] According to these changes, the positive obligation of the state to achieve gender equality became a Constitutional provision. The death penalty was completely abolished, including in times of war and imminent threat of war. The constitutional rights of the press were increased. Moreover, the priority of international agreements over national law was recognised. The representation of the Chief of Staff in the University Education Council was ended. Lastly and very importantly, the State Security Courts were abolished. In June 2003, the President confirmed the ratification of the United Nations Twin Covenants.

In July 2004, a Law on Compensation on Losses Resulting from Terrorist Acts was adopted. In June 2004, the ten years arrest of Leyla Zana and her friends ended with their release. Turkish state television started broadcasts in local languages including Kurdish. In August 2004, a civilian was appointed to the Secretariat of the National Security Council for the fist time. A completely renewed Penal Code was accepted on 26 September 2004.[27] At the same time, the Law on Intermediate Courts of Appeal was enacted as well. Although there were problems with the implementation of reforms, the government indicated its strong will for compliance. Fortunately, there was not a major backlash in response to the reforms in society and the government did not meet powerful opposition in either parliament or society as far as many issues are concerned. However, as stated above, the identity transformation of Turkey has not been completed yet in the absence of a social peace with the Kurdish people and different religious groups. The question of minorities, protection of secularism and the Cyprus issue are still considered primarily security issues by representatives of the state elite, especially by the armed forces.

Conclusion: Democracy or Conflict?

The appearance of the new Turkish identity will be clear in the future. The democratic achievements are considerable gains for everyone in society as long as they are implemented and tolerated. In this manner, the Turkish people can socialise themselves in a way distant from threat and security-oriented state policies, but rather approaching, digesting and internalising the benefits of democracy that they deserved long ago.

[26] Only eight MPs voted against, whereas six abstained. Visit http://www.eutukey.org.tr/ abportal/category.asp?TreeID=246&VisitID={6CBEB806-4B3D-4C8D-8BE8868FEC3A02DC} &Time =131 (10 October 2005).

[27] The new law brought the provisions of the criminal law in line with European standards. Especially through related articles, persons having committed honour killings will not be able to enjoy any reductions in their crimes, but on the contrary they may be punished to the maximum. This issue had been a main concern of many human rights organizations as it undervalued women's lives.

In 2004, the Commission finally decided that with the adoption and introduction of some new legislation, Turkey will fulfill the Copenhagen criteria and consequently accession negotiations can be opened. The Commission report in 2004 found the progress made by the government overall satisfactory.[28] The report stated some ongoing problems, such as corruption, numerous claims of torture, use of disproportionate force in demonstrations, problems of non-Muslim minorities especially in their legal personality, property rights, internal management and property rights, non-recognition of Alevis as a Muslim minority, child labour, lack of strategy for closing the economic and social gaps between regions and integration of people who returned to their homes.

2005 has witnessed the emergence of social tensions. In spite of support of the government, the so called 'Armenian Conference' held to discuss the fate of Ottoman Armenians was postponed because of growing reactions in the society. Later, it was forbidden by a local court decision. Eventually, while the conference was held in another venue in Istanbul in September 2005, it was overshadowed by demonstrations and protests. Additinally, the PKK attacks against military and civilians started again, especially in the south eastern regions. The attempts of the Kurdish intelligentsia to establish a new political party have not yet been fruitful. Because of the awakening of terror and insensitive remarks of Kurdish politicians, there have been growing reactions, demonstrations and protests against the Kurdish political groups and the PKK. This increased the strain between the two groups. Although the AKP did not pay particular attention to the Kurdish people in the first two years of its governance, in August 2005, a speech made by Tayyip Erdoğan in the biggest Kurdish city, Diyarbakır was assessed as a positive attempt toward reconciliation. The speech did not only prompt the PKK to establish a temporary cease-fire, but it was also welcomed by the Kurdish people and the European Union states. In his speech Erdoğan restated his decisiveness to continue the reform process. He also said that states can make mistakes, but a big state is a state which faces its mistakes and sins. He added that the 'Kurdish problem' was not the problem of only a part of Turkey, but it belonged to everyone. Hence, for the first time a Turkish Minister named the 'Kurdish problem' as such and accepted the responsibility of the state for the failure to resolve the Kurdish question.[29]

In general, in 2005 the reformation process lost momentum in comparison with previous years. A group of European Parliamentarians asked Ali Babacan, chief negotiator of Turkey questions concerning apparent slow-down in reforms in July 2005.[30] The Progress report of the European Commission has been issued in November 2005. Although the report confirms that Turkey fulfilled the Co-

[28] http://europa.eu.int/comm/enlargement/report_2004/pdf/rr_tr_2004_en.pdf (12 October 2005)
[29] "Kürt Sorunu Benim Sorunum!" *Hürriyet*, 18 August 2005.
[30] http://www.europarl.eu.int/omk/sipade3?PUBREF=-//EP//TEXT+PRESS+NR-20050713-1+0+DOC+XML+V0//EN&LEVEL=2&NAV=S

penhagen criteria, it also states that the implementation of reforms have been uneven and slow in 2005, including those concerning the retrial procedures of formerly accused people including Öcalan.[31] Government authorities claim that further reforms including rights of non-Muslim associations, churches and foundations will take place soon and old reforms need time to be implemented. Yet, it seems that non-resolved issues of internal politics such as insurgencies in Kurdish areas, reactionary demonstrations of nationalist groups, the re-emergence of PKK terror and arguments between secular groups and the government are occupying a more central place in parliamentary and public debates.

It is clear that the Turkish membership process will not be smooth considering the strengthening of the nationalist groups who demand more securitisation rather than democracy in Turkey. According to Barkey, "the process of transition to the European Union--even if success is a long way off--is likely to force Turkey to undertake significant changes that will make the state smaller, more efficient, less repressive and intrusive and, yet, genuinely stronger" (2000: 87).

Both EU-sceptics in Turkey and Turkey-sceptics in the EU are unintentionally serving voices against reforms and democracy in Turkey. From this perspective, to receive positive messages from the European Union is very important both for the people living in Turkey longing for democracy and the government which has the power and will to transform the country. At the same time, the credibility and prestige of the European Union depends on its decisions on Turkey, which will be given on objective basis rather than internal political concerns. Although there are still problems of democratic sufficiency and lack of consensus on identity issues, Turkish governments have worked very hard to comply with the Copenhagen criteria. Many members of civil society, universities and media have provided support for democratic reforms. Now it remains a question whether the Union states remember their commitment and if they will do their best to prepare themselves and their public for Turkey's membership.

As Günter Verheugen, the former Commissioner responsible for enlargement warned the European Union states;

> If the promise to Ankara to start negotiations will not be kept, the reform process in Turkey will be seriously weakened. If your message is 'You do whatever you want, but we will never accept you', why would the Erdogan government continue with the painful reforms? Those who give such messages should know what kind of responsibility they are taking.[32]

[31] http://www.europarl.eu.int/registre/docs_autres_institutions/commission_europeenne/sec/2005/1426/ COM_SEC(2005)1426_EN.pdf, last checked in November 2005.
[32] "Verheugen: AB Sözünden Cayarsa Türkiye`ye Darbe Vurulur," *Hürriyet*, 8 August 2005.

Macedonia – The Imperative of Success

Harald Schenker

From the very onset of its short history as an independent country, the Republic of Macedonia[1] has been struggling with its internal stability. While a series of external factors[2] continue to be a threat often disconsidered by the international community or treated merely in the regional context, the internal stability has been subject to a massive international intervention. This article looks at the role of the international community, with a specific emphasis on the European Union, in the effort of post-conflict stabilisation of the Republic of Macedonia and in the on-going process of European integration.

Background

Macedonia has been facing ethnic tension and the threat of conflict ever since the state was created in 1991 in the process of the break-up of Yugoslavia. From the start the state definition was that of a national state, hence a referendum for a new constitution was boycotted by large parts of the ethnic Albanian minority, which also refused to participate politically in the first government and elections.

Given the naked figures based upon the 2002 census, it is difficult to talk about a national state in the classic sense, with one nation dominating, without this being contested by more than one third of the population.

A lot of factors influenced the lack of loyalty among ethnic Albanians to the new state, of which the cutting of contacts to neighbouring Kosovo – the centre of Albanian culture and life in former Yugoslavia - may have been the most important one.[3]

Very little was done on the Macedonian side to ensure this loyalty. The Albanian minority was regarded with some suspicion and as a hindering moment to fulfilling the national dream. A vicious circle started with a series of protests and clashes, culminating in what is widely interpreted as an armed inter-ethnic conflict in 2001.

The deployment of UN troops (UNPREDEP) on the country's borders between 1992-1999 was a measure to avoid a spill-over effect from the wars in former Yugoslavia. This was backed by a small OSCE and ECMM (now EUMM) presence. While the spill-over did not happen in a military way, too little attention was given to the internal development of the country, where a

[1] Internationally recognised in 1993 as the "former Yugoslav Republic of Macedonia" or FYRoM, hereafter referred to as Macedonia in this article.

[2] Bulgaria does not recognise the Macedonian language, Greece does not recognise the name of the people and country, Serbia does not recognise the Macedonian Orthodox church and Kosovo is considered a threat to the territorial integrity of the country.

[3] Macedonians 65,18%, Albanians 25,17%, and others 10,65%.

series of confrontations over issues of participation and education, heated up by nationalist rhetoric on both sides, led to clashes in several instances. One of the few institutions taking the situation in Macedonia seriously was the OSCE HCNM (then Max van der Stoel), whose involvement over most of the 90's attempted to find feasible compromises in order to get out of the political impasse a rigid government and a rigid Albanian block had manoeuvred themselves into.

Following parliamentary elections in 1998, a coalition of two "nationalist" parties, the Macedonian VMRO-DPMNE[4] and the ethnic Albanian DPA[5] managed to make the first steps. One of the first decisions of the government, however, the Taiwan adventure[6], brought the mandate of UNPREDEP to a sudden end. They had to leave in spring 1999, just weeks before the spill-over happened: more than 350,000 refugees from Kosovo.

The coalition, in which for the first time Albanians were real partners and not just a pretext, initiated important reform steps. In fact, most of the provisions of the 2001 peace settlement were already in government or parliament procedure, except for the language provisions. One major success was the new law on higher education, passed in 2000, which allowed the establishment of a private university with teaching in Albanian language (along with English and Macedonian). This university is still financed by the international community and represents an example of successful intervention in order to ameliorate conflictual situations. The credit for brokering this break-through goes to Max van der Stoel.

At the same time, the government period of 1998-2001 was marked by a high level of corruption and government backed criminal activity, probably not more massive than the previous government's fraudulent privatisation of the state industries, but lacking the sophistication of structures coming from within the state sector. The government of this period was formed mainly by persons who had not held key functions before and displayed little experience and capacity in managing state affairs. Many of them had access to state resources for the first time and little to no mechanisms and political will were in place to prevent personal financial ambitions from being realised at the expense of the common good. This open self-service attitude of government officials combined with the

[4] Internal Macedonian Revolutionary Organisation – Democratic Party for the Macedonian National Unity.

[5] Democratic Party of the Albanians

[6] In a strangely naïve or cynical decision, the government recognised the statehood of Taiwan in exchange to what was believed to be a billion dollars worth of investment. Soon it became clear that solely the commissions cashed by several high ranking politicians were high amounts and that Taiwan intended to invest over a long term period a much smaller sum. The decision, which was never endorsed by then President Boris Trajkovski, has in the meanwhile been revoked. The immediate effect however was that China vetoed the extension of the UN blue helmets' mandate in early 1999 in the UN Security Council, provoking an immediate withdrawal.

traditional patterns of clientelism produced massive frustrations within the population. This goes for the majority ethnic Macedonian as for the largest minority population, the ethnic Albanians.

The conflict that broke out in early 2001 was widely interpreted as an inter-ethnic one. Given that policy towards ethnic Albanians was starting to bear results, there was little reason for an armed uprising. I tend to see the conflict more as the attempt of one group to provoke a change of elites among ethnic Albanians. In this sense, it was an intra-ethnic one as well. The ruling DPA's openly expressed hostility against the insurgents speaks for itself. Part of the explanation for the conflict is also a struggle among Albanian interest groups linked to political formations over the control over one of the most lucrative smuggling routes to Kosovo and Serbia proper. This route leads through the area of North-Western Macedonia, where the conflict broke out.

The armed conflict ended in August 2001 with an internationally brokered peace settlement, the so-called "Ohrid Framework Agreement". Apart from the immediate cessation of hostilities and the decommissioning provisions, agreement laid down a number of measures leading to constitutional changes. These thoroughly changed the character of the Republic of Macedonia, turning it into a multi-ethnic state, with a number of power-sharing mechanisms in place in order to assure adequate minority participation.

A census and parliamentary elections were held in parallel to a massive legislative overhaul, in which legal reality was to follow the newly created constitutional reality. The government formed after the 2002 elections involves the Social Democratic Union of Macedonia (SDSM) and its smaller allies and the ethnic Albanian Democratic Union for Integration (DUI), a party formed by leaders of 2001's insurgent "National Liberation Army"[7].

This government has filed an application for EU candidacy in March 2004, trying to force a faster approach of the EU, comparable to Croatia, which would somewhat detach Macedonia from the other countries of the so-called Western Balkans. The results of this process are still to be expected.

The following two sections of the article will look first at the international involvement before, during and after the 2001 conflict and second at the process of European integration.

From Prevention to Rehabilitation

For almost ten years until after the end of the Kosovo crisis, the Macedonian example was viewed as a success story in terms of international crisis prevention and diplomacy. The aforementioned deployment of UN blue helmets, OSCE and

[7] The Albanian acronym UÇK (for Ushtria Çlirimtare Kombëtare) is similar to the one used by the "Kosovo Liberation Army" (KLA), although the name is slightly altered. This was certainly done in order to boost support from local and Kosovo Albanians as well as the diaspora, by inventing a line of continuity.

EC monitors was regarded as a sufficient and effective tool in deterring possible appetites of Macedonia's neighbours. And indeed, this part of the story can be viewed as a success. No force from outside the country acted openly against it in a military way. A lesser successful part is the fact that Macedonia was not internationally recognised under its constitutional name of *Republic of Macedonia*, but under the preliminary name of *The former Yugoslav Republic of Macedonia*, due to Greece's refusal. It is not understandable why EU countries and their allies have given in to Greece's pressure, knowing that this situation would have the potential of provoking conflicts.

Following Macedonia's compliant role[8] in dealing with the Kosovo refugee crisis, the EU decided to award the government by opening the negotiations about a Stabilisation and Association Agreement. This was done in spite of the fact that very few of the conditions to implement such an agreement were in place then. The gesture was clearly seen as a political act of good will, meant to help further stabilising the country.

All international involvement at that point was aiming at boosting the economic growth and encouraging reforms such as the decentralisation. Substantial funds flew in country from the EU, the USA and other bilateral donors and had an immediate impact in optimistic statistics and hopes for substantial growth. Too little attention was given here to the vast amounts of funds which disappeared into the pockets of implementers and later materialised among others as rather large and luxurious villas in the residential part of Skopje or well hidden in private compounds outside the city.

Although a plethora of projects financed by international donors wore the label "inter-ethnic relations", little attention was given to the ethnic Albanian underground movement that began to form itself from former KLA combatants, frustrated and marginalised individuals and persons who suffered from the "business" policy of the ruling DPA.

Despite a number of classic warning signals such as attacks on police stations and on police patrols or on military objects – some of which caused material damage only, others resulted in casualties and even killed police officers, both the government and the international community continued to portray the situation in country as stable, ignoring reports coming from the field. The formula, repeated in mantra like repetitions left the impression that the incidents were isolated and could not affect the internal stability of the country, which was marked by improving inter-ethnic relations. While all this was true, little or no attention was given to the fact that the country's institutions, including the security and defence systems were by far not functioning properly.

[8] After initial hesitation, Macedonia allowed more than 360,000 refugees from Kosovo into country and allowed NATO troops to use the country as a logistical base for its Kosovo operation.

Consequently it was sufficient that a small group of around 50 combatants were activated, which were later joined by up to maximum 2000 other recruited persons and mercenaries, which brought the country to the brink of implosion.

At the beginning of the conflict, in the first three-four months of 2001, the personality-driven coordination between the representatives of the international community on the ground was exemplary, especially between EU, OSCE, NATO and USA. The communication with the government was less than ideal, which is why a decision has been taken to regard the President as the leading political force (in his function of supreme commander of the armed forces and as head of the National Security Council). A number of bilateral embassies were instrumental in enhancing this perception. When an all-party coalition government was formed in spring of 2001 it became obvious that the President would have to take on a role much stronger that most political players would have liked to, in order to keep the fragile coalition and by that the very state together.

At the insistence of the international community the government made some desperate last minute efforts to limit the attraction of the insurgents with the ethnic Albanian population, with partial success. Especially those who knew the provenance of the insurgents knew to be weary.

Most of this effort was too little, too late, though. Warning signals sent e.g. by the OSCE mission starting as early as summer 2000 had been ignored and now disenfranchised youth from areas with almost 100% youth unemployment started filling the ranks and file of the NLA, spreading the conflict beyond its initial zone.

It was the ambivalence of the US policy due to its close ties to the Kosovar KLA and the failure of its first mediator, OSCE envoy Robert Frowick, that cost the international community a lot of credibility. The idea to bring the ethnic Albanian parties at one table with the rebels was not bad as such, it was the lack of coordination and information that made this attempt look like giving legitimacy to the insurgent NLA.

Although the regional dimension was clear from the onset, and the NLA could have never started and carry out the operation without strong logistical support from and in Kosovo, the international community insisted to call the conflict an internal one, fearing that a potential acknowledgement of the involvement of interest groups and armed groups from Kosovo would escalate the conflict. This only opened the space for conspiracy theories on the Macedonian side, where the Prime Minister was speaking about an attack by the Kosovo Protection Corps, totally ignoring the internal element. A more thorough analysis in the beginning and more openness towards the public would have helped to set straight some of these misconceptions. This not having been done, the international community was targeted several times by angry and incited demonstrators: cars were destroyed and set on fire, fire was set to embassy buildings, etc.

What followed was a very intense phase of shuttle diplomacy on highest level by EU, NATO, US and OSCE, aiming at ending the armed conflict and reaching a settlement. While the US and others were acting behind the scenes, it was the tandem of EU and NATO envoys, who brokered first a cease-fire and then a peace settlement.

Following a ceasefire in late June 2001, negotiations about a peace agreement commenced in Skopje. The political negotiations were conducted under the auspices of the president. The offer to relocate to a place outside the country was turned down by the president, who insisted in a gesture of sovereignty. As the situation in Skopje became untenable with substantial information leaking to the media, a new venue was found in a rather secluded presidential summer residence on lake Ohrid in the south of the country. The treaty hence received the name of "Ohrid Framework Agreement".

The proposed remedy to the conflict consisted in an agreement brokered by the EU and US, transforming the state from a national state in the make to a multi-national structure. Little expertise and a lot of political negotiation brought about a document full of terminological mistakes, which now constitutes the basis of Macedonia's political identity. Its provisions have been translated and adopted as amendments into the constitution.

The establishment of a EU Special Representative office enhanced the role of the international community as a guarantee that the provisions would be implemented. Backed by the US as the other guarantee power, the EUSR office coordinates the efforts of the international community to assist Macedonia with the reform process. It often acts as a direct adviser to the government, thus ensuring stream-lined communication channels.

The establishment of the office however raised the confusion about the role of the various EU agencies in country. Apart from the EUSR, there is a delegation of the European Commission active in Skopje, mainly charged with the implementation of the EU programs of the type of CARDS and others. The third large agency is the European Agency for Reconstruction, which is also implementing programs, but which come from different sources. Apart from these, a number of programs have been and continue to be implemented by other EU agencies, such as Europe Aid and others. It is very difficult for Macedonian public and potential beneficiaries of funds to keep an oversight over who does what. The problem is aggravated by open competition and personal animosities carried out in public, which only contributed to the confusion and poor image of the European Union in country, despite considerable assistance in funds and expertise, from which Macedonia has profited for more than a decade. This does however not constitute a Macedonian problem only, but the confusion caused over the years is exemplary. The decision to appoint one person in late 2005, who will be both EUSR and head of the EC delegation is an attempt to clarify some of this confusion.

Other international organisations involved in assisting Macedonian institutions, like the OSCE, the Council of Europe or the Stability Pact for South Eastern Europe are often also mistaken for bodies of the European Union and numerous information campaigns, seminars, information tours and a multitude of other tools have had little effect with the public, but also with the media, which continue to confuse labels, thus contributing to the perpetuation of a false picture.

First a census and later the parliamentary elections in September 2002 passed peacefully and showed that the hot phase of the conflict was over and a peaceful political transition took place, bringing the oppositional SDSM into a coalition with the DUI, a party that emerged from the ranks and file of the NLA. The quality of both operation was questioned by experts as well as by political analysts. This did not however lead to major contestant's movements among either of the ethnic communities. The fact that also the 2005 local elections failed to live up to a number of international standards shows the continuity of weaknesses in the system, which are not addressed despite repeated appeals from the international organisations involved. The elections showed however as well that a certain degree of stability can be maintained if there is political will to do so.

The main challenge for all layers of government as well as for the legislative was the tremendous amount of legislation to be passed within a short time, in order to reflect the new constitutional set up. With massive assistance from foreign experts and accompanied by marathon sessions of the Parliament, most of the more than 160 laws were passed within a reasonable time, allowing the largest reform to commence in summer 2005: the decentralisation.

While considered as crucial for the country's eligibility as EU candidate, the decentralisation process is probably the most sensitive of the reforms undertaken so far. Derogation of power from a highly centralised system to the municipal level is the positive side. Lack of financial resources and the problems connected to this complex is the negative one. Furthermore, the decentralisation process involved a redefinition of municipal administrative boundaries, and here it became obvious that the ethnic factor often prevailed over economic or rational arguments. By drawing ethnic municipalities, the danger of a further segregation of the population has become imminent. The international community did nothing to prevent this trend, leaving the decision fully in the hands of politicians, whose short-term interest in political and financial profit is obvious, but whose capacity of a larger political vision combined with the capacity of imposing this vision is clearly lacking.

The implementation of the decentralisation laws will produce a great deal of confusion and frustration, and it will be necessary that the international players, especially the European Union and the OSCE monitor this process carefully and direct assistance to where it is really needed. One particular focus in all this complex environment will have to be the pressure towards what is called "soft" ethnic cleansing, meaning the creation of ethnically "pure" areas, not by conflict, but by encouraging the "others" to leave in much more subtle ways.

This brings me to a major point of criticism directed to those who authored the Ohrid Framework Agreement. In most of its provisions, the agreement ensures adequate minority participation in the administration and in other spheres of public life, even introducing the rather sophisticated concept of qualified majority for parliament decisions impacting on ethnic communities. This is certainly a major step forward for Macedonia, meaning that minorities have to agree before legislation concerning them can be passed, thus ensuring that their wishes have to be taken into account. What is completely missing is a set regulations defining the protection of minorities. Although Macedonia has signed and ratified all major international documents concerning this issue, these remain vague. The situation created now is one in which pressure on ethnic groups can be exercised outside parliament in order to have them agree to political decisions. Furthermore, the decentralisation process has created a situation, in which one ethnic group forming the majority locally can exercise pressure upon the local minorities, without fears of being sanctioned. Given that nationalism is very strong still and will remain so in the absence of economic development, this may give way to the above mentioned processes of creating ethnically "clean" areas. Whether this will contribute to the internal cohesion and stability of the entire country remains to be seen.

The immediate next challenges for the internal coherence of the Macedonian state will be the introduction of partial bilingualism and the debate on new national symbols. Given the sensitivity of these issues anywhere and especially in the Balkans, the international attention will have to remain high and the readiness to broker mutually acceptable agreements will have to be there on the side of the EU and especially the OSCE. In the wake of this process, and with a steady rapprochement of Macedonia towards the European Union, the ridiculous and futile issue of the country's official name will have to be resolved soon, the position of Greece, which is imposing its position on the entire UN and EU becoming more and more untenable.

On the Path towards Euro-Atlantic Integration

NATO

Macedonia has been a country of special focus for NATO, not only because of its role in the Kosovo crisis, but especially because it was acknowledged that stabilisation of the country also had to include a reform and modernisation of its security structures. At the moment of independence, Macedonia was left practically without a functioning military force and the crisis of 2001 found all security structures utterly unprepared for such a situation, which partially explains the success of the uprising.

Being an early member of NATO's Partnership for Peace program, Macedonia has strived to reform its military according to NATO standards. The process was accompanied by a number of ups and downs, but at the moment it looks likely that the country will be offered full NATO membership in 2006. Given the unstable situation on parts of its border, this will certainly contribute in a major way to the stabilisation of the country, which is also dependent from psychological processes. Having the security that a political and military alliance is protecting the country's territorial integrity may free potential and resources towards other burning issues, among which the economy is probably the gravest one.

European Union

The Republic of Macedonia was the first country in the region to start with the negotiations on the Stabilisation and Association Agreement and the first country to conclude and sign the Agreement in April 2001. The Agreement came into force in April 2004, after having been ratified by all EU member states. In March 2004, Macedonia applied for EU membership, applying the Croatian model of not waiting for the SAA to come into force. After Macedonia having completed and handed over the EU questionnaire in February 2005, and answered to additional questions in September 2005 it is expected that the European Commission will form an opinion by the beginning of November and the European Council will pass a decision in December 2005.

The Macedonian development is somewhat typical for the prevailing political drive behind the Stabilisation and Association process. The early successes in negotiating the Agreement were related more to the country's positive role during the Kosovo crisis and to an attempt to stabilise the country as much as possible, given its immediate vicinity to Kosovo and the fact that one quarter of the population is ethnic Albanian.

The armed uprising in early 2001 tied up most of the energy of the country for most of that year and beyond. The fact that the SAA was signed in April 2001 indicates yet another political gesture, aiming at stabilisation of the country, rather than the conclusion of a reform process in which merit has been awarded.

Following the 2001 conflict, all international actors, including the EU focussed almost exclusively on the implementation of the Ohrid Framework Agreement. A major reform exercise started, re-defining most of the country's legislation according to the principle of multi-ethnicity, while at the same time streamlining it with EU standards.

The country Stabilisation and Association report for 2004 acknowledges the reform efforts made, but also states that: *In many areas, the reform process is still in its infancy and will need further efforts to be converted into concrete changes and bring the expected benefits.*[9]

In a nutshell, the situation in Macedonia has progressed considerably, if the absence of conflict is a sign of stability. The political landscape has changed, minority participation has become not only reality, but one of the driving political motives for reform. This is certainly true for the upcoming process of decentralisation, which will be the stepping stone for political actors in country, but also for the assessment of Macedonia's readiness to become a candidate country for EU accession.

Other areas mentioned in the report, in which reform is under way but where the efforts need to be sustained are rule of law, good governance, transformation of the administration and of the security sector, and last, but definitely not least, the economic situation, where *notably serious weaknesses in the functioning of the economy, business climate, competitiveness and enforcement of property rights, is increasingly a challenge for the country's successful transition.*[10]

In such a situation, the Macedonian government made a bold decision to apply for full membership, overriding the process as it is envisaged by the EU and imposing a position that demanded reaction from the EU side. Although it is more than obvious and all actors are conscious that the largest part of the work is still to be done, and that genuine ownership of the process is not fully realised, it is expected that Macedonia's request will not be refuted by the European Union. In the light of the failure of the European constitution, which is partially attributed by many analysts to a perceived "enlargement fatigue" of the European Union population, and in the light of little real and tangible progress especially in the area of economic growth, it becomes more and more unlikely that Macedponia will receive a fully positive *avis*. It is more likely that the answer will at best translate into some form of conditioned candidate status, with a long list of issues to be resolved still or will encourage the government to undertake more efforts and reapply within a given period of time.

Either way, the government will have to explain to its citizens why the full candidate status could not be obtain, which may provoke a political crisis to some degree. In 2006 parliamentary elections are to be held and this issue will certainly contribute to heating up the electoral campaign.

On the other hand, the European Union will have to do its utmost not to endanger its own success story in the region. As much as it is true that the work to be done by the Macedonian government remains substantial, the expectations have continuously been raised by the EU's policy of granting Macedonia a probably premature arrangement with the Stabilisation and Association Agree-

[9] Commission of the European Communities: SEC(2004) 373, Commission Staff Working Paper, Former Yugoslav Republic of Macedonia. Stabilisation and Association Report 2004, p. 3.
[10] Idem.

ment and by allowing the request for candidate status to be filed. To fall back behind the dynamics that the integration process has shown in the past years would not only damage the credibility of the European Union in Macedonia and the entire region, but would also pose a threat to the very stability of the country.

A continuity in the integration process remains vital and would enhance regional stability and the internal coherence of the state at the same time. In the wake of further security problems to be expected in Kosovo, the loyalty of ethnic Albanians in Macedonia to their state will remain an important issue to improve. Apart from finding ways out of the dire economic situation, the internal integration of the country is an issue to be closely scrutinised and encouraged by the international factor. The Ohrid Framework Agreement was imposed by the international community, against maximalist wishes of both parties to the conflict. The changes to the country's internal structure are far reaching and have stretched the capacity of local actors to a maximum. But the process is just at its start. Creating a new legal reality does not change the attitudes, mentalities and patterns of behaviour and action over night. This process will have to be paralleled by an educational effort, trying to impose what is usually called "European values" to fill the existing void, which has occurred in the transformation process. This implies much more attention to the long-term processes like the reform of the education system, an area where the impact cannot be measured but in the dimension of generations.

The European Union and Human Rights in Bulgaria

Katina Boncheva

The early 1990s were a period of radical democratic transformations in the Bulgarian state and society. The post-totalitarian state declared itself to be democratic but the perception and protection of human rights as a supreme value and an innate characteristic of democracy remained a mere vain pretence.

In addition to the collapsing economy and the political crisis, the communist regime left the legacy of a society in distress and people "unaccustomed to" genuine rights, the responsibilities for their protection, and efficient enforcement. Inbred in this society is the tendency to ignore marginalising grave human rights' problems such as sexual and ethnic discrimination, domestic violence and police misconduct. The predominant part of the Bulgarian society, brought up in the context of planned economy and a permanent deficit of goods, remained accustomed and insensitive to the lack of effective consumer rights' protection mechanisms and to the problems caused by the abuse of the monopoly position of state power-transmission companies. Post-totalitarian people are not used to demanding information about the activities of the ruling circles, and yet, they willingly divulge their personal data not only to the governmental bodies authorised to access them but also to private trading companies, thus preconditioning misuse themselves. Moreover, the existing sub-cultural concepts of power "use" combined with the absence of democratic traditions and efficient mechanisms for civil control of state administration contribute to the legal unreliability inhibiting the development of Bulgarian society.

Proclaiming its intention to turn citizens into a sovereign, the Bulgarian Constitution of 1991 envisages two "pylons" safeguarding individual rights: the direct application of constitutional provisions and the judicial primacy of ratified international acts over national legislation. The former allows the prosecution of claims, grounded directly in the Constitution. The latter prioritises international human rights' law above domestic law. Based on these changes and since its ratification on 7 September 1992, The Convention for the Protection of Human Rights and Fundamental Freedoms has become a powerful and directly applicable legal instrument for the protection of human rights in Bulgaria. Thereby, the state has voluntarily restricted its sovereignty, acknowledging the obligatory jurisdiction of the European Court of Human Rights and guaranteeing the right to individual complaints filed with this court. By declaring its commitment to common European democratic and human rights' values, Bulgaria has undertaken the international public duty to observe and guarantee the fundamental rights and freedoms enshrined in the Convention. A few months later, a new important step was made reinforcing democracy and the protection of human rights. On 8 March 1993, the European Agreement between Bulgaria and the member states of the European Communities was signed. It went into effect in

1995. On 14 December 1995, the Republic of Bulgaria submitted its application for membership in the European Union. Henceforth, the negotiation process, the requirements set before the state, the regular annual reports and the pre-accession programmes of the EU, as well as the mandatory decisions of the European Court of Human Rights have become the main leading mechanism of the democratic process in terms of the export of European policy standards having to do with human rights.

The following expose, laying no claim to be exhaustive, aims to track the main spheres of influence of the European Union on the process of democratisation in Bulgaria. The analysis is made through the prism of the condition of human rights as testifying to the maturity and humanity of the Bulgarian society.

The 'Copenhagen criteria'

The basis of any social system is defined by standards of behaviour. The willingness of the EU member states to keep and further develop their legal performance naturally presupposes their need to make sure that the candidate-countries have the potential to become part of their community.

Soon after the fall of the Berlin wall, during the early 1990s, the European Community and its member states concluded Association Agreements with several countries of Central and Eastern Europe, which wanted to become EU members. As mentioned above, Bulgaria was among these countries. In the context of the new political situation, at the June 1993 European Council in Copenhagen, Denmark, two fundamentally new decisions were taken: that the associated countries in Central and Eastern Europe will become EU members if they express such a desire and they comply with a certain minimum of conditions, the so-called 'Copenhagen criteria'. According to the Copenhagen Presidency conclusions:

> *Membership requires that the candidate country has achieved stability of institutions guaranteeing democracy, the rule of law, human rights and respect for and, protection of minorities, the existence of a functioning market economy as well as the capacity to cope with competitive pressure and market forces within the Union. Membership presupposes the candidate's ability to take on the obligations of membership including adherence to the aims of political, economic and monetary union.*

What human rights guarantees is a question, to which the answer changes with the development of the society. In Europe the basic standards are set by the European Court of Human Rights, which, through the interpenetrations given in its judgements, makes the Convention for the protection of Human rights and Fundamental Freedoms a 'living' and actual instrument for the protection of human rights. The approach of the Court is well summarised in the Judgement of the case *Ireland v. United Kingdom*, where it is stated that its "judgements in fact serve not only to decide those cases brought before the Court but, more generally, to elucidate, safeguard and develop the rules instituted by the Convention, thereby contributing to the observance by the States of the engagements undertaken by them as Contracting States".

Although some decisions of the Court, ruled in connection to cases versus Bulgaria, have acted as catalysing agents stimulating changes in the legislation, thus bringing about the institutionalisation of human rights protection in the respective area, this cause-effect mechanism is far from being the rule. In most cases, the state is content with the payment of the applicants' damages. Unfortunately, the Continent-type legal system adopted by Bulgaria, complemented by the long-established traditions and idiosyncrasies of this country's law enforcement and government, requires that the code of conduct be guided by normative acts in a written form. In this sense, although setting European standards concerning the observance of human rights in Bulgaria, the decisions of the Court are unable fully to perform their function, viz. not only protect the applicant's violated rights but also be the norm of state conduct. Due to the said idiosyncrasies, despite its not being a human rights document and its remaining technically outside the Copenhagen criteria, *the acquis communautaire* seems to be able to partially compensate for this deficit and provide a strong impetus for the advancement of human rights protection in Bulgaria.

Thus, the most tangible impact of the EU with respect to human rights is on the legislation of the Republic of Bulgaria. In order to implement its commitments to the EU, Bulgaria has adopted a comprehensive number of laws and pieces of secondary legislation establishing qualitative, new Bulgarian conditions, rights and mechanisms for their efficient protection. The most important of them will be summarised below.

Adopting Acquis Communautaire

With considerable delay and after dramatic parliamentarian debates, the Protection against Discrimination Act became effective on 1 January 2004. Its adoption was reported by the Government in the context of Chapter 13 of Bulgaria's EU accession negotiations, titled "Social Policy and Employment". The content of the act is obtained mainly from Directive 2000/43 and Directive 2000/78. This is a general anti-discrimination act, providing against any direct or indirect discrimination on the grounds of "gender, race, nationality, ethnicity, human genome, citizenship, origin, religion or belief, education, convictions, political affiliation, personal or social status, disability, age, sexual orientation, marital status, property status, or on any other grounds established by law or by an international treaty to which the Republic of Bulgaria is a party".

The enforcement of the act has evoked quite a controversial response. A lot of people considered it solely as a reply to "European pressure", but not as a response to a society necessity. Regardless of the obvious and repeatedly ascertained problems with discriminatory provisions and practices, the opinion that there is no discrimination in Bulgaria and that this act will not find application is common even in juridical circles. The long-expected anti-discrimination act has been accepted with hope mainly by non-governmental organisations active in the field of human rights. It has introduced for the first time a detailed definition of the concept of discrimination and its manifestations in addition to positive measures for ensuring equality. Besides the detailed regulations in the field of substantive law, it has also introduced a series of procedural safeguards. The opportunity for a non-governmental organisation in public interest to initiate legal action against discrimination on its own behalf when a number of persons are aggrieved or to serve an intervening cause in an already instituted court proceedings is a new phenomenon in Bulgarian law. The free-of-charge proceedings and the burden of proof distribution facilitating the people seeking protection from discrimination are also a significant relief.

One disadvantage of this law is the comprehensive list of the grounds on which unequal treatment is inadmissible. Though significant in number, the indicated grounds cannot cover all instances of discrimination. Both the variety and dynamics of social relations, as well as the development of the sciences will inevitably put on probation the "closed" definition of the discrimination grounds. In support of the above-mentioned comes the fact that the grounds have been supplemented with the prohibition of discrimination on the grounds of human genome, which became effective on 1 January 2005.

In conformity with European requirements, the new act envisages the existence of a Commission for Protection against Discrimination whose functions include the investigation of reported instances of discrimination, the enactment of decisions concerning the presence or absence of discrimination and imposing sanctions on violators. The Commission is a specialised body which, by the idea of the law, shall research into discrimination acts quickly, efficiently and free of charge. An important role for achieving the goal of the act is assigned to the power of the Commission to initiate investigations and impose sanctions, on its own initiative, on discrimination acts. Unfortunately, the idea of this authority being a prompter and more effective alternative of the court is overshadowed by the method, stipulated by the law, of establishing the Commission whose members are appointed by two state bodies, the National Assembly and the President. The lack of opportunity for direct civil participation in this body may undermine the perception of the objectivity and impartiality of its activities, especially when an anti-discrimination procedure is initiated against the Parliament or the President who are the actual employers of the Commission members. The formation of the Commission itself has proved to be an unexpected problem. As a result of the adoption of anti-discrimination measures only as part of the "adherence to commitments made to Europe", almost two years after the act came into effect, this body has not started functioning yet. The Parliament and the Government share the responsibility for this delay. It took the Parliament eighteen months to elect the Commission's Chairperson. The Commission members were appointed by the respective institutions in April 2005 but the Government has not provided the Commission with physical offices Therefore, two years after the law became operative the Commission was still not effective.

The first actions of the judiciary with respect to the newly adopted law are discouraging, as well. Bordering on resistance against the law, the judicial conservatism is mainly displayed through the refusal of some magistrates to comply with the provisions of the law concerning proper relief. Of frequent occurrence is the phenomenon of imposing payment of legal costs justified by the judges' power to assess themselves the legal grounds of the claim. On the grounds that the facts described fall under the hypothesis of regulations belonging to other laws in which the legal proceedings are not free of charge, persons seeking protection against discrimination often also become the victims of judicial misconduct. Despite the mandatory provisions, there are many cases when judges do not allow non-governmental organisations in public interest to participate as litigants in lawsuits filed under the Protection against Discrimination Act. Many actions taken by such organisations and provoked by the public interest to solve a problem concerning a great number of people, are dismissed. Shifting the burden of proof is also rather unfamiliar to many law-enforcing authorities in Bulgaria. The problem with the instrument of evidence is interesting, as well. In the process of discussing the bill, expert committees insisted that the "sandwich test", which allows the discrimination treatment to be easily and efficiently proved, should be used as an instrument of evidence in discrimination cases. The position that traditional testimonial evidence can play a role in this test since participants in the test can speak out their perceptions as witnesses finally overweighed the others. As it could be expected, the difference between the two methods of proof has become visible in practice. Some of the judges have expressed their negative attitude towards witnesses who have "checked" whether there has been a different treatment of plaintiffs. They consider these "out-court" checks an incitement to discrimination and do not credit their testimony.

Although the Protection against Discrimination Act is a good start, it is not able, without the relevant changes in social attitudes, to solve grave human rights problems, evolving from the traditions and practices of non-equal treatment. The core of the problem is to be found in the way society responds to existing acts of discrimination and in the attitude to their victims. The series of seminars and conferences held to promote and clarify the new law have provided a relatively thorough picture of the attitude of various social groups towards the new law, including local government representatives, heads of educational institutions, police officers, legal practitioners and minority representatives. Few participants in the working meetings have really understood the aim and meaning of the law and its public indispensability. Purely discriminatory views have been repeatedly expressed. Minority groups which are the usual victims of discrimination have found it difficult to accept the rights and the guarantees for their protection as real and capable of bringing about positive change. Thus, changes, democratic in their form, have collided with archaic stereotypes and living totalitarian practices characterised by the disrespect for human dignity and the zero tolerance to personal differences and individual needs. In this context, one can easily understand the following statement published on the website of the Bulgarian Ministry of Foreign Affairs as part of a summary of the achievements made within Chapter 13 of the accession negotiations "Social Policy and Employment":

> *The efforts made by Bulgaria have led to the adoption of one of the most up-to-date laws in Europe in this direction – The Protection against Discrimination Act. Now the bigger challenge stands both for the society in general and for each one of us. It is a challenge for the society because the first step is to accept that discrimination exists as a phenomenon and not to allow this law to become a shop window which is empty at the back. It is a challenge for everyone because everyone should reconsider some aspects of our behaviour, especially the way we bring up our children.*[1]

Regardless of the difficulties outlined, this act is a good juristic basis, on which the problems regarding discrimination could be thought over and eventually solved. Before it was adopted, there had been rare cases of lawsuits filed on the grounds of Art. 14 of the Convention for the Protection of Human Rights and Fundamental Freedoms and Art. 6 of the Constitution of the Republic of Bulgaria banning some aspects of unequal treatment. Despite the direct application of the two regulations, few judges were inclined to base guilty judgments on acts of discrimination. There was also a problem with the proof of discrimination acts because of the application of the traditional allocation of the burden of proof which fell entirely over the victims of discrimination. The unsuccessful attempts of taking actions against discrimination without a special law led to the conclusion that the regulations of the Convention and the Constitution do not constitute a sufficiently effective domestic-law mechanism of protection within the meaning of Art. 13 of the Convention. The impossibility for receiving protection from

1 "Chapter 13: Social Policy and Employment." http://www.evroportal.bg/edocs/ChapterDocs/ch13.doc (7 Dec. 2005).

the national law resulted in the initiation of a great number of actions at the European Court of Human Rights in Strasbourg.

Unlike the Protection against Discrimination Act, the Ombudsman Act, which came into force on 1 January 2004, among all, has responded to deliberated social needs. Under totalitarianism, the administration becomes a mighty power "for its own benefit", capable of imposing arbitrary rule. During the years of transition to democracy, this characteristic feature of administration in Bulgaria could no longer be tolerated. In this respect, the establishment of the ombudsman as an institution that has proven its capacity to safeguard human rights has filled a painful void in the Bulgarian citizens' expectations concerning human rights, apart from its being an important European Union membership criterion. A multitude of discussions and roundtables have been organised with the aim of clarifying the substance of a normative document which would reflect in the utmost degree the European acquis projected in the Maastricht Treaty of 1995, Recommendation R /85/13 of 23 September 1985 regarding the institute of the ombudsman and Resolution /85/8 of 23 September 1985 on cooperation among member states. The awakening civil society has already started to realise its role for settling a democratic living environment. The adoption of the Ombudsman Act arranges and makes meaningful a large number of complaints randomly addressed to the President, the Prime Minister or other state organs whom citizens trust emotionally. The powers of the ombudsman stipulated by the law - receiving detailed information about problems he or she is referred to, making recommendations and proposals to the authorities against which there are complaints, reporting to the National Assembly the results of his or her activities - not only aid the solution of specific problems but also constitute an explicit signal for the administration that it is responsible for the nonfeasance or malfeasance of its obligations.

The Ombudsman Act, together with the special Act on the Liability Incurred by the State for Damage Inflicted on Citizens and the Access to Public Information Act, form the basic "set" of civil rights and the reciprocal responsibilities of the state necessary for maintaining a democratic society by exercising control on the administration.

The Access to Public Information Act is another piece of legislation reflecting the *acquis communautaire*. According to the motives of the bill, "the approximation of Bulgarian legislation to EU legislation and practices is directly dependent on the application of the principles included in the recommendations of the Council of Europe because this is the only European institution of which Bulgaria is a full-fledged member". Although it is relatively new – it has been effective since July 2000 - the Access to Public Information Act is an operating law lined with a serious court practice. Soon after it came into force, the initial confusion of institutions, caused by their unwonted communication with citizens, was replaced by polite manners and a decreasing number of ungrounded refusals to provide public information. Related to this law, as long as it also regulates the scope of the right to access to information, is the Personal Data Protection Act, effective as of 1 January 2002. It is part of the National Strategy for the Development of the Information Society and an immediate result of Bulgaria's efforts to meet the requirements of the EU regarding the harmonisation of Bulgarian legislation with European legislation in the domain of human rights protection. The act adopts the principles and concepts of the Council of Europe Convention 108 of 1981 for the protection of individuals with regard to automatic processing of personal data and EC Directive 46/95 on the protection of individuals with regard to processing of personal data and on the free movement of such data. According to the assessments of the European Commission, by adopting this law and ratifying the Council of Europe Convention 108 of 1981, Bulgaria has successfully accomplished the process of harmonising its national law with European legislation in the field of personal data protection, an important element of the process of harmonisation in the area of justice and interior affairs. Although the law is already "working", there remain some strange legal provisions and practices which could discredit undermine its purpose. One example of this is the posting of what has been called "electoral lists" in public places. The purpose of these lists is to assure citizens that on the election day they can go to the polls in due course. Pursuant to the laws regulating the election of President, deputies to the National Assembly, mayors and municipal councilors, the electoral lists include the full names of voters, their personal identification numbers, addresses and the types and full numbers of their ID documents. High magistrates are among those who refuse to conform to the law. Less than a year ago, the Appellate Prosecutor of Plovdiv, Rosen Dimov, issued an order stipulating that owners of Internet cafés were bound to file in special registers the full names and the personal identification numbers of their customers, how long they stayed in the café and which PC they used. The procurator's view is that the aim of this measure is to prevent multiplying defamatory statements sent by email to politicians, statesmen and magistrates and to counteract terrorist threats received in emails sent from these institutions. It is necessary to point out that besides being individual and unique, the personal identification number in Bulgaria has become a universal code for accessing information. It is the individualising data for the authorities and a multitude of private trading partnerships: mobile phone operators, banks and other financial institutions, etc. Trading partnerships often issue what they call "client's cards" and require a full copy of their customer's ID document which also contains this number. In this sense, anyone having another person's personal identification number can receive limited information about their financial status, complete information about their liability at the National Social Security Institute, tax liability and the number and type of imposed administrative violations. Irrespective of the outlined problems, the number of civil cases initiated with regard to violations under the Personal Data Protection Act is small. Bulgarian society has still not customarily viewed and protected personal data as part of the right to a private life.

There is an important and socially disregarded human rights problem with respect to Bulgaria's immigration and asylum policy. It is a fact that Bulgarian legislation has introduced into domestic law the fundamental norms regulating this substance. With the amendments of April 2003, the Foreigners in the Republic of Bulgaria Act (promulgated in State Gazette No. 37/22.04.2003) was set in conformity with the requirements of the Convention Implementing the Schengen Agreement and Directive 2001/51/EC, supplementing the provisions of Article 26 of the Convention. The Asylum and Refugees Act was amended and supplemented in April 2005. It distinguishes between grounds for refusal, refugee status and humanitarian status determination procedure discontinuation, and refugee status termination and revocation.

The Regular Reports of the European Commission have also acknowledged that this field of Bulgarian legislation corresponds to Community law. European observers, however, point out that Bulgaria should direct its efforts to the effective implementation of adopted legislation. In support of the latter come the warnings made by influential human rights organisations which point out the disrespect of human rights in these areas. In its Annual Report on the Human Rights in Bulgaria in 2004, the Bulgarian Helsinki Committee evaluates Bulgaria's asylum and refugee policy as follows:

Neither accelerated proceedings nor any other form of proceedings were conducted at the border for the recognition of refugee status. Neither of the two transit centres planned for this purpose by the State Refugee Agency is functioning as yet. The BHC (Bulgarian Helsinki Committee) found that no actions have been undertaken to even begin building the centre at the village of Pustrogor, on the Bulgarian-Turkish border, which is the main overland point of entry, nor the one at the village of Busmantsi, near the Sofia Airport, which is the main point of entry by air. The authorities denied NGOs the possibility of observing the border detention centres. /.../ For this reason there were no practical guarantees of compliance with the principle of non-refoulement as per Art. 33, Para. 1 of the Geneva Convention on the status of refugees and people seeking asylum at the border. The lack of NGO ability to observe the National Border Police Service detention centres led to the registration of eight cases of denial of entry (refoulement) in violation of Art. 3 of the European Convention on Human Rights of persons seeking asylum on the Bulgarian-Greek border, four of whom were unaccompanied children.[2]

[2] Bulgarian Helsinki Committee. "Human Rights in Bulgaria in 2004: Annual Report by the Bulgarian Helsinki Committee." March 2005. http://www.bghelsinki.org/index.php?module =pages&lg =en&page=reports (7 Dec. 2005).

The cases of unreasonable expulsions of foreigners residing legally in the territory of the country are not an isolated phenomenon. Under the cover of the universal formula of being a "menace to national security", people are summoned to police stations for identity checks and in a couple of hours are taken out of the country, even without being provided with the opportunity to contact their families. The good news is that with respect to these cases the court has recently responded with corresponding to European standards set in the case of Al Nashif v. Bulgaria and has overruled orders because of groundlessness.

As a whole, the adoption of EU *acquis communautaire* provides a general outline for achieving a fair balance between individual and community interests. The development of this outline is a task for Bulgarian society. The "life" of a law providing for human rights protection depends, to a great extent, on the active participation of citizens whose rights are infringed upon and on the activities of law-enforcement bodies. The lack of tradition and effective mechanisms for interaction among state bodies, causing the inefficiency of democratic-in-their-form institutions, is typical of post-totalitarian countries. Thus, European values and standards enshrined in some new Bulgarian laws quite often come into dramatic legal and moral collision with the living totalitarian mentality of people in whose power lies the implementation of the "new law". In the absence of an accomplished civil society and in the context of a retrograde judicial system, the engine for the actual implementation of the new pro-European legislation is now played by human rights organisations whose activities are targeted at conducting lawsuits in public interest.

On the other hand, an important place in the development of the EU is occupied by the conclusions of the Tampere European Council (15-16 October 1999) which provide the fundament for the efforts of creating an area of freedom, security and justice in the EU. A main principle of cooperation in this field is the safeguarding of impartial justice. Stability and effective operation of the judicial system are key prerequisites for the consolidation of democracy, human rights protection and, consequently, Bulgaria's prospective membership in the EU. Pursuant to the statement of Mr. Christof Stock, First Secretary of the Delegation of the European Commission to Bulgaria, 20 million Euro have been allocated for the Bulgarian judicial system reform for the period 1995 – 2005. The training of magistrates which aims at preparing them for the implementation of European standards in law has been widely covered, along with the technical equipment and premises' improvement assistance. Curricula in European Law have been developed which newly appointed "junior magistrates" have been using for their six-month training at the specialised National Institute of Justice. Also, training seminars and conferences for active magistrates have been organised and held on a regular basis.

Indirect as it is, an objective assessment of the results of these efforts can be provided through the analysis of judicial documents decreed for actions initiated under the newly adopted legislation based on the *acquis communautaire*. In most cases, the contents of the judicial documents show a fundamental lack of understanding of the social and moral meaning of these laws. Quite often, through their inadequate procedural behaviour and acts, some magistrates discourage citizens for pursuing such claims. This expose has already summarised the negative experience of lawsuits filed under the Protection against Discrimination Act. The content and the tone of the judicial decisions often reveals the unlawful "solidarity" of some courts with state institutions which have denied public information to citizens. It took years for the first claims of disabled people in wheelchairs against the state to be gained. People claimed that the public and architectural environment in towns and cities they lived in was hostile and turned them into social outsiders. These claims were pursued by legal experts of the Association for European Integration and Human Rights in the period 2000 – 2003 under the Protection, Rehabilitation and Social Integration of Disabled Act (now revoked). The provisions of this law, though not utterly adequate to European criteria in the field they regulated, laid down some European human rights standards. Often, within these "new" lawsuits, lawyers base their arguments on the practice of the European Court of Human Rights, because of the commitment of the Bulgarian court to the norms of the Convention for the Protection of Human Rights and Fundamental Freedoms and the similarity between human rights standards shared by the European Court of Human Rights and those incorporated in European law. Unfortunately, with a view to the human rights results of the implemented trainings, it turns out that a significant part of Bulgarian magistrates do not have the will or professional capacity to reform which would make the Bulgarian judicial system an institution safeguarding full protection of constitutional-state principles and effective enforcement of European law. The essence of the genuine judicial reform involves changes in mentality and attitudes towards human rights and human beings in general. This reform is unimaginable without an effective system of incentives and sanctions, clear rules for personal accountability and transparent criteria for certification and professional development of magistrates.[3] People's mistrust and alienation from the state are a natural result of poorly administered justice. In this specific socio-economic situation, the shortcomings of the judicial system represent the most serious impediment to Bulgaria's accession to the EU. They have been unambiguously stated both by the Bulgarian society and by international observers. It is not accidental that surveys indicate only 8-10 % of public trust in judicial institutions. However, a judicial reform has been imitated in Bulgaria for more than 10 years now. When there is no clear political will to overcome this situation, one of the ways to inspire a democratic change is civil pressure for changes in

[3] Ekimdjiev, M. (2004). "Who Seeks the Justice of the European Court in Strasbourg and Why". *Trud Daily*: 12, August.

the Constitution and in the legislation and regulating the functioning of the judicial organs and their interrelations with the other institutions and the civil society.

Development of human rights protection in Bulgaria through the perspective of the European Commission

The three key incentives for the improvement of human rights conditions in Bulgaria include the willingness to keep undertaken commitments for harmonisation of national with European legislation, active assistance on the part of the EU regarding the adherence to undertaken commitments by means of pre-accession programmes and the European Commission's regular assessment projected in its Regular Reports on Bulgaria's Progress towards Accession to the European family.

In December 1997, the Council of the European Union declared in Luxemburg that the Commission's reports on the candidate-countries' progress towards accession would serve as a basis for making necessary decisions regarding the negotiation process. An important element of these reports is the evaluation of the level of human rights protection in the respective candidate-country. The European Commission reports the stage of coping with existing problems in Bulgaria on an annual basis and its negative repercussions is a clear indication that measures should be taken in order to overcome established discrepancies with international standards. Discrimination in all its manifestations, i.e. minority protection, police violence, trafficking in human beings, conditions in prisons and mental hospitals, access to legal protection, freedom of speech and the attitude of the state towards asylum seekers and homosexuals, are all understandable highlights in the observations of the European Commission in Bulgaria.

A comparative analysis of the European Commission's assessments of the above-mentioned issues included in its last four reports would be beneficial to this expose and would also outline the significance of these reports for the development of human rights protection in Bulgaria. The Commission's annual general conclusion is that, as a whole, Bulgaria respects human rights and fundamental freedoms. Nevertheless, three main groups of problems, which are especially stressed upon in the reports, are easily distinguished. The first group includes solved problems, the second one problems which the state is trying to resolve by undertaking certain measures, and the third one ignored problems.

Of all the above-mentioned, the European Commission regards as solved only the human rights problem of unequal treatment of homosexuals in Bulgarian penal legislation. After discrimination provisions were criticised by the Commission, the age under which the homosexual and heterosexual acts are criminalised, was made equal by the adoption of amendments to the Penal Code in September 2002. The criminal treatment of persons inciting homosexual and heterosexual prostitution has also been made equal. Unfortunately, homosexual orientation is still a common reason for discrimination or harassment. However, the adoption of the Protection against Discrimination Act can lead to the assumption that there is a trustworthy mechanism available for protection against unequal treatment. This can be demonstrated by the first judgement delivered in response to a discrimination complaint on the grounds of sexual orientation. In that case, "St. Kliment Ohridsky" University of Sofia, the oldest and the most authoritative higher education institution in Bulgaria, has been convicted of discrimination manifested against homosexual students.

The European Commission has drawn the annual conclusion that living conditions and attitude of staff towards detainees in Bulgarian prisons and investigation detention facilities contradict European human rights standards. Findings indicate that cells are overcrowded, food is insufficient and of poor quality, and sanitary conditions are extremely poor. In its 2002 Report, the Commission also emphasises that "besides a lack of financial resources, inadequate management and organisation /of centres of detention/ are also contributing factors". The regular reports and visits of the European Committee for the Prevention of Torture and Inhuman or Degrading Treatment or Punishment, established for the application of the European Convention for the Prevention of Torture and Inhuman or Degrading Treatment or Punishment, are also targeted at solving the above-mentioned problem. For the period 2003-2005, the European Court of Human Rights has rendered five judgements in Bulgarian cases and thus has stated that both the conditions in some Bulgarian prisons and investigation detention facilities, and the penitentiary regime of serving imprisonment terms in some cases are excessively cruel, which constitutes a violation of Article 3 of the Convention for the Protection of Human Rights and Fundamental Freedoms, abolishing torture, inhuman and degrading treatment or punishment. In execution of these judgements, the Bulgarian state has been convicted to pay the amount of 26 000 Euro as complainants' damage and costs.

As a result of this permanent, varied and gradating international pressure, Bulgaria has started to make steps towards solving the mentioned problem. Four new prisons have been built, three prisons have been reconstructed, a great number of the underground investigation detention facilities have been closed down and there have been ongoing renovation programmes.

One of the gravest problems mentioned in the Regular Reports is police violence to detainees. Traditionally in Bulgaria, police and investigation detention facilities are used as a non-procedural instrument for obtaining "confessions" or testimony of questionable procedural value. There are three fundamental functional shortcomings allowing of police misconduct: the legal regulation of using arms, conditioning the excess use of force; the reluctance of the judiciary, in the person of Military Procurator's Office and Military Courts, to investigate and punish malfeasances committed by police officers; and the tolerance towards discrimination on the grounds of ethnicity. Cases, in which investigation of police officers is conducted in a way aiming not to expose but rather disguise the crimes, are not isolated. The European Court of Human Rights has rendered such a conclusion in four claims against Bulgaria – Assenov, Velikova, Anguelova and Nachova.[4]

Legislation does not regulate explicitly the terms for using firearms and this lies at the root of the problem of the excessive use of force. The law also allows using arms by police officers against unarmed and unresisting persons, who do not pose a threat to anyone. In its 2002 Report, the European Commission stresses this problem and the necessity of adopting international standards for the use of force. The Report takes into account the progress achieved in the processes of human rights training for police officers and providing representation of minorities in police authorities. The state has continued to implement this course in following years. A special unit for involving citizens of Roma origin in service of the national police has been established. Amendments to the Ministry of Interior Act have been made stipulating that firearms may be used upon detention only if resistance of law is offered or the suspect attempts an escape. Europeanisation of legislation and human rights training are, undoubtedly, positive changes but significant strides toward solving the problem of police brutality would be possible only after the establishment of an effective system for investigation and adequate sanctioning of crime. The "colleague" solidarity of some military magistrates with manifestations of police violence only perpetuates the feeling of impunity and the lack of respect for the law. In this context, the number of warnings by non-governmental organisations regarding violence during detention and inquisition quite naturally remains unchanged. According to records of human rights activists, the share of Roma people who claim to be victims of violence performed by law-enforcement bodies in police stations is significantly higher than the average.

Minority protection provides a separate focus in European Commission's Reports. In fact, the problem in this field is related mainly to protecting the rights of the Roma community. The state treats Roma people in an ambiguous and contradictory way.

Segregation and discrimination against Roma people are in fact tolerated by the authorities in the most significant social spheres, i.e. education, healthcare and employment. The differentiation of Roma neighbourhoods, Roma schools and occupations "appropriate" to Roma, is a result of a long-term state policy and institutional practices of long standing. The everyday confrontation of Roma

[4] European Court of Human Rights. Case of Assenov and others v. Bulgaria, Application No 24760/94, Judgement of 28.10.1998, Reports 1998-VIII; Case of Anguelova v. Bulgaria, Application No 38361/97, Judgement of 13.06.2002, Reports of Judgements and Decisions 2002-IV; Case of Velikova v. Bulgaria, Application No 41488/94, Judgement of 18.05.2000, Reports of Judgements and Decisions 2002-VI; Case of Nachova and others v. Bulgaria, Application No 43577/98, No 43579/98, Judgement of 06.07.2005, Grand Chamber. http://www.echr.coe.int (7 Dec. 2005).

people with the attitude of the administration, police and law-enforcement bodies creates the painful feeling that the state is prejudiced against them and it does not protect their rights as properly and vigorously as it does for other citizens.

As a result of mainly international interference and in conflict with dominant social attitudes, the state has initiated sporadic activities of Roma population integration. In 1999, Bulgaria adopted the Framework Programme for Equal Integration of Roma People into Bulgarian Society and the Action Plan for the implementation of the Framework Programme. There are some municipal projects initiated on the construction of houses for limited numbers of Roma people and for improving the infrastructure in Roma residential districts. National programmes targeted at coping with long-term unemployment of Roma people have been developed. Measures to preserve Roma culture and identity have been taken. A long-term action plan has been launched under the Decade of Roma Inclusion initiative, envisaging cooperation among EU countries, candidate countries and countries outside the accession process.

Unfortunately, despite the apparent activity, certain considerable flaws in the anti-discrimination programmes leave the impression that they are a means of simulating willingness for the integration of Roma in society. The 2003-2004 Action Plan for implementing the Framework Programme encompasses the activities necessary to achieve the programme objectives, an implementation timeframe and a budget. However, some of the objectives of this plan are not financially provided for. In addition, it does not envisage relevant legislation reforms in sensitive areas such as education, healthcare and housing. The Ministry of Education and Science has issued instructions for the desegregation of Roma in schools for 2002-2003 but "there appears to be little commitment to devise a specific policy in this area over the short to long term"[5]. The functions of the National Council on Ethnic and Demographic Issues at the Council of Ministers remain mostly screening in view of the fact that this body does not have the powers for the effective protection of minorities.

The divided attitude of the state towards Roma people condemns undertaken measures to failure in the long run since qualitative change of Roma people's social environment will only happen after overcoming discrimination attitudes of the majority towards the minority which inevitably reflect on state policy.

The judgement of the European Court of Human Rights of 5 October 2000 regarding the case of *Varbanov v. Bulgaria* put into focus the international criticism of the commitments in psychiatric hospitals in Bulgaria. Pursuant to Article 61, Paragraph 2 of the operative at that time Public Health Act, the prosecutor is entitled to order, without any medical evidence of a mental disease, a compulsory outpatient examination or commitment in a specialised medical institution for an in-patient forensic medical expertise. According to Paragraphs 3 and 4 of

[5] European Commission (2004). Regular Report on Bulgaria's Progress towards Accession: pp.26.

the same Article, the commitment may last up to six months. There is no opportunity for appealing in court against this type of detention. This problem was not omitted by European observers in the 2001 Regular Report on Bulgaria's Progress towards Accession. The European Commission therein highlighted the necessity of legislative measures for filling in normative gaps and stated that intentions expressed by the Government to amend the Public Health Act were still not reality. The posed question of confinement in psychiatric institutions also provoked the examination of living conditions in these public institutions. It was found that residents live in inhuman conditions: in buildings built to serve as workers' dormitories, schools, agricultural structures, etc., which do not allow for sufficient personal space, space for personal belongings or even appropriate conditions to maintain personal hygiene. There are cases of isolating mentally ill people in special premises and the only treatment is pharmaceutical. Complaints about the use of physical force on residents by staff members are frequent.[6]

The unambiguous evaluations of the European Court of Human Rights and the European Commission, and the warnings signaled by human rights organisations have caused changes. A new Healthcare Act was adopted in August 2004 and it entered into force on 1 January 2005. It contains more reliable guarantees against arbitrary restrictions of personal freedom. The role of the prosecutor's office has been reduced to the power of request with the district court to render a judgement of commitment and treatment in a psychiatric institution. Within the initiated procedure, the person whose commitment is requested receives a copy of the request and has the right to lodge an objection and provide evidence in his or her defence. A psychiatrist and a counsel for the defence take part in the proceedings. The court may solely, after a psychiatrist is heard, institute a psychiatric expert examination report and the deadline for its preparation may not be longer than fourteen days.

There is no tangible progress in improving living conditions in psychiatric institutions. However, a programme has been developed and actions have been taken to reconstruct or close down institutions which do not correspond to basic sanitary requirements.

Although still insufficient, measures have been launched for combating the traffic of human beings which, in addition to being the stumbling block in negotiations under Chapter 25 of "Justice and Home Affairs", is also a grave human rights issue. There are issues though, which, despite the criticism of the European Commission, the state seemingly prefers to disregard. An example of this is the lack of guaranteed legal assistance for all defendants and the existence of heavy punitive sanction against libel on the part of journalists which directly affects freedom of speech by causing self-censorship.

[6] Bulgarian Helsinki Committee. "Human Rights in Bulgaria in 2004: Annual Report by the Bulgarian Helsinki Committee." March 2005. http://www.bghelsinki.org (7 Dec. 2005).

The ambiguity in the process of assessing the quality of managing problems specified by the European Commission is due to the conflict between the two mutually exclusive approaches of state policy towards human rights. On the one hand, it declares that human rights protection is one of its keystone priorities. On the other hand, the rampancy of "visible" crime and related feelings of uncertainty and mistrust in institutions are used by "force" institutions for promoting before the public ideas about the necessity of restricting citizens' rights and freedoms. Through their powerful propaganda centres, they suggest the thesis of antagonism between public security and individual rights. The absence of democratic traditions makes broad social circles persuadable to these suggestions threatening the fragile civil society in Bulgaria. The judiciary system, instead of being a corrective of the executive, has constructed itself to be a stronghold of outdated views on the inviolability of the state and its servants. Within this unfavourable social context, the enforcement of the European standards, objectified in the "new" laws is left to reside in the hands of non-governmental human rights organisations. Pursuing strategic claims is a proven, yet an extreme method of popularising law, encouraging disadvantaged people and accomplishing greater social equity. In this respect, the adoption of the European *Acquis* in the form of new legislation, though forced from the international pressure, rather than realised as a necessity, creates a reliable instrument for human rights protection, i.e. legal proceedings in the public interest. Using law as a means of making impact on institutions, Association for European Integration and Human Rights Foundation has won the first dozens of cases in which the state has been convicted to pay damage to disabled people on account of inaccessible architectural environment in big Bulgarian cities. After the Protection against Discrimination Act, which explicitly qualifies existing architectural barriers as discrimination, became effective, Legal Alternative Foundation has initiated a new series of legal actions taken by disabled people whose aim is to multiply the accomplished success. The Access to Public Information Act is an operating law the credit for which should be given to Access to Information Programme Foundation whose activities, in addition to taking legal action against illegal denial of information, include trainings and seminars for promoting the act. The number of non-governmental organisations pursuing claims under the Protection against Discrimination Act is large: Romani Baht Foundation and Bulgarian Helsinki Committee which are entirely devoted to discrimination against Roma, Gemini Organisation and Foundation Queer which files lawsuits against discrimination on the grounds of sexual orientation, and Association for European Integration and Human Rights Foundation which has initiated actions against discrimination on the grounds of ethnicity, gender, disability, and social status.

In conclusion, on account of the lack of democratic traditions, and the fragile civil society in Bulgaria, the mightiest engine for importing the European standards in the field of the human rights, is the aspiration towards accession to the

European Union. The leading role for "working out" these standards is assigned to the non-governmental organisations. This conclusion imposes itself unconditionally on the background of the ineffective and poorly working state institutions and the extremely vital post-totalitarian mentality, dominating among magistrates, on which the enforcement of the new, "European" laws depends.

CHAPTER V

ON THE LIMITS OF THE HUMAN RIGHTS APPROACH

Taking Human Rights to its Limits or Why We Need a Critical Review
David Chandler

Introduction
This paper seeks to critique the human rights discourse from a different position from that more commonly taken. Most criticism has originated largely within the human rights discourse itself. The policy-makers and institutional actors have been criticised for failing to act on behalf of human rights in some areas of the world, or when they have acted, have been criticised for being too slow to respond or for merely taking half-measures. Much of this criticism has also been focused on the slow level of institutional change at the international level, for example: the UN Security Council composition and power of veto; UN Charter restrictions on international intervention; the slow development of an International Criminal Court; the lack of institutional integration of NGOs in international decision-making; and the remaining outdated privileges of state sovereignty.

As Alex de Waal has noted, 'to date most sociological study of humanitarian action implicitly accepts the axioms of the humanitarian international'. Statements of human rights NGOs and states and international institutions acting in the name of human rights are often taken at face value as if the nobility of aim conferred immunity from sociological analysis or political critique. He sums up the strength of consensus by analogy: 'It is as though the sociological study of the church were undertaken by committed Christians only: criticism would be solely within the context of advancing the faith itself' (1997a: 65).

Instead, this chapter first of all considers the theoretical and political justifications for universal human rights claims and raises the problematic nature of these claims against traditionally conceived civil and political rights. The following sections consider the nature of the human rights-based critique of existing international practices and discuss how current conceptions of human rights tend to empower dominant institutions and leading states rather than ostensible human rights victims. The concluding sections focus on some of the mechanisms through which the human rights discourse reinforces current international inequalities, for example, through increasing human rights conditionality, the legitimisation of external regulation over the domestic political process in selected states and international protectorates, and the legitimisation of increasingly militarised international relations.

Justifying Human Rights

Initially it would appear that there is little justification necessary to uphold the importance of universal human rights. Human rights are commonly understood, literally, as the rights we have because we are human and from this flows their universality. They must be equal rights because either one is a human being, and therefore entitled, or not. It also follows that human rights are inalienable, as one cannot stop being a human being, and they cannot be denied, or put aside.

This approach seems to be the one taken in the major international treaties and statements which are the founding documents for human rights campaigners. The Universal Declaration, the UN Covenants and the Vienna Declaration only provide a 'thin' answer to the basic conceptual and theoretical justification for human rights (Donnelly 1999: 8). The source of internationally recognised human rights is identified as the inherent (moral) nature of the human being. Every person, simply as a human being, is entitled to human rights. The Universal Declaration, Article 1, states: 'All human beings are born free and equal in dignity and rights'. The Economic and Social and the Civil and Political Covenants of the UN assert that 'these rights derive from the inherent dignity of the human person'. The Vienna Declaration, in similar wording, states that 'all human rights derive from the dignity and worth inherent in the human person'. The same terminology is used by UN Secretary-General Kofi Annan, who asserts that: 'they derive from the intrinsic value and dignity of each and every human being' (1997a: 1). 'All human rights for all' was the motto of the Office of the High Commissioner for Human Rights for 1998, the fiftieth anniversary year of the Universal Declaration (Donnelly 1999: 10).

The need for some theoretical grounding or justification for transcendental human rights arises only when one seeks to go beyond the circular reasoning of having human rights because we are human. When the advocates of human rights seek to use the concept to question the international political order, they are confronted with the need to go beyond abstract justification for their demands. It is here that some problems become apparent. Although human rights are assumed, by definition, to be universal and indivisible there is little unanimity over their universal grounding. State-grounded political rights, as considered below, assume as their foundation an individual capable of self-government. The advocates of human rights start from the assumption that this is a false universal subject. There are a number of well-established theoretical approaches that lend support to their critique of the political rights thesis. It is undoubtedly true that the equality of political and civil rights relies on the formal separation of the public and private spheres. The formal equality of the legal and political sphere necessarily abstracts from differences and inequality in the social and economic sphere.

This separation forms the basis of the radical critique that the sphere of formal political rights excludes and marginalises many people that lack the capacities and resources necessary for self-government. Before a court of law or at the ballot box every citizen is treated as an equal, equally capable of taking responsibility for their actions and their political decision-making. Yet this does not mean that the inequalities of the private sphere will be progressively overcome. Inequalities in the social and economic sphere are not necessarily resolved through political rights and many would argue that they are perpetuated through them. David Beetham, for example, suggests that the proper subjects of human rights, as distinct from civil and democratic rights, are those individuals who lack the capacities to act in a politically independent way. He argues that political and civil rights are 'of little value if individuals lack the personal capacities or resources to make use of the freedoms in question, and that legally established rights will be largely formalistic if the means necessary to exercise them are beyond people's reach' (1999: 96). As Michael Ignatieff notes, we are increasingly made aware that it is man's wretchedness that necessitates the universal protections of human rights:

> Nothing good has come of these experiments [in international intervention] except perhaps the consciousness that we are all Shakespeare's "thing itself": unaccommodated man, the poor, bare forked animal. It is "the thing itself" that has become the subject – and the rationale – for the modern universal human rights culture (1998: 5).

Neil Stammers also observes that the idea of human rights is premised on the '*vulnerability* of individuals...people require human rights to protect them from potential violations arising from the social contexts in which they find themselves' (1995: 491). Ken Booth, who locates the subject of human rights in 'ethical communities' defined by exclusion from the political process, rather than political communities bounded by the state, takes the same approach:

> Universal human rights are supposed to be invalid because there is no universal ethical community. But there is: the ethical community of oppressed women, the ethical community of under-classes; the ethical community of those suffering from racial prejudice; the ethical community of prisoners of conscience; the universal ethical community of the hungry...and on and on (1999: 61).

This perspective is given greater weight by a feminist critique of the political rights tradition which sees the majority of the population, women as a whole, as marginalised and oppressed, and therefore denied the formal capacities claimed by the democratic rights thesis. A slightly different approach is to assert that the problem lies not with a lack of recognition of the marginalised or oppressed groups within society but with the concept of the self-governing individual itself. James Nickel, for example, claims that even the individuals, which are able to play a full role in policy-making, lack the moral capacity for self-government. In this case, the need for human rights derives from the fact that 'unaided conscience will not generally provide fully adequate beliefs about how people ought to behave and how society ought to be organized' (1987: 41).

The rejection of the concept of the self-governing political subject of necessity brings us back to the problem of grounding human rights on the basis of the innate characteristics of being a human being. This universal capacity has been theorised in a diverse variety of ways. For example, on 'an identification of the needs and capacities common to all humans, whatever the differences between them'; a universal 'capacity for moral understanding and progress'; the 'thin' conception of rationality proposed by John Rawls; or the speech and listening capacities identified by Jean-Francois Lyotard (Beetham 1999: 93; Nickel 1987: 41; Mendus 1995: 14; Lyotard 1993: 138). For many of today's human rights advocates this essentially boils down to a capacity for moral reciprocity, 'feeling the pain' of others, or in the words of Michael Ignatieff: 'imagining the pain and degradation done to other human beings as if it were our own' (1999b). However, having rejected the universal grounding of political and democratic rights for exaggerating human capacities or for ignoring the social and economic inequalities in society, the 'common needs and capacities' are necessarily those at the lowest level of human society. This approach inevitably tends towards a minimalist view of the human subject, where capacities are minimised and needs maximised (for example, Gerwith 1981; Doyal and Gough 1991).

Whichever approach is chosen, the human rights-bearing subject is qualitatively different from the subject of state-based political rights. The universal subject of human rights has much less capacity, for either self-government or self-determination, than the rational individual assumed by modern representative democracy. It is this perspective of the minimal subject, incapable of meaningful action in the political sphere, which leads to a pre-political justification for human rights (Zizek 1999: 171). All advocates of universal human rights necessarily have to posit a moral dimension to their claims for universal rights. As Nigel Dower notes: 'Since a human right is independent of actual conventions in society, the basis for its existence must be found elsewhere, and the natural place to find this is moral theory'(1997: 88). For example, Jack Donnelly asserts that human rights can 'be relatively easily derived from many moral theories'. He suggests that they could be derived from natural law or that teleological ends-based theories may be able to ground human rights in their tendency to further human good or flourishing (1999: 12). Donnelly is not unusual in his reluctance to substantiate which moral grounds he is actually standing on. Attempts to ground abstract human rights in an overtly moral context reveal the problems of deriving a modern conception of right from the pre-political or anti-political sources of moral philosophy.

Modern conceptions of rights, the state-based civil and political rights, can only be justified on the basis of the political equality of rational self-governing individuals, and necessarily eschew any moral basis of external judgement. Moral philosophy sets itself as above or prior to political conceptions of equal rights between self-governing subjects. For this reason, it is not possible to argue cogently for political rights on a moral basis. Neither the categorical imperative of Kantian theory nor the ends-based teleology of Bentham's utilitarianism, for example, would justify universal human rights claims. For Kant, duty comes before human rights and for Bentham the good of society would come prior to human rights. Moral philosophy can logically derive duties but not rights, it can morally justify a universal duty to the common good but can justify neither universal human rights nor political and civil rights, which depend on the capacity for self-determination (Freeman 1995: 31). As Donnelly is forced to concede, the category of rights-based moral theories has 'historically been an empty one' (1999: 12).

The concept of human rights appears to straddle the division between morality and politics in a way that prevents a consistent moral or political grounding to the subject of the rights concerned (Henkin 1990: 6). It has been widely noted that the lack of theoretical cogency has been no barrier to the revival of human rights theory, creating a gap between political theory and political practice (Mendus 1995: 10). As the vast majority of governments have accepted the concept of human rights, despite the lack of plausible fundamental principles, many influential commentators openly state that the question of theoretical consistency is of little importance (Bobbio 1996: 10; Rawls 1993: 68). This uncritical acceptance of human rights is highlighted by the public disavowal of theory in the resort by some theorists to the tautology of grounding human rights solely 'in the fact of their recognition' or by 'leaving open the question of justification' (Chesterman 1998: 117; Nickel 1987: 9; Waldron 1987: 163).

In fact, the conceptual ambiguity of human rights allows advocates of the concept to have the best of both worlds. The moral 'human' emphasis helps to abstract the concept from disputed political terrain, while the political 'rights' side of the concept helps to skate over the divisions within moral philosophy. The abstract subject of human rights appears to be the perfect moral/political category because the inherent ambiguity within it means that it can be taken up across the moral and political divisions of society. As Donnelly notes, the vague grounding of universal human rights helps overcome disputes over moral foundations and provides a common ground between different political perspectives (1999: 13, see also Charvet 1998; Klug 1997).

However, there is a fundamental difference between deriving rights from the capacity of human subjects and deriving them from the incapacity of human subjects. The central component of all democratic systems of rights or legal systems, and their theoretical starting point, is the individual's capacity for self-government. The subject of the modern law is a person assumed to be a moral agent or self-willing actor. As a rights-bearing subject the person is not simply coerced into accepting the law by forces outside their influence. The law is seen to be freely accepted and to derive from their own will. The framework of regulation of the modern democratic system is historically and logically derived from the formal assumption of equal self-governing individuals, responsible and accountable for their actions and capable of rational decision-making. All modern doctrines of the enforcement of contract, the punishment of crime, the election of governments and the state system of international law rest on this core assumption (Heartfield 1996). This can be usefully highlighted by a brief consideration of the different facets of a modern state's rights-framework or legal system.

Civil law is the clearest expression of the derivation of the law from the will of the self-governing subject. In enforcing the law of contract, civil law does not impose an alien or external goal onto individuals. In fact, the civil law only binds individuals to their word; this is an expression of the will of the legal subject as the contract is voluntarily made. There is no compulsion to higher policy goals or ends; the only object of the law is the contract between two equal contracting parties. Of course, it could be argued that it is unfair to hold a person to an earlier word against a later decision, however, that word was part of a social contract with another person who acted on the basis of it. The law is justified in holding an individual responsible and accountable for a promise freely given and the basis of another's actions. The implicit assumption is that we are not only all equally free to engage in contractual obligations but that we are all equally responsible for keeping our side of a contractual promise, i.e., that we are all equally moral and autonomous agents.

Criminal law also assumes the equality and free will of the legal subject. The accused is represented at the court in the same way as for breaches of civil law. The citizen has the right to defend his or her interests in court equal to any other citizen. The law is binding on the individual as if it were a contract, although there is no formal contract beyond the assumption of assent to membership of a law-bound community (mythologised in social contract theory). This is clearly only notional assent, but it is through this fiction of consent that the equal rights of defendants before the law are enshrined. The defendant is recognised as a moral agent, responsible for his own actions. Just as under the civil law, punishment is for a free act of will; there is no liability if the defendant acted without free will, for example, under duress or if suffering from mental impairment. Despite the lack of voluntary contract, the criminal law formally enforces the will of the offender, as a law-abiding citizen, against his or her actions. As a moral agent, the offender is responsible for his decision to break the law, just as if he had broken a civil contract. The possibility of punishment, as opposed to mere repression, derives from this recognition of the autonomy of the offender. The law is legitimate and not repressive because it is based on the assumption of a free autonomous and self-determined individual.

In constitutional law, the notional social contract is given content. As a people, the electorate is the subject from which the authority of the state is derived. There are many forms of deriving constitutional authority from the people, including, for example, constitutional monarchies, presidential systems, or consociational federal bodies, and within these a variety of forms of separation of powers between the executive, legislature and the judiciary. For all its limitations, the principle of popular sovereignty is a thoroughly radical conception of authority from the people. It argues that the state's authority derives exclusively from the people, without any external source of either power or legitimacy.

This idealised picture reveals the centrality, to all aspects of the modern framework of rights, of the rights-bearing individual with the capacity for self-government. The source of particular state-based rights is the autonomous legal subject, rather than abstract humanity. As the German MP Uwe-Jens Heuer and his colleague Gregor Schirmer point out:

> [T]he sphere of law ("Right") and human rights are (conceptually) separated from the state and from politics. But Right, and with it law, is a social product, the result of social struggles, and only comes to be when it is set out as law and sanctioned by the state... But the separation of Right from the state and politics leads to its mystification. It now seems to come from the heavens above (1998: 8).

As Hannah Arendt noted the 'inalienable rights' of abstract humanity would mean claimants falling back 'upon the minimum fact of human origin' (1979: 300). She cogently argued that the concept of rights could not exist independently of political society. For Arendt:

> Equality, in contrast to all that is involved in mere existence, is not given us, but is the result of human organisation... We are not born equal; we become equal as members of a group on the strength of our decision to guarantee ourselves mutually equal rights (1979: 301).

Even if the universal subject of human rights were clearly identifiable, it would be impossible to connect the abstract universal denominator of humanity with the concept of rights in any coherent way. Norman Lewis notes:

> Placing the concept 'human' in front of 'rights' may represent a quantum leap up. But this is only in the abstract. No matter how these rights are presented, what they have in common is the fact that they are not derived from legal subjects (1998: 85).

This central distinction in approach to the rights-subject explains why the two different rights approaches have an opposing conception of the importance of the political sphere and its institutions at the level of the state and international society. This difference is highlighted in the following section, considering the radical nature of the human rights critique of the political sphere and the problems this poses for any practical alternative.

The poverty of normative philosophy

As David Beetham notes, the essence of normative theory is the 'critical component' which asks two questions: 'How far are the criteria or principles entailed by the concept realised in a given situation or set of institutions? and How far does practice measure up to a justifiable normative standard or ideal?'(1996: 28) The normative critique of international society, based on the challenge of human wrongs is a very powerful one. Wheeler, for example describes:

> ...a world where, protected by the non-intervention principle, 123 states practice torture or ill-treatment of prisoners; where genocide occurs and goes unpunished; where 40,000 children die daily of preventable diseases; and where millions – especially women – live hopeless and wretched lives (1996: 131).

As long as there are victims of human wrongs then existing institutions and legal frameworks are open for criticism and seen as vulnerable to the call for change. The commitment of normative international relations theory to 'placing the victims of the society of states at the centre of theorizing' has produced a stark moral critique of international society, sometimes referred to as 'critical international society theory'. Nicholas Wheeler argues: 'Critical international society theory places suffering humanity at the centre of its theoretical project exploring how the society of states might become more hospitable to the promotion of justice in world politics.'(1996: 127) For Ken Booth, this approach is 'an ethics for the emancipation of victims across the world' (1995: 116). This theory is not just thoroughly critical it is also thoroughly radical, against the realist concern with power relations and states, 'especially important here is critical theory's project of placing the powerless and dispossessed at the heart of theory and emancipatory political practice' (Wheeler 1996: 128).

The moral critique of existing practices is always a thoroughly radical one. But, as with any critique that starts from ethics rather than existing society, there is little need for serious consideration of the real and the profane:

> Westphalia, in its time, had represented a sort of anchorage, after the ravaging wars of religion. But the grammar of the system of state sovereignty and statism constructed from the seventeenth to the twentieth century led inexorably to the Holocaust and atomic warfare... In the killing fields at the apogee of Westphalia – Dachau and Hiroshima – 'Hell was here'.(Booth 1999: 65)

According to this study it is the striving for democracy and state sovereignty, allegedly the 'amoral' politics of 'realist' Machiavellism, which has led to the horrors of the twentieth century. If the political sphere is the cause of warfare and oppression, there is clearly little positive about politics or democratic government. The human rights critique is in many ways a stunningly confident attack on the political sphere under the cover of ethics and morality. Transcendental moral values are portrayed as the progressive solution to the problems of the narrow political sphere: 'This is the hope of progressively leaving behind the politics of the concentration camp – the ultimate sovereign space – for a cosmopolitan democracy aimed at reinventing the global human being – being human globally...and badged with a common humanity.'(Booth 1999: 65-6)

Interestingly, this point is the exact opposite of that made by Hannah Arendt in her acclaimed study *The Origins of Totalitarianism*, originally published in 1951. She made the vital point that state rights were taken away from the Jews and other minorities prior to their internment, that in fact it was the loss of political and legal rights that were the crucial precondition for the horrors of the concentration camp (1979: 296-7). She further demonstrated, that for those lucky enough to escape, the stateless refugees, 'the only practical substitute for a nonexistent homeland was an internment camp', in reality the only guarantor of rights was the nation-state (1979: 284). The truth of this was confirmed by my grandfather's experience on escaping Buchenwald for British India, when he was interned in Ahmadnagar, one of the original concentration camps established by the British during the Boer War. Because human rights can only imply dependency on others, persecuted people, from the Jews in the 1940s to the Kosovo-Albanians in the 1990s, claimed not human rights but political rights and fought for the establishment of the state of Israel and for an independent Kosovo (1979: 292-9).

Normative human rights theory, however, argues for a rejection of the existing framework of international society and the political sphere of the states which compose it. The theorists that are most critical of existing international society are those that are more concerned with blue-prints for a future moral world order than an analysis of the problems of the existing one. This theory is powerful as a critique but the problems appear when the theory addresses alternatives, the institutional arrangements which can be derived from the starting moral precepts (Beetham 1996: 29). Human wrongs are the central empirical support for this critique, which condemns the fact that 'many states do not provide for the security of their citizens' (Wheeler 1996: 127). However, the description of 'wrongs' provides little explanatory depth and the link from being critical of human wrongs to a positive human rights framework is not straightforward, even in theory let alone practice. As Mary Midgley notes:

> To talk of rights is, by contrast, to talk directly about the people who need relief. It aims to lay a burden publicly on anyone who stands in the way of relieving them – a burden which cannot be dodged by passing the can. The quasi-legal language invokes the broad impersonality of the law. It makes it much harder to say 'this is none of my business' (1999: 167).

The problem is that, having written-off states from acting in a morally responsible way, the moral agent, whose 'burden' or 'business' it is to enforce human rights, is difficult to locate. Where the political rights of the public sphere are non-specific as to ends or content, the human rights thesis is non-specific regarding the means of guaranteeing or implementing rights. For the founders of political and civil rights theory, rights could only be guaranteed by the subjects of the rights themselves (Rosenberg 1999). If a right could not be protected, or exercised, by its bearers then it could no longer be a right, an expression of self-government. Democratic rights theorists developed this conception of the active and self-determining subject of rights in opposition to pre-modern hierarchical conceptions of rights as privileges bestowed on the deserving from above.

For the advocates of human rights, the legitimacy of the claim stands independently of, and sometimes in inverse relation to, the capacity of the subject. Because the human subject is defined as being without autonomy some external source has, of necessity, to be looked to. The theorists of human rights find it difficult to come up with a cogent answer as to the external source that can be trusted to implement and guarantee human rights. In reinterpreting rights as a moral category, as opposed to a legal or political one, a contradiction appears between the enforcement and guarantee of human rights and the formal legal and political framework. The ambitious nature of the concept of human rights, which establishes the content of those rights independently from the capacity of its subjects, means that this gap between claim and capacity lies at the heart of the question of implementation.

The lower the capacity of the human subject the greater the need for some form of external assistance or grant of resources or regulatory power, yet the incapacity of the subject makes this grant entirely arbitrary and by no means guaranteed. Fiona Robinson rightly argues that 'the right to food' or the 'right to housing' cannot guarantee anything more than an absence of discrimination, a formal freedom. To make these rights a duty of provision by the state or another actor, they require much more than a statement of right (1998: 65). The 'right to food' or 'the right to housing' or 'right to development' are meaningless in terms of rights, as they are abstract claims which say very little about who or what must act to ensure they occur. As David Beetham notes, the International Covenant on Economic and Social Rights 'can at most be a statement of aspirations or goals rather than properly of *rights*' (1999: 116):

> They confuse the fundamental with the merely desirable or with that, which is specific to the advanced economies (holidays with pay, free higher education, and the continuous improvement of living conditions). Even those that are fundamental can not be defined in a justiciable form. At what level can the deprivation of nutrition, sanitation or healthcare be sufficient to trigger legal redress? (1999: 116)

With little agreement on the substance of human rights, or the means of implementing them, it is easy to see why the claims made are often declared to be normative 'wish lists'. To achieve the good ends of human rights advocates, as Donnelly notes, is 'to reshape political and social relations so that this moral vision will be realised': 'Human rights thus are simultaneously a 'utopian' vision and a set of institutions – equal and inalienable rights – for realizing at least an approximation of that vision'(1999: 16).

The lack of an autonomous human subject means that human rights advocates' aspirations for a better and more just society must necessarily focus on a beneficent agency, external to the political sphere, to achieve positive ends. There may be a duty to act to fulfil human rights needs but there is no politically accountable institution that can be relied upon. In order to help bridge this gap, between the ideal critique of the real and solutions which are necessarily part of the profane reality, human rights advocates tend to privilege the role of institutions which can stand above politics.

In the world of realist political and international relations theory, the focus is on existing institutional arrangements. This focus makes it difficult to accept the possibility of institutions that stand independent from social and political pressures. When addressing practical alternatives, the advocates of human rights are forced either to take existing political institutions, at state or inter-state level, out of the political sphere or to posit some form of alternative institutional arrangement, which is independent of politics. For some theorists of human rights, the solution is to bring the state back into the analysis. But, of course, only if the political sphere is subordinated through the institution of forms of regulation independent of elected government. This can occur through political actors being bound by a Bill of Rights and therefore capable of acting morally, that is, independently from the economic pressure of the world of business and the political pressure of parliamentary competition.

The idea of the state acting morally to guarantee a set of moral ends seems to fly in the face of the democratic political conception of the state, based on the need to achieve consensus between competing interests within society. To justify the subordination of politics to moral ends, human rights theorists often stress the protective and morally progressive role of the state as the guarantor of democratic political rights as well as potential human rights. Donnelly, for example, as considered earlier, asserts that the 'negative' anti-state conception of political rights is misplaced as the state has to play a central role in the implementation of civil and political rights. Active institutional intervention is seen as necessary to implement legislation against discrimination, to ensure the procedural rights of individuals in the courts, and to create an environment conducive to the development of civil and political freedoms. Once democratic rights and civil liberties are seen to be dependent on the beneficent nature of state protection, as opposed to the reflection of the self-governing activity of the historical subject, it is then easy to assert an external mandate for the state, or other institutions, as the guarantor of human rights. The anti-political critique of the human rights theorists, shifts from condemning the 'concentration camp' of the politically-tied state to concluding that the morally-engaged state can be the guarantor of human rights. For some commentators, for example David Held (1995), Martin Shaw (1994), Bikhu Parekh (1993), Michael Walzer (1997) and Fred Halliday (1994), the leading Western states can act as the moral agents of humanity and have the duty to ensure the protection of human rights in those states that cannot be so easily trusted (see further Chapter 5).

Once the distinct guarantor of democratic rights, the active rights-bearing subject, is removed from the analysis, rights of self-government become indistinguishable from privileges granted by the tolerance and understanding of the powerful. As Neil Stammers notes, the imperative of action to defend human rights ironically entails a *realpolitik* which is highly state-centric and, in fact, not only reflects but also reinforces the highly uneven balance of existing power relations (1999: 992). Under the logic of the human rights discourse, determined by the abstract and ahistorical view of a degraded subject, even the 'negative' freedoms against state interference are seen as guaranteed by the state itself. Once this tautological conception is accepted, rights to 'freedom' are indistinguishable from a licence for external regulation. If 'negative' freedoms entail dependency on an external will, human rights, regardless of their specific content, would necessarily entail far greater external regulation as the breadth of their moral claims makes their implementation a far more ambitious project. As A. Belden Fields and Wold-Dieter Narr note:

> If people are not aware of the historical and contextual nature of human rights and are not aware that human rights become realized only by the struggles of real people experiencing real instances of domination, then human rights are all too easily used as symbolic legitimizers for instruments of that very domination (Cited in Stammers, 1999: 980).

Not all human rights theorists are willing to grant the state the capacity for moral action. For more radical international relations theorists the Western-led 'international community' is still too tied to the political sphere and incapable of being led by the moral human rights impulse (Booth, 1995: 121). For the more radical human rights theorists, if even the leading Western states cannot be trusted to act morally, then there is little hope that international society as it is constituted can guarantee human rights (Wheeler 1996: 127).

The Problem of Agency

Underlining the consequences of the human rights discourse's dismissal of the active political subject is the question of agency: 'which social or political groups might plausibly act as bearers, protagonists or beneficiaries of the values in question?' (Beetham 1996: 29) At first appearances the human rights thesis seems to adhere to the view of the historical agency of collective humanity. For Ken Booth: 'The discourse of human rights is potentially crucial to human history because it is part of the language of the human species' self-creating emancipation from natural and societal threats'(1999: 31). A deeper consideration reveals that this is far from the case.

What was lost in the promulgation of human rights theory in the 1990s was the connection between rights and subjects that can exercise those rights, which was at the core of political accountability and democracy. Once the historical and logical link between rights and the subjects of these rights is broken, then democracy is a meaningless concept. The epistemological premise of democracy is that there are no final truths about what is good for society that can be established through the powers of revelation or special knowledge. As David Beetham argues: 'the only criterion for the public good is what the people freely organised, will choose, not what some expert or prophet decrees on the basis of superior knowledge' (1999: 35). If we accept that people are the best judges of their own interests, then only self-determination can be the basis for collective self-government. Democracy therefore is only a means to an end, to the realisation of the public good because it allows people to define what that good is, as well as to control the process by which it is realised (Beetham 1999: 13).

Democracy does not guarantee that everyone will equally support, or equally gain from, the outcomes of collective decision-making. Democracy merely ensures that everyone has an equal say in that outcome. The predominance of some form of majority say in policy-making, through the electoral process, is a product of the underlying principle of equality, the basis of 'everyone counts for one and none for more than one'. If we are all equal, but have an infinite variety of different individual views of what the public good should be, and how it should be served, the only way to decide is by process of an equal say. The system of representative government attempts to ensure that the individual perspectives of the public good coalesce into a broader social perspective through a variety of processes by which a public will is manifested. There are a several stages in approximating this public will, which can vary with constitutional frameworks, but usually include political party competition at the polls and the debate and vote of elected members of the legislature, or parliament, on legislation.

Fiona Robinson's treatment of the problems of human rights gets to the heart of the issue, the difference between democratic rights without moral ends and human rights defined by moral ends. Robinson privileges ends over means in a direct way through the introduction of a distinction between 'the right' and 'the good'. She defines 'the good' as a substantive moral goal, or end in itself:

> ...'the right' by contrast, is that which is decided simply by its instrumental significance for achieving that good. The right is negative, procedural, rule-like notion; the 'good' by contrast, is that which gives the point of the rules which define the right (1998: 65).

If human rights, 'the goods', stand on their own as a moral end then there is little need for 'rights' in the decision-making process. Donnelly, similarly, recognises the implications of the human rights discourse for democracy. He argues that democracy is concerned with who ought to rule and human rights are concerned with what the rulers of the people do and how they rule. He asserts that in this sense human rights are 'profoundly anti-democratic', because their aim is to frustrate the will of the people when it diverges from human rights (1999: 41). This separation of rights from their subjects leads to the redefinition of both rights and subjects through the human rights discourse. In fact, the logical conclusion of human rights policy would be the end of politics as a sphere for the resolution of social questions of the distribution of goods and policy-making. Even David Beetham, a leading proponent of the human rights thesis, balks at its consequences:

> While we may reasonably require of them [non-Western governments] to refrain from torturing their citizens, it is not obvious that we can equally require them to guarantee them all a livelihood, adequate accommodation and a healthy environment. Moreover, for them to do so, it is contended, would require a huge paternalistic and bureaucratic apparatus and a corresponding extension of compulsory taxation, both of which would interfere with another basic right, the right to freedom (1999: 116).

All human rights advocates share the view that social justice, the righting of 'human wrongs' should stand above the formal political equality of liberal democracy. The protection of women, national minorities, children, the environment, peace, multi-ethnic society and many other rights-causes are considered, by their advocates, to be too important to be left to the traditional instruments of domestic and international government. Whereas representative government works to realise the derivation of the state from the will of the people, human rights theorists seek to subordinate the will of the people to ethical or moral ends established by a less accountable elite. The traditional conservative critique of democracy was that of the 'despotism of the multitude', today's human rights advocates dress these nineteenth century arguments in the twenty-first century garb of normative rights theory.

Wheeler's critical international society theory places an important emphasis on public involvement in the 'ethical content and purpose of foreign policy' (1996: 128). But not the public as constituted through the political process. In place of the democratic participatory society, assumed as the basis of the political conception of rights, the role of the individual is a much less empowered and passive one. In place of politics, we have the moral advocacy of a liberal elite. The voices of the human rights victims and politically excluded are not expressed through the ballot box but are the raw material for their self-appointed liberal advocates in the media, academia and the international NGOs.

The preference for elite activism over democratic involvement has been central to the anti-politics of the normative human rights revival. The elite assumptions behind this approach were expressed clearly in Michel Foucault's address at the launch of a human rights initiative to send naval vessels into the Gulf of Thailand on behalf of the Vietnamese boat people, at the Intercontinental Hotel, Geneva, in June 1981:

> We are here only as private individuals, who have no other claim to speak, and to speak together, than a certain shared difficulty in accepting what is happening… Who, then, has commissioned us? No one. And that is precisely what establishes our right… Amnesty International, Terre des Hommes, Médecins du Monde are

> initiatives which have created this right: that of private individuals actually to intervene in the order of international politics and strategies. The will of individuals has to inscribe itself in a reality over which governments have wanted to reserve a monopoly for themselves – a monopoly which we uproot little by little every day (Cited in Keenan 1997: 156-7).

For Booth, the problem with those who are critical of the moral advocacy of the liberal elite is that they are too concerned with the political framework of the state system to be sensitive enough to appreciate the emerging moral and ethical constituencies of the human rights discourse. These NGOs and liberal cosmopolitans are the basis of the 'new social movements' which the human rights advocates claim to represent:

> Universal human rights are solidly embedded in multiple networks of cross-cutting universal ethical communities. The fundamental weakness of the critics of universality is that they take too territorial a view of the idea of human community, human political solidarity and human social affinity. Their perspective is conservative, overdisciplined by constructed notions of states and cultures (Booth 1999: 61).

'Global civil society' is to be the moral arbiter of policy, not the party competition and struggle for representation of the political sphere (Archibugi 2000). Policy 'is best tested by listening to victims and trying not to offend global civil society, the nearest we have to a conscience of world society' (Booth 1999: 57). For Mary Kaldor, 'global civil society' can be located in 'the cosmopolitan young people to be found in almost every city from Sarajevo to New York' or the people active in NGOs, international organisations or the international media.

The human rights advocates, who listen to the voices of the oppressed and the cosmopolitan-minded, envisage themselves as the moral gatekeepers to policy-making discussion, under the guise of empowering the excluded. Mary Kaldor expresses this preference for liberal opinion to replace representative democracy in choosing who is entitled to have a say in policy discussion:

> Civil society thus consists of groups, individuals and institutions which are independent of the state and state boundaries, but which are, at the same time, preoccupied with public affairs. They are, in effect, the guarantors of civil behaviour both by official institutions (states and international institutions) and in the world at large. Defined in this way, civil society does not encompass all groups or

> associations independent of the state. It does not include groups which advocate violence. It does not include self-organised groups and associations which campaign for exclusivist communitarian concepts. Nor does it include self-interested private associations...(1999a: 210).

To be granted the right of inclusion into the policy-debate, Kaldor insists people must pass the test of respect for 'global human rights culture'. Naturally this test involves agreement with the all the ethical causes that Mary happens to espouse herself (1999a: 210). This makes a mockery of the globally inclusive rhetoric of human rights theorists, like Ken Booth, who assert that 'a good place to start thinking about politics is to ask the victims'. The question of agency reveals the central flaw of the normative human rights theorists. Their replacement of an historical social subject of rights with an abstract ethical subject inevitably leads to their own self-appointment as agents of change. Far from giving a voice to the excluded, the elite advocates are empowered on the basis of their vicarious association with moral causes.

Highlighting the centrality of the self-governing or autonomous human subject to the concept of rights sharply reveals the flaw of the burgeoning human rights discourse and the reason for its inability to establish a foundation for the substance and character of the new rights it proclaims. The redefinition of rights from neutral means to ethical and value-laden ends, or claims on an external authority, removes the universality and democratic content of rights. Neither the discussions over the substance or content of human rights, nor the means of implementing and guaranteeing them, are resolvable through democratically accountable mechanisms because these political questions of power and distribution are reposed as moral absolutes open to external or juridical interpretation through international institutions or domestic and international courts.

Once humans are universalised, not as competent and rational actors capable of determining their own view of the 'good' but, as helpless victims of governments and the forces of the world market or globalisation, then democratic freedoms and civil liberties appear meaningless. Under the guise of 'ethical' universalism the human subject is degraded to the lowest level, in need of paternalist guidance from the 'great and the good' who can establish a moral agenda of human rights to guide, educate and 'empower' the people. The assumptions and processes of representative democratic government are turned on their head.

Empowering Victims?

Human rights intervention to support victims' rights or needs tends to empower the forces that are acting on their behalf rather than the victims themselves. As Hannah Arendt noted, this relationship of external assistance for victims is the opposite of a right, it is a charitable act, there is no law or right that could force intervention of this sort (1979: 296). As with all cases of claims not based on rights: 'Privileges in some cases, injustices in most, blessings and doom are meted out to them according to accident and without any relation whatsoever to what they do, did, or may do'(1979: 296).

International intervention in the Balkans demonstrates clearly how this process reinforces the inequalities of power between the international actors and the purported victims themselves. It is the intervening powers, which define the victim and prescribe the rights, which they are choosing to uphold. The use of human rights to directly undermine democratic rights in this region was demonstrated in discussions on the selective use of humanitarian aid in Serbia in 1999 and 2000. The European Union proposed to only provide certain types of humanitarian aid to Serbian municipalities run by opposition parties (see Chapter 2). The first selective aid programme was 'Energy for Democracy', where humanitarian shipments of heating fuel were directed to cities such as Nis, Kraljevo and Kragujevac. This was followed by similar aid programmes such as 'Schools for Democracy', 'Roads for Democracy' and 'Milk for Democracy' (ESEM, 2000; Rozen, 2000a). This selective approach of aiding some 'victims' while the rest of Serbia suffered international sanctions did little to empower the 'victims' but rather attempted to manipulate them to support a political project favoured by Western governments.

Perhaps the clearest example of the manipulation of victims' rights in the region was in response to the Kosovo crisis. Firstly, the NATO powers established the need for intervention and a prolonged bombing campaign on the basis of protecting the human rights of the ethnic-Albanian community, alleged to be the victims of genocidal policies by the Serbs. During the bombing campaign US Defence Secretary William Cohen claimed 100,000 ethnic-Albanian men 'may have been murdered', David Scheffer the US envoy for war crimes put the figure as high as 225,000 (Steele 2000b). The lowest NATO government estimate of the number of ethnic-Albanians massacred by Serb forces, by Geoff Hoon at the British Home Office, was 'at least 10,000' (Steele 2000a; 2000b). These figures were in marked contrast to the ICTY's preliminary conclusions, in August 2000, that the final total death toll of the civil conflict would be between 2,000 and 3,000.

The victim status of the ethnic-Albanians, that allowed them to gain the support of NATO states, was not enough to allow them a say in the post-war government of the province. Once the Serb state had been forced to relinquish sovereign powers over the territory, NATO was concerned that the victims would 'fill the vacuum' with their own institutions (Zizek 2000: 59). After waging war for ethnic-Albanian rights to autonomy and self-government, the NATO and UN officials felt that the ethnic-Albanians could not be trusted to rule in their own name, let alone take over the administration of schools, hospitals and the media (Chandler 2000b). An extensive bombing campaign that was waged for the rights of Balkan victims, as the most public example of ethical human rights-led foreign policy resulted in little gain for the people of the region. Michael Mandelbaum makes the point in *Foreign Affairs* that 'Western leaders declared that they were fighting for the sake of the people of the Balkans, who nevertheless emerged from the war considerably worse off than they had been before.'(Cited in Littman 1999:ii-iii)

Once ethical policy is presented as action in the cause of others, any policy failure can only have limited political repercussions. This was demonstrated time and again over Balkan policy. Even the worst results of international meddling in the region were interpreted, not as evidence of US and NATO policy-failure, but rather, in the words of President Clinton, as 'we gave them a chance to make their peace and they blew it' (Rose 1998: 65). One month, if developments in the region looked positive, it would be 'a test case' of America's ability to promote human rights; the next month, if things were going less well, the Balkans would become 'an intractable "problem from hell" that no one can be expected to solve' (Woodward 1995: 307). Any complaints over policy outcomes were met with the moral exculpation that 'we' tried and 'they' failed to make the most of it (Ignatieff 1998: 99).

Accountable to None

The upholding or promotion of human rights represents a major shift away from the UN Charter framework of international regulatory mechanisms, precisely because it replaces an enforceable equal standard of state sovereignty with an abstract universality that can never be realised within the confines of contemporary society. Human rights, within these parameters can unfortunately be nothing more than an empty concept whose function is, at best, the legitimisation and perpetuation of the existing mechanisms of international regulation, and, at worst, the legitimisation of a new more divisive international framework based on economic and military power.

The modern system of law (whether international or domestic) depends in two vital respects on the concept of formal equality between its subjects. At the most basic level, that of derivation, all international institutions, including the UN, OSCE and NATO, derive their authority from inter-state agreements. International law derives its legitimacy from the voluntary assent of nation-states, which are to be bound by it. Without a notion of consent, the distinction between law (based on formal equality) and repression (based on force and arbitrary power) disappears (Dicey 1959: 202-3; Heartfield 1996). International law, as expressed in the resolutions of the United Nations, explicitly relies on this conception. Sovereign equality is also essential for the application of international law. Law cannot exist without equality of application, without formal equality under the law. If states were not treated as equals, then the universal quality of law would be eroded. Rights of weaker states could be infringed on the basis that the law does not fully apply in their cases, or more powerful states would claim immunities from prosecution due to their 'special case' situation.

This extension of 'international justice' is in fact the abolition of international law. There can be no international law without equal sovereignty, no system of rights without equality between rights-bearing subjects. Without sovereign equality, and the resolution of differences through mechanisms of the United Nations, different states would be free to declare their own particular interests as law, leading to the end of certainty and consensus about international law. Because international law cannot be based on the new conception of 'international justice', the gulf between state practice and the UN Charter is growing (Shaw 1994: 174).

Leading advocates of 'international justice' in fact challenge the concept of international law itself. For example, Roy Gutman and David Rieff, the editors of Crimes of War: What the Public Should Know (1999), allege that international law is 'frustratingly counterintuitive' and cannot address 'which side was right and which side was wrong' (1999: 11). For this reason, Albrecht Schnabel and Ramesh Thakur, editors of the United Nations University study 'Kosovo and the Challenge of Humanitarian Intervention', argue for the ad hoc and arbitrary application of international human rights protections:

> A code of rules governing intervention would be likely in the early 21st Century to limit rather than help effective and responsible action on the part of the international community... Any attempt to get general agreements would be counter-productive... It may be inevitable, possibly even preferable, for responses to international crises to unfold selectively (2000).

The NATO bombing campaign over Kosovo symbolises the transition of international law from 'hard law' to 'soft law'. The US government and NATO have not sought to justify their actions on legal grounds (Wedgewood 1999: 829; Charney 1999: 836; Franck 1999: 859). Theorists like Nigel Dower assert that a moral view of international relations means that 'one cannot simply support the law', opposition to evil must be higher duty (1997: 107). Rights-interventionists, like Richard Falk, argue that the ethical imperative has 'superseded legalistic restraints'. International law has to move with the times and assume more of an ad-hoc character: 'Otherwise, the self-marginalisation of international law and international lawyers is assured in contemporary situations involving claims to use force, consigning their vocational fate to the demeaning roles of "apologist" or "utopian."'(Falk 1999: 853) Those who upheld international law against NATO's bombing campaign were indeed condemned as 'apologists' for genocidal policies or as out of touch 'utopians'. The UK House of Commons Foreign Affairs Committee confirmed Falk's view that the ethical imperative must come before the law, concluding that although the war was 'of dubious legality' it was, however, 'justified on moral grounds' (UKFAC 2000c: par.138).

Human rights conditionality

Today, human rights concerns are central to most international treaties and held to justify a wide range of conditions, which have to be met for membership of the European Union and other international bodies. At the same time, an increasing variety of human rights conditions have been integrated into inter-state agreements on aid and trade and for economic development aid from international institutions. The comprehensive nature of human rights allows conditionality to cover nearly every aspect of government policy once economic and social development are included under the human rights rubric. This can involve subjecting economic and social policies to 'independent external evaluation' and the development of a set of conditions, such as the reduction of military budgets, taking steps to combat political corruption, or spending more on education and welfare (Felice 1998). This trend towards external accountability could in effect spell the end of independent economic and social policy-making in the less-developed world, subjecting areas of traditional domestic policy decision-making to international bodies which can dictate policy (Robertson 1999: 149). Nigel Dower argues that: '[I]f any country manifestly fails to realise the basic rights of people of a political, civil or economic nature, through deliberate policies of oppression, unequal treatment or discrimination, then actions can be legitimately taken to put pressure on such a country to mend its ways'(1997: 105).

Unconditional humanitarian aid is seen to be problematic today because non-Western states are increasingly seen to be unable to rule themselves. Radical critics condemn aid programmes as supporting governments more than the poor, and see aid as increasing corruption. For Geoffrey Robertson, international aid, which is conditional on human rights policies, can hardly be seen as 'human rights imperialism' rather, it is a 'sensible step in global governance' as it is based on empowering the people that are worst affected by poverty: 'transforming them from passive recipients of aid into plaintiffs who had obtained their due by asserting before the international community their human right to a remedy for the hopelessness of their collective life' (1999: 150).

Moves in this direction can already be seen in the 'holistic approach' to development taken in the Comprehensive Development Framework presently being implemented in several African states, which the World Bank launched in 1999 as an alternative to the failed policies of structural adjustment (Pender 2000). As Gordon Crawford notes, bilateral and multi-lateral aid from the private sector, governments, the World Bank and the IMF, is becoming conditional on agreed reform packages which leave developing countries with less and less influence over policy decisions (1996: 36-7). Bradlow and Grossman state that the impact of greater human rights conditionality means that power and influence is exercised more unevenly in international affairs because it is the poorer and weaker states that are most dependent on the financing services of these institutions (1995: 427-8).

The introduction of human rights concerns into the policy-making powers of international financial institutions, such as the World Bank and the International Monetary Fund has created a new range of *ad hoc* powers. These institutions operate independently from the United Nations and effectively have the power of independent decision-making on all financial issues. The inclusion of human rights concerns under the financial mandate has, in effect, given greater unaccountable powers to these leading international institutions. For example, the Articles of Agreement of the International Bank for Reconstruction and Development (part of the World Bank Group) preclude it from intervening in the 'political affairs' of its member states, requiring it only to take 'economic considerations' into account in decision-making. It is entirely up to the bank to interpret which human rights issues impact on economic development and therefore are not purely 'political', in this context it has made loans conditional on the suppression of female genital mutilation but not, for example, on the prevention of torture. As Bradlow and Grossman note, the inclusion of human rights in the mandates of these institutions introduces a completely *ad hoc* factor which gives these institutions arbitrary powers over domestic affairs: 'The arbitrary nature of this situation becomes clear when one takes into account the connection between freedom of the press and hunger, and between freedoms of speech and association, transparent and accountable governance, and economic development'(1995: 431-2).

With the development of human rights-conditionality clauses in international agreements between major economic powers and other states, existing relations of formal equality between states in the West and the developing world are brought into question. Political equality and independent policy-making capacities are being undermined by Western paternalism in the cause of human rights. Nigel Dower suggests that criticisms of external interference in the promotion of human rights tend to 'overwork' the appeal to democracy:

> No theory of democracy says that no-one either inside or outside a community, may for moral reasons, seek to influence the way democratic preferences turn out. But at a more fundamental level, it seems to me that there is a false contrast being drawn between what a fundamental morality demands and what a genuinely democratic procedure would select as basic rights to be protected (1997: 106).

The conflation of external human rights regulation with democratic outcomes legitimises the elitist perspective that external institutions are better suited to making policy-decisions than non-Western governments and their electorates.

Direct protectorates

The extension of the logic of conditionality can be seen in the developing UN agenda of civil administration over post-conflict states. Until the end of the Cold War, UN peace operations had no direct mandates to reshape the political sphere. Over the last decade the UN's peace operations have increasingly extended to the political sphere, under the rubric of 'peacebuilding', building the 'foundations of something that is more than just the absence of war' (UN 2000c: 3). This new programme is part of a people-centred framework in which the human rights component of a peace operation is seen as critical to its long-term effectiveness (UN 2000c: 7). The August 2000 Brahimi Panel report defines peacebuilding as including, but not limited to: rebuilding civil society; strengthening the rule of law, through police restructuring and judicial and penal reform; improving the human rights situation by monitoring, educating and investigating abuses; democratic development including election and media regulation; tackling corruption; HIV/AIDS education and control; and promoting conflict resolution and reconciliation (UN 2000c: 3).

Regarding the rule of law, the UN panel emphasised the importance of the international reform and restructuring of the penal and judicial system in post-conflict societies, and the need to involve international judicial experts, penal experts and human rights specialists. The panel also suggested a 'doctrinal shift' in the role of civilian police in post-conflict operations (UN 2000c: 7). In the past this role was a monitoring one, documenting behaviour and, by their presence, attempting to discourage unacceptable behaviour. This was now seen as a 'somewhat narrow perspective'. Instead, the panel report proposed that the UN police should reform, retrain and restructure local police forces and have the capacity to take over their role if necessary, responding to civil disorder.

The panel also emphasised the danger of seeing post-conflict elections as marking the end of the period of international administration. It warned that 'elections merely ratify a tyranny of the majority' until democratisation and civil society-building processes have been completed and a 'culture of respect for human rights' has been established (UN 2000c: 7). Because of the perceived lack of legitimacy of post-conflict governments, elected or not, the panel suggested that the economic reconstruction programme should be kept under UN control, with no direct aid or investment, as the UN 'should be considered the focal point for peace building activities by the donor community' (UN 2000c: 8). The panel further recommended that 'quick impact projects' were established, to overcome hostility to the UN's regulation of economic reconstruction and 'help establish the credibility of a new mission' (UN 2000c: 7).

The logical conclusion of the focus on extending peace building regulation in post-conflict societies is the extension of the mandates of the 'transitional' civil administrations headed by the UN. The first fully developed peace building mandate of this sort was established in 1995, when the UN effectively took over the civil administration of Bosnia. This was originally a one-year mandate, but was extended indefinitely after two years (Chandler 2000a: 158). This was followed in 1999, by indefinite formal mandates of civil administration over Kosovo and then East Timor. These missions have revealed that the peacebuilding project is highly likely to be a long-term one, during which, state sovereignty is effectively surrendered by the post-conflict state. As the Brahimi Panel noted, the UN has been given responsibility for micro-managing these societies: making and enforcing the law, establishing customs services, collecting business and personal taxes, attracting foreign investment, adjudicating property disputes, reconstructing and operating public utilities, creating a banking system and running the schools (UN 2000c: 13).

The panel suggested that the UN Security Council should establish a centre of responsibility for the tasks of transitional administration to manage future direct mandates. It also suggested that the UN draw up a 'justice package' with an interim legal code to avoid the difficulties of establishing 'applicable law'. This would solve the problems of Kosovo where the UN was formally working under Federal Yugoslav law but allowed their appointed judges to overrule it while NATO troops and UN police initially worked according to their own conflicting national laws (Chandler 2000a: 210).

Once the non-Western state is no longer seen as a political equal the trend is for greater levels of external regulation, as can be seen by the establishment of international protectorates in Bosnia, Kosovo and East Timor. As Michael Ignatieff notes: 'The United Nations once oversaw discrete development projects. Now it takes over the political and administrative infrastructure of entire nations and rebuilds them from scratch'.(1998: 79) The advocates of human rights, of course, dispute any connection between their perspective of long term management as a transition to self-government and that of Great Power domination in the past.

The problem with the 'freedoms' campaigned for, by the first internationally appointed colonial governor of Kosovo, is that they are won through the radical restriction of the political sphere. The protectorate solution is a logical outcome of the human rights discourse but clearly demonstrates the limits of this perspective, which holds that external regulation can manage society better than democratic involvement in decision-making. The result is that under the new international protectorates, the human rights subjects have little possibility of taking ownership of political issues (Waal 1997a: 221). As Christine Chinkin notes, regarding Kosovo: 'The internationalization of the internal dispute by the commission of human rights abuses and the military action has displaced the agency of the local players and made them passive objects of international proposals' (1999: 845). The consequence of international regulation under the rubric of human rights protection is not merely the formal removal of democratic accountability. The central problem with regulation in East Timor, Bosnia and Kosovo has been that the political sphere has been colonised by external regulation with negative consequences for any self-sustaining solution.

In all the UN administrations, the vast network of human rights protections leaves little space for any local accountability. As Seth Mydans noted in the *New York Times*, one critical problem with the UN protectorate's nation-building attempts, involving an overhaul of every aspect of East Timorese society, has been that 'relatively few local people are being given important roles in the planning and running of the reconstruction effort' (2000). While UN bureaucrats have taken on the roles of district administrators, the leading political group in East Timor, the National Council for Timorese Resistance (CNRT), were ignored by the UN and refused office space in the capital Dili (*Financial Times* 1999). There have been daily protests at the UN's high-handed rule over the territory. José Ramos Horta, CNRT vice president, complained: 'We saw time going by and no Timorese administration, no civil servants being recruited, no jobs being created.'(Cited in Aglionby 2000)

The Bosnian example is probably the most revealing, as after six years of international rule the problems of external regulation are becoming clearer. The constantly expanding role of the multitude of international organisations has inevitably restricted the capacity of Bosnian people to discuss, develop and decide on vital questions of concern. At state level the Bosnian Muslim, Croat and Serb representatives can discuss international policy-proposals under the guidance of the Office of the High Representative, but at the most can make only minor amendments or delay the implementation of externally-prepared rules and regulations. Even this limited accountability has been diminished by the High Representative who has viewed democratic consensus-building in Bosnian state bodies such as the tri-partite Presidency, Council of Ministers and State Parliament as an unnecessary delay to imposing international policy. Compared to the swift signature of the chief administrators' pen, the working out of democratic accountability through the joint institutions was seen as 'painfully cumbersome and ineffective' (OHR 1997b). At the end of 1997, the 'cumbersome' need for Bosnian representatives to assent to international edicts was removed and the High Representative was empowered both to dismiss elected representatives who obstructed policy and to impose legislation directly. The international community thereby assumed complete legislative and executive power over the formally independent state.

The Dayton settlement for Bosnia, like the Rambouillet proposals for Kosovo, promised the decentralisation of political power and creation of multi-ethnic administrations in order to cohere state institutions and provide security to ethnic minorities and safeguard their autonomy. However, the experience of Dayton suggests that the outcome of the framework imposed will inevitably belie any good intentions that lie behind it. Minority protections, promised to the three constituent peoples under Dayton, have not been delivered under the international administration. At state, entity, city and municipal levels a clear pattern has emerged where elected majorities have been given little control over policy making. However, this power has not been decentralised to give minority groups security and a stake in government but transferred to the international institutions and re-centralised in the hands of the High Representative. Today the international community regulates Bosnian life down to the minutiae of local community service provision, employment practices, school admissions and sports (OHR 1997d: par.5.7). Multi-ethnic administrations exist on paper, but the fact that the consensus attained in these forums is an imposed one, not one autonomously negotiated, is important. Compliance with international edicts imposed by the threat of dismissals or economic sanctions does little to give either majorities or minorities a stake in the process, nor to encourage the emergence of a negotiated accountable solution that could be viable in the long term.

The institutions of Bosnian government are hollow structures, not designed to operate autonomously. The Bosnian state Council of Ministers with the nominal role of assenting to pre-prepared policy has few staff or resources and is aptly described by the Office of the High Representative as 'effectively, little more than an extended working group' (OHR 1997a: par.24). Muslim, Croat and Serb representatives have all argued for greater ethnic autonomy in policy-making, and have attempted to uphold the rights protected in the 'letter' of the Dayton Agreement against the *ad hoc* reinterpretation of international powers under the 'spirit of Dayton' (Woodger 1997). As an advisor to Bosnian President Alijah Izetbegovic noted, there is a contradiction between the stated aims of the international protectorate and its consequences: 'A protectorate solution is not good, because the international community would bring all the decisions which would decrease all the functions of Bosnia-Herzegovina institutions. The High Representative's mandate is actually, an opposite one, to strengthen the Bosnia-Herzegovina institutions' (OHR 1997c).

The frailty of Bosnian institutions has perpetuated the fragmentation of political power and reliance on personal and local networks of support which were prevalent during the Bosnian war. Both Susan Woodward and Katherine Verdery provide useful analyses of the impact on Bosnian society of the external undermining of state and entity centres of power and security (Woodward 1995: 136-7; Verdery 1996: 82-3). The lack of cohering political structures has meant that Bosnian people are forced to rely on more narrow and parochial survival mechanisms, which has meant that ethnicity has maintained its wartime relevance as a political resource.

It would appear that the removal of mechanisms of political accountability has done little to broaden Bosnian people's political outlook. The removal of sites of accountable political power has in fact reinforced general insecurity and atomisation which has in turn led to the institutionalisation of much narrower political relations in the search for individual links to those with influence and power. The narrowing of the political sphere and reliance on individual survival strategies has assumed a generalised pattern across society. The 'new feudalism' noted by some commentators and the continued existence of weak para-state structures in Muslim and Croat areas of the Federation are symptomatic of the vacuum of integrative institutional power at state and entity level rather than some disintegrative dynamic (Deacon and Stubbs 1998).

The dynamic of the Dayton process has been to institutionalise fears and insecurities through high-handed international rule disempowering Bosnian people and their representatives. With little influence over, or relationship to, the decision-making process there is concern that entity boundaries or rights to land, employment and housing can easily be brought into question. The extended mandates of the international institutions have undermined the power of the main political parties and their elected representatives but have not created the political basis of a unitary Bosnia, except in so far as it is one artificially imposed by, and dependent upon, the international community.

Under the human rights international protectorates there is a high level of external regulation but little democracy and no mechanisms through which the rights-administrators can rebuild fragmented societies. While mainstream commentators conflate human rights with empowerment, self-determination and democracy there are few critics who highlight that the human rights discourse of moral and ethical policies is essentially an attack on the public political sphere and democratic practices. The result is a 'hypertrophied public realm' with the political sphere reduced to a narrow one of international officialdom with extensive powers wielded in isolation from broader society, and an 'atrophied public realm' in the sense of a loss of citizenship with collective political society reduced to reliance on personal and parochial networks (see Weintraub 1997; Garcelon 1997). In fact, the time scales for external administration have been extended as society becomes increasingly atomised (Chandler 1998). In Bosnia, Kosovo and East Timor external regulation has been highly destructive of the political sphere as increasing levels of civil interaction have come under regulatory control.

Military Humanitarianism

The rights-based critique of humanitarianism has provided the military in Western states with the opportunity to portray their actions as increasingly ethical in the 1990s. Ironically, this occurred at the same time as armed interventions moved away from the UN 'Blue Helmet' approach that overlapped with the humanitarian principles of neutrality, impartiality and consent (Pugh 1998: 348; UN 2000c). As Michael Pugh observes, 'military humanism' is no longer an oxymoron because military action has increasingly been justified through defending human rights goals (1998: 342). From the perspective of the military establishment, this new role is important and the cultures of the military and the human rights activist are increasingly being brought together through the idea of helping the 'victim', as can be seen from recruitment advertising in Britain and the United States. The humanitarian motives for military action have been so heavily stressed that some critics have warned that the British army is danger of being flaunted as 'the military wing of Oxfam' (Norton-Taylor 2000a).

This convergence between 'ethical foreign policy', carried out through military action, and humanitarian assistance was only made possible through the concept of human rights-based humanitarian intervention. Several commentators argue that the division between humanitarianism and militarism was decisively eroded in 1991 with Security Council Resolution 688 concerning humanitarian provision in Iraq at the end of the January-February 1991 war (Ramsbotham and Woodhouse 1996: 13). Under the banner of 'humanitarianism', the supporters of UN Resolution 688 linked human rights with international peace and security, arguing that failure to protect the Kurds would threaten the security and sovereignty of other countries (Mills 1997: 286). Once the protection of human rights was linked to international security the UN Charter framework of non-intervention in internal affairs was implicitly undermined. Matters of domestic jurisdiction could now be re-framed through the human rights discourse as 'just cause' for military action (Black 1999b).

The military intervention in Somalia in 1992 and the dispatch of UN and NATO forces to Bosnia was also justified in the UN Security Council as a response to a 'threat to the peace' (Roberts 1993: 440). During the 1990s, the connection between rights-based humanitarianism and military intervention was cemented, through the UN Security Council's broad definition of international peace to include concerns which would have been earlier classed as internal questions (Forsythe 2000: 57-62). Despite this manoeuvre the Security Council did not recognise a formal right of military intervention purely on human rights grounds. The NATO assault on Kosovo was the first internationally sanctioned military action in the name of human rights and internal questions of governance, rather than international security.

The blurring of the distinction between military action and humanitarian intervention, through the human rights discourse, has seen the questioning of every traditional humanitarian principle (MacMillan 2000; Thomas 2000). The UNHCR has blurred the distinction between being a warring party or an impartial humanitarian actor by suggesting that through the NATO mandate being one of peace-enforcement it is therefore maintaining the principles of neutrality and impartiality. NGO analyst, Ed van Mierop, however notes that NATO dictated the terms of co-operation with the UNHCR and that the NGO community as a whole has accepted NATO co-operation (2000). As Robert Hayden observes, the concept of humanitarianism has been transformed: 'instead of protesting the application of state violence on non-violent dissidents, activists are demanding the application of massive violence on states deemed to be inferior'. He terms this development 'humanrights-ism' to demonstrate the repudiation of traditional humanitarian principles (2000). Thomas Weiss also argues that the human rights community have redefined humanitarianism as its opposite: 'These actions are, by definition, coercive and partial. They are political and humanitarian; they certainly are not neutral, impartial, or consensual.'(1999: 21)

Conclusion

It is only post-1989 that the agenda of human rights interventionism has become both possible and necessary with the end of super-power rivalry and the old international political framework. During the 1990s, the ethical human rights agenda has become an important mechanism for cohering Western governments and international institutions, bereft of any clear political agenda of their own. This drive to resolve questions of legitimacy and coherence through ethical policy, has led national governments and international bodies to institutionalise the once marginal concerns of human rights advocacy groups and international lawyers.

The lack of accountability involved in ad hoc denunciations of human rights abuses and the ease with which this leads to selective actions against targeted states, has been facilitated by the human rights discourse. Pushing the idea of the victim to the fore and presenting a much diminished view of the capacity of societies to rule themselves, the rights-based NGOs presented a coherent picture of the degraded non-Western subject and thereby legitimised a new sphere of 'ethical' or non-political policy-making (Johnstone 1998). By blurring the boundaries of domestic and foreign policy they have facilitated the creation of a new sphere of activism for institutions and governments seeking to demonstrate their importance and legitimacy in the post-Cold War world.

The ethical foreign policy of criticism is an 'aspiration' or 'principle', which stands on the moral high-ground. However, the ethics of coercive universalism have resulted in an increasingly divided world in which a few select states are held up for condemnation, punishment and external intervention. Even in the select cases, where coercive action is taken in the cause of human rights, it seems that the motivation for these actions has less to do with the development of human rights in these countries than the symbolisation of what Western states and institutions stand for. The sanctions and denunciations are more for the purposes of domestic and international credibility than intended to improve the situation for the worst-off citizens in the selectively targeted states. The reality of selective scapegoating and irrational policy-making is obscured by the human rights discourse, enabling the human rights road-show to move on from Somalia to Bosnia to Kosovo to East Timor to Sierra Leone with 'demands for action' and little accounting of the outcome of intervention (Chomsky 1999; Maren 1997; Chandler 2000b).

References

Aden, H. (2002) "Die Auswahl der normsetzenden Institutionen im Prozess der Globalisierung des Rechts. Organisierte Kriminalität und Klimawandel als Beispiele für Modethemen bei der internationalen Normsetzung", in Nahamowitz and Voigt (eds), *Globalisierung des Rechts II: Internationale Organisationen und Regelungsbereiche*, Baden-Baden: Nomos, 281-318.

Aden, H. (2001). "Der Etat de droit der V. französischen Republik und seine Begrenzung durch große exekutive Handlungsspielräume", in *Deutsch-Französisches Institut* Albertin, Asholt, Bock, Christadler (eds), Frankreich-Jahrbuch 2001, Opladen: Leske + Budrich, 65-79.

Aden, H. (1998). *Polizeipolitik in Europa. Eine interdisziplinäre Studien über die Polizeiarbeit in Europa am Beispiel Deutschlands, Frankreichs und der Niederlande*, Opladen/Wiesbaden: Westdeutscher Verlag.

Aglionby, J. (2000). "Bungled UN Aid Operation Slows East Timor's Recovery", *Guardian*, 30 August.

Annan, K. (1997). "Strengthening United Nations Action in the Field of Human Rights: Prospects and Priorities", *Harvard Human Rights Journal*, 10, 1-9.

Alston, P. (ed.) (1999). *The EU and human rights*. Oxford et al.: Oxford University Press.

Alter, K.J. (2001). *Establishing the Supremacy of European Law: The Making of an International Rule of Law in Europe*, Oxford: Oxford University Press.

Aral, B. (2001). "Dispensing with Tradition: Turkish Politics and International Society During Özal Decade, 1983-93", *Middle Eastern Studies*, 37,1, 72-88.

Archibugi, D. (2000). "Cosmopolitical Democracy", *New Left Review*, Vol.2, No.4, 137-150.

Arendt, H. (1979). *The Origins of Totalitarianism* (new edn), New York: Harvest.

Aschenbrenner, J. B. (2000). *Menschenrechte in den Außenbeziehungen der Europäischen Union*. Frankfurt am Main et al.: Lang.

Barany, Z. D. (2002). *The East European Gypsies: Regime Change, Marginality, and Ethnopolitics*. Cambridge: Cambridge University Press.

Barkey, H. J. (2000). "The Struggles of a Strong State", *Journal of International Affairs*, 54, 1, 87-106.

Barnes and Olsthoorn (1999). *The Framework Convention for the Protection of National Minorities. A Guide for Non-Governmental Organizations*. London: Minority Rights Group.

Beetham, D. (1996). "Theorising Democracy and Local Government", in King and Stoker (eds) *Rethinking Local Democracy*, London: Macmillan, 28-49.

Beetham, D. (1999). *Democracy and Human Rights*, Cambridge: Polity Press.

Bellamy and Schönlau (2004). "The normality of Constitutional Politics - An Analysis of the Drafting of the EU Charter of Fundamental Rights", in *Constella tions*, 11, 3, 412-433.

Bellamy and Castiglione (2001). "Tra retorica e simbolismo: La Carta europea dei diritti fondamentali", *Quaderni Forum*, No. 2.

Biering, K. (2003). "Efforts and Possibilities of the OSCE in Combating Terrorism", in *OSCE Yearbook 2002*, Institute for Peace Research and Security Policy at the University of Hamburg/IFSH (ed.), 31-38. Baden-Baden: Nomos.

Binder, J. (2001). *The Human Dimension of the OSCE: From Recommendation to Implementation.* Wien: Verlag Österreich.

Birkenbach, H.-M. (2000). "Half Full or Half Empty? The OSCE Mission to Estonia and its Balance Sheet 1993-1999", *ECMI Working Paper # 7*.

Black, C. (1999). "An Impartial Tribunal, Really?", November. Available from: http://www.swans.com/library/art5/zig036.htm

Bloed, A. (ed.) (1993). *The Conference on Security and Co-operation in Europe. Analysis and Basic Documents, 1972-1993*. Dordrecht/Boston/London: Kluwer.

Bloed, A. (1991). "A New CSCE Human Rights 'Catalogue", *The Human Dimension of the Helsinki Process - The Vienna Follow-up Meeting and its Aftermath. (International Studies in Human Rights, vol. 20)*, Bloed and Van Dijk, 54-73. London: Martinus Inhofe.

Bobbio, N. (1996). *The Age of Rights*, Cambridge: Polity Press.

Boer-Buquicchio, M. de (2003). "Klarstellung zum Status des Europäischen Gerichtshofs für Menschenrechte und seiner Beziehungen zum Europarat", *Europäische Grundrecht-Zeitschrift,* 30 No. 17-20, 561–563.

Boden, D. (2004). "Whither the OSCE?", *OSCE Yearbook 2003*, Institute for Peace Research and Security Policy at the University of Hamburg/IFSH (ed.), 43-49. Baden-Baden: Nomos.

Bölke and Gostomzyk (2005). "Die Auswirkungen der Caroline-Entscheidung des EGMR auf die Bildberichterstattung nach deutschem Recht", *Juristische Ausbildung,*27,5, 336 – 338.

Booth, K. (1995). "Human Wrongs and International Relations", *International Affairs*, 71, 1, 103-126.

Booth, K. (1999). "Three Tyrannies", in Dunne and Wheeler (eds) *Human Rights in Global Politics,* Cambridge: Cambridge University Press, 31-70.

Borko, Y. (2001). "The European Union's Common Strategy on Russia: a Russian View", in *The EU Common Strategy on Russia. Learning the Grammar of the CFSP,* H. Haukkala, et al. (ed.), 117-143. Helsinki: Finnish Institute for International Affairs.

Börzel, T. A., et al. (2004). One Size Fits All! EU Policies for the Promotion of Human Rights, Democracy and the Rule of Law. Paper prepared for the Workshop on Democracy Promotion, Oct. 4-5, 2004, Center for Development, Democracy, and the Rule of Law, Stanford University. http://iis-db.stanford.edu/pubs/20747/Risse-Borzel-stanford_final.pdf [02.02.2005].

Bouloc, B. (2001). "La durée des procédures: un délai enfin raisonnable?" *Revue de science criminelle et de droit pénal comparé*, 55-64.

Bradlow and Grossman (1995). "Limited Mandates and Interwined Problems: A New Challenge for the World Bank and the IMF", *Human Rights Quarterly*, 17, 411-442.

Brandtner and Rosas (2001). "The EU as an external human rights actor", in *International human rights monitoring mechanisms. Essays in honour of Jakob Th. Möller*, Alfredsson, Gudmundur/Grimheden, Jonas/Ramcharan, Bertrand G./Zayas, Alfred de (eds.), 667-678. The Hague at al.: Nijhoff.

Breucking, D. (2000)."Schutz der Menschenrechte und soziale Grundrechte", in Uwe Holz (ed.) 50 Jahre Europarat, Baden Baden: Nomos, 139-149.

Breuer, M. (2004). "Offene Fragen im Verhältnis von EGMR und EuGH" *Europäische Grundrechte-Zeitschrift*, 31, No. 8-10, 429-434.
Breuer, M. (2004a). Zur Anordnung konkreter Abhilfemaßnahmen durch den EGMR", *Europäische Grundrechte-Zeitschrift*, 31 No. 9-12, 257–263.
Breuer, M. (2004b). "Urteilsfolgen bei strukturellen Problemen – Das erste „Piloturteil" des EGMR", *Europäische Grundrechte-Zeitschrift*, 31, No. 16-18, 445-451.
Brimmer, E. (2002). *The United States, the European Union, and international human rights issues*. Washington, D.C.: Center for Transatlantic Relations.
Brosig, M. (2005a). "Integration der Desintegrierten? Zu den Perspektiven einer europäischen Minderheitenpolitik" *Arbeitspapiere und Materialien – Forschungsstelle Osteuropa*, Bremen, Nr. 70 Integration und Ausgrenzung im Osten Europas, Beiträge für die 13. Tagung junger Osteuropa Experten, 111-114.
Brosig, M.(2005b)."Am Rande Europas, Mehrheiten und Minderheiten in Estland" *Pogrom* (231_3/2005) 36-39.
Brosig, M. (2005c)."Normdiffusion als Prozess der Europäisierung: Die Slowakei und europäische Minderheitenstandards" in Salimi-Asl, Wrasse, Schuch (eds) *Die Transformation nationaler Politik Europäisierungsprozesse in Mitteleuropa*, DGAP-Schriften zur internationalen Politik, 225-245.
Browning, C. (2005). "The Region-building Approach Revisited: The Continued Othering of Russia in Discourses of Region-Building in the European North", *Geopolitics* 8,1, 45-71.
Brummer, K. (2004)."Umstrittene Menschenrechte: der Europarat, Russland, Tschetschenien", *Gegenwartskunde, Zeitschrift für Gesellschaft, Wirtschaft, Recht und Bildung, 437-447*
Buerstedde, D. (2005). "Violence in Kosovo Calls for a Fresh Look at the Mission's Priorities", in *OSCE Yearbook 2004*, Institute for Peace Research and Security Policy at the University of Hamburg/IFSH (ed.), pp. tba. Baden-Baden: Nomos (forthcoming).
Bulgarian Helsinki Committee. "Human Rights in Bulgaria in 2004: Annual Report by the Bulgarian Helsinki Committee." March 2005. http://www.bghelsinki.org.
Bulgarian Helsinki Committee. "Human Rights in Bulgaria in 2004: Annual Report by the Bulgarian Helsinki Committee." March 2005. http://www.bghelsinki.org/index.php?module=pages&lg=en&page=reports.
Bundesministerium der Justiz (2005). "Bericht über die Rechtsprechung des EGNR in Verfahren gegen Deutschland im Jahr 2004", *Juristische Ausbildung*, 27,7, 449 - 452.
Callewaert, J. (2003)."Die EMRK und die EU-Grundrechtecharta, Bestandsaufnahme einer Harmonisierung auf halben Weg" *Europäische Grundrechte Zeitschrift*, 30, No. 7-10, 198-206.
Capotorti, F. (1979). "Study on the Rights of Persons Belonging to Ethnic, Religious, and Linguistic Minorities", *UN Doc. E/CN.4/Sub.2/283/Rev. 1*, United Nations, New York.
Chandler, D. (2003). "The Bureaucratic Gaze of International Human Rights Law," paper presented at the UCL Conference *The Legalization of Human Rights* April 25/26th London.
Chandler, D. (2000a). *Bosnia: Faking Democracy After Dayton* (2nd edn), London: Pluto Press.

Chandler, D. (2000b). "Bosnia: Profile of a Nato Protectorate", in T. Ali (ed.) *Masters of the Universe?: Nato's Balkan Adventure,* London: Verso, 271-84.

Charney, J. I. (1999). "Anticipatory Humanitarian Action in Kosovo", *American Journal of International Law*, 93, 834-841.

Charvet, J. (1998). "The Possibility of a Cosmopolitan Ethical Order Based on the Idea of Universal Human Rights", *Millennium*, 27, 3, 523-41.

Chandler, D. (1998). "Democratization in Bosnia: The Limits of Civil Society Building Strategies", *Democratization*, 5, 4, 78-102.

Charities Aid Foundation (2000). Evaluation of the Joint Programmes between the European Union Commission and the Council of Europe for strengthening federal structures and local government, introducing human rights protection mechanisms, and supporting reforms of the law and legal systems in the Russian Federation and Ukraine. Final Report. Brussels: European Commission.

Charter of Paris for a New Europe, Paris, 21 November 1990, www.osce.org/documents/mcs/1990/11/4045_en.pdf (23 Aug. 2005).

Chesterman, S. (1998). "Human Rights as Subjectivity: The Age of Rights and the Politics of Culture", *Millennium*, 27, 1, 97-118.

Chinkin, C. M. (1999). "Kosovo: A "Good" or "Bad" War?", *American Journal of International Law*, 93, 841-7.

Chomsky, N. (1999). *The New Military Humanism: Lessons From Kosovo*, London: Pluto Press.

Chrysogonnos, K. (2001) "Zur Inkorporation der Europäischen Menschenrechts-konvention in den nationalen Rechtsordnungen der Mitgliedstaaten", *Europarecht*,36, 1, 49-61.

Clapham, A. (1999). "Where is the EU's human rights common foreign policy, and how is it manifested in multilateral fora?", in *The EU and human rights*, Alston, P. (ed.), 627-683. Oxford et al.: Oxford University Press.

Claude, P. R. (2005). "The Right to Education and Human Rights Education", *SUR,* 2, 2, pp. 37-59. São Paulo: Prol Editora Gráfica Ltda.

Commission on Security and Cooperation in Europe. (1997). *Human Rights and Democratization in Slovakia*. Washington, DC: Commission on Security and Cooperation in Europe.

Communities of the European Union and its Member States (1997). Agreement on Partnership and Cooperation establishing a partnership between the European Communities and their Member States, of the one part, and the Russian Federation, of the other part, JOCE L 327, Nov. 27, 1997.

Concluding Document of Budapest, Towards a Genuine Partnership in a New Era (Budapest Decisions), 6 December 1994, www.osce.org/documents/mcs/1994/12/4048_en.pdf (23 Aug. 2005).

Concluding Document of Helsinki - The Fourth Follow-up Meeting, The Challenges of Change (Helsinki Decisions), Vienna, 10 July 1992, www.osce.org/documents/mcs/1992/07/4046_en.pdf (23 Aug. 2005).

Concluding Document of Vienna - The Third Follow-up Meeting, Vienna, 19 January 1989, www.osce.org/documents/mcs/1989/01/16059_en.pdf (23 Aug. 2005).

Cornell, S. E. (1999). "International Reactions to Massive Human Rights Violations: The Case of Chechnya", *Europe-Asia Studies* 51, 1, 85-100.

Cortell and Davis Jr. (1996). "How do international institutions matter? The domestic impact of international rules and norms", *International Studies Quarterly*, 40, 451-478.

Council of Europe (CoE, 2004). *Explanatory Report to the CETS 194.* http:// conven tions.coe.int/Treaty/EN/Reports/Html/194.htm

Council of Europe (2003). Compass – A Manual on Human Rights Education with *Young People*. Strasbourg Cedex, (first published 2002): Council of Europe Publishing.

Council of Europe/Conseil de l'Europe (2001). *Accession of the European Union to the European Convention on Human Rights. Reflection paper prepared by the Secretariat*, Strasbourg (DG-II(2001)02).

Council of Europe. (1999a). *Report Submitted by the Czech Republic Pursuant to Article 25, Paragraph 1 of the Framework Convention for the Protection of National Minorities*. Strasbourg: Council of Europe.

Council of Europe. (1999b). *Report Submitted by the Slovak Republic Pursuant to Article 25, Paragraph 1 of the Framework Convention for the Protection of National Minorities*. Strasbourg: Council of Europe.

Council of Europe. (1995). *Framework Convention for the Protection of National Minorities.* Strasbourg: Council of Europe.

Council of Europe Parliamentary Assembly (1995). Report on procedure for an opinion on Russia's request for membership of the Council of Europe. Doc. 7372, Strasbourg, 11.11.1995.

Council of Europe (1992). Charter for Regional and Minority Languages, ETS N. 148, 5 November, 1992, entry into force 1 March, 1998.

Council of Europe Parliamentary Assembly (2000): Exchange of correspondence between the Secretary General of the Council of Europe and the Minister for Foreign Affairs of the Russian Federation under Article 52 of the European Convention of Human Rights, Doc. No. 8704, Strasbourg, 05.04.2000.

Council of the European Union, "Presidency Conclusions," 2004, http://ue.eu.int/ueDocs/cms_Data/docs/pressData/en/ec/83201.pdf (5 September 2005).

Council of the European Union (1999a). Common Strategy of the European Union on Russia, 4 June 1999. (1999/414/CFSP), in: Official Journal of the European Communities L 157/1, 24.06.1999.

Council of the European Union (1999b). Council Regulation (EC, EURATOM) No 99/2000 of 29 December 1999 concerning the provision of assistance to the partner States in Eastern Europe and Central Asia, in: Official Journal of the European Communities, L 12/1, 18.1.2000.

Council of the European Union (1999c). Presidency Conclusions. Helsinki European Council, 10 and 11 December 1999. Bulletin of the EU 12/999. http://europa.eu.int/council/off/conclu/dec99/dec99_en.htm [15.03.2005].

Crawford, G. (1996). "Promoting Democracy, Human Rights and Good Governance Through Development Aid: A Comparative Study of the Policies of Four Northern Donors", *Working Papers on Democratization*, No.1, Centre for Democratization Studies, Leeds University.

Cremer, H.-J. (2005). "Zur Bindungswirkung von EGMR-Urteilen", *Europäische Grund rechte Zeitschrift*, 32, No. 19-21, 683 – 700.

CRC - Committee of the Rights of the Child (2005). Concluding Observation: Finland, CRC/C/15/Add. 272, 20 October, 2005, para. 44 and 45.

Danilov, D. (2005). "Russia and European security", in *What Russia sees. Chaillot Paper Nr. 74,* D. Lynch (ed.), 79-98. Paris: Institute for Security Studies.

Danish Institute for Human Rights (2003a). Discrimination and Prevention on Torture. Collected Papers from the First Roundtable under the EU –Iran Human Rights Dialogue, Tehran, 16-17 December 2002, Copenhagen.

Danish Institute for Human Rights (2003b). *Rule of Law and Fair Trial. Collected Papers from the Second Roundtable under the EU –Iran Human Rights Dialogue*, Brussels, 14-15 March 2003, Copenhagen.

Danish Institute for Human Rights (2004a). *The Right to Freedom of Expression and the Right to Development. Collected Papers from the First Roundtable under the EU – Iran Human Rights Dialogue*, Brussels, 8-9 October 2003, Copenhagen.

Danish Institute for Human Rights (2004b). *Administration of Justice and Promotion International Cooperation and Solidarity in the Field of Human Rights. Collected Papers from the First Roundtable under the EU –Iran Human Rights Dialogue*, Tehran, 14-15 June 2004, Copenhagen.

Davidová, E. (1995). *Romano Drom: Cesty Romů, 1945-1990*. Olomouc: Univerzita Palackého.

Deacon and Stubbs (1998). "International Actors and Social Policy Development in Bosnia-Herzegovina: Globalism and the "New Feudalism"", *Journal of European Social Policy*, 8, 2, 99-115.

Dekker, I. (2003). "Declaration on the Fight Against Terrorism and the Protection of Human Rights - A Resolvable Conflict", in *Helsinki Monitor*, 2003 No. 4, 321-327.

De Schutter, O. (2004). "The Implementation of the EU Charter of Fundamental Rights through the Open Method of Coordination", *Jean Monnet Working Paper* 07/04, NYU School of Law.

DeSpiegeleire, S. (2001). "The Implementation of the EU's Common Strategy on Russia", in *The EU Common Strategy on Russia. Learning the Grammar of the CFSP,* H. Haukkala, et al. (ed.), 81-116. Helsinki u.a.: Finnish Institute of International Affairs.

Deutsch, K. W. (1957). *Political Community and the North Atlantic Area. International Organizations in the Light of Historical Experience*. Princeton: Princeton Univ. Press.

Deutscher Bundestag (Referat Öffentlichkeitsarbeit) (2001). "Die Charta der Grundrechte der Europäischen Union - Berichte und Dokumentationen", *Zur Sache* 1/2001, Berlin.

Development Researchers' Network (2000). An evaluation of the TACIS Country Programme in Russia. Final synthesis report, January 2000. Brussels: European Commission.

de Waal, A. (1997). *Famine Crimes: Politics and the Disaster Relief Industry in Africa*, Oxford: James Curry/ Indiana University Press.

Dietrich, J. (2001). "Turkey and Europe: Ongoing Hypocrisy?", *Copenhagen Peace Research Institute Working Papers,* www.ciaonet.org/frame/wpsfrm.html (10 October 2003).

Diez, T. (2005). "Constructing the Self and Changing Others: Reconsidering 'Normative Power Europe'", *Millenium*, 33, 613-636.

Dicey, A. V. (1959). *Introduction to the Study of the Law of the Constitution*, London: Macmillan.
Document of the Copenhagen Meeting of the Conference on the Human Dimension of the CSCE, Copenhagen, 29 June 1990, www.osce.org/documents/odihr/1990/06/13992_en.pdf (23 Aug. 2005).
Document of the Moscow Meeting of the Conference on the Human Dimension of the CSCE, Moscow, 3 October 1991, www.osce.org/documents/odihr/1991/10/13995_en.pdf (23 Aug. 2005).
Donnelly, J. (1999). "Ethics and International Human Rights", *Human Rights Working Papers*, No. 1, University of Denver Graduate School of International Studies, December.
Donnelly, J. (1986). "International human rights: a regime analysis", *International Organization*, 40, 599-642.
Dostál, O. (1998). "Národnostné menšiny", in *Slovensko 1997: Súhrnná správa o stave spoločnosti a trendoch na rok 1998*, Bútora M. and Ivantyšyn, M. (eds), 155-170. Bratislava: Inštitút pre verejné otázky.
Dower, N. (1997). "Human Rights and International Relations", *The International Journal of Human Rights*, 1, 1, 86-111.
Doyal and Gough (1991). *A Theory of Human Need*, London: Macmillan.
Dunay, P. (2005). "Improve What You Can – Ignore What You Can't: Reform and the Prospects of the OSCE", in *OSCE Yearbook 2004*, Institute for Peace Research and Security Policy at the University of Hamburg/IFSH (ed.), pp. tba. Baden-Baden: Nomos (forthcoming).
Duve, F. (2005). "Six Years as OSCE Representative on Freedom of the Media – An Assessment", in *OSCE Yearbook 2004*, Institute for Peace Research and Security Policy at the University of Hamburg/IFSH (ed.), pp. tba. Baden-Baden: Nomos (forthcoming).
Ehlers, D. (2003). "Die Europäische Menschenrechtskonvention – Allgemeine Lehren", in *Europäische Grundrechte und Grundfreiheiten*, Ehlers, D. (ed.), 21 – 46, Berlin: De Gruyter.
Eide, A. (1998). "Multicultural Education and Minority Rights", in: Spiliopoulou Akermark, S. (ed) *Human Eights Education, Achievements and Challenges*, Finnish National Commission for UNESCO, Turku, 53-66.
Eiff, H. (2000). "The OSCE Mission in Kosovo", in *OSCE Yearbook 1999*, Institute for Peace Research and Security Policy at the University of Hamburg/IFSH (ed.), 283-300. Baden-Baden: Nomos.
Elvers, J. (2000). "Der Europarat und die Russiche Föderation", in *50 Jahre Europarat*, Holtz (ed.), 11 – 36. Baden-Baden, Nomos Verlagsgesellschaft.
Ekimdjiev, M. (2004). "Who Seeks the Justice of the European Court in Strasbourg and Why". *Trud Daily*, August 2004.
Engel, N. P. (2003). "Status, Ausstattung und Personalhoheit des Inter-Amerikanischen und des Europäischen Gerichtshofs für Menschenrechte", *Europäische GrundrechteZeitschrift*, 30, No. 4-6, 122-133.
Ergil, D. (2000). "Identity Crises and Political Instability in Turkey," *Journal of International Affairs,* 54 (1), 43-63.
ESEM (2000). *Europa South-East Monitor*, No.12, Centre for European Policy Studies, Brussels, June.

European Commission (2005). Proposal for a Council Regulation Establishing a European Union Agency for Fundamental Rights, Com (2005) 280 final. European Commission (2004). Regular Report on Bulgaria's Progress towards Accession.

European Commission (2001a). Country Strategy Paper 2002-2006 and National Indicative Programme 2002-2003 Russian Federation, Brussels, 27.12.2001.

European Commission (2001b). European Initiative for Democracy and Human Rights Programming Document 2002-2004. Commission Staff Working Document, REV 1 - Final, Brussels, 20.12.2001.

European Commission (2003). Communication from the Commission to the Council and the European Parliament: *Wider Europe — Neighbourhood: A New Framework for Relations with our Eastern and Southern Neighbours.* COM(2003) 104 final, Brussels, 11.03.2003. Brussels:

European Commission (2004a). *Communication from the Commission to the Council and the European Parliament on relations with Russia.* COM(2004) 106, Brussels, 09.02.2004.

European Commission (2004b). *Towards a new Tacis concept and regulation: outline of issues for web-based consultation.* http://europa.eu.int/comm/external_relations/consultations/cswp_tacis.htm#I.%20Key%20developments%20since%201999 [30.09.2004].

European Commission against Racism and Intolerance (1997). *Report on the Czech Republic.* Strasbourg: Council of Europe.

European Commission against Racism and Intolerance (1998). *Report on Slovakia.* Strasbourg: Council of Europe.

European Commission against Racism and Intolerance (2000a). *Second Report on the Czech Republic.* Strasbourg: Council of Europe.

European Commission against Racism and Intolerance (2000b). *Second Report on Slovakia.* Strasbourg: Council of Europe.

European Commission against Racism and Intolerance (2004a). *Third Report on the Czech Republic.* Strasbourg: Council of Europe.

European Commission against Racism and Intolerance (2004b). *Third Report on Slovakia.* Strasbourg: Council of Europe.

European Council (2001). *Declaration on the Future of the EU*, Annex to the Conclusions of the presidency, Laeken, 14/15.12.2001.

European Council (2000). *Declaration on the Future of the Union*, Annex IV to the Nice Treaty, Nice, 10.12.2000.

European Council (1999). Decision on the drawing up of a Charter of Fundamental Rights of the European Union, Conclusions of the Presidency, Cologne, 04.06.1999.

European Council (1985). A People's Europe: Report from the ad hoc Committee, [chairman: Pietro Adonnino], to the European Council (part I 29/30.03.1985, Brussels; part II 28/29.06.1985, Milan) in *EC Bulletin* Supplement 7/85 (1985), 7-32.

European Court of Human Rights/Cour Européenne des Droits de l'Homme (2006). *Survey of Activities 2005*, Strasbourg: Information document issued by the Registrar of the European Court of Human Rights.

European Parliament (2000). Committee on Foreign Affairs, Human Rights, Common Security and Defence: Policy: *Report on the Implementation of the Common Strategy of the European Union on Russia.* Rapporteur: Arie M. Oostlander. A5-0363/2000 final, Strasbourg, 29.11.2000.

European Parliament, Commission and Council (1977). "Joint Declaration on Human Rights", *OJC* 103 of 27.04.1977.

European Roma Rights Center (1999). *A Special Remedy: Roma and Schools for the Mentally Handicapped in the Czech Republic.* Budapest: European Roma Rights Center. http://www.errc.org/cikk.php?cikk=1698 (31 May 2005).

European Union (2004). Treaty establishing a Constitution for Europe, Art. I-2, CIG 87/2/04 Rev. 2, 29 October, 2004.

European Union (2001a). *Communication from the commission to the Council and the European Parliament. The European Union's role in promoting human rights and democratisation in third countries*, Brussels, COM (2001) 252 final.

European Union (2001b). *Communication on Promoting Core Labour Standards and improving Social Governance in the Context of Globalisation*, COM (2001) 416 final http://europa.eu.int/comm/external_relations/human_rights/doc/com01_252_en.pdf

European Union (2002a-2004a). *Annual Report on Human Rights 2002-2004.* Brussels. Internet: http://ue.eu.int/uedocs/cmsUpload/DEHR2004.pdf

European Union (2003b). *Communication from the Commission to the Council and the European Parliament. Reinvigorating EU actions on Human Rights and democratisation with Mediterranean partners. Strategic guidelines*, Brussels, COM (2003) 294 final.
http://europa.eu.int/comm/external_relations/human_rights/doc/com03_294.pdf.

European Union (2003c). *Guidelines on Protection of Civilians in EU-Led crisis management operations.* http://register.consilium.eu.int/pdf/en/05/st08/st08373-re03.en05.pdf.

European Union (2004b). *Implementation of the Commission Communication*, Brussels (COM (2001) 252 final). Commission staff working document.

European Union (2004c). *EU Guidelines on Children and Armed Conflict*, http://ue.eu.int/uedocs/cmsUpload/GuidelinesChildren.pdf.

European Union (2005). *Generic Standards of Behaviour for ESDP Operations* http://register.consilium.eu.int/pdf/en/05/st08/st08373-re03.en05.pdf.

European Union (2000). *EU Adopts TACIS 2000 Core Action Programme for Russia and TACIS 2000 Special Action for the Baltic Region.* Press Release 28 June 2000. www.eur.ru/en/news_493.htm [20.04.2003].

European Union (2003). *Eleventh EU-Russia Summit*, St. Petersburg 31.05.2003. IP/03/768, Brussels, 28.05.2003.
http://europa.eu.int/comm/external_relations/russia/sum05_03/ip03_768.htm [05.03.2005].

European Union (2005). *EU-Russia Summit Moscow*, 10 May 2005 - Conclusions. http://europa.eu.int/comm/external_relations/russia/summit_05_05/index.htm [15.05.2005].

European Union/Russian Federation (2003). *Joint Statement EU-Russia Summit St. Petersburg*, 31 May 2003.
http://europa.eu.int/comm/external_relations/russia/sum05_03/js.htm [07.05.2005].

Evers, Kahl, Zellner (eds) (2005). *The Culture of Dialogue. The OSCE Acquis 30 Years after Helsinki*. Hamburg/Vienna: Manz Crossmedia, www.core-hamburg.de/documents/30Years_OSCE_Booklet.pdf (23 Aug. 2005).

Everts, D. W. (2002). "The OSCE Mission in Kosovo", in *OSCE Yearbook 2001*, Institute for Peace Research and Security Policy at the University of Hamburg/IFSH (ed.), 137-148. Baden-Baden: Nomos.

Ewing, K.D. (2002). "The EU Charter of Fundamental Rights: Waste of Time or Wasted *Opportunity?* ", Institute of Employment, London.

Falk, R. A. (1999). "Kosovo, World Order, and the Future of International Law", *American* Journal of International Law, 93, 847-857.

Federacii (2000). Strategija razvitija otnos*enij Rossijskoj Federacii s Evropejskim Sojusom na srednesroc'nuju perspektivu (2000-2010 gody). Tekst predstavlennyj Predsedatelem Pravitel'stva Rossii V.V. Putinym na sammite RF-ES v Chel'sinki 22.10.99, in: Sovremennaja Evropa 1(2000): online version, http://www.ieras.ru/journal/journal1.2000/9.htm [20.05.2005].

Fierro, Elena (2003). *The EU's approach to human rights conditionality in practice*. The Hague et al.: M. Nijhoff.

Finnemore and Sikkink (1998). "International Norm Dynamics and Political Change", *International Organization*, 52 887-918.

Finnish National Board of Education (2004a). *National Core Curriculum for Basic Education intended for pupils subject to compulsory education*, unofficial translation; Helsinki.

Finnish National Board of Education (2004b). *National Core Curriculum for General Upper Secondary Education Intended for Young People*, unofficial translation; Helsinki.

Felice, W. F. (1998). "Militarism and Human Rights", *International Affairs*, 74, 1, 25-40.

Forsythe, D. P. (2000). *Human Rights in International Relations*, Cambridge: Cambridge University Press.

Franck, T. M. (1999). "Lessons Of Kosovo", *American Journal of International Law*, 93, 857-60.

Freeman, M. (1995). "Are There Collective Human Rights?", *Political Studies*, 43, Special issue, 25-43.

Friedman, V.A. (1999). "The Romani Language in the Republic of Macedonia: Status, Usage, and Sociolinguistic Perspectives", *Acta Linguistica Hungarica* 46, No. 3-4, 317-339.

Fromont, M. (2005). "Die Bedeutung der Europäischen Menschenrechtskonvention in der französischen Rechtsordnung", *Die Öffentliche Verwaltung*, 58, 1, 1-10.

Frowein, J. A. (2002). "Der europäische Grundrechtsschutz und die deutsche Rechtsprechung", *Neue Zeitschrift für Verwaltungsrecht* , 21, 1, 29-33.

Fritzsche, K. P. (2004). *Menschenrechte* Paderborn: UTB.

Gál, K. (2000). "The Council of Europe Framework Convention for the Protection of National Minorities and its Impact on Central and Eastern Europe", *Journal on Ethnopolitics and Minority Issues in Europe*, Winter 2000.

Garcelon, M. (1997). "The Shadow of the Leviathan: Public and Private in Communist and Post-Communist Society", in J. Weintraub and K. Kumar (eds) *Public and Private in Thought and Practice: Perspectives on a Grand Dichotomy*, Chicago: University of Chicago Press, 303-332.

Garcia, Ricardo Alonso (2002). "The General Provisions of the Charter of Fundamental Rights of the European Union", *Jean Monnet Program Working Paper* 4/02, NYU School of Law.

Geistlinger and Kirch (1995). *Estonia – A new framework for the Estonians majority and the Russian minority*, Vienna, Wilhem Braumüller.

General Affairs Council (1999). Northern Caucasus/Chechnya - Conclusion. 2217th Council Meeting - General Affairs - Brussels, 15 November 1999 (part) - PRES/99/344.

Gerwith, A. (1981). "The Basis and Content of Human Rights", in Pennock and Chapman (eds) *Human Rights*, New York: New York University Press, 119-47.

Gilbert, G. (1996). "The Council of Europe and Minority Rights", *Human Rights Quarterly*, 18, 175.

Gomien, D. (2000). *Short guide to the European Convention on Human Rights*, Stras bourg, Council of Europe Publishing.

Gowan, D. (2001). *How the EU can help Russia*. London: Centre for European Reform.

Gower, J. (2000). "Russia and the European Union", in *Russia and Europe: Conflict or Cooperation*, M. Webber (ed.), 66-98. New York: St. Martin's Press. *Menschenrechte vom Atlantik bis zum Ural*, F.-J. Hutterer, et al. (ed.), Baden-Baden: Nomos.

Grabenwarter, C. (2004). "Auf dem Weg in die Grundrechtsgemeinschaft? " *Europäische Grundrechte-Zeitschrift*, 31, 19, 563–583.

Gras, J. (2000). *The European Union and Human Rights Monitoring*, The Erik Castrén Institute of International Law and Human Rights, Research Reports 5/1999, Helsinki University Press, 2000.

Gries, T. and Allewedt (eds.) (2004). *Human Rights within the European Union* Berliner Wissenschafts-Verlag, Berlin.

Gutman and Rieff (1999). "Preface", in Gutman and Rieff (eds) *Crimes of War: What the Public Should Know*, New York: W. W. Norton, 8-12.

Guy, W. (2001). "The Czech Lands and Slovakia: Another False Dawn?" in *Between Past and Future: The Roma of Central and Eastern Europe*, Guy, W. (ed.), 285-323. Hatfield: University of Hertfordshire Press.

Haaland Matlary, J. (ed.) (2002). *Intervention for Human Rights in Europe*. New York: Palgrave.

Human Rights Watch (2004). "Failure to Protect. Anti-Minority Violence in Kosovo, March 2004", *Human Rights Watch Publications*, July 2004, 16, 6 (D), New York: HRW, http://hrw.org/reports/2004/kosovo0704/kosovo0704.pdf (23 Aug. 2005).

Hale, W. (2003). "Human Rights, The European Union and The Turkish Accession Process," in Ali Carkoglu and Barry Rubin (eds), *Turkey and the European Union: Domestic Politics, Economic Integration and International Dynamics*, Frank Cass& Co. Limited, London, 107-126.

Halliday, F. (1994). *Rethinking International Relations*, London: Macmillan.

Haltern, U. (2004). "Integration through Law", in *European Integration Theory*, Wiener and Diez (eds), Oxford, Oxford University Press, 177–196.

Harmsen, R. (2001). "The European Convention on Human Rights after Enlargement", *The International Journal of Human Rights*, 5, 18-43.

Haukkala, H. (2000). *"The Making of the European Union's Common Strategy on Russia", UPI Working Papers 28/2000*. Helsinki: Finnish Institute of International Affairs.

Haukkala, H. (2005). *The Relevance of Norms and Values in the EU's Russia Policy. UPI Working Papers 52/2005*. Helsinki: Finnish Institute of International Affairs.

Hayden, R. M. (2000). *UN War Crimes' Tribunal Delivers a Travesty of Justice*, Woodrow Wilson International Centre for Scholars.

HCNM (2005a). "Factsheet on the High Commissioner on National Minorities 2005", www.osce.org/publications/hcnm/2005/05/14784_378_en.pdf (23 Aug. 2005).

HCNM (2005b). "High Commissioner on National Minorities – Feature: Ten Years of Reducing Ethnic Tensions", www.osce.org/hcnm/item_2_129.html (23 Aug. 2005).

Heartfield, J. (1996). "Rights and the Legal Subject", Freedom and Law discussion paper.

Heinz, W. S. (2002). *Die Menschenrechtsorientierung in der Entwicklungs-zusammenarbeit der Europäischen Union. Anspruch und Wirklichkeit*, in: epd-Dokumentation, 30.9.2002, 41, 4-17; http://www.epd.de/dokumentation/dokumentation_index_10102.htm.

Heinz, W. S. (2003). *The European Union Human Rights Policy*, Bonn: Friedrich Ebert Foundation, Internet: http://library.fes.de/fulltext/id/01713.htm.

Heinz, W. S. (2004). "Die Menschenrechtsorientierung in der Entwicklungszusammen-arbeit der Europäischen Union. Anspruch und Wirklichkeit", in *Menschenrechte und Entwicklungszusammenarbeit. Anspruch und Wirklichkeit*, Selchow and Hutter (eds.) Wiesbaden: Verlag für Sozialwissenschaften, 69-86.

Heintze, H.-J. (2002). "Human Rights and Political Interest - Is there a Double Standard?", in *OSCE Yearbook 2001*, Institute for Peace Research and Security Policy at the University of Hamburg/IFSH (ed.), 219-236. Baden-Baden: Nomos.

Heintze, H.-J. (2001). "The Lund Recommendations on the Effective Participation of National Minorities in Public Life", in *OSCE Yearbook 2000*, Institute for Peace Research and Security Policy at the University of Hamburg/IFSH (ed.), 257-270. Baden-Baden: Nomos.

Held, D. (1995). *Democracy and the Global Order: From the Modern State to Cosmopolitan Governance*, Cambridge: Polity Press.

Helsinki Final Act of the Conference on Security and Co-operation in Europe, Helsinki, 1 August 1975, www.osce.org/documents/mcs/1975/08/4044_en.pdf (23 Aug. 2005).

Henkin, L. (1990). *The Age of Rights*, New York: Columbia University Press.

Herrberg, A. (1998). "The European Union and Russia: Toward a New Ostpolitik?" in *The European Union in the World Community*, C. Rhodes (ed.), 83-104. London u.a.: Lynne Rienner.

Heuer and Schirmer (1998). "Human Rights Imperialism", *Monthly Review*, March, 5-16.

Holtz, U. (2000)."50 Jahre Europarat - Eine Einführung", in *50 Jahre Europarat*, U. Holtz (ed.), 11-36. Baden-Baden: Nomos.

Hughes and Sasse (2003). "Monitoring the Monitors: EU Enlargement Conditionality and Minority Protection in the CEECs", *Journal on Ethnopolitics and Minority Issues in Europe*, Issue 1/2003, 10-12.

Human Rights Watch (1996). *Roma in the Czech Republic: Foreigners in their Own Land*. New York: Human Rights Watch.

Human Security Network (2003). Understanding Human Rights – Manual on Human Rights Education, Graz: ETC.

Hutterer, F.-J., et al. (1998). "Bürgergesellschaft und Nationalismus im "gemeinsamen Haus Europa". Eine Einleitung", in *Das gemeinsame Haus Europa.*

Ignatieff, M. (1998). The Warrior's Honor: Ethnic War and the Modern Conscience, London: Chatto & Windus.

Ignatieff, M. (1999). "Human Rights: The Midlife Crisis", *New York Review of Books*, 20 May, 58-62.

Incerti, Kurpas, and Schönlau (2005). "What Prospects for the Ratification of the Constitutional Treaty?", *EPIN-Working Paper* No. 12, Brussels.

ISA Consult (1997). Evaluation of the PHARE and TACIS Democracy Programme 1992 - 1997. Final Report. Brussels: European Commission.

Jaeger, R. (2005) "Menschenrechtsschutz im Herzen Europas. Zur Kooperation des Bundesverfassungsgerichts mit dem Europäischen Gerichtshof für Menschenrechte und dem Gerichtshof der Europäischen Gemeinschaften", *Europäische Grundrechte-Zeitschrift*, 32, No. 8-10, 193-204.

Järve, P. (2000). "Ethnic Democracy and Estonia: Applications of Smooha's Model", *ECMI Working Paper* # 7.

Jobard, F. (2003). "Counting violence committed by the police: Raw facts and narratives", *Policing and Society*,13, 4, 423-428.

Jobard, F. (2002) *Bavures policières? La force publique et ses usages*, Paris: La Découverte.

Johnston, A. I. (2001). "Treating International Institutions as Social Environments", *International Studies Quarterly*, 45, 487-515.

Johns, Michael (2003). "Do As I Say, Not As I Do: The European Union and Minority Rights", paper prepared for the *International Studies Association*, 2003 Portland.

Johnstone, D. (1998) "Seeing Yugoslavia Through a Dark Glass: Politics, Media and the Ideology of Globalization", *Direct Action Quarterly*, Fall, No.65. Available from: http://www.caq.com/.

Joubert and Bevers (1996). *Schengen investigated. A Comparative Interpretation of the Schengen Provisions on International Police Cooperation in the Light of the European Convention on Human Rights*, Deventer: Kluwer Law International.

Jurová, A. (1993). *Vývoj rómskej problematiky na Slovensku po roku 1945*. Bratislava: Goldpress Publishers.

Kadelbach, S. (2005). "Der Status der Europäischen Menschenrechtskonvention im deutschen Recht", *Juristische Ausbildung*, 27,7, 480–486.

Kahl, M. (2004)."Welche Grenzen für die EU?", in *Neues Europa - alte EU? Fragen an den europäischen Integrationsprozess*, J. Varwick, et al. (ed.), 133-148. Opladen: Leske + Budrich.

Kaldor, M. (1999). "Transnational Civil Society", in T. Dunne and N. J. Wheeler (eds) *Human Rights in Global Politics*, Cambridge: Cambridge University Press, 195-213.

Karaosmanoglu, A. (2000). "The Evolution of the National Security Culture and the Military in Turkey", *Journal of International Affairs*, 54, 1, 199-217.

Kartusch, A. (2003). "Trafficking in Human Beings - A Human Rights Challenge for the OSCE", in *OSCE Yearbook 2002*, Institute for Peace Research and Security Policy at the University of Hamburg/IFSH (ed.), 259-274. Baden-Baden: Nomos.

Keenan, T. (1997). *Fables of Responsibility: Aberrations and Predicaments in Ethics and Politics*, Stanford, California: Stanford University Press.

Keller and Bertschi (2005). "Erfolgspotenzial des 14. Protokolls zur Europäischen Men schenrechtskonvention", *Europäische Grundrechte-Zeitschrift,* 32, No. 8-10, 204-229.

Kelly, M. (2004). *ECRI, Ten years of combating racism.* Strasbourg / Council of Europe.

Kemp, W. (2004). "Breaking the Crime-Conflict Nexus: A Challenge for the OSCE", in *OSCE Yearbook 2003*, Institute for Peace Research and Security Policy at the University of Hamburg/IFSH (ed.), 301-318. Baden-Baden: Nomos.

Khazinyan, Hovannisyan, and Harutyunyan, (eds) (2001). Human Rights, Textbook for 8th grade, Yerevan. (in Armenian).

Kieschke, O. (2003). *Die Praxis des Europäischen Gerichtshofs für Menschenrechte und ihre Auswirkungen auf das deutsche Strafverfahrensrecht*, Berlin: Duncker & Humblot.

Kilian, D. (1994). *Die Bindungswirkung der Entscheidungen des Europäischen Gerichtshofs für Menschenrechte auf die nationalen Gerichte der Mitgliedstaaten der Konvention zum Schutze der Menschenrechte und Grundfreiheiten vom 4. November 1950*, Frankfurt/M.: Lang.

King, T. (1999). "Human Rights in European Foreign Policy: Success or Failure for Post-modern diplomacy?" *European Journal of International Law*, 10, 2, 313-337.

Kirch, A. (1997). *The Integration of Non-Estonians into Estonia society: History, Problems and Trends*, Estonian Academy Publishers Tallinn 1997.

Klebes, H. (1995). "The Council of Europe´s Framework Convention for the Protection of National Minorities", *HRLJ*, 16, No. 1-3, 92-98.

Kl'učka, J. (1995). *Porovnávacia štúdia vnútroštátnych právnych poriadkov členských štátov Rady Europy o ochrane národnostných menšín*. Košice: B'nai B'rith.

Klug, F. (1997). "Can Human Rights Fill Britain's Morality Gap?", *Political Quarterly*, 68, 2, 143-152.

Kodakondsus- ja Migratsiooniamet, Estonian Citizenship and Migration Board, Annual Report, Tallinn 2003.

Koenig, M. (2005). *Menschenrechte.* Frankfurt / New York: Campus Verlag.

Krehl and Eidam (2006). "Die überlange Dauer von Strafverfahren", *Neue Zeitschrift für Strafrecht* , 26, 1, 1-10.

Krivý, V. and Mesežnikov, G. (2001). "Politické strany a ich prívrženci", in *Krajina v pohybe: Správa o politických názoroch a hodnotách ľudí na Slovensku*, Gyárfášová, O. et al. (eds.), 53-146. Bratislava: Inštitút pre verejné otázky.

Krüger and Polakiewicz (2001). "Vorschläge für ein kohärentes System des Menschenrechtsschutzes in Europa", *Europäische Grundrechte-Zeitschrift* 28, No. 4-6, 92-105.

Krauss, S. (2000). "The European Parliament in EU External Relations: the Customs Union with Turkey", *European Foreign Affairs Review,* 5, 2, 215-237.

Kühling, J. (2003). "Grundrechte", in: von Bogdandy, A. (ed), *Europäisches Verfassungsrecht*, Berlin/Heidelberg/New York: Springer, 583-630.

Lagerspetz, M. (2001) "Consolidation as Hegemonization: the Case of Estonia", *Journal of Baltic Studies*, 32, 402-420.

Lappenküper, U. (1990). "Rolle und Zusammenwirken der Organe des Europarates", in *Vierzig Jahre Europarat*, Schmuck (ed.), 81 – 98. Bonn, Europa Union Verlag.

Laubner, T. (2004). "Relieving the Court of its success? Protocol No. 14 to the European Conventions on Human Rights", *German Yearbook of International Law*, 47, 691–721.

Laue, C. (2005). "Die Rechtsprechung des Europäischen Gerichtshofs für Menschenrech te zum strafrechtlichen Beschleunigungsgebot", *Juristische Ausbildung*, 27,2, 89-97.

Leben, C. (1999). "Is there a European Approach to Human Rights?" in Alston (ed.) *The EU and Human Rights*, Oxford University Press, 69-99.

Legro, J. (1997). "Which Norms Matter? Revisiting the „Failure" of Internationalism " *International Organization*, 51, 31-63.

Lehnhart, V. (2003). *Pädagogik der Menschenrechte*, Opladen: Leske + Budrich.

Lerch, M. (2004). *Menschenrechte und europäische Außenpolitik: eine konstruktivistische Analyse*, Wiesbaden: Verlag für Sozialwissenschaften.

Lerch and Schwellnus (2003). "Europe's Role as a Promoter of International Human Rights: Modes and dynamics of justifying supranational foreign policy", paper prepared for the *2nd ECPR General Conference*, Marburg Germany 18-21

Lewis, N. (1998). "Human Rights, Law and Democracy in an Unfree World" in T. Evans (ed.) *Human Rights Fifty Years On: A Reappraisal*, Manchester: Manchester University Press, 77-104.

Liebich, A. (1998). "Ethnic Minorities and Long-Term Implications of EU Enlargement", *EUI, Working Paper* RSC Not 98/49.September.

Light, M. (2001). "The European Union's Russian Foreign Policy", in *Russia and Europe in a Changing International Environment*, K. Malfliet, et al. (ed.), 13-24. Leuven: Leuven Univ. Press.

Lippert, B. (1995). Menschenrechtspolitik, in: Weidenfeld and Wessels (eds), *Europa A-Z*, Bonn, 263-266.

Lohrenscheit, C. (2002)."Zum Zusammenhang von Menschenrechten und Bildung", *ZEP*, 25,4, 2-5. Frankfurt, M.: Verlag für Interkulturelle Kommunikation (IKO).

Ludlow, P (2002). *The Laeken Council*, EuroComment, Brussels – European Council Commentary Vol.1, No 1.

Littman, M. (1999). *Kosovo: Law and Diplomacy*, London: Centre for Policy Studies.

Lynch, D. (2005a). "Misperseptions and divergence", in *What Russia sees. Chaillot Paper Nr. 74*, D. Lynch (ed.), 7-22. Paris: Institute for Security Studies.

Lynch, D. (2005b). "Struggling with an indispensable partner" in *What Russia sees. Chaillot Paper Nr. 74*, D. Lynch (ed.), 115-136. Paris: Institute for Security Studies.

Lyotard, J. (1993). "The Other's Rights", in S. Shute and S. Hurley (eds) *On Human Rights*, New York: Basic Books, 135-48.

MacMillan, L. (2000). "Ascribing Responsibilities for Ensuring Refugee Protection", *Talk Back*, The Newsletter of the International Council of Voluntary Agencies (ICVA), 2, 1, 18 February.

Mahler and Toivanen (2004). "Nationale und ethnische Minderheiten im Prozess der Erweiterung der Europäischen Union", *Europa Ethnica* 1/2, 16-20.

Mahler C. and Mihr, A. (eds) (2004). *Menschenrechtsbildung Bilanz und Perspektiven.* Wiesbaden: Sozialwissenschaftlicher Verlag.

Mahler, Claudia (2004). "Menschenrechtsbildungsprogramme im Bereich des Europarates", in Mahler and Mihr (eds) *Menschenrechtsbildung: Bilanz und Perspektive.* Wiesbaden: VS Verlag für Sozialwissenschaften.

Mahlmann, M. (2002). "Die Grundrechtscharta der Europäischen Union", *Zeitschrift für europarechtliche Studien*, 419 – 444.
Malfliet, K. (2001). "Russia and the European Union: Towards a Strategic Partnership?" in *Russia and Europe in a Changing International Environment*, K. Malfliet, et al. (ed.), 161-176. Leuven: Leuven Univ. Press.
Mann, A. B. (1995). "Premeny spoločenského postavenia Rómov na Slovensku po roku 1989", in *Rómovia na Slovensku a v Európe*, 36-44. Bratislava: Informačné a dokumentačné stredisko o Rade Európy.
Manners, I. (2002). "Normative Power Europe". *Journal of Common Market Studies* 40 , 2, 235-258.
Maren, M. (1997). *The Road to Hell: The Ravaging Effects of Foreign Aid and International Charity*, New York: Free Press.
Martín Estébanez, M.A. (1999a). *Minority Protection and the Organisation for Security and Co-operation in Europe.* In: *Minority Rights in the 'New' Europe.* Cumper, P. / Wheatley, S. (eds), 31-52. The Hague / London / Boston: Martinus Nijhoff Publishers.
Martin Estebanez, M. A. (1999b). "The OSCE and Human Rights", in *An Introduction to the International Protection of Human Rights. A Textbook*, Second Edition, Hanski, and Suksi (eds), 329-350. Turku: Abo Akademis Tryckeri.
McCrudden, C. (2002). "The Future of the EU Charter of Fundamental Rights", *UACES On-line Reflection Papers*, No. 1, February 2002, www.uaces.org.
Merlingen, Mudde, and Sedelmeier (2001). "The Right and the Righteous? European Norms, Domestic Politics and the Sanctions against Austria", *Journal of Common Market Studies*, 39, 1, 59-77.
Mendus, S. (1995). "Human Rights in Political Theory", in D. Beetham (ed.) *Politics and Human Rights*, Oxford: Blackwell, 10-24.
Merino, P. (1999). "The Office for Democratic Institutions and Human Rights", in *OSCE Yearbook 1998*, Institute for Peace Research and Security Policy at the University of Hamburg/IFSH (ed.), 383-392. Baden-Baden: Nomos.
Meyer-Ladewig and Petzold (2005) "Die Bindung deutscher Gerichte an Urteile des EGMR", *Neue Juristische Wochenschrift*, 58, No. 1-2, 15-20.
Meyer-Ladewig, J. (2003). *Konvention zum Schutz der Menschenrechte und Grundfreiheiten*, Nomos Verlagsgesellschaft, Baden-Baden.
Midgley, M. (1999). "Towards an Ethic of Global Responsibility", in T. Dunne and N. J. Wheeler (eds) *Human Rights in Global Politics*, Cambridge: Cambridge University Press, 160-174.
Mierop, E. S. van (2000). "The Entanglement of Humanitarians and the Military", *Talk Back*, The Newsletter of the International Council of Voluntary Agencies (ICVA), 2, 1, 18 February.
Mihr, A. (2004). "Human Rights Education: Methods, Institutions, Culture and Evaluation", *Discussion papers of the Otto-von-Guericke-Universität Magdeburg*, Institut für Politikwissenschaft, Band 4, 2004.
Mihr, A. (2005). Die UN-Dekade für Menschenrechtsbildung – eine Bilanz, Frech and Haspel (eds) Menschenrechte, 189-210. Schwalbach/Ts.
Mihr, Mkrtichyan, Mahler, Toivanen, (eds) (2005). *Armenia: A Human Rights* Perspective for Peace and Democracy, University of Potsdam.

Mills, K. (1997). "Reconstructing Sovereignty: A Human Rights Perspective", *Netherlands Quarterly of Human Rights*, 15, 3, 267-290.

Moravcsik, A. (2000) "The Origins of Human Rights Regimes: Democratic Delegation in Postwar Europe", *International Organization*, 54, 2, 217-252.

Murrills, R. (2001). *Human Rights in Europe, A study of the European Convention on Human Rights*, Manchester University Press 2001.

Ministry of Education, Tamoyan, H. and Tamoyan, A. (Eds.) (2005). Alphabet of Yezidi, Yerevan 2005.

Mitchell, S. (2001). "Human Rights in Kosovo. January to December 1999", in *OSCE Yearbook 2000*, Institute for Peace Research and Security Policy at the University of Hamburg/IFSH (ed), 241-256. Baden-Baden: Nomos.

Mommsen, M. (2002). "Die Europäische Union und Russland", in *Europa-Handbuch*, W. Weidenfeld (ed), 671-687. Gütersloh: Bertelsmann.

Möller, C. (2004). "Press Freedom in the OSCE Area and the Activities of the OSCE Media Representative", in *OSCE Yearbook 2003*, Institute for Peace Research and Security Policy at the University of Hamburg/IFSH (ed.), 323-336. Baden-Baden: Nomos.

Müller, L. (1999). "Menschenrechtserziehung in Deutschland. Ziele, Erfolge, Perspektiven", in *Menschenrechte und Frieden*, , Sommer, Stellmacher, and Wagner. (eds), 349-355. Marburg: IAFA.

Müller, L. (2002)."Menschenrechtserziehung an Schule und Hochschule", *Arbeits-*gemeinschaft Menschenrechte Universität Trier Occasional Paper No. 6, 2002.

Mydans, S. (2000). "Ruined East Timor Awaits a Miracle", *New York Times*, 22 April.

Mykola and Busch (2003). *Die Bedeutung der Europäischen Menschenrechtskonvention für den Grundrechtsschutz in der Europäischen Union*, Nomos Baden Baden.

Netherlands Helsinki Committee (ed.) (2005). *Ideas on Reforming the OSCE. (Drafted with the Input of the Helsinki Committee of the International Helsinki Federation for Human Rights)*. May 2005, The Hague: NHC (Draft).

Neukirch, Simhandl, and Zellner (2004). "Implementing Minority Rights in the Framework of the CSCE/OSCE", in *Mechanisms for the implementation of minority rights*. Council of Europe, 159-181. Strasbourg: Council of Europe.

Nickel, J. W. (1987). *Making Sense of Human Rights: Philosophical Reflections on the Universal Declaration of Human Rights*, Berkley: University of California Press.

Norman, P. (2003). The Accidental Constitution- the Story of the European Convention, EuroComment, Brussels.

Norton-Taylor, R. (2000). "From Killing to Cuddling", *Guardian*, 17 August.

Nowak, M. (1999). "Human Rights 'Conditionality' in Relation to Entry to, and Full Participation in, the EU", in *The EU and Human Rights*, Alston, Philip (ed) 687-698. Oxford: Oxford University Press.

Nowak, M. (1999). "Das Recht auf Bildung", *Teaching Human Rights*, 4/1999, 10–13.

Oberleitner, G. (1999). "Minority Protection and the Organisation for Security and Co-operation in Europe", *in Minority Rights in the 'New' Europe*. Cumper and Wheatley, (eds), 71-88. The Hague / London / Boston: Martinus Nijhoff Publishers.

Oberschmidt, R. (2002). "Ten Years of the Office for Democratic Institutions and Human Rights - An Interim Assessment", in *OSCE Yearbook 2001*, Institute for Peace Research and Security Policy at the University of Hamburg/IFSH (ed.), 387-400. Baden-Baden: Nomos.

ODIHR (2005a). "Office for Democratic Institutions and Human Rights - Organisational Structure", www.osce.org/odihr/13406.html (23 Aug. 2005).
ODIHR (2005b). "Office for Democratic Institutions and Human Rights - Upcoming Events/ Past Events", www. org/odihr/events.html (23 Aug. 2005).
ODIHR (2005c). "Office for Democratic Institutions and Human Rights - Meetings", www.osce.org/odihr/13414.html (23 Aug. 2005).
Oellers-Frahm, K. (2005). "Verbindlichkeit einstweiliger Maßnahmendes EGMR – Epi log", *Europäische Grundrechte-Zeitschrift*, 32, No. 13-16, 347-350.
Oellers-Frahm, K. (2003)."Verbindlichkeit einstweiliger Maßnahmen: Der EGMR voll zieht – endlich – die erforderliche Wende in seiner Rechtsprechung", *Europäische Grundrechte-Zeitschrift*, 30, No. 22-23, 689–693.
Oeter, S. (2004). "The European Charter for Regional or Minority Languages", in *Mechanisms for the implementation of minority rights*. Council of Europe, 131-157. Strasbourg: Council of Europe.
OHCHR (2000a). Mid-term Evaluation of the Decade for Human Rights Education, Spain. Unpublished questionnaire. Geneva.
OHCHR (2000b). Mid-term Evaluation of the Decade for Human Rights Education, Estonia. Unpublished questionnaire, EUR/GOV/EST. Geneva.
OHR (1997a). *Report of the High Representative for Implementation of the Bosnian Peace Agreement to the Secretary General of the United Nations*, 11 July. Available from: http://www.ohr.int/reports/r970711a.htm.
OHR (1997b). *Office of the High Representative Bulletin*, 62, 11 October. Available from: http://www.ohr.int/bulletins/b971011.htm.
OHR (1997c). *Bosnia and Herzegovina TV News Summary*, 10 November. Office of the High Representative e-mail service.
OHR (1997d). *Return and Reconstruction Task Force Report*, December. Office of the High Representative. Available from: http://www.ohr.int/rrtf/r9712.htm.
Okresek, W. (2003). "Die Umsetzung der EGMR-Urteile und ihre Überwachung. Probleme der Vollstreckung und der Behandlung von Wiederholungsfällen", *Europäische Grundrechte-Zeitschrift*, 30, No. 4-6, 168-174.
Ombudsperson Institution in Kosovo (ed.) (2005). *Quarterly Information Sheet, Jan-Mar 2004*. Pristina: Ombudsperson Institution in Kosovo, www.ombudspersonkosovo.org/doc/Quarterly%20Newsletter/Informatori01_english.pdf (23 Aug. 2005).
OMIK (ed.). 1999. *Kosovo/Kosova. As Seen, As Told, Part II. A Report on the Human Rights Findings of the OSCE Mission in Kosovo, June to October 1999*. Pristina: OSCE Mission in Kosovo/Schaeffer, www.osce.org/documents/mik/1999/11/1622_en.pdf (23 Aug. 2005).
OMIK (ed.) 2004. *Human Rights Challenges Following the March Riots*. Pristina: OSCE Mission in Kosovo, Department of Human Rights and Rule of Law, 25 May 2004, www.osce.org/documents/mik/2004/05/2939_en.pdf (23 Aug. 2005).
OMIK (2005a). *OSCE Mission in Kosovo - Fact Sheet*, www.osce.org/documents/mik/2004/10/3821_en.pdf (23 Aug. 2005).
OMIK (2005b). *OSCE Mission in Kosovo - Factsheet. Human Rights and Rule of Law*, www.osce.org/publications/mik/2005/06/14881_379_en.pdf (23 Aug. 2005).
OMIK (2005c). *OSCE Mission in Kosovo - Documents*, www.osce.org/kosovo/documents.html (23 Aug. 2005).

OMIK (2005d). *OSCE Mission in Kosovo - Human Rights Expert Programme*, www.osce.org/kosovo/13424.html

OMIK Human Rights Department (ed.) (2003). *Departmental Guide*, May 2003. Pristina: OSCE Mission in Kosovo, Human Rights and Rule of Law Department.

Onis, Z. (2000). "Neoliberal Globalization and the Democracy Paradox: The Turkish General Elections of 1999", *Journal of International Affairs,* 54 (1), 283-306.

Onis, Z. (2003). "Domestic Politics, International Norms and Challenges to the State: Turkey-EU Relations in the Post-Helsinki Era," in Carkoglu and Barry (eds), *Turkey and the European Union: Domestic Politics, Economic Integration and International Dynamics,* Frank Cass& Co. Limited, London, 9-43.

Open Society Institute (2001a). "Minority Protection in the Czech Republic", in *Monitoring the EU Accession Process: Minority Protection*, 121-174. New York: Open Society Institute.

Open Society Institute (2001b). "Minority Protection in Slovakia", in *Monitoring the EU Accession Process: Minority Protection*, 429-492. New York: Open Society Institute.

Open Society Institute (2002a). "Minority Protection in the Czech Republic: An Assessment of Governmental Policy Towards Members of the Roma Community Supporting Their Integration into Society" in *Monitoring the EU Accession Process: Minority Protection*, 123-87. Budapest: Open Society Institute.

Open Society Institute (2002b). "Minority Protection in Slovakia: An Assessment of the Strategy for the Solution of the Problems of the Roma National Minority and the Set of Measures for Its Implementation - Stages I and II" in *Monitoring the EU Accession Processs: Minority Protection*, 527-87. Budapest: Open Society Institute.

OSCE (2005). *Survey of OSCE Long-term Missions and other OSCE Field Activities*. SEC.INF/33/05. Vienna: OSCE.

OSCE (2004). Supplementary Human Dimension Meeting "Human Rights Education and Training" Final Report, Vienna, 25-26 March 2004, ODIHR.GAL/33/04.

OSCE (2002). *OSCE Handbook.* Third edition. Vienna: OSCE.

OSCE (ed.) (2000). *Handbook.* Third Edition. Vienna: Secretariat of the Organization for Security and Co-operation in Europe, www.osce.org/publications/osce/2005/04/13858_222_en.pdf (23 Aug. 2005).

OSCE/ODIHR (eds) (2003). *Individual Human Rights Complaints. A Handbook for OSCE Field Personnel.* Warsaw: ODIHR, www.osce.org/publications/odihr/2003/10/12354_162_en.pdf (23 Aug. 2005).

OSCE/ODIHR (eds) (2001). *OSCE Human Dimension Commitments. A Reference Guide.* Warsaw: Le Graph, www.osce.org/publications/odihr/2001/01/12366_161_en.pdf (23 Aug. 2005).

OSCE/ODIHR (eds) (1999). *Kosovo/Kosova. As Seen, As Told. An Analysis of the Human Rights Findings of the OSCE Kosovo Verification Mission, October 1998 to June 1999.* Warsaw: Office for Democratic Institutions and Human Rights/Pressoor Moutier SA, www.osce.org/documents/mik/1999/11/1620_en.pdf (23 Aug. 2005).

OSCE Parliamentary Assembly/Swiss Foundation for World Affairs (eds) (2005). *Report. Colloquium on "The Future of the OSCE". (A Joint Project of the OSCE Parliamentary Assembly and the Swiss Institute for World Affairs)*, Washington, 5-6 June 2005 (forthcoming).

Pache, E. (2004)."Die Europäische Menschenrechtskonvention und die deutsche Rechts ordnung", *Europarecht*, 39, 3, 393–415.

Pan, Christoph (2003). "Minderheitenschutz in Europa und in der EU: Theorie und Praxis", *europa ethnica*, 60, 3-9.

Parekh, B. (1993). "Beyond Humanitarian Intervention", in Cullen, Kritsiotis and Wheeler (eds) *Politics and the Law of Former Yugoslavia*, Hull: European Research Unit/ University of Hull.

Park, A. (1995). "Russia and Estonian Security Dilemmas", *Europe-Asia Studies*, 47, 27-45.

Patten, C. (1999). Declaration on Chechnya. Speech by the Rt Hon Chris Patten, CH. European Parliament, Strasbourg, 17 November 1999. Speech 99/166.

Patten, C. (2002). EU-Russia relations. Speech by The Rt Hon Chris Patten, CH. European Business Club (EBC) Conference 'Shaping Russian-European Integration in the 21th Century - Moscow, 28/05/02 - SPEECH/02/235.

Pender, J. (2000). "From "Structural Adjustment" to "Comprehensive Development Framework": Conditionality Transformed?", paper presented to the African Studies Association of the UK Biennial Conference, 'Africa: Past, Present & Future', Trinity

Peers and Ward (eds) (2004) The European Union Charter of Fundamental Rights, Hart Publishing, Oxford/ Portland.

Pentassuglia, G. (2004). "Minority Rights, Human Rights : A Review of Basic Concepts, Entitlements and Implementation Procedures under International Law", in *Mechanisms for the implementation of minority rights*. Council of Europe, 9-28. Strasbourg: Council of Europe.

Pentassuglia, G. (2002). *Minorities in international law*. Strasbourg: Council of Europe.

Pentassuglia, G. (1999). "Monitoring Minority Rights in Europe: the Implementation Machinery of the Framework Convention for the Protection of National Minorities – With Special Reference to the Role of the Advisory Committee", *International Journal on Minority and Group Rights*, 6, 417-461.

Pentikäinen and Scheinin (1993). "A Comparative Study of the Monitoring Mechanisms and the Important Institutional Frameworks for Human Rights Protection within the Council of Europe, the CSCE and the European Community". In: *Monitoring Human Rights in Europe – Comparing International Procedures and Mechanisms. (International Studies in Human Rights, 30)*, Bloed, A./et al., 93-120. London: Martinus Nijhoff.

Pernice and Kanitz (2004) "Fundamental Rights and Multilevel Constitutionalism in Europe", Berlin: *Walter Hallstein-Institut für Europäisches Verfassungsrecht, Paper* 7/04.

Permanent Council Decision No. 193, 5 November 1997. 137th Plenary Meeting, PC Journal No. 137, Agenda item 1 – Mandate of the OSCE Representative on Freedom of the Media, www.osce.org/documents/mcs/1997/12/4167_en.pdf (23 Aug. 2005).

Peters, A. (2003) *Einführung in die Europäische Menschenrechtskonvention*, München: Beck.

Petitville, F. (2003). "Exporting "Values"? EU External Cooperation as "Soft Diplomacy"", in *Understanding the European Union's External Relations*, M.

Pettai, I. (2002). "Estonians and Non-Estonians: A Typology of Tolerance," in Proceedings of Conference '*Multicultural Estonia*', October 24-25, 2002, Tallinn, Estonia, 103-124.

Phillips, A. (2004). *The Framework Convention for the Protection of National Minorities (FCNM)*, in *Mechanisms for the implementation of minority rights*. Council of Europe, 109-129. Strasbourg: Council of Europe.

Pippan, C. (2002). *Die Förderung der Menschenrechte und der Demokratie als Aufgabe der Entwicklungszusammenarbeit der Europäischen Gemeinschaft*, Frankfurt am Main u.a.: Lang.

Polakiewicz, J. (1999). *Treaty-Making in the Council of Europe*. Strasbourg, Council of Europe Publishing.

Poleshuk and Semjonov (2000). "Report, International Seminar „Minorities and Majorities in Estonia: Problems of Integration at the Threshold of the EU", Tallinn, Estonia 8-9 January 1999.

Prague Document on Further Development of Institutions and Structures, Second Meeting of the Council of CSCE, Prague, 1992, www.osce.org/documents/mcs/1992/01/4142_en.pdf (23 Aug. 2005).

Prodi, R. (2002). Wider Europe, Peace, Security And Stability International Dialogue and the Role of the EU. Sixth ECSA-World Conference. Jean Monnet Project, Brussels, 5-6 December 2002.

Prodi, R. (2004). Russia and the European Union: enduring ties, widening horizons. Speech held by Romano Prodi Speech/04/198, Tretyakov Gallery Moscow 23 April 2004.

Pugh, M. (1998). "Military Intervention and Humanitarian Action: Trends and Issues", *Disasters*, 22, 4, 339-351.

Radičová, I. (2001). *Hic Sunt Romales*. Bratislava: Fulbrightova komisia SR/Nadácia S.P.A.C.E.

Ramsbotham and Woodhouse (1996). *Humanitarian Intervention in Contemporary Conflict: A Reconceptualization*, Cambridge: Polity Press.

Raun, T. (2003). "Nineteenth- and early twentieth-century Estonian nationalism revisited", *Nations and Nationalism*, 9, 129-147.

Rawls, J. (1993). "The Law of Peoples", in S. Shute and S. Hurley (eds) *On Human Rights*, New York: Basic Books, 41-82.

Reinikainen, J. (1999). "Right against Right, membership and justice in post-society Estonia", *Stockholm Studies in Politics* 65, University of Stockholm.

Reljic, D. (2002). "The OSCE Representative on Freedom of the Media", *OSCE Yearbook 2001*, Institute for Peace Research and Security Policy at the University of Hamburg/IFSH (ed.), 377-386. Baden-Baden: Nomos.

Representative on Freedom of the Media (2005). "Mandate", www.osce.org/fom/13028.html (23 Aug. 2005).

Ress, G. (2004). "Die europäische Grundrechtskonvention. Brauchen wir eine verbindliche Europäische Grundrechtscharta?" in Herzog and Hobe (eds) *Die Europäische Union auf dem Weg zum verfassten Staatenverbund: Perspektiven der europäischen Verfassungsordnung*, München: Beck.

Risse, T., et al. (1999). "The Socialization of International Human Rights Norms Into Domestic Practice: Introduction", in *The Power of Human Rights. International Norms and Domestic Change,* T. Risse, et al. (ed.), 1-38. Cambridge: Cambridge Univ. Press.

Roberts, A. (1993). "Humanitarian War: Military Intervention and Human Rights", *International Affairs*, 69, 3, 429-449.

Robertson, A. H. (1961). "The Council of Europe, its Structure, Functions and Achieve ments", in *The Library of World Affaires*, Keaton and Schwarzenberger (eds), 32, 24–40. London.

Robertson, G. (1999). *Crimes Against Humanity: The Struggle for Global Justice*, London: Allen Lane/ Penguin Press.

Robinson, F. (1998). "The Limits of a Rights-Based Approach to International Ethics", in T. Evans (ed.) *Human Rights Fifty Years On: A Reappraisal*, Manchester: Manchester University Press, 58-76.

Robinson, M. (1998). "Foreword", The United Nations Decade for Human Rights *Education 1995-2004, Lessons for Life,* Geneva: United Nations Publication HR/PUB/DECADE/1998/1.

Rose, G. (1998). "The Exit Strategy Delusion", *Foreign Affairs*, 77, 1, 56-67.

Rosemann, N. (2002). "Die Rechtlichen Grundlagen von Menschenrechtsbildung, in *ZEP* 25, 4, 22-26. Frankfurt, M.: Verlag für Interkulturelle Kommunikation (IKO).

Rosenberg, J. (1999). "Just War and Intervention: The Challenge of the International for Social and Political Thought", paper presented at Sussex University International Relations/Social and Political Thought joint seminar series, *The Kosovo War: Perspectives from Social, Political and International Theory*, Summer. Available from: http://www.sussex.ac.uk/Units/SPT/seminars/kosovo/seminar1.

Rotfeld, A. D. (2004). "Does the OSCE Have a Future?", in *OSCE Yearbook 2003*, Institute for Peace Research and Security Policy at the University of Hamburg/IFSH (ed.), 31-42. Baden-Baden: Nomos.

Roth, M. (2004). "Europarat", in *Jahrbuch der Europäischen Integration 2003/2004*, 447 –454.

Royen, C. (1999). "*Der Westen und Rußland - Leben aus der Krise*", Osteuropa 49, 7, 79-88.

Rozen, L. K. (2000). "Humanitarian Aid", *Boston Globe*, 30 July.

Ruffert, M. (2004). "Die künftige Rolle des EuGH im europäischen Grundrechtsschutz system", *Europäische Grundrechte-Zeitschrift*, 31, No. 14-16, 466–471.

Rumford, C. (2003). "Resisting Globalization", *International Sociology,* 2003, 18, 2, 379-394.

Rupel, D. (2005). "Cold War Echoes". *Washington Post*, 7 March 2005, p. A19.

Sands and Klein (2001). *Bowett's Law of International Institutions*. London: Sweet & Maxwell.

Sandoval, V. (2002). "OSCE Human Dimension Implementation Meeting. Warsaw, 9-19 September 2002", *papers in the Theory and Practice of Human Rights*, no. 36, University of Essex: Human Rights Centre (ed), 10-30.

Satzger, H. (2005). "Die Rspr des EGMR als Motor der europäischen Strafprozessrechts harmonisierung", *Juristische Arbeitsblätter*, 2005, No. 8-9, 656–658.

Sbírka zákonů České republiky (1993a). *Ústavní zákon České národní rady ze dne 16. prosince 1992 č. 1.* Prague: Sbírka zákonů České republiky.

Sbírka zákonů České republiky (1993b). *Zákon č. 40 ze dne 29. prosince 1992 o nabývání a pozbývání státního občanství České republiky*. Prague: Sbírka zákonů České federativní republiky.

Sbírka zákonů České republiky (1995). *Zákon č. 152, kterým se mění a doplňuje zákon č. 140/1961 Sb., trestní zákon, ve znění pozdějších předpisů, zákon č. 141/1961 Sb., o trestním řízení soudním (trestní řád), ve znění pozdějších předpisů, zákon České národní rady č. 283/1991 o policii České republiky, ve znění pozdějších předpisů, zákon č. 189/1994 Sb., o vyšších soudních úřednících, a zákon č. 59/1965 Sb., o výkonu trestu odnětí svobody, ve znění pozdějších předpisů*. Prague: Sbírka zákonů České republiky.

Sbírka zákonů České republiky (1996). *Zákon č. 139 ze dne 26. dubna 1996, kterým se mění a doplňuje zákon České národní rady č. 40/1993 Sb., o nabývání a pozbývání státního občanství České republiky, ve znění zákona č. 272/1993 Sb. a zákona č. 140/1995 Sb.* Prague: Sbírka zákonů České republiky.

Sbírka zákonů České republiky (1999). *Zákon č. 194 ze dne 29. července 1999, kterým se mění zákon č. 40/1993 Sb., o nabývání a pozbývaní státního občanství České republiky, ve znění pozdějších předpisů*. Prague: Sbírka zákonů České republiky.

Sbírka zákonů České republiky (2002). *Zákon č. 134/2002 Sb., kterým se mění zákon č. 140/1961 Sb., trestní zákon, ve znění pozdějších předpisů*. Prague: Sbírka zákonů České republiky .

Scheeck, L. (2005) *Solving Europe's Binary Human Rights Puzzle. The Interaction between Supranational Courts as a Parameter of European Governance*, Paris: Centre d'études et de recherches internationales/Sciences Po, Questions de Recherche No. 15.

Scheinin, M. (2003). "Minority rights or added protection", in *Human Rights and Criminal Justice for the downtrodden*, Bregsmo, M. (ed.), 486-504. Leiden/Boston: Martinus Nijhoff Publishers.

Schenker, H. (2004). "Violence in Kosovo and the Way Ahead", *ECMI Brief*, no. 10, European Centre for Minority Issues (ed), March 2004, Flensburg: ECMI, www.ecmi.de/download/brief_10.pdf (23 Aug. 2005).

Schimmelfennig, F. (2003)."Internationale Sozialisation: Von einem "erschöpften" zu einem produktiven Forschungsprogramm? " , *Die neuen Internationalen Beziehungen. Forschungsstand und Perspektiven in Deutschland*, G. Hellmann, et al. (ed.), 401-427. Baden-Baden: Nomos.

Schimmelfennig, F., et al. (2003). "Costs, Commitment and Compliance: The Impact of EU Democratic Conditionality on Latvia, Slovakia and Turkey", *Journal of Common Market Studies* 41, 3, 495-518.

Schmidt, S. (1999). *Die Demokratie- und Menschenrechtsförderung der Europäischen Union unter besonderer Berücksichtigung Afrikas*. München: Forschungsstelle Dritte Welt am Geschwister-Scholl-Institut für Politische Wissenschaft der Ludwigs-Maximilians-Universität.

Schmitz, T. (2004). "Die Grundrechtecharta als Teil der Verfassung der Europäischen Union", *Zeitschrift Europarecht*, 39, 5, 691-713.

Schmolke, O. (org.) (1999). *Human rights and civil society in the Mediterranean. Report of the Euro Mediterranean Partnership Conference*, Stuttgart, 15 - 16 April 1999, Bonn.

Schmuck, O. (1987). "The European Parliament's Draft Treaty Establishing the European Union (1979-1984)" in R. Pryce (ed.) *The Dynamics of European Union*, Croom Helm, (reprinted by Routledge, London/ New York 1989).

Schnabel, A. and Thakur, R. (2000). "Policy Brief: Lessons from the Kosovo Conflict", summary in A. Schnabel and R. Thakur (eds) *Kosovo and the Challenge of Humanitarian Intervention: Selective Indignation, Collective Intervention, and International Citizenship*, Tokyo: United Nations University, 7-12. Summary available from: http://www.unu.edu/p&g/kosovo_full.htm.

Schönlau, J. (2005). Drafting the EU Charter: Rights, Legitimacy and Process, Palgrave-Macmillan, Basingstoke.

Schönlau, J. (2003). "New Values for Europe? Deliberation, Compromise and Coercion in Drafting the Preamble to the EU Charter of Fundamental Rights", in Eriksen, Fossum and Menendez (eds) *Chartering Europe*, Nomos, Baden-Baden.

Schwarze, J. (2005). "Der Schutz der Grundrechte durch den EuGH", *Neue Juristische Wochenschrift*, 58, 48, 3459-3466.

Schwimmer, W. (2000)."Zwölf Sterne für Europa – Warum der Europarat für ein friedliches und demokratisches Europa unersetzlich ist", in *50 Jahre Europarat*, Holtz (ed.). Baden-Baden, Nomos Verlagsgesellschaft.

Secretariat of the Council for National Minorities of the Government of the Czech Republic (1999). *National Minorities in the Czech Republic.*

Shaw, M. (1994). *Global Society and International Relations: Sociological Concepts and Political Perspectives,* Cambridge: Polity Press.

Sikk, A. (2003). "A Cartel Party System in a Post-Communist Country? The Case of Estonia, " *2nd ECPR General Conference, Marburg.*

Simma, Aschenbrenner and Schulte (1999). "Human Rights Considerations in the Development Co-operation Activities of the EC", in *The EU and human rights*, Alston, P. (ed.), 571-626. Oxford et al.: Oxford University Press.

Simon, G. (2002). "Allianz für die Freiheit oder Potomkinsche Dörfer" *Europäische Rundschau* 30, 4, 59-65.

SIPRI/Stockholm International Peace Research Institute (2005). *Armaments, Disarmament and International Security*, Oxford: Oxford University Press.

Smith, David J. (2003). "Minority Rights, Multiculturalism and EU Enlargement: the Case of Estonia", *Journal on Ethnopolitics and Minority Issues in Europe*, Issue1/2003

Smith, David J. (1998). "Russia, Estonia and the Search for a Stable Ethno-Politics", *Journal of Baltic Studies*, 29, 3-18.

Smith, M. (1996). "The European Union and a A Changing Europe: Establishing the Boundaries of Order", *Journal of Common Market Studies* 34, 1, 5–28.

Smith, R. K. M. (2003). *International Human Rights*. Oxford: Oxford University Press.

Sobotka, E. (2001). "Crusts from the table: Policy formation towards Roma in the Czech Republic and Slovakia", *Roma Rights* 6, No. 2-3.

Spanger, H.-J. (2004). *Modernisierung contra Demokratisierung. Putins russischer Weg. HSFK-Report 12/2004*. Frankfurt am Main: Hessische Stiftung für Friedensforschung und Konfliktforschung.

Spiliopoulou Åkermark, A (1998) (ed). Human Rights Education – Achievements and *Challenges*. Åbo / Turku.

Spiliopoulou Åkermark, A. (1997). *Justifications of Minority Protection in International Law*. Uppsala: Iustus Förlag.

Splidsboel-Hansen, F. (2002). "Russia's Relations with the European Union: A Constructivist Cut", *International Politics* 39, 4, 399-421.

Stammers, N. (1995). "A Critique of Social Approaches to Human Rights", *Human Rights Quarterly*, 17, 488-508.

Stammers, N. (1999). "Social Movements and the Social Construction of Human Rights", *Human Rights Quarterly*, 21, 980-1008.

Steele, J. (2000a). "Serb Killings Exaggerated By West", *Guardian*, 18 August.

Steele, J. (2000b). "Motivated to Believe the Worst", *Guardian*, 18 August.

Stefánsson, S. M. (2001). "Human rights in EU and EEC law", in *International human rights monitoring mechanisms. Essays in honour of Jakob Th. Möller*, Alfredsson, Gudmundur/Grimheden, Jonas/Ramcharan, Bertrand G./Zayas, Alfred de (eds), 795-801. The Hague et al.: M. Nijhoff.

Steinacker, G. (2004). "The Role of the OSCE as a Regional Security Organization in Combating International Terrorism", in *OSCE Yearbook 2003*, Institute for Peace Research and Security Policy at the University of Hamburg/IFSH (ed.), 89-93. Baden-Baden: Nomos.

Stopp, A. H. (1994). Die Behandlung ethnischer Minderheiten als Gleichheitsproblem. Baden-Baden: Nomos.

Strauß, E. (2002). "Protection of Minorities", in *A Concise Encyclopedia of the United Nations*, Volger, H. (ed.), 373-378. The Hague: Kluwer Law International.

Tannous, I. (2002). Menschenrechtspolitik, in: Weidenfeld and Wessels (eds): *Europa von A-Z*, Bonn.

Tardu, M.(2003). "The European Systems for the Protection of Human Rights", in *Hu man Rights: International Protection, Monitoring, Enforcement*, Symonides (ed.), 135–164, Bodmin, MPG Books Ltd.

Thiele, C. (2005). *Citizenship as a Requirement for Minorities*. E.H.R.L.R., 3, 277–289.

Thio, L. (2003). *Developing a 'Peace and Security' Approach towards Minorities' Problems*, 52 I.C.L.Q. 115-150.

Thomas, M. (2000). "Co-ordination in Kosovo: A Failure of Multilateralism", *Talk Back*, The Newsletter of the International Council of Voluntary Agencies (ICVA), 2, 1, 18 February.

Thompson, W.ayne (1998). "Citizenship and Borders: Legacies of Soviet empire in Estonia", *Journal of Baltic Studies*, 29, 109-134.

Thornberry, Martín Estébanez (2004). *Minority rights in Europe*. Strasbourg: Council of Europe.

Thürer and Doldt (2005). "Rassismus und Rule of Law / Erstmalige Verurteilung wegen Rassendiskriminierung durch den Europäischen Gerichtshof für Menschenrechte", *Europäische Grundrecht- Zeitschrift*, 32, No. 1-3, 1–12.

Timmermann, H. (1996). "Relations between the EU and Russia: The Agreement on Partnership and Co-operation", *Journal of Communist Studies and Transition Politics* ,12, 196-223.

Timmermann, H. (2000a). "European-Russian Partnership: What Future?" *European Foreign Affairs Review* 5 (2): 165-174.

Timmermann, H. (2000b). "Rußlands Politik gegenüber der EU (II). Konzeptionen und Handlungsmuster der "Mittelfristigen Strategie"". *Osteuropa* 50, 8 885-901.

Timmermann, H. (2002). "Strategische Partnerschaft: Wie kann die EU Russland stärker einbinden?", *Integration* 25, 4, 297-310.

Timmermann, H. (2004). "Innenpolitische Voraussetzungen für eine Partnerschaft Russ land - Europäische Union", in *Wohin steuert Russland unter Putin?: Der autoritäre Weg in die Demokratie,* G. Gorzka, et al. (ed.), 343-359. Frankfurt am Main: Campus.

Toivanen, R. (2005). "Das Paradox der Minderheitenrechte in Europa", *SWS-Rundschau*, 45, 2, 185-207.

Toivanen, R. (2006). "Unwissen, Vorurteile und andere „Gewohnheiten" – Notizen aus einer Feldforschung mit Roma in Estland", in *Roma in Europa*, Toivanen and Knecht (eds). Berliner Blätter 1/2006. Forthcoming.

Tomaševski, K. (2003). *Education Denied – Costs and Remedies*. Zed Books.

Tomaševski, K. (2001). *Human Rights obligations: making education available, accessible, acceptable and adaptable, Right to Education Primers No. 3.* Gothenburg: Novum Grafiska AB.

Tomaševski, K. (2000). *Responding to Human Rights Violations 1964-1999.* London: Kluwer Law (Martinus Nijhoff Publishers).

Topidi, K. (2004). "European Union Standards and Mechanisms for the Protection of Minorities and the Prevention of Discrimination", in *Mechanisms for the implementation of minority rights*. Council of Europe, 183-202. Strasbourg: Council of Europe.

Trautmann, L. (1995). *Russland zwischen Diktatur und Demokratie. Die Krise der Reformpolitik seit 1993*. Baden-Baden: Nomos.

Trifunovska, S. (ed.) (2001). *Minority Rights in Europe: European Minorities and Languages*. The Hague: T.M.C. Asser Press.

Tulkens, F. (2001) Les droits de l'homme en détention, in: Revue de science criminelle et de droit pénal comparé, 881-890.

Uerpmann, R. (2003). "Völkerrechtliche Nebenverfassungen", in: von Bogdandy, Armin (ed.), *Europäisches Verfassungsrecht*, Berlin/Heidelberg/New York: Springer, 339-371.

Uibopuu, H.-J. (1998). "The new Estonian Constitution of 1992 in the Context of European Law", in Talavs J. (ed) *The Baltic States at Historical Crossroads*, 214-231.

United States General Accounting Office (2000): Foreign Assistance. International ef forts to aid Russia's transition have had mixed results. Report to the Chairman and to the Ranking Minority Member, Committee on Banking and Finance, House of Representatives. Washington D.C.: GAO.

UKFAC (2000). *Fourth Report*, Session 1999-2000, United Kingdom House of Commons Foreign Affairs Committee, 23 May. Available from: http://www.publications.parliament.uk/pa/cm199900/cmselect/cmfaff/28/2802

United Nations (1948). *Universal Declaration of Human Rights*, adopted and proclaimed by the UN General Assembly resolution 217 A (III) of 10 December, 1948.

UN ICCPR (1966). International Covenant of Civil and Political Rights, GA. Res. 2200 A (XXI), UN Doc. A/6316 (1967), December 16, 1966.

UN Doc. (2005). *Revised draft plan of action for the first phase (2005-2007) of the World Programme for Human Rights Education*, A/59/525/Rev.1, 2 March, 2005.

UN Doc. (2005). Resolution adopted by the General Assembly [without reference to a Main Committee (A/59/L.65 and Add.1)] 59/113. World Programme for Human Rights Education A/RES/59/113 B, 5 August, 2005.

UN (2000). *Report of the Panel on United Nations Peace Operations*. United Nations General Assembly Security Council, 21 August. Available from: http://www.un.org/peace/reports/peace-operations/.

Úřad vlády České republiky (2003). *Zpráva o situaci národnostních menšin v České republice za rok 2002*. Prague: Úřad vlády České republiky.

Uzun, A. (2002). "Siyasi Kriterler Cercevesinde Katilim Ortakligi ve Ulusal Programin Karsilastirilmasi," in Cengiz Aktar (ed.), *Avrupa Birliginin Genisleme Sureci*, Iletisim Yayinlari, Istanbul, 77-99.

Van der Stoel, Max (1998). "Conflict Prevention in Situations Involving National Minority Issues", *The Polish Quarterly of International Affairs*, vol. 7 no. 3, 59-72.

Vaňo, B. (2001). *Demografická charakteristika rómskej populácie v SR*. Bratislava: Výskumné demografické centrum.

Varenness de, F. (2004). *Using the European Court of Human Rights to protect the rights of minorities*, in *Mechanisms for the implementation of minority rights*. Council of Europe, 83-108. Strasbourg: Council of Europe.

Vašečka, M. (1999a). "Rómovia", in *Slovensko 1998-1999: Súhrnná správa o stave spoločnosti*, Mesežnikov. G. and Ivantyšyn, M. (eds), 757-776. Bratislava: Inštitút pre verejné otázky.

Vašečka, M. (1999b). "Rómovia a parlamentné voľby 1998", in *Kto? Prečo? Ako? Slovenské voľby '98*, Bútora, M. et al. (eds), 289-298. Bratislava: Inštitút pre verejné otázky.

Vašečka, M. (2003). "Roma", in *Slovakia 2002: A Global Report on the State of Society*, Kollár, M. et al. (eds), 163-182. Bratislava: Institute for Public Affairs.

Vašečka and Džambazovič (2000). "Socio-Economic Situation of Roma in Slovakia as Potential Migrants and Asylum Seekers in EU Member States", in *Social and Economic Situation of Potential Asylum Seekers from the Slovak Republic*, 17-69. Bratislava: International Organization for Migration.

Verdery, K. (1996) "Nationalism, Postsocialism, and Space in Eastern Europe", *Social Research*, Vol.63, No.1, 7-96.

Vláda České republiky (1994). *Governmental Approach to National Minorities in the Czech Republic (Government Resolution 63)*. Prague: Úřad vády České republiky.

Vláda České republiky (1997a). *Usnesení vlády České republiky č. 686 ke Zprávě o situaci romské komunity v České republice a k současné situaci v romské komunitě*. Prague: Úřad vlády České republiky.

Vláda České republiky (1997b). *Usnesení vlády České republiky ze dne 15. října 1997 č.640 o Statutu Meziresortní komise pro záležitosti romské komunity*. Prague: Úřad vlády České republiky.

Vláda České republiky (1998). *Usnesení vlády České republiky ze dne 9. září 1998 č. 580 o odvolání a jmenování předsedy Rady pro národnosti vlády České republiky a předsedy Meziresortní komise pro záležitosti romské komunity a o změně statutů těchto orgánů*. Prague: Úřad vlády České republiky.

Vláda České republiky (2000). *Usnesení vlády České republiky č. 599 ke Koncepci politiky vlády vůči příslušníkům romské komunity, napomáhající jejich integraci do společnosti*. Prague: Úřad vlády České republiky.
Vláda České republiky (2002). *Usnesení vlády České republiky ze dne 23. ledna 2002 č. 87 k informaci o plnění usnesení vlády týkajících se integrace romských komunit a aktivního postupu státní správy při uskutečňování opatření přijatých těmito usneseními ke dni 31. prosince 2001 a k návrhu Koncepce romské integrace*. Prague: Úřad vlády České republiky.
Vláda České republiky (2003). *Usnesení vlády České republiky ze dne 12. března 2003 č. 243 k Informaci o plnění usnesení vlády, týkajících se integrace romskúch komunit a aktivního postupu státní správy při uskutečnění opatření přijatých těmito usneseními k 31. prosinci 2002*. Prague: Úřad vlády České republiky.
Vláda České republiky (2004a). *Informace o plnění usnesení vlády týkajících se integrace romských komunit a aktivního postupu státní správy při uskutečňování přijatých těmito usneseními ke dni 31. prosince 2003*. Prague: Úřad vády České republiky.
Vláda České republiky (2004b). *Koncepce romské integrace, 2004*. Úřad vády České republiky.
Vláda České republiky (2004c). *Zpráva o stavu romských komunit v České republice*. Úřad vády České republiky.
Vláda Československé socialistické republiky. (1996). "Usnesení vlády ČSSR ze dne 13. října 1965 č. 502 o opatřeních k řešení otázek cikánského obyvatelstva". In: *Rómska problematika 1945-1967: Dokumenty*, vol. 4, Jurová, A. (ed.), 809-811. Prague: Ústav pro soudobé dějiny AV ČR.
Vláda Slovenskej republiky (1991). *Zásady vládnej politiky Slovenskej republiky k Rómom prijaté uznesením vlády Slovenskej republiky č. 153 dňa 9. apríla 1991*. Bratislava: Úrad vlády Slovenskej republiky.
Vláda Slovenskej republiky (1995). *Štatút splnomocnenca vlády Slovenskej republiky na riešenie problémov občanov, ktorí potrebujú osobitnú pomoc (Uznesenie vlády Slovenskej republiky č. 668 dňa 10. augusta 1995)*. Bratislava: Úrad vlády Slovenskej republiky.
Vláda Slovenskej republiky (1996). *Uznesenie vlády Slovenskej republiky k návrhu úloh a opatrení na riešenie problémov občanov, ktorí potrebujú osobitnú pomoc, na rok 1996, č. 310 dňa 30. apríla 1996*. Bratislava: Úrad vlády Slovenskej republiky.
Vláda Slovenskej republiky (1997a). *Koncepčné zámery vlády SR na riešenie problémov Rómov v súčasných spoločensko-ekonomických podmienkach (Uznesenie vlády Slovenskej republiky č. 796 dňa 3. novembra 1997)*. Bratislava: Úrad vlády Slovenskej republiky.
Vláda Slovenskej republiky (1997b). *Správa o plnení úloh a opatrení na riešenie problémov občanov, ktorí potrebujú osobitnú pomoc v roku 1996 a návrh opatrení na riešenie problémov občanov, ktorí potrebujú osobitnú pomoc na rok 1997 (Uznesenie vlády Slovenskej republiky č. 335 dňa 6. maja 1997)*. Bratislava: Úrad vlády Slovenskej republiky.
Vláda Slovenskej republiky (1998). *Uznesenie vlády Slovenskej republiky 861 dňa 2. decembra 1998 k návrhu na odvolanie PaedDr. Branislava Baláža z funkcie splnomocnenca vlády Slovenskej republiky na riešenie problémov občanov, ktorí potrebujú osobitnú pomoc*. Bratislava: Úrad vlády Slovenskej republiky.

Vláda Slovenskej republiky (1999a). *Stratégia Vlády Slovenskej republiky na riešenie problémov rómskej národnostnej menšiny a súbor opatrení na jej realizáciu - I. etapa (Uznesenie vlády Slovenskej republiky č. 821/1999)*. Bratislava: Úrad vlády Slovenskej republiky.
Vláda Slovenskej republiky (1999b). *Štatút splnomocnenca vlády Slovenskej republiky na riešenie problémov občanov patriacich k rómskej menšine (Uznesenie vlády Slovenskej republiky č. 127)*. Bratislava: Úrad vlády Slovenskej republiky.
Vláda Slovenskej republiky (2000). *Rozpracovaná stratégia vlády SR na riešenie problémov rómskej národnostnej menšiny do súboru konkrétnych opatrení na rok 2000 - II. etapa (Uznesenie vlády Slovenskej republiky č. 294 dňa 3. maja 2000)*. Bratislava: Úrad vlády Slovenskej republiky.
Vláda Slovenskej republiky (2002). *Priorities of the Government of the Slovak Republic with regard to Roma Communities for 2002 (Government Resolution 357/2002)*. Bratislava: Vláda Slovenskej republiky.
Vláda Slovenskej republiky (2003). *Základné tézy koncepcie politiky Vlády SR v integrácii rómskych komunít*. Bratislava: Vláda Slovenskej republiky.
Vláda Slovenskej republiky (2004a). *Uznesenie vlády Slovenskej republiky č. 397 z 28. apríla 2004 k vyhodnoteniu základných téz koncepcie politiky vlády v integrácii rómskych komunít za rok 2003 a Priority vlády SR v integráci rómskych komunít na rok 2004*. Bratislava: Úrad vlády Slovenskej republiky.
Vláda Slovenskej republiky (2004b). *Vyhodnotenie Základných téz koncepcie politiky vlády SR v integrácii rómskych komunít za rok 2003*. Bratislava: Úrad vlády Slovenskej republiky.
Vogel, H. (1995). "Partnership with Russia: some lessons from Chechnya", *The World Today* 51 (4): 64-67.
von Bogdandy, A. (2000). "The European Union as a Human Rights Organization? Human Rights and the Core of the European Union", *Common Market Law Review*, 37, 1307-1338.
Waldron, J (ed.) (1987). *Nonsense Upon Stilts: Bentham, Burke and Marx on the Rights of Man* London: Methuen.
Wallace, W. (2003). "Looking after the Neigbourhood: Responsibilities for the EU-25. Groupement d'Études et de Recherches Notre Europe", *Policy Paper 4, July 2003*. Brussels: Groupement d'Études et de Recherches Notre Europe.
Walzer, M. (1997). *Just and Unjust Wars: A Moral Argument with Historical Illustra tions* New York: Basic Books.
Wedgewood, R. (1999). "Nato's Campaign in Yugoslavia", *American Journal of International Law*, 93, 828-34.
Weiler, J.H.H. (2002). "A Constitution for Europe? Some Hard Choices", *Journal of Common Market Studies*, 40, 4, 563-580.
Weiler, J.H.H. (2000) "Does the European Union Truly Need a Charter of Rights?", Editorial in *European Law Journal*, 6, 2, 95-97.
Weiler, J.H.H. (1999). "Fundamental Rights and Fundamental Boundaries: On the Conflict of Standards and Values in the Protection of Human Rights in the European Legal Space", in Weiler, *The Constitution of Europe*, Cambridge University Press, 102-129.

Weiler, J. H.H. (1999). *The Constitution of Europe: "Do the new clothes have an emperor?" and other essays on European integration*, Cambridge: Cambridge University Press.

Weiler, J. (1993). "Journey to an Unknown Destination: A retrospective and Prospective of the European Court of Justice in the Arena of Political Integration", *Journal of Common Market Studies* 31, 4, 417 – 446.

Weiler, J.H.H. (1997). "The Reform of European Constitutionalism", *Journal of Common Market Studies,* 35, 1, 97-131.

Weintraub, J. (1997). "The Theory and Politics of the Public/Private Distinction", in Weintraub Kumar (eds) *Public and Private in Thought and Practice: Perspectives on a Grand Dichotomy* Chicago: University of Chicago Press, 1-42.

Weiss, T. G. (1999). "Principles, Politics and Humanitarian Action", *Ethics and International Affairs*, 13, 1-22.

Weiß, N. (2004). "Sind Minderheitenrechte Menschenrechte", in *Menschenrechtsschutz im Spiegel von Wissenschaft und Praxis*, Mahler C. and Weiß, N. (eds), 292-320. Berlin: Berliner Wissenschafts Verlag.

Weiß, N. (2000). *Die Bedeutung von Menschenrechtsklauseln für die Außenbeziehungen und Entwicklungshilfeabkommen der EG/EU*, Potsdam: Menschenrechtszentrum der Univ. Potsdam.

Weissbrodt, D. (2003). *Final report of the rights of non-citizens—Regional Activities.* E/CN.4/Sub.2/2003/23/Add. 2, May 26, 2003.

Wheatley, Steven (2002). "Non-Discrimination and Equality in the Rights of Political Participation for Minorities", *Journal on Ethnopolitics and Minority Issues in Europe*, Issues3/2002.

Wheeler, N. J. (1996). "Guardian Angel or Global Gangster: A Review of the Ethical Claims of International Society", *Political Studies*, 44, 1, 123-135.

White, N. D. (1996). *The law of international organisations*. Glasgow, Bell & Bain Ltd.

Williams, A. (2004). *EU Human Rights Policies*. A Study in Irony, Oxford et al.: Oxford University Press.

Wilson, D. (2002). Minority Rights in Education. Lessons for the European Union from Estonia, Latvia, Romania and the Former Yugoslav Republic of Macedonia. Lund.

Windmeißer, A. (2002). *Der Menschenrechtsansatz in der Entwicklungszusammenarbeit. Menschenrechte, Demokratie, Rechtsstaatlichkeit und "good governance" in der Entwicklungszusammenarbeit. Das Beispiel der AKP-EU-Beziehungen*, Vienna: Verlag Österreich.

Wiener and Wobbe (2002). "Norm Resonance in Global Governance – Contested Norms in the Process of EU Enlargement", paper prepared for the *Annual Meeting of ISA*, New Orleans.

Wiener, A. (2000). "Legitimate Governance by Enlargement, The dual quality of Norms", paper prepared for the workshop, *Governance by Enlargement*, Darmstadt.

Wiener, A. (1998). European Citizenship Practice - Building Institutions of the non-*State*, Westview Press, Boulder, Colorado.

Wlachovský, M. (1998). "Zahraničná politika", in *Voľby 1998: Analýza volebných programov politických strán a hnutí*, Mesežnikov, G. (ed.), 63-75. Bratislava: Inštitút pre verejné otázky.

Wolchik, S.L. (1997). "Democratization and Political Participation in Slovakia", in *The Consolidation of Democracy in East-Central Europe*, Parrott, B. and Dawisha, K. (eds), 197-244. Cambridge: Cambridge University Press.

Woodger, W. (1997). "The Letter of Democracy and the Spirit of Censorship: The West Runs the Media in Bosnia". Unpublished paper, October.

Woodward, S. L. (1995). *Balkan Tragedy: Chaos and Dissolution after the Cold War* Washington, DC: Brookings Institution.

Yavuz, H. M. (2000). "Cleansing Islam from Public Sphere", *Journal of International Affairs*, 54, 1, 21-43

Žáček, R. (1997). "Národnostní menšiny v českých zemích v historické retrospektivě", in *Právní nástroje k ochraně národnostních menšin: Postavení národnostních menšin v České republice a jejich ochrana*, 9-24. Prague: Rada Evropy.

Zannier, L. (2004). "A New Focus on Borders", in *OSCE Yearbook 2003*, Institute for Peace Research and Security Policy at the University of Hamburg/IFSH (ed.), 225-235. Baden-Baden: Nomos.

Zbierka zákonov Slovenskej republiky (1992). *Ústava Slovenskej republiky.* Zbierka zákonov Slovenskej republiky.

Zbierka zákonov Slovenskej republiky. (1993). *Zákon Národnej rady Slovenskej repub liky č. 40 z 19. januára 1993 o štátnom občianstve Slovenskej republiky.* Bratislava: Zbierka zákonov Slovenskej republiky.

Zbierka zákonov Slovenskej republiky (2001). *Ústavný zákon zo dňa 23. februára 2001*. Bratislava: Zbierka zákonov Slovenskej republiky.

Zellner, W. (ed.) (2005). *Managing Change in Europe. Evaluating the OSCE and Its Future Role: Competencies, Capabilities, and Missions*. Hamburg: Centre for OSCE Research, www.core-hamburg.de/documents/CORE_Working_Paper_13.pdf (23 Aug. 2005).

Zimmermann, A. (2002). *Die Charta der Grundrechte der Europäischen Union zwischen Gemeinschaftsrecht, Grundgesetz und EMRK: Entstehung, normative Bedeutung und Wirkung der EU-Grundrechtecharta im gesamteuropäischen Verfassungsraum*, Baden-Baden: Nomos.

Zizek, S. (2000). *The Fragile Absolute or, Why is the Christian Legacy Worth Fighting For?* London: Verso.

Zizek, S. (1999). *The Ticklish Subject* London: Verso.

Internet Resources

Council of the European Union:
http://europa.eu.int/institutions/council/index_en.htm

Directorate-General Development:
http://europa.eu.int/comm/development/index_en.htm

Directorate-General External Relations:
http://europa.eu.int/comm/external_relations/index.htm

European Court of Human Rights:
http://www.echr.coe.int

European Parliament:
www.europarl.eu.int/home/default_en.htm

The EU's Human rights & Democratisation Policy:
http://europa.eu.int/comm/external_relations/human_rights/intro/index.htm

The European Initiative for Democracy and Human Rights:
http://europa.eu.int/comm/europeaid/projects/eidhr/index_en.htm

FSC
www.fsc.org
MIX
Papier | Fördert gute Waldnutzung
FSC® C083411

Kolibri 360 GmbH
Ferdinand-Jühlke-Straße 7
99095 Erfurt, Deutschland
produktsicherheit@kolibri360.de

Druck:
CPI Druckdienstleistungen GmbH
im Auftrag der
Kolibri 360 GmbH
Ferdinand-Jühlke-Str. 7
99095 Erfurt